# Theorizing American Literature

# THEORIZING

Hegel,

# AMERICAN

the Sign,

# LITERATURE

and History

*Edited by*
*Bainard Cowan & Joseph G. Kronick*

· · · · · · · · · · · · · · ·

LOUISIANA STATE UNIVERSITY PRESS
*Baton Rouge and London*

Designer: Rebecca Lloyd Lemna
Typeface: Janson
Typesetter: Graphic Composition, Inc.
Printer and binder: Thomson-Shore, Inc.

Library of Congress Cataloging-in-Publication Data
Theorizing American literature : Hegel, the sign, and history /
  Bainard Cowan and Joseph G. Kronick, [editors].
    p. cm.
  Includes bibliographical references and index.
  ISBN 0-8071-1628-9
    1. American literature—History and criticism—Theory, etc.
  2. Hegel, Georg Wilhelm Friedrich, 1770–1831—Aesthetics.
  3. Semiotics and literature.   I. Cowan, Bainard.   II. Kronick,
  Joseph G.
  PS25.T47    1991
  810.9—dc20                                      90-49723
                                                    CIP

Excerpts from Wallace Stevens' poetry are taken from
*The Collected Poems of Wallace Stevens* and
*Opus Posthumous* by Wallace Stevens.
Reprinted by permission of Alfred A. Knopf, Inc., and
by permission of Faber and Faber Ltd.

# Contents

# Preface and Acknowledgments

The past few decades have witnessed a steady revival and revision of Hegel. Throughout this century his readers have retrieved the particularity of his writings from the blurry, largely symbolic perception of his work as project and system that dominated in the nineteenth century. In Germany, the Frankfurt School reexamined his formulations of the historical dialectic for its negative implications, while hermeneutic theory saw in his critique of subjective spirit a path beyond positivism. French thought developed itself extensively around his master-slave model on the one hand, while on the other it took his models of subjectivity and knowledge as the final formulations of an entire Western philosophical tradition in need of reevaluation or overthrow. Small wonder, then, that the movement of literary theory toward what is now known as textuality has come to recognize its inescapable engagement in the work of the author whom Jacques Derrida has called "the last philosopher of the book and the first thinker of writing."

Although dismissed and ridiculed from time to time, Hegel has not lost his status as the imposing dead or dying father who prophesies to his sons and daughters what they will do even before they revolt against him and only fulfill his prophecy. If the image of the father is still ineradicable, however, the change in his other image from the great system builder to the philosopher of language allows his heirs to focus their negative labor by means of a fundamental questioning of literary language and literary history. The problematic of the relation between language, thought, and history implicit in Hegel's writings is in essence the contemporary problematic both of philosophy and of critical theory. In writing about language, Hegel's thought demonstrates this problematic. The dialectical model of consciousness, which has certainly been Hegel's trademark, prescribes the relation of subjectivity to history, subsuming contradiction and heterogeneity under the unifying synthesis of consciousness. His analysis of the sign, however, amounts to a competing and subversive model, for in retaining its materiality the sign resists the interiorization of the sensory world as pure thought and implies a non-unifiable relation of language to history. Thereby a contradiction is forged between the concept of literary history and literary language itself, a contradiction strong enough to generate a history of its own in modern literature and its criticism.

For European thinkers Hegel offered a new alignment for old knowledge; if he was understood more thoroughly on the Atlantic's eastern shore, he may have remained too familiar. In America, Walt Whitman saw a stranger, perhaps more dangerous, *poetic* potency when in *Democratic Vistas* he called for "poets consistent with the Hegelian formulas." As Whitman intuited, Hegelianism finds affinity with American literature in their common insistence on the immanent and concrete development of the spirit within history. The theoretical critique of this connection thus remains anything but a matter of the philosophical salon; American culture and literature finds itself in a position of already having lived the Hegelian assumptions and, in so doing, to have subjected them to the harshest critique, namely the critique of historical experience. To understand the path of the *notion* of spirit in history, along with its consequences in language, then, is the task and the aim of theorizing American literature.

This volume aims therefore to explore the intersections of Hegelian thought, contemporary theory, and American literature, in order to counter a Hegelianism that has long ensnared American literary history and cultural thought and to clear the way for a new understanding of the American text and its complex involvement in history.

This work of many hands has incurred a number of debts that we are glad to acknowledge. We owe thanks first of all to Beverly Jarrett, former executive editor at Louisiana State University Press and now director of the University of Missouri Press, for her encouragement and good counsel during this book's preparation. Margaret Dalrymple, editor-in-chief at LSU Press, and Julie Schorfheide, copy editor of the book, have been helpful and perceptive in dealing with the completed manuscript. Meetings at the MLA and the Hegel Society helped develop our plans and drafts. Besides the authors of the essays included herein, David Stern provided valuable commentary, as did Rodolphe Gasché, John Pizer, Gary Shapiro, Gary Lee Stonum, and, as he has done so often in the past, Lewis Simpson. Thanks go also to the College of Arts and Sciences at LSU and to Graham McGill for assistance in material and research.

# Introduction
## The Unreadable Translation—Toward Thinking American Writing

• • • • • • • • • • • • • • • • •

*Bainard Cowan*


### ADVENTURES OF HEGEL IN AMERICA

The criticism of American literature, of its forms, its history, and the conditions of its culture has labored under a double forgetting of Hegel. I call it forgetting rather than ignoring because the study that has gone into producing this volume has uncovered so many and such consistent traces of Hegel in American writing and cultural activity that it seems America has never been entirely ignorant of Hegel; indeed, if one follows Mitchell Breitwieser's remarkably convincing establishment of connections, Hegelian thought was already present in Puritan America before it was present in Hegel's own person. Moreover, this forgetting of what our writing already knows is unquestionably to our disadvantage, less a liberation from European clerical intellectualism and a discovery of a properly American identity than a prolonged misunderstanding of identity itself. In America's case, forgetting Hegel is not a salutary inner act that frees the power of imagination but rather a repression: a denial of the complex web of human interrelations, a denial to support which the largely unmarked landscape of the new world has been pressed into service as a mythic image, a double denial of the sign and of history.

The more accessible of these two collective acts of forgetting is marked by the absence of the name of Georg Wilhelm Friedrich Hegel from accounts of American intellectual history. This omission has only recently begun to be addressed, and it is no simple matter, since it involves not merely the reinvestigation of ignored documents but the reading of writers' denunciations of Hegel according to a logic that seems much like Oedipal denial.[1] The widening circle that one discov-

---

1. See the important study by Paul Edward Gottfried, *The Search for Historical Meaning: Hegel and the Postwar American Right* (DeKalb, Ill., 1986), especially 16, 22–23,

ers on examining the history of education and political interpretation in the nineteenth century only begins to confirm all the more strongly Paul de Man's remark that "whether we know it, or like it, or not, most of us are Hegelians and quite orthodox ones at that."[2]

Before Hegel arrived in American universities in the twentieth century, bound closely to Marx by Alexandre Kojève and the Frankfurt School, his writings had been appropriated first of all by conservatives and centrist liberals in America, and the values into whose service they impressed him were inseparable from his Europeanness and the historical method. Hegel was seen and used to affirm historical continuities and stabilities within American life and the deep links of American society to the long-accumulated wisdom of European civilization. A circle of thinkers, socially activist and influenced by Ralph Waldo Emerson, had formed in Cincinnati in the 1850s and included the abolitionist-freethinker Moncure Conway and the socialist revolutionary August Willich. Far more organized, persistent, and influential, however, in working to spread Hegelian thought in America was the St. Louis Philosophical Society. Henry C. Brokmeyer, William Torrey Harris, and Denton J. Snider, the three founders in 1866 of the group of some fifty participants, were outstanding civic and educational leaders in post–Civil War America. Harris was perhaps the most prominent of them, serving as lifetime director of the National Education Association and as United States commissioner of education from 1889 to 1906. Brokmeyer became lieutenant governor and, for a time, acting governor of Missouri; Snider was the organizer of the kindergarten program in American education. All three were prolific authors in philosophy, education, and history, and Snider authored more than forty books, mostly on Hegelian thought. Harris and Snider founded the *Journal of Speculative Philosophy*, which became the premier philosophical periodical in America.

As it expanded, the group came to be known as the St. Louis Movement and wrote into its rolls many of the leading professors in

63–64, and 131–32, from which many of the details in my account are taken. Earlier, more chronicle-like sources include: Henry A. Pochmann, *New England Transcendentalism and St. Louis Hegelianism: Phases in the History of American Idealism* (Philadelphia, 1948); Loyd David Easton, *Hegel's First American Followers: The Ohio Hegelians* (Athens, Ohio, 1966); William H. Goetzmann, *The American Hegelians: An Intellectual Episode in the History of Western America* (New York, 1973).

2. Paul de Man, "Sign and Symbol in Hegel's *Aesthetics*," *Critical Inquiry*, VIII (Summer, 1982), 763.

the humanities, including G. S. Morris at the University of Michigan, George Herbert Palmer, chairman of the philosophy department at Harvard University, and George Holmes Howison of the University of California. Harris corresponded with Charles Sanders Peirce on the subject of Hegel. Thus the notion of philosophy as the queen of all university disciplines and as their ultimate legitimator—a notion that was part of Wilhelm von Humboldt's world-exported plan for the University of Berlin, where Hegel taught—holds true for America as well.[3] Philosophy was the ultimate recourse for authority on education and other subjects, and Hegel came to dominate American philosophy departments.

Two of the movement's critical characteristics were its interest in Hegel as a political theorist and its belief in his special relevance for the American people. It was the unwavering conviction of the fervent Hegelians who founded both the Society and the Movement that America would realize the vision of a free society based on ever-expanding institutional relationships. The St. Louis Hegelians saw the historical dialectic as culminating in the American nation state. The highest stage of the dialectic could not be attained on the European continent, where nations still struggled for mastery over each other. Only the Anglo-American world, and preeminently its American part, was realizing the Hegelian ideal of harmonizing individual will and the public good, private activity and communal norms, civil society and political authority. From his writings it is clear that Harris, like Snider and other American Hegelians, sought administrative power in order to create public policy. The St. Louis Hegelians pressed for a national program of public education that would stress individual discipline and the transmission of inherited cultural values. Harris himself was explicit in advocating the study of Hegel's social philosophy in public schools.

The extent to which Hegelian schematism has been successful in invisibly restructuring American self-interpretation can be seen in Snider's biography of Lincoln. Snider presented his subject as a world-historical individual who understood fully the spirit of the American regime. Snider's Lincoln wished to reconcile the two founding principles of the Republic, the will toward national government and the will toward states' rights, but History forced him to raise both into a

---

3. See Jean-François Lyotard, *The Postmodern Condition: A Report on Knowledge*, trans. Geoff Bennington and Brian Massumi (Minneapolis, 1984), 32–34.

new synthesis. By his "serious, patient, suffering" labor—to use Hegel's evocative language in the *Phenomenology* about the crucial importance of the negative in the dialectic of spirit—Lincoln canceled the burden of slavery and arrived at a new, transcendent sense of nationhood. The lineaments of Napoleon in Lincoln are often seen but seldom recognized for what they are. This belief in renewal was reinforced by the hegemonic interpretation of the Civil War in general as an arduous and bloody, though irrepressible, "labor of the negative" through which a higher unity was formed and a greater freedom achieved. Even Frederick Jackson Turner's frontier theory of American society, often presented as marking America's differentiation from European institutional models, has been shown to have been greatly influenced by the Italian social economist Achille Loria, who, steeped in Hegelian thought, tried to correlate the course of the American regime to the availability of frontier land, which he held to be the safeguard of American liberty.[4]

Not only American historical understanding has tended to fall into Hegelian patterns. Hegel was present in prospect, as well as in retrospect, in the minds and plans of many of the makers of American civilization. The very notion and shape of American aspiration may in fact be Hegelian, and its shape may be that of a bridge. The deep Hegelianism of John Augustus Roebling, the visionary designer of Brooklyn Bridge, is evident in his writings. Roebling is one figure discussed by Joseph Riddel in this volume as part of the American sense of the endless poetic project. A more direct connection with the St. Louis Movement would be James Eads, the builder of the Eads Bridge in St. Louis, the first major rail-crossing over the Mississippi River. During the construction of this great steel bridge, the most marveled at in America in its time, Snider said it symbolized the concrete universal in America. The bridge can be seen as a symbol representing the collective reading of Hegel by American civilization, a reading that, Riddel reminds us, goes not at all far enough if it fails to disclose the bridge as an abyss as well.

Eads too was a Hegelian, a charter member of the St. Louis Movement, and was responsible as well for opening the lower Mississippi to oceangoing vessels and for designing the first armor-clad gun-

4. Gottfried, *Search*, 63–64; see also Lee Benson, *Turner and Beard* (Glencoe, Ill., 1980).

boats in the Civil War. The city of St. Louis itself seemed to Snider to unite the Hegelian sense of historical destiny with the American heartland. A historian of the Movement writes that to Snider, "the bustling city with its overflowing German population and its bourgeois energy signified the working-out of Hegel's destiny for man."[5]

Aggressive westernism and American exceptionalism combined with the engineer's sense of a categorical imperative for concrete achievement of the beautiful to make this democratic, expansionist view of culture also a powerfully exclusionary one for anyone who opposed the specific concretizations selected to advance the course of history. One sees a familiar stigmatization of opposing views: "The leadership [of the Movement] inveighed against the Marxist adaptation of the Hegelian dialectic, and it distinguished its members from European 'negative Hegelians.' In 1901 Snider went so far as to ascribe radical or socialist Hegelianism to a non-Western consciousness present among some Europeans. Marx, for example, had strayed from authentic Hegelian teachings because his Jewish background had given him a propensity for Oriental collectivism."[6]

These considerations began to complicate the narrative of aspiration woven out of Hegelianism and American exceptionalism. Furthermore, when the view of the Movement shifts from events to texts, interesting, if anomalous, patterns begin to appear, and one encounters a different history from that of the progress of the consciousness of freedom. The first of Hegel's texts to arrive west of the Mississippi, in St. Louis, was a translation by Brokmeyer, dictated to Harris, of the *Wissenschaft der Logik*, often called the "Greater *Logic*." The American *Logic* was born, in Snider's account, as if in answer to the dialectical conflict of the Civil War itself. Part of the manuscript of the translation is inscribed "Finished August 16, Thursday, 1861—25 minutes to 6 P.M."—seemingly a gesture indicating an awareness of the historic nature of their time and their labor. Later, Snider would comment on the forming of the St. Louis Philosophical Society in 1866:

> The Civil War had just concluded, in which we all had in some way participated, and we were still overwhelmed, even dazed partially by the grand historic appearance. What does it all mean? was quite the

5. Goetzmann, *American Hegelians*, 14.
6. Gottfried, *Search*, 16.

universal question. . . . A great world-historical deed had been done
with enormous labor and outer panoramic pageantry. What lay in it for
us and for the future? So we began to grope after the everlasting veri-
ties, the eternal principles, the pure essences [*reine Wesenheiten*] as they
are called by our philosophic authority. These transcendent energies of
man and of the world were said to be collected and ordered in one
book—Hegel's Logic.[7]

The *Logic* was felt to be a redemptive text—a conviction the St.
Louis Hegelians shared with, or passed on to, Walt Whitman, as Kathryne Lindberg notes in her essay in this volume—but its life-clarifying
potential needed to be unlocked somehow. The *Logic* had the reputation
as "the hardest book in the world, the one least accessible to the ordinary human mind even when academically trained." Reading was out
of the question; access to the text had to be gained through a ready-to-
hand algorithmic method. This conviction removed the emphasis of
study from theory to practical application, as Harris recalls:

> Mr. Brockmeyer . . . impressed us with the practicality of philosophy,
> inasmuch as he could flash into the questions of the day, or even into
> the questions of the moment, the highest insight of philosophy and
> solve their problems. Even the hunting of wild turkeys or squirrels was
> the occasion for the use of philosophy. Philosophy came to mean with
> us, therefore, the most practical of all species of knowledge. We used it
> to solve all problems connected with school-teaching and school man-
> agement. We studied the "dialectic" of politics and political parties and
> understood how measures and men might be combined by its light.[8]

To the St. Louis Hegelians, the issue of making Hegel available
to the people at large became a prominent concern and the occasion for
a number of imaginary musings and plans. Brokmeyer remarked that

7. John O. Riedl, "The Hegelians of Saint Louis, Missouri and Their Influence in
the United States," in *The Legacy of Hegel*, ed. J. J. O'Malley *et al.* (The Hague, 1973),
272; Denton Jacques Snider, *The St. Louis Movement in Philosophy, Literature, Education,
Psychology, with Chapters of Autobiography* (St. Louis, 1920), 27–28, quoted *ibid.*, 268. I rely
on Riedl's account for several details concerning Brokmeyer, Harris, and the founding of
the St. Louis group.
8. William Torrey Harris, *Hegel's Logic. A Book on the Genesis of the Categories of the
Mind. A Critical Exposition* (Chicago, 1890), xi–xiii, quoted in Riedl, "Hegelians," 274–
75.

Hegel ought to be able to be read and understood at a rate commensurate with the speed of the steam engine. In an essay titled "Why Hegel should be Popular," he wrote:

> There can be no doubt . . . that the increased speed, the haste at which we have arrived, would have been no detriment to the general usefulness of the book. As it is, I fear it never will be of much value as a source of popular entertainment. . . . But it does seem to me that if there is a theme in nature, art or science that ought to be popular, that ought to be thoroughly familiar to everybody, it is the one treated in this book: for it treats of nothing but human knowing. . . . Or, is it true that we live habitually out of doors and are strangers nowhere so much as in our own house?[9]

The final sentence of this quoted passage gives expression, in strikingly Emersonian language, to a theme repeatedly encountered in readings of Hegel. Jean Hyppolite, for example, claims that Hegel's great concern is to make ordinary consciousness recognize itself in philosophic consciousness and vice versa.[10] The popularization of Hegel was a notion that came from the heart of the liberal and right-Hegelian position, as espoused not in Europe, however, but in America.

A kind of cult developed around the *Logic*. It was the book that Brokmeyer, the inspirational leader of the St. Louis Hegelians, swore by, and it was the book with which he attempted to convert thinkers into believers in the Hegelian system, as he had done to Harris. *It is at this point, early in the history of the St. Louis Movement, that the second, deeper level of the forgetting of Hegel manifests itself, as if it were the return of the repressed: the material linguistic sign that is forgotten in reading Hegel is reasserted, remembered, by the text of Hegel itself, even despite itself.* As if in resistance to the fluidity Brokmeyer wished to confer on the *Logic*, the text itself remained stranded in a crabbed translation by Brokmeyer himself—a translation that Snider recalls "was on the whole very lit-

9. Henry C. Brokmeyer, *A Mechanic's Diary* (Washington, D.C., 1910), 55–56 (note the populist title), quoted in Riedl, "Hegelians," 271.

10. Jean Hyppolite, "The Structure of Philosphic Language According to the 'Preface' of Hegel's *Phenomenology of the Mind*," in *The Structuralist Controversy: The Languages of Criticism and the Sciences of Man*, ed. Richard Macksey and Eugenio Donato (Baltimore, 1972), 165. *Cf.* Hyppolite, *Genesis and Structure of Hegel's "Phenomenology of Spirit*," trans. Samuel Cherniak and John Heckman (Evanston, Ill., 1974), 4.

eral—so literal that I often had to turn back to the German, in order to understand the English."[11] Harris had studied stenography and had copied down the graphic signs of phonography as Brokmeyer dictated to him, but the dialectic between speech and writing was never able to reach transcendence. The sign remained a foreign body imported into their midst.

The inaugural American translations of the *Logic* and the *Phenomenology* were so unreadable that no publisher would accept the manuscripts. A drama seems to be unfolding here in which the Hegel of the concrete universal is directly countered by his own writing and by writing itself, as manifested in literal translation. The curious but telling result is that Hegel proves incapable of entering the concretely universalizing realm of publication in the English-speaking world. Of course almost all of his texts, including the *Logic*, have eventually been translated and published, yet the intrinsic difficulty encountered in St. Louis seems to have had two determining consequences in Anglo-America at large: the long failure of English philosophy to take other than a dismissive stance toward Hegel, and the invisibility of Hegel's influence in American culture and American universities—an imperceptibility that was compounded when English predispositions overtook American philosophy departments in the twentieth century, ousting the continental tradition of inquiry.

The St. Louis parable (parabola?) of Hegel suggests a further twist. In a countermovement to what one might call the invisible American path of Hegelian "spirit," the letter—Hegel's writing—became reified and fetishized in the hands of his St. Louis cult: the unreadable translation of the *Phenomenology* was kept in manuscript in a tin box, to be brought out faithfully, scripturally at each meeting of the Society. Moreover, as a curious side effect, the unreadable translation began to be overwritten as a cultural and biographical document, ghostwritten or *Geist*-written, as it were, through association with its translator. The text of the *Logic* became, in a sense, a palimpsest over which was drafted a decidedly romantic narrative that blended transcendental thought, life rhythms, and politics. Snider gives the reader all the materials needed to see Hegel transformed, through the charismatic Brokmeyer, into the American Spirit in dialectic with itself: "I found Brokmeyer re-translating the original on his return from the in-

---

11. Snider, *St. Louis Movement*, 13, quoted in Riedl, "Hegelians," 279.

dians in the early nineties. And I saw him thumbing over the manuscript only a few days before his death in 1906. It was his one Supreme Book, his Bible; it meant to him more than any other human production, and was probably the source of his greatest spiritual transformation from social hostility and inner discord and even anarchism, to a reconciliation with his government and indeed with the World-Order, after his two maddened flights from civilization."[12] Brokmeyer seems to have enacted a microcosmic narrative of American history, with Hegel's *Logic* functioning repeatedly as the Book in which, like Saint Augustine at the moment of conversion, he reads his own—America's—destiny. Such reconciliation would seem to accord with the deep inner reconciliation that Hegel considered to be the goal of his philosophy of spirit.

After Brokmeyer died, his friends proposed to the editor of the Library of Philosophy that he publish the translation, "accompanied with a short biography of the translator . . . to partake of the character of a tribute to his memory both as a philosopher and as Governor of the State of Missouri." But, the editor goes on to recall, though the manuscript had a "romantic history," the translation was not of high quality, and hence the only motive to publish it would have been to devote a sentimental tribute to the translator. Thus the editor had to concede that it was "impossible" for him to accept it for publication, "as it seemed inappropriate to have a volume of this kind included in a series devoted to the pure study of philosophy."[13] The *Logic* not appropriate to the pure study of philosophy! The accent in this remark might properly be shifted to the word *study*, for as the translated text becomes purer it becomes more impossible to study, to appropriate as meaning-for-oneself.

Ironically, substance and subject repeatedly fail to unite in the vicissitudes of Hegel in St. Louis: the unapproachable manuscript and the romantic life remain bound together without interblending; the text with a universal message remains mute and must be coupled with a sentimental tribute that would convert the resultant book into a commodity with only private appeal. Jacques Derrida's proclamation that Hegel is the "last philosopher of the book and the first thinker of writing" takes on unexpected meaning in a country where Edward Dahl-

12. *Ibid.*
13. John Henry Muirhead, Editor's Note to *Hegel's Science of Logic*, trans. W. H. Johnston and W. G. Struthers (London, 1929), 17–18, quoted in Riedl, "Hegelians," 282.

ing" takes on unexpected meaning in a country where Edward Dahlberg has remarked, with a mixture of scorn and wonder, that the cult of the book is our secret passion.[14] Allegorically, unconsciously, the episode of Brokmeyer's unreadable translation enacts the problem of Hegel for literary theory, as well as for cultural and educational policy, namely, that the very medium that makes it possible to think the project of spirit is itself the most resistant element in that project: the sign, the concretization that to Hegel *makes* thought, is decodable, translatable, but unreadable—inappropriable, unreturnable to ordinary consciousness. Any attempt to read appropriable meaning out of a text thus necessarily takes on the character of a palimpsest, a "romantic history," a narrative that may be full of meaning but is about someone or something else.

## SPIRITLESS THINKING

A bridge is said to be a trans-lation, a carrying-across from point of origin to destination. It is a matter of renewing the life of civilization: Aeneas makes a bridge of himself in carrying Anchises, and the flight from Troy to Rome is known as the *translatio imperii*. A translation, for its part, is supposed to be a bridge, allowing an opening up of a previously unfamiliar region to civilization and its commerce. Beneath the syntheses of St. Louis—and whether marked by bridge or arch, this city has repeatedly implied Hegel in its symbolism—lurks a repressed conflict that is at once more real and more theoretical, more difficult to trace because it has not been incorporated into intellectual discourse until the last two decades. This is a repression in which Hegel himself takes part and which might be called, for the sake of brevity and clarity, the forgetting of the "semiological" Hegel by the "cultural" Hegel. The semiological Hegel is hardly one that Hegel himself would have acknowledged, yet it is written so distinctly into his text that Derrida calls him "*also* the thinker of irreducible difference," adding that "he rehabilitated thought as the *memory productive* of signs," *i.e.*, the *produc-*

14. Jacques Derrida, *Of Grammatology*, trans. Gayatri Chakravorty Spivak (Baltimore, 1976), 24–26; Edward Dahlberg, *Alms for Oblivion* (Minneapolis, 1964), 79, 86: "Underneath our genius, which is not really political, is the crust of cult, for we turn every doctrine into a Bible, sex, or geographic screed. . . . American radicalism . . . is half Bible socialism, half sex cult." See also pp. 62–63, on the question "How important have books been to the republic?"

*tive Gedächtniß,* or productive memory, which produces nothing but signs or marks.[15]

The kernel of Derrida's approach to Hegel may be found in the closing pages of the first subsection of the *Grammatology,* titled "The End of the Book and the Beginning of Writing," where Derrida follows the itinerary of Hegel's ambivalent attitude in the *Encyclopedia* toward writing. Writing in itself is abstraction, alienation, loss of the self, pure exteriorization, the denial of interiority. However, phonetic writing subdues this tendency, mastering writing by making it work in the service of voice. Voice is the expression of interiority and, seen through Western political history, the expression of the deliberation that issues in the will of the people; to capture it and preserve it for study means to follow its development with more intense devotion, to bring the movement of spirit before the tribunal of conscious intelligence. Thus Hegel reasons: "It also follows from what has been said, that learning to read and write an alphabetic script is to be regarded as an infinitely rewarding means of education [*unendliches Bildungsmittel*], a means moreover, which has been insufficiently appreciated, for it leads spirit from what is sensuously concrete into awareness of the more formal nature of the spoken word and its abstract elements, and does what is essential in order to establish and purify the basis of inwardness within the subject" (*PSS,* Sec. 459).

Alphabetic writing is the greatest instrument in service of the expansion of education and culture, specifically a culture of interiority. But when writing is not married to voice through phonetic script, Hegel sees in it the very essence of that which is against life, against the life of spirit, and against history, insofar as history is seen as the path of the development of spirit. In its proper nature, without being tamed and subordinated to the service of speech, writing is exegetical and not spontaneous; it does not allow expression or "spiritual creation" to take place; it is dependent, parasitic on another's word. This trait makes it also antidemocratic, inasmuch as Hegel finds these elements together

15. In working to uncover this level of Hegel, I am relying chiefly on Derrida's sketch of this split Hegel in *Grammatology,* 24–26 (translation altered slightly), more thoroughly worked out in Derrida, *Margins of Philosophy,* trans. Alan Bass (Chicago, 1982), 69–108, and on de Man's "Sign and Symbol." Quotations of Hegel's *Encyclopedia* in German and English are taken from G. W. F. Hegel, *Hegel's Philosophy of Subjective Spirit,* trans. M. J. Petry (3 vols.; Boston, 1978), Vol. III, Sec. 458. Further references will cite this edition as *PSS* in the text. I have altered the translation where it seemed necessary to conform more closely to Hegel's literal word choice.

in the elitist, "exegetic" (*statarisch*) culture of the Chinese: "The written hieroglyphic language of the Chinese is adapted only to the exegetic nature of this people, and in any case this kind of written language can only be cultivated by the minority which maintains its exclusive possession of a people's spiritual culture" (*PSS*, Sec. 459).

Still, Hegel insists that the sign, with its fundamental property of alienability from its material context, is "something great" (*etwas Großes*), a "great advance" over the symbol, whose meaning, like utterance, remains tied to the context of its production (*PSS*, Addition to Sec. 457). He then goes on to consider closely the heterogeneity of meaning to the material sign. He now characterizes the bringing together of two radically distinct elements in the sign as the "unity deriving from intelligence . . . of independent presentation and an intuition" (*PSS*, Sec. 458). The material of the intuition is "immediate or given," he goes on, but it does not represent itself: "It is an image, which has received into itself as its soul or *significance*, an independent presentation of intelligence. This intuition is the *sign*":

> The *sign* is a certain immediate intuition, presenting a content which is wholly distinct from that which it has for itself;—it is the *pyramid* in which an alien soul is ensconced and preserved.

The choice of the pyramid metaphor here—the house of the dead—may seem dissonant, since Hegel's intent seems to be to show that by signification the intelligence gains in *Bildung* (culturedness), hence in power, and, presumably, therefore in life: "In its use of intuition therefore, intelligence displays more wilfulness and sovereignty in *designating* than it does in symbolizing" (*PSS*, Sec. 458). Yet the metaphor is apt, for the imposition of a foreign representation on a material entity necessarily disrupts or cancels its own self-representation. For an entity to become a signifier it must to that extent cease being a subject; it must lose its freedom and become a pure load-carrier. Seen in this way, signification is a process of enslavement; "subjection" now takes on a double meaning. In the sign, the intelligence "gives its independent presentations a definite determinate being, *treating* the filled space and time of the intuition *as its own*." The signified, for its part, as the precious cargo carried, has had to be harvested from the intuitions of independently existent entities in order to be entered into its realm of universality ("the vague mine and universality") by the intelligence. The signified undergoes death, in this sense; as Hegel will say in the *Aesthetics*, the pyramid manifests the truth that "the inward indeed [is] the negative of life, as death."[16] Its existence in signification is only an afterlife; it can only be "conserved." The sign no longer has for its model the dynamic figure of the bridge as pure opportunity, the aspiring model that productive imagination supplies in its (to Hegel comparatively blind) undertaking. Instead, the figurative image for the sign is the duo of pyramid and mummy, and Hegel will argue in his *Aesthetics* that these artifacts are a testimony of the self-limitation and impotence of a civilization. This model, however, is what the sign looks like upon its completion, under the aspect of mechanical memory.

In his lectures on aesthetics, Hegel discusses Egyptian art under the developmental phase he calls "symbolic," and he finds evidence everywhere in Egyptian artifacts that the ancient Egyptians did not achieve a conception of life as freedom. They "have only reached the threshold of the realm of freedom." They intuited the immortality of the soul and detached the spirit from its imprisonment in nature, but they did not allow it through struggle to emerge in new life. The "realm of death" is the inward, "the negative of life," meaning. But the Egyptians have succeeded in realizing only one side of its truth, "and that a formal one, namely that of being removed from immediate existence; and so this realm is primarily only Hades, not yet a life which, even if liberated from the sensuous as such, is still nevertheless at the same time self-existent and therefore in itself free and living spirit." He concludes, "The Pyramids are such an external environment in which an inner meaning rests concealed." Taken together, the *Encyclopedia* and the *Aesthetics* seem to imply that for Hegel it is necessary to forget the sign in order to achieve life, spirit, and history—or to produce their illusions in philosophical consciousness.

At first regard, the outlook for America in the history of the progress of spirit seems to be good indeed. The section "Geographic Basis of History," which forms part of the prefatory matter in Hegel's *Philosophy of History*, is the place of the famous comment about America as the "land of the future" that so directly influenced the St. Louis Hegelians. A closer examination of this section, however, reveals that Hegel sees America as the site of repeated misadventures of the dialectic

16. G. W. F. Hegel, *Aesthetics: Lectures on Fine Art*, trans. T. M. Knox (2 vols.; Oxford, 1975), I, 355–56.

of history. To find the wisdom in this text, one must follow his argument with patience, for he asserts several received and reigning opinions as true that today are found distasteful and manifestly false. As other critics have sometimes found, Hegel's racist comments are places at which he is likely to say something most unintendedly insightful about his entire system, for the subject of race, like the subject of geography, is tied to material existence.[17] In this light, the title itself, "Geographic Basis of History," can be reread as conceding the material basis of idealism.

For example, Hegel employs an allegation that Thomas Jefferson had already refuted, namely, that native Americans are physically weak, in order to generalize about the fate of spirit in America. The substance of American soil is so weak that it does not have the capacity to produce a native subject (in the sense of the subject of history, the equivalent of European man). "America has always shown itself physically and psychically powerless, and still shows itself so. . . . The weakness of the American physique was a chief reason for bringing the negroes to America, to employ their labor in the work that had to be done in the New World; for the negroes are far more susceptible of European culture than the Indians."[18] Hegel is discoursing on the failure of a synthetic dialectic between the subject of history—the European—and its new substance—America—to form on its own. The term mediating the oppositions, performing the labor of concretization, should be accomplished by the exteriorization of the subject himself. But instead the mediating term must be imported from elsewhere; the agents of concretization are neither European nor American but African, outside history, according to the treatment of Africa he gives (typically bigoted as it is) later in this section; they remain irrevocably foreign. *The negroes* is hence the element through which the historical subject tells itself it is accomplishing history, yet it is also the element that bars the subject from making, or participating in, history.

17. James A. Snead's comments in "Repetition as a Figure of Black Culture," in *Black Literature and Literary Theory*, ed. Henry Louis Gates, Jr. (New York, 1984), 62–65, are particularly perceptive. For Hegel's racism, see Sander L. Gilman, "The Figure of the Black in the Thought of Hegel and Nietzsche," *German Quarterly*, LIV (March, 1980), 141–58.

18. G. W. F. Hegel, *The Philosophy of History*, trans. J. Sibree (1899; rpr. New York, 1956), 82. I am using the translation that was most influential on American readers rather than the newer, more accurate translation by H. B. Nisbet. Further references will cite the Sibree translation as *PH* parenthetically in the text.

Another potential for mediation arises from the contrast between North and South America and the chief religions that characterize their cultures:

> From the Protestant religion sprang the principle of the mutual confidence of individuals—trust in the honorable dispositions of other men; for in the Protestant Church the entire life—its activity generally—is the field for what it deems religious works. Among Catholics, on the contrary, the basis for such a confidence cannot exist; for in secular matters only force and voluntary subservience are the principles of action; and the forms which are called Constitutions are in this case only a resort of necessity, and are no protection against mistrust. (*PH,* 84)

*Trust* is the mediating term that Protestants have and Catholics lack. It might be said that trust is mediation par excellence. It allows politics to take place in the form of the interiorization of the state, the necessary preamble for spirit to engage in its historical activity. In South America, Hegel has noted, "the state was merely something external for the protection of property," and hence the activity of spirit could never find its way to the center stage of world history. (After reading John Carlos Rowe in this volume, it should be apparent just how well Hegel's description of South America fits the United States as it appears in Herman Melville's *Pierre.*)

But trust as pure mediation also has its problems. Hegel goes on to sketch a brief portrait of *idées reçues* about American life, one that turns out to invert trust into its opposite, all because the chief activity of Americans is so *purely* subjective: "If, on the one side, the Protestant Church develops the essential principle of confidence, as already stated, it thereby involves on the other hand the recognition of the validity of the element of feeling to such a degree as gives encouragement to unseemly varieties of caprice" (*PH,* 85). Trust as mediation thus comes to seem less a bridge than a slippery floor, or plane, of encounter. Hegel has just mentioned the penchant of "American merchants" for "dishonest dealings." The inverted world of trust seems to dictate that the subject of history in North America will be replaced by the Confidence Man. That this development anticipates Melville hardly needs to be said, the more so since this passage in its entirety can be taken to imply that the poetics of the American novel will be a poetics of caprice. (Thus, also, it is far from coincidental that one of the scapegoat figures for the destabilization of confidence seized upon by the conversationalists aboard the *Fidèle* is the Jesuit missionaries, supposedly the *ne plus ultra* of Catholics, who, in Hegel's words, recognize "only force and voluntary subservience.")

If slave importation characterizes and prevents the American subject of history in the South, the mercantile reliance on confidence continually undermines the production of the historical subject in the North. Finally, in what amounts to a third snapshot taken on tour, Hegel looks to a recognizable cliché of the American West, where he finds that America lacks the internal tensions and developments that are necessary to develop the European state: "America is hitherto exempt from this pressure, for it has the outlet of colonization constantly and widely open, and multitudes are continually streaming into the plains of the Mississippi. By this means the chief source of discontent is removed, and the continuation of the existing civil condition is guaranteed. . . . Had the woods of Germany been in existence, the French Revolution would not have occurred" (*PH*, 86). It is the element of discontent that leads to the linked boons of self-alienation, exteriorization, the production of the sign in the service of speech, and, ultimately, the European model state. It is striking that Hegel is arguing nothing like Turner's thesis of the frontier as safeguard of American liberty, a thesis arrived at through the mediation of Loria's Hegelianism. Here the frontier serves not as a block to the operation of the historical dialectic that will produce the state, the subject of history, but as a kind of fuse, which, once it is burned out, will allow the elements of discontent to mix and ferment into history. Until this happens, America will be a strange civil society with the idea of the state interiorized but not produced—written in glorious script but not uttered (*geäußert*). The frontier is the postponement, not the cancellation; the deferral, not the *Aufhebung*, of history. It is, therefore, what makes America strange and literally unspiritual. It is a soft, pliant wall off which the dialectic cannot rebound. In America, the dialectic neither operates nor stands still; it fizzles.

This factor of delay in the frontier is what leads Hegel to arrive at his famous formulation:

> America is therefore the land of the future, where, in the ages that lie before us, the burden of the World's History shall reveal itself—perhaps in a contest between North and South America. It is a land of

desire for all those who are weary of the historical lumber-room of old Europe. (*PH*, 86)

The ringing first words of this passage thus take on a different meaning in the context of Hegel's argument. At first glance they would appear to contrast diametrically with another famous sentence of Hegel's, the knell sounded at the beginning of the *Aesthetics:* "In all these respects art, considered in its highest vocation, is and remains for us a thing of the past." If that sentence summarizes how art must henceforth have become thought, however, the formulation in "Geographic Basis of History" announces how spirit in America will forever be unrealizable: it will never have entered into that authentic dialectic called concretization or self-alienation, *Äußerung.* "As a Land of the Future, it has no interest for us here, for . . . in regard to *Philosophy,* . . . we have to do with that which (strictly speaking) is neither past nor future, but with that which *is,* which has an external existence—with Reason" (*PH*, 87). Being "of the future" means to lack the mediation that allows spirit to emerge out of subject and substance. Instead, historical spirit will be unrealizable, thought will exist in its unmediated, alien, Egyptian/African form, revealing its semiological essence but preventing history.

The very inauthenticity of the "expression" of spirit in America, however, allows a curious development to take place in that back door to the dialectic that has been identified as Hegel's semiology: "What *has* taken place in the New World up to the present time is only an echo of the Old World—the expression of a foreign Life" (*PH*, 86). The foreignness of life in the New World recalls Hegel's assertion in the *Encyclopedia* that the sign presents "a content which is wholly distinct from that which it has for itself;—it is the *pyramid* in which an alien soul is ensconced and preserved." Living its labor only substitutively or allegorically; subject to a nondialectical, counterhistorical antinomy of trust and caprice; deferred continually from collective reflection by the frontier, America is then such a pyramid: impossible for philosophy or history to produce its proper political dialectic, and dead and embalmed until it does. America is a sign: the signifier is a slave; the signified is dead, "only an echo of the Old World." All that can happen is, in D. H. Lawrence's seriocomic phrase, "post-mortem effects." [19]

19. D. H. Lawrence, *Studies in Classic American Literature* (New York, 1977), 172, 173.

Hegel's comments on slavery, the atmosphere of Protestant mercantilism, and the frontier have a certain insightful relevance to the phenomena themselves, partly because Hegel is unfailingly attentive to the operation of real dialectics in practice between operating human subjects. The conclusion I read here, however, has more to do with the place of America in Hegelian thought, and hence with the implicit terms that American cultural discourse has adopted for itself. Hegel's passage on America shows the role that America plays in his thought, as the dismantler of his system, or as the name of the place that gives rise to the realization of how every place escapes the history of spirit. Thus, paradoxically, America does have a specific nature, but it is in the realm of thought: it is the place where thinking was discovered to run counter to the errand of spirit everywhere.

It is just such a pyramidic structure—of thought as alien content, conserved sterilely in a wrapping of expression or history—that Hegel's *Logic* reveals itself to be, in the hands of the St. Louis Hegelians, and, as Joseph Kronick argues in "Romance and the Prose of the World," that Blithedale or Boston becomes, as enacted in Nathaniel Hawthorne's romances. Far from being a self-reflexive, self-founding form, argues Kronick, both philosophy and romance are subsumable under the category of *prose*, Hegel's extensive term in the *Aesthetics* for a discursive practice whose aim and performance are not artistic but critical, "exegetical." Kronick concludes that America is eminently prosaic.

## THE PERILS OF HISTORICIZING

That the *Logic* should be Hegel's carte d'entrée across the Atlantic has a peculiar appropriateness. As Snider relates, "This Logic was declared to be the movement of the pure essences of the world, stripped from their outer illusory vesture."[20] The *Logic* attempts to give the conceptual structure of the Idea independently of its gradual revelation in the experience of nature and history: "in logic," writes Hegel in introducing his work, "the presupposition is that which has proved itself to be the *result* of that phenomenological consideration" in the phenomenology of spirit; "in the said result, *the Idea has determined itself to be the*

---

20. Snider, *St. Louis Movement*, 7, quoted in Riedl, "Hegelians," 273.

*certainty which has become truth*, the certainty which, on the one hand, no longer has the object over against it but has internalized it, *knows it as its own self*—and, on the other hand . . . *has divested itself of this subjectivity and is at one with its self-alienation*."[21] The Constitution announced implicitly that the United States was to be a nation begun with eyes open, not coming gradually to itself through the twists and turns of historical experience but deduced, defined, and inaugurated by a collective performative act of writing. The opening of the *Logic*, furthermore, announcing that pure being is in fact nothing and that therefore pure nothing is pure being, could seem to an expatriated European on the midwestern plains to announce a path into a new level of insight into reality and a new vista of concretization, a path that did not have to take the bloody road of history. As Kronick reasons in his essay in this volume, the notion of self-founding that serves as the urgent goal of the *Logic* could be said to be everything that the modern conception of American politics, as well as of poetry and philosophy, is about.

Most of the essays in this volume examine the ways in which America has imagined itself through the medium of Hegel. Henry Sussman's essay in this volume virtually unmasks the word *America* as both a philosophical and an ideological construct. Hegel's logic of supersession, ultimately deriving from the New Testament/Old Testament relation in Christian exegesis, finds its ideological extension as a recipe for civilizational annexation. Sussman shows that America's description of itself vis-à-vis Europe, for former Europeans of all nationalities, has followed the logic of the *Aufhebung:* supersession, preservation, and cancellation. For Sussman, the modern age is marked by a tendency to do all historical thinking, including poetic solutions or evasions, in Hegelian terms—and the Hegel Sussman sees at work in this tendency is a master ideologue of Euro-American hegemony by means of the logic of superimposition. Similarly, for Riddel both modernism and the notion of the unending poetic project that modernism and the postmodern hold in common derive from Hegel. Both Roebling and Hart Crane expose their involvement with Hegel's dynamic through the figure of the bridge.

Gregory Jay shows that critical discourse has also reacted to Hegel, but in a more complex, less courageous way. American literary

---

21. G. W. F. Hegel, *Hegel's Science of Logic*, trans. A. V. Miller (London, 1969), 69 (emphasis added).

history has been conceived in right-Hegelian terms but has refused to face Hegel; its implicit adoption of Kantian epistemology and aesthetics is, as Hegel read Kant, a retreat from the task of confronting and transforming reality. Jay's careful following of Hegel's distinctions seems to insist that American criticism can hardly claim to be ready for deconstruction or what presumably lies beyond it, since it has never grasped Hegel's construction of the dialectic that unlocked the formalist impasses of Kant—impasses that take refuge in the cult of the sublime and in the intuitionism of transcendentalism.

After these broad views of ideology, poetry, and criticism, the essays in Part II examine specific episodes of Hegel in the American text. In "Early American Antigone," Breitwieser gives ample evidence, through an astute analysis of the ideological history of American Puritanism, that Hegelianism in American culture runs deep and works hard to suppress and marginalize insistent dissonant elements. Puritanism was not a negative theology but a repressive reliance on exempla in the manner of Sophocles' Creon. Such a logic represses mourning and in practice consigns the work of mourning to the slave rather than the master, to woman rather than man, so that man can delude himself that he is going about his mission unencumbered by the mute protests of earth. Hegel's dictate of assimilating mourning characterizes a Euro-American assumption that Puritan American literature both asserts and questions.

The Hegel that Lindberg finds in Whitman has grown far more robust, becoming a generalized figure of salvation. The imaginary Hegel uncovered in "Whitman's 'Convertible Terms'" is a fully orchestrated version of the imaginary Hegel of St. Louis, a wand-bearing angel of Imagination, a Yes to the problem. He seems nothing short of an allegorical figure of Hope when Whitman writes of the reconciliation of individualism and patriotism: "I have no doubt myself that the two will merge, and will mutually profit and brace each other, and that from them a greater product, a third, will arise." He seems to enter the text of Whitman's notebooks always along with the very notion of *"Warnings (encouragements too, and of the vastest,) from the Old World to the New."* [22] He stands for this grandfatherly figure, apparently, who dissolves the guilt and anger of the father-son relation in subl(im)ated de-

---

22. Walt Whitman, *Prose Works 1892*, ed. Floyd Stovall (2 vols.; New York, 1963–64), II, 373; *ibid.*, I, 262.

tachment. But Lindberg is concerned too with how Whitman uses his imaginary construction of Hegel to help him define his version of the poetic *anti*populism that has played a determinative role in American literary history. In brief, this ideology has to do with the surpassing of the old landed, cultured elite by a new race of men (and the term *men* is used advisedly) trained for superiority by exposure to superior ideas.

For Whitman, in what becomes the American divergence from Hegel's orthodoxy, "literature" takes the place of "Spirit" as the ultimate stage of self-consciousness as well as the motive force of history. Literary historians have taken their cue from this reorientation in portraying both a national sensibility and a modernist literature as inevitable products of the self-contained infinite progress of reason. Hegelian historicism tends to represent modernism as at once a culmination of a European past and a radically new beginning for a mode of consciousness without precedent and with infinite potential. Marked by a naïve notion of perfectibility, this geneticist version of Hegel's concept of history reduces Emerson to the flawed source of an original American literature: his disjointed and diffuse works provide the basis for an aesthetic that is perfected in Thoreau, Whitman, and Dickinson. American literature comes to be taken as an a priori entity that unfolds itself throughout history in the various authors canonized as the tradition. In addition to expressing itself in a progressivist concept of history, this ideology also determines the isolationist and insular attitude of American studies programs, the periodization of literary movements, and the presupposition of a distinctly "American" identity for a literature that begins in the questioning of the very concepts of origin, identity, and history.

In retrospect, Hegel's St. Louis reception presents itself as something of an allegory of the difficulty of reading his text, especially of reading it without succumbing to the unceasing temptation to resort to the self-affirming formulations that American literary history has repeatedly put forward. This difficulty could be called a struggle between the sign and historiographic ideology, or between reading and thematizing or historicizing. In any case, it is the very struggle that has occupied with increasing emphasis the reading of Hegel in Europe, whether through Marx and various Marxist philosophies of negativity (notably T. W. Adorno's) or through Kojève and the French thought arising from his reading of Hegel's master-slave dialectic. Georges Bataille, Derrida, Michel Foucault, René Girard, and Gilles Deleuze form a spectrum of response whose thought transforms, critiques, undermines, or attacks the dialectic.[23] The grand projects identified with Hegel—expounding the Idea as the concrete universal, and incarnating reason in and as history—now mark him as the last philosopher of the Logos. To this "Hegel," history proper is the philosophy of history, and the task of historical investigation is simply and supremely the application of thought to history. Reason is self-supporting, the material of its own operation, and will complete history by transforming it into Reason's own image. Even Maurice Merleau-Ponty, characterizing the liberalization of Hegel's mission in the philosophical movements of the twentieth century, cannot escape this formulation when he writes that it was Hegel "who started the attempt to explore the irrational and integrate it into an expanded reason, which remains the task of our century."[24]

The chronic oversimplifications in this model of the totalizing process of history have often led modern intellectuals to conclude that the Hegelian dialectic of history cannot avoid a homogenization that grossly falsifies particular, contingent reality, especially as it occurs in historical events. This assessment has operated with the mission of defending the site of real, independent existence from the danger, in principle, of extinction—a danger that in the twentieth century has expanded beyond the metaphysics textbook to the front page of political reality. Hegel's *Philosophy of History* and the *Phenomenology*, insofar as it is read as a document of the evolution of concrete consciousness as history *tout court*, are especially vulnerable to this critique. As the minor voice objecting to Hegel's stance of majority takes on historical and political substance, one comes to see it as a positive duty to read Hegel against himself.

Early in this century, Franz Rosenzweig charted the course Judaism would have to take to oppose such a monomyth of history. For Rosenzweig, "history in the 19th-century sense" is the development and realization of the spirit through its metamorphoses, at once necessary and intelligible, its judgments belonging to Reason itself.[25] In

23. For the tracing of much of this line of intellectual inheritance see Judith Butler, *Subjects of Desire: Hegelian Reflections in Twentieth-Century France* (New York, 1987).

24. Maurice Merleau-Ponty, "Hegel's Existentialism," in Merleau-Ponty, *Sense and Non-Sense*, trans. H. L. Dreyfus and P. A. Dreyfus (Evanston, Ill., 1964), 63.

25. Franz Rosenzweig to Eugen Rosenstock, quoted in Stéphane Mosès, "Hegel pris au mot: La critique de l'histoire chez Franz Rosenzweig," *Revue de métaphysique et de morale*, XC (1985), 328–29.

1910, he insists, Hegel could not be read otherwise than as chief ideologist of the Bismarckian state. History had come to mean the proving ground of what is rational and what is not, *i.e.*, what has to disappear with no regrets.

At the core of Rosenzweig's critique of Hegel's philosophy of history is the assertion that "Christianity becomes for Hegel the archetype of the accord between the rational and the real." In other words, Christianity—by which Hegel always means its most extensive realization in society, what Kierkegaard will call, scathingly, "Christendom"—is the phenomenon to be explicated and, at the same time, the law of its own explication. Thus it must always leave out those realities that fall outside its ordering. The very principle that Rosenzweig names, the "accord between rational and real," recodes in broader terms the unity of signified and signifier that Jean Hyppolite takes to be the definition of thought in Hegel. Through Rosenzweig's perspective, the formula "rational = real" can come to be seen as a recipe for the self-willed blindness of the powerful. For Rosenzweig, the tyranny of history and the tyranny of the Logos, now understandable either as Reason or as Word, S/s, are two sides of the same oppression.[26]

At the beginning of the First World War, shortly after Rosenzweig's magisterial *Hegel und der Staat* (1910), George Santayana wrote *Egotism in German Philosophy* (1915) and moved briskly from an epistemological and ethical assessment of egotism to its political implications, with results strikingly similar to Rosenzweig's critique, for all his differences in political vulnerability, tradition, and tone. As an international and an agnostic, strongly favoring Catholic culture, Santayana found himself triply marginalized from the program for the realization of *Geist* in America, a project he viewed with distaste in any case. Santayana was undoubtedly reacting against the entrenched Hegelianism of American academic philosophy and educational policy. The "egotism" he sees in Hegel (a term so *rébarbatif* to his French editor that he advised changing it in the French translation to the more neutral *erreur* with a neatly indicative subtitle added: "*je suis, donc tu n'es pas*") is much more to the point when seen as addressing the American acceptation of Hegel. Santayana's assessment of Hegel would have been dismissed by any Hegelian, who might have labeled it the view of an

26. *Ibid.*, 341; Hyppolite, "Structure of Philosophic Language," 160: "for Hegel himself there is no thought outside the unity of signifier and signified"; Mosès, "Hegel pris au mot," 335–36.

aestheticist, a pessimist, and an inactivist. Yet it bears reexamining for its peculiar resonance with Rosenzweig's critique and even, implicitly, with Derrida's.

Santayana's objections to the sweep of spirit through history and culture stem from an aesthetic devotion to particularity rather than from an alternative conviction of redemptive history. To be sure, his comments seem insufficiently aware of how thoroughly "languaged" the human environment is and thus how logocentric it is to oppose language to reality. But when he upbraids Hegel by disclosing that "he made discourse the key to reality," one may read such a remark against the grain of its apparent intent as a realist jeer at idealism and see an insight despite itself: Hegel is true insofar as he is read as giving the structure of language—that is, grammar—not of experience.[27] Through Hegel's linguisticism, Santayana is detecting the indelible one-sidedness of the dialectical method that purports to be so all-inclusive: "The favourite tenet of Hegel that everything involves its opposite is also a piece of egotism; for it is equivalent to making things conform to words, not words to things" (*EGP*, 89). Further, Hegel is unable to contact or recognize otherness through the dialectic of subject and substance, since "his substance is but his grammar of discourse" (*EGP*, 92). Hegel "fancied himself deeply sympathetic because he saw in everything some fragment of himself. But no part of the world was that; every part had its own inalienable superiority, which to transcend was to lose for ever" (*EGP*, 94). The use of the word *inalienable* shows Santayana had read his American history well enough to hint at an alternative alignment between American politics and Hegelianism. In this passage, Santayana also exposes the irony and danger of the notion of sympathy, which when allied with power can annihilate existents by appropriating or transcending them.

Thus what Santayana finds in Hegel's philosophical accounts of culture and history is the rationalization not of the real but of ideology: "what we know little or nothing about seems to us in Hegel admirably characterized: what we know intimately seems to us painted with the eye of a pedantic, remote, and insolent foreigner. It is but an idea of his own that he is foisting upon us, calling it our soul" (*EGP*, 93). And it is this "foreign" idea for which human lives must in the end be sac-

---

27. George Santayana, *Egotism in German Philosophy* (2nd ed., London, 1939), 84, hereinafter cited parenthetically in the text as *EGP*.

rificed, "the sacrifice of the natural man and of all men to an abstract obsession, called an ideal" (*EGP*, 97). Thus, he continues, "he seems to proclaim the moral government of the world, when in truth he is sanctifying a brutal law of success and succession."

## BEYOND HEGEL?

Breitwieser shows in passing that Hegel's dialectic of transcendence amounts basically to a sacrificial agreement, all the way up to reading the Christ story sacrificially: sacrificing a victim is necessary in order to have the synthesis and dialectical progress of concretization/redemption. In a sense, Hegel is the repressed and repressive figure who has already been exposed brilliantly and vehemently by Bataille: if not himself a sacrificial priest, Hegel supports the work of the man of sacrifice and looks at the truth of Negativity revealed by sacrifice.[28]

In "Romancing the Stone," Rowe, too, like Breitwieser, sees Hegel as repressing what an American author works to expose. Rowe, however, demonstrates how a Marxian critique of Hegel would engage an American text that finds itself intricated in a web of American idealism. For Rowe, both literature and the family, as institutions and in their capacity to lend themselves to ideological representation, naturalize oppression and inequality. In *Pierre*, Melville understands family and social relations to function dialectically; but he casts a sharply critical light on the idealized, unsexual family of Hegel's scheme centering on brother and sister, a relation whose incompleteness characterizes the family sphere for Hegel and necessitates the move outward toward the state. Like Marx, Melville sharply critiques the synthetic philosophy of society (family, culture, state) given by Hegel, but Rowe's Melville fails to arrive at an interventionist program as Marx did. Melville's struggle with idealism eventuates in his late ironic style, aware that romantic rhetoric and Hegelian/Emersonian idealism are unsuited to articulate a real politics.

The problems that Sussman, Breitwieser, and Rowe detect are

---

28. See Georges Bataille, "Hegel, la mort et le sacrifice," *Deucalion*, V (October, 1955), 21–43, and *Inner Experience*, trans. Leslie Ann Boldt (Albany, N.Y., 1987). On Bataille's reading of Hegel, see Jacques Derrida, *Writing and Difference*, trans. Alan Bass (Chicago, 1978), especially 257–58 and 334*n*6.

not just in Hegel: his work is only the most imposing theodicy for an aggressive Western culture-machine that can no longer afford to see itself as hero of a monodrama. But if Hegel is the most complete ideologue of the modern West, he is also the one who has examined its logic most deeply. The best readings of Hegel are aware of this: mount virtually any critique of the Western system, and Hegel has been there first. It is impossible to remain modern and not be a Hegelian of some stamp or other. But forgetting Hegel is not an easy move to make, nor would it necessarily be desirable: "the postmodern," whatever forms of organization it takes, will collapse into a naïve self-assertion if it does not bear a monitory image of Hegel in mind. Any new discursive epoch will need more than this: it will need the real Hegel's text, his awareness and irony, in order to foresee its own pitfalls. The canniest strategists will grow strong by enlisting Hegel in the struggle against Hegelianism. One does well—especially in light of the St. Louis Hegelians—to peruse this notoriously difficult dictum of Maurice Blanchot: "One cannot 'read' Hegel, except by not reading him. To read, not to read him—to understand, to misunderstand him, to reject him—all this falls under the authority of Hegel or doesn't take place at all. Only the intensity of this nonoccurrence, in the impossibility that there be such a thing, prepares us for a death—the death of reading, the death of writing—which leaves Hegel living: the living travesty of completed Meaning."[29] The implication at the very least is that whoever wants intensely to be free of this totalistic, totalitarian Hegel must undergo death. But what kind of death is acceptable besides the final one? Blanchot proposes, if I may suggest a clarification, the death that is reading and the death that is writing. To submit with full awareness to what reading is—to say nothing of writing—will entail leaving Hegel behind in a deserted land, the land of completed meaning. Letting go of the project of meaning is a reorientation of intellectual life profound enough to merit the name of death.

Blanchot's characterization of "Hegel living" is curiously compatible with a notion of Hegelianism as lifeless, however. Sussman cites the passage in *The Philosophy of History* in which Hegel refers to the union of the substantive and subjective moments of freedom and then asserts, "The sole end of all spiritual activity is to attain consciousness

29. Maurice Blanchot, *The Writing of the Disaster*, trans. Ann Smock (Lincoln, Nebr., 1986), 46–47.

of this union, and hence of freedom."[30] This highmindedness is the target of the exclamation of Fyodor Dostoevsky's Ridiculous Man, aimed at Russian journalistic Hegelianism: "'The consciousness of life is higher than life, the knowledge of happiness is higher than happiness'—that is what we have to fight against!" To make such consciousness and knowledge the goal at the expense of what escapes them is, as the Ridiculous Man learns, tantamount finally to a sad narcissism.

No apologies need be made for digressing on Dostoevsky in a book on American literature: Sussman's discussion of *The Count of Monte Cristo*, like Kronick's placing of Hawthorne's poetics of romance within the context of German romanticism, demonstrates that the analysis of American literature can no longer afford to take an insular path. Two points that must emerge in confronting the Hegelianism implicit in American literature and culture are, first of all, that the coherence of a collective self-understanding can no longer be taken for granted and, furthermore, that the "American moment" in cultural history is to be understood as an instance, not in the progressive history of Spirit, but in the development of a modern Euro-American ideology. One cannot recognize this pattern if American phenomena are viewed in implicit isolation.

To root out Hegelian historicism, to reject the temptations of the Hegelian myths of the self and of Absolute Knowledge—these seem incredibly easy and even quaint tasks when one states them thus, as if dry scholars were out on the field arming themselves against long-dead dragons. The problem is that we are all still caught within the orbit of Hegel: "all this falls under the authority of Hegel or doesn't take place at all." Sussman takes Hegel to be the origin of the modern human disciplines, as well as of their intercommunicability.[31] How are we to do thinking without him? And when we succeed in doing that, how can we recognize it as thinking without returning thinking to the orbit of self-centered pseudo-recognition called "self-othering"?

The notion of "history" itself has great difficulties avoiding the "egotism" Santayana excoriates. Whenever history is hypostatized, turned into a subject, the single point of view still masquerades, in a "living travesty," as the view of all. To attempt to escape implied nar-

30. G. W. F. Hegel, *Lectures on the Philosophy of World History. Introduction: Reason in History*, trans. H. B. Nisbet (Cambridge, Eng., 1975), 104.

31. See also Henry Sussman, *The Hegelian Aftermath: Readings in Hegel, Kierkegaard, Freud, Proust, and James* (Baltimore, 1982).

ratives of history altogether, on the other hand, would be to blind one-self to the way in which such narratives and a communal subject tend to find their way into discourse, whether their referents exist or not. Rather than attempt to extirpate these fundamental elements, one should situate them in differing scenarios of power and opportunity and adjust them according to their contexts. For the beneficiaries of power—and here intellectuals are automatically included—the question is rather one of learning how to *defer* coherence, to have patience with what doesn't make sense, to grant it the right to be, to its own alien subjectivity, until such time as an opening appears that will not obliterate or maim either side.

In this light, the poetry of Wallace Stevens as examined here by Judith Butler affords an interesting contrast with Lindberg's Whitman: the imaginary healing angel Hegel is gone, replaced by a continuance of dialectical method that dares to look starkly at the absence of a synthesis. In Butler's reading of "The World as Meditation," we see Stevens moving the dialectical activity—in this case, the poetic process, "meditation" or "essential exercise"—away from a subject-centered location toward an interactive, situation-centered model; away, too, from a clear terminus and object toward an interminable process of the kind Riddel finds typical of all American modernism.

Butler ends by claiming that Hegel's philosophy of language, of history, and of negation have "yet to be fully reconsidered within contemporary criticism" and "will reveal a Hegel who . . . sought a mode of thinking that would not capture its object, but let it live" (Butler, 287). Such deferral or deference can be detected in Hegel the more emphasis one places on "the seriousness, the suffering, the patience, and the labour of the negative" in reading his text, as he himself enjoins in the Preface to the *Phenomenology*.[32] After considering Hegel in St. Louis, one would have to add that this passage can be read in the mode of *différance*, but it can also be—and demonstrably has been—read as a sanction for holy war. To redeem Hegel's text from Hegelianism may be the task particularly suited to poetics and its commentary at the end of this most warlike century.

Both Riddel's and Butler's essays here read modernist poetics as a finer attunement to "the way in which absence works, the way in

32. G. W. F. Hegel, *Phenomenology of Spirit*, trans. A. V. Miller (Oxford, 1977), Sec. 19.

which history persists, the way in which all manner of 'not being' organizes experience and allows for the poetic affirmation of mere being" (Butler, 283). Whereas undoing Hegel's logic of affirmation and synthesis often defines the object of the most strenuous poetic effort, Hegel's philosophy of language and of negation may still be discerned behind the very effort to bring forth the labor of the negative and to reveal not only the "dialectic at a standstill," in Walter Benjamin's phrase, but the path toward the authentic recognition of a multiplicity of subjects and the beginning tools to a conceptual description of the configurations they make.

# I POETICS OF HISTORY

# An American History Lesson
## Hegel and the Historiography of Superimposition

· · · · · · · · · · · · · · · · · ·

*Henry Sussman*

The nineteenth century was crowned by the international expositions whose medallions adorn the labels of the liquors, jellies, and sauces that we continue to eat and drink. The spirit of internationalism enabled the destinies of continents, nations, and individuals to be yoked in tandem, so that to smear a certain marmalade on one's toast was to step, however tangentially and provisorily, into the spotlight of history.

We remember Hegel for, among other things, the efficiency and mechanical perfection with which, at the outset of that fateful century, he effected a fusion between the temporal articulation of history and the spatial subdivisions interacting on a vast historical chessboard. Time and space are different substances, or perhaps they are forms. They have a markedly different feel about them. To isolate a structure according to which time and space can translate easily into each other is no mean feat, and yet this gesture is emblematic of Hegel's achievement in his writings on history, preeminently a structural accomplishment. The following remarks may succeed in breaking away from the Hegelian schematism; they may occasionally fall back inside it as well. They never stray far from Hegel's structural experimentation, which constitutes the philosopher's primary link to modern literature and art.

In the Introduction to *The Philosophy of History*, Hegel writes: "We began with the assertion that, in the History of the World, the Idea of Spirit appears in its actual embodiment as a series of external forms [*als eine Reihe äußerlicher Gestalten erscheint*], each one of which declares itself as an actually existing people [*deren jede sich als wirklich existierendes Volk kundgibt*]. This existence falls under the category of Time as well as Space, in the way of natural existence; and the special principle, which every world-historical people embodies, has this principle at the same time as a *natural* characteristic."[1] A particular nation could embody the Idea of Spirit in a specific form, which would in turn encompass and coordinate temporal and spatial facets. Hegel has not only formulated a common set of criteria, related to the evolution of consciousness and reason, according to which the state of culture at the most diverse ends of the globe could be coordinated. He has achieved some measured degree of success in fusing this panoptical view of cultural development in wide-flung theaters to a centralized evolutionary schema of normative and necessary steps. It is possible not only for every location in a widely heterogeneous global stage-set to have a common conceptual ground linking it to the others, but also for each *stage* of cultural development, preserved in artifacts as well as in historical documents, to be fixed to a moment within an evolutionary process encompassing a universal world-culture.

History has evolved from a narrative process, postulating links between events splayed diachronically, into a conceptual machine, a food processor, so to speak, of historical material, of events that have resisted oblivion. The efficiency of the machine of which I write is of course qualified by the turns in the language that has made it possible. Yet it is worthwhile to dwell on the conditions making this machinework possible, even with its qualified validity, if for no other reason than the powerful influence that Hegel's historiography exerted on subsequent social and literary thought.

At the end of our own century, whose greatest intellectual achievements have included a prodigious refinement, and then questioning, of structural thought, Hegel emerges as a powerful avatar and master mechanic of structuralism. It is not excessive to identify Hegel as, among other things, the first modern structuralist, a herald of the structural fabulation so decisive to modernist literature and art. (Here *modernity* and *structuralism* embrace historical and performative dimensions. They correspond only approximately to any historical moment; it is possible at the same time to speak of a certain text-configuring performance extending to major artifacts of modernism involving a kaleidoscopic variation of structures.) Historically, the seminal deliberations on the nature of an American national identity coincided with

1. G. W. F. Hegel, *The Philosophy of History*, trans. J. Sibree (1899; rpr. New York, 1956), 79. English citations throughout the present essay derive from this edition, hereinafter cited parenthetically in the text as *PH*. German introjections refer to Hegel, *Werke in zwanzig Bänden*, Theorie Werkausgabe (Frankfurt, 1970), XII.

certain structuralist alignments of historical material effected by Hegel and others. In a sense, the American nation may be described as metanational, already resulting from a historiographic meditation on nationality. It is precisely the recurrent and retrospective quality of the emergent American myth that made American historiography, almost from the outset, so susceptible to the analogies and superimpositions effected by Hegel's structuralist model of history.

Among Hegel's lasting achievements may be numbered first the isolation and then the orchestration of structures capable of marshaling the diverse moments and materials of thought in rhythm with the march of time. The fate of Hegel in twentieth-century thought follows the fate of structuralism. Only by virtue of this structuralistic finesse could Hegel's writings have survived well into the midst of the twentieth century as an intellectual paradigm, well beyond the credibility of their devotions to Spirit. History seems to move in circles, and this appearance is no accident when we consider the degree to which Hegelian historiography first conditioned a milieu for social and critical thought, which then welcomed the innovations of structural anthropology, linguistics, and literary explication. So strong is the momentum of this mode of thinking that major portions of the work of Georges Bataille and Maurice Blanchot hover at its outer limits while resisting it. In the case of Bataille, for example, a text such as "The Pineal Eye" abounds with Hegelian imagery—the sun, trees, the horizon—at the same time that it disrupts the Hegelian schematism. Blanchot, in such a pivotal essay as "Literature and the Right to Death," not only makes Hegel a major player in demarcating literary space but also situates himself at the limit of Hegelian boundaries: "By negating the day, literature recreates day in the form of fatality; by affirming the night, it finds the night as the impossibility of the night."[2] To the degree to which Hegelian speculations on history had conditioned American culture's most powerful images of itself, the American academy was primed both to receive and to debunk the findings of twentieth-century structuralism.

2. In addition to "The Pineal Eye," see "The Critique of the Foundations of the Hegelian Dialectic" in Georges Bataille, *Visions of Excess: Selected Writings, 1927–1939*, trans. Allan Stoekl *et al.*, ed. Allan Stoekl (Minneapolis, 1985), 79–90, 105–15. See Maurice Blanchot, "Literature and the Right to Death," in Blanchot, *The Gaze of Orpheus*, trans. Lydia Davis (Barrytown, N.Y., 1981), 48. See also pp. 23–24, 28, 33, 39, 42, 61–62.

The Hegelian axes upon which the diverse possibilities for thought and action are displayed may well be more metaphysically charged than their twentieth-century descendants. The interplays between universality and particularity, the East and the West, the internal and the external, spirituality and materiality, and the subject and the object are decisive to the structural solutions that Hegel devises. In the work of Roland Barthes, say, such axes are linguistically, rather than ontotheologically, constituted: they play between paradigm and syntagm, between connotation and denotation, but their axial structure is just as central to the enterprise at hand. Hegelian thought has thus demonstrated the capacity to perpetuate itself on a subliminal level even where it has been overtly discredited on another plane; its seemingly radical innovations tend to fall prey to the continuity implemented by mechanical efficiency. In this latter respect, there is an unmistakable hermeneutic bent to the progress of Hegelian history, yet as this works itself out, the potentially explosive results of intertextuality are muted in favor of historical and dialectical consistency.

Structures reside at the interstice between logic and form. A structure is a contour that has been placed into a specific logical relationship with other categories in some sense analogous to it. The field in which structures interact is a gridwork determined by the axes common to the categories invoked. The Foucauldian notion of the episteme implies that each intellectual age, to the extent that we can employ this notion, marshals its own categorical gridwork or structuralism. Especially when we keep in mind the historical sophistication evident in an essay such as Paul de Man's "Literary History and Literary Modernity," in which modernity is less a specific moment than a sliding perspective of generation and improvisation, it becomes fruitless to limit either structuralism or modernity to the period inaugurated by Hegel.[3] One can nonetheless either credit or blame Hegel for inspiring a sequence of intellectual generations characterized by breathtaking sophistication in the deployment of structures. Surely the periods that we refer to as "ancient philosophy" and "the Renaissance" also delimited knowledge by the use of structures and structural grids. It still remains possible to hold in a privileged admiration the unique facility and dynamism of the Hegelian and post-Hegelian structuralism.

---

3. See Paul de Man, *Blindness and Insight: Essays in the Rhetoric of Contemporary Criticism* (2nd ed.; Minneapolis, 1983), 142–44, 148, 150, 152, 164–65.

By the time of Hegel's *Philosophy of History*, the prodigious coordination of narrative perspectives, cognitive and conceptual stages, and logical operations first rehearsed in *The Phenomenology of Spirit* has undergone considerable lubrication. One could indeed argue that in the earlier work, the arbitrariness of this massive yoking becomes a substantial element of the subject matter: dysfunctions in conceptual evolution, such as the "differences which are no differences" produced by Understanding, are considered to be an important result of philosophical speculation. *The Philosophy of History* is not nearly as taken with the grindings and squealings that result from the welding together of various functions performed by conceptual machinery. Pursuing at all times the Sun, which directs the trajectory of History from East to West, this work constitutes a conceptual gridwork allowing for diverse stages of World History, taking place in far-flung historical theaters, to be superimposed upon each other. The gridwork supplies the common terms according to which the different moments and locations may be evaluated, or placed in communication with each other.

This spatial configuration is powered, motivated, by the progressive thrust rehearsed in *The Phenomenology of Spirit* in terms of the evolution of philosophical consciousness. In *The Philosophy of History*, it is the realization of Spirit in a number of nations, national cultures, and world-historical personalities that furnishes the temporal articulation, the forward thrust. Yet one might well argue that the ultimate model for the supersession of certain empires, cultures, and personalities by others is a hermeneutic one. Hegelian historiography is implemented by the gridwork that supplies the terms according to which different cultures and productions may be played off against each other in the drama of history. History itself proceeds by a dynamic of marginal insertion or "reading in," by which each successive crystallization locates itself within, and declares its independence from, the lacunae limiting and immobilizing its predecessors. The fundamental test case in Western thought of one civilization's hermeneutically disqualifying and superseding its predecessor is of course the New Testament's isolation of its own justification and necessity quite literally within the margins of the Old Testament.[4] The gridwork of Hegelian historiography thus facilitates and feeds a process of hermeneutic sublation.

4. For a fuller discussion of this dynamic, see Henry Sussman, "Kafka in the Heart of the Twentieth Century: An Approach to Borges," in *Kafka's Contextuality*, ed. Alan Udoff (New York, 1986), 177–233.

The roots of the Hegelian historiography run deep in the tradition of Western theological thought. Crucial to its method is the retrospective annexation or appropriation of diverse locations and moments in the service of a predetermined necessity, whether designated as God, reason, Spirit, or national destiny. The Egyptian pyramids, Hinduism, classical Greek art, and European romanticism each occupy a point, are each accorded a distinct moment or setting, within a map or closed combinatorial machine whose coordinates can, and indeed must, be known from the outset. The strategic model for this historiography, which Hegel did not so much invent as endow with its highest, near-seamless and transparent refinement, is the calculated assault on the Old Testament by the New, the irresistible manner in which the latter manifesto abolishes the former compendium, all the while basing itself upon it, preserving it, and ostensibly defending its necessity. The Hegelian historiography, even where its telos is Reason or Absolute Knowing rather than Christ, is an all-too-recognizable descendant of the method devised for the paradigmatic hermeneutic annexation at the basis of Western theology.

In light of the preceding discussion, it is perhaps not so difficult to envision how Hegel could have delivered so decisive a history lesson to an emergent American culture. North American culture and literature of the nineteenth century, with their own need to celebrate a break with tradition and the possibility for the realization of an unprecedented destiny, were particularly receptive to hermeneutic schemes that effectively devour the past while culminating it. To the extent that the American nation saw itself as the realization of prior historical and cultural stages and as the amalgamation of existing populations, a historical program combining structural comprehensiveness with theological conviction furnished a highly attractive national scenario. The Hegelian historiography could assign a distinctive, messianic place to the American nation. "America is therefore the land of the future, where, in the ages that lie before us, the burden of the World's History shall reveal itself" (*PH*, 86). It could retrospectively construct the foundations for American history within the evolution of world culture; and not only could it justify any American nationalism, but it could articulate the conceptual conditions under which that nationalism would arise.

Hegelian historiography thus coordinates superimposition and hermeneutic supersession. The act of superimposition is made possible by the application of an axial gridwork to diverse cultures, moments, and artifacts. Superimposition enables philosophy to crystallize the conceptual criteria that will realign the otherwise jumbled detritus of human activity. It instruments alignments that would otherwise be impossible. It effects a seemingly seamless welding of disparate spatial and temporal contexts.

In Hegel's *Aesthetics*, the relation between content and form is a touchstone placing Egyptian, Persian, Greek, Oriental, and Romantic artifacts in communication with each other. *The Philosophy of History* applies to the ages and artifacts it considers a complicated conceptual meshwork, whose axes include East and West, Light and Darkness, subjectivity and objectivity, freedom and determination, morality and despotism, and spirituality and materialism. In this latter work, it is the realization of individual destiny in the fate called, of all things, the freedom of a nation that provides a common ground for American, Asian, African, and European political tendencies. Hegelian superimposition emphasizes the commonality of destiny and the homogeneity of cultural experience at the expense of what Derrida would call the local difference.[5] In *The Philosophy of History*, as in Foucault's tabulated space, exceptions drop off the map or become the basis for the next grand episode in the collective adventure.[6] The mutations along the path of cultural evolution are possessed of weak blood. "History requires Understanding," insists Hegel when characterizing the oriental world: "the power of looking at an object in an independent objective light [*den Gegenstand für sich freizulassen*], and comprehending it in its rational connection with other objects. Those peoples therefore are alone capable of History, and of prose generally, who have arrived at that point of development . . . at which individuals comprehend their own existence as independent" (*PH*, 162).

History demands, and is a form of, Reason. It is ultimately self-reflexive: "But History presents a people with their own image in a condition which thereby becomes objective to them" (*PH*, 163). Pity the poor Indians, then, who simply lack the conceptual hardware to join history and to augment its record. "The Hindoos [*Inder*] on the contrary are by birth given over to an unyielding destiny [*einer substan-*

---

5. See, for example, Jacques Derrida, *Of Grammatology*, trans. Gayatri Chakravorty Spivak (Baltimore, 1976), 251, 260, 268.

6. For more on tabulated space, see Michel Foucault, *The Order of Things: An Archaeology of the Human Sciences* (New York, 1973), 133–35, 152–57, 160, 234–39, 264, 274–76, 316–22.

*tiellen Bestimmtheit zugeteilt*], while at the same time their Spirit is exalted to Ideality [*zur Idealität erhoben*]; so that their minds exhibit the contradictory processes of a dissolution of fixed rational and definite conceptions in their Ideality, and on the other side, a degradation of this ideality to a multiformity of sensuous objects. This makes them incapable of writing History" (*PH*, 162). Lacking historical pedigree, the Indians are fated to remain beyond the pale of historical memory. They undergo the historical equivalent of genetic extinction. Yet their naïve idealism and their uncontrollable sensuality survive on the map—as historical possibilities, even if untenable ones, as recurrent mutations with no future in themselves.

The axial gridwork that is the instrument of Hegelian superimposition transforms philosophical speculation and historical recollection from purely observational pursuits into a *critical* enterprise, in its tendentious, as well as its functional, dimensions. There is an optimal point on each of the axes that goes to make up the gridwork of history: there is an ideal degree of independence felt by a people (which the Chinese lack) and an ideal sense of cultural Beauty (which the Athenians possess). The structural matrix of historical and cultural alignment is iterable; it is exportable. It furnishes an occasion not only for the gathering of materials but for their evaluation, their judgment. The multi-axial grid is not only the tool for historical investigation; it is a rationale for vocational criticism, criticism as vocation, in cultural analysis. In a tangible sense, this grid is an instrument of judgment.

As suggested above, the history of Hegelian superimposition runs well into the twentieth century. Under different guises, superimpositional acts can be located in works as diverse as Freud's *Studies on Hysteria*, Proust's *Recherche*, Kafka's "Description of a Struggle," Joyce's *Ulysses*, and the essays of Walter Benjamin. One thinks of the Freudian "*successions* of *partial* traumas and *concatenations* of pathogenic trains of thought," or the concentric arrangement of themes "round the pathogenic nucleus": "The most peripheral strata contain the memories (or files), which, belonging to different themes, are easily remembered and have always been clearly conscious. The deeper we go the more difficult it becomes for the emerging memories to be recognized."[7] Proust grafts a homosexual love story, involving Baron Charlus and Morel,

---

7. Josef Breuer and Sigmund Freud, *Studies on Hysteria*, trans. James Strachey (New York, 1955), 288–89.

upon the paradigmatic heterosexual romances between Swann and Odette, Marcel and Albertine. Joyce superimposes the details of Bloom and Stephen Dedalus' contemporary "lives"—and the perspectival dialectic between these characters—upon certain pivotal events in Homer's *Odyssey*.

Yet modernist superimposition, as practiced by Benjamin in "On Some Motifs in Baudelaire," emphasizes systematic collapse rather than ineluctable continuity. What Benjamin aligns in that crucial essay are not nations or art works but contemporary schools of thought. His feat is early on to place the perspectives of psychoanalysis, phenomenology, historiography, and Proustian memory in tandem with each other by virtue of the breakdown of a certain defensive shield common to them all. What configures the common elements is not a destiny but an intellectual structure, in Benjamin's case the constitution of organisms and organs through resistance and blockage rather than receptivity. The instances of shock that he elicits and subsequently describes in the essay shatter, among other things, the parallelism of the initial schematization. Benjamin's telling examples of this structure in modern experience—shock, gambling, photography, casual sex—all impede the momentum that Hegelian superimposition would make only too easy. Benjamin's essay thus *performs* the full cycle of structural assembly and demolition epitomizing modern experience and the major productions of modernism.

"The History of the World," asserts Hegel from a universal point of view, "travels from East to West [*geht von Osten nach Westen*], for Europe is absolutely the end [*das Ende*] of History" (*PH*, 103). Within this global sweep, the "general aim" of the History of the World is "the realization of the Idea of Spirit [*daß der Begriff des Geistes befriedigt werde*]" (*PH*, 25). "The State is . . . the embodiment of rational freedom," and "the Idea of Spirit is the external manifestation [*Äußerlichkeit*] of human Will and its Freedom" (*PH*, 47). The state, for Hegel, is both the manifold for subjective identity and consciousness and the shifter transforming compliance with the law into a form of freedom. As Hegel elaborates the interaction between the individual and the state, he dramatizes the superimposition effected by his thought while justifying this intellectual *modus operandi* for the citizens of his age.

The State is the Idea of Spirit [*die geistige Idee*] in the external manifestation of human Will and its Freedom. It is to the State, therefore, that

change in the aspect of History indissolubly attaches itself [*fällt daher
. . . die Veränderung der Geschichte*]; and the successive phases [*die Mo-
mente*] of the Idea manifest themselves in it as distinct political *principles*.
The Constitutions [*die Verfassungen*] under which World-Historical
peoples have reached their culmination [*worin die welthistorischen Völker
ihre Blüte erreicht haben*], are peculiar to them. . . . From comparison
therefore of the political institutions of the ancient World-Historical
peoples, it so happens, that for the most recent principles of a Constitution . . . nothing . . . can be learned. . . .
We observe, therefore, an essential union [*eine Vereinigung*] between the
objective side—the Idea [*dem Begriffe*]—and the subjective side—the
personality that conceives and wills it.—The *objective* existence of this
union is the State, which is therefore the basis and centre [*die Grundlage
und der Mittelpunkt*] of the other concrete elements in the life of a
people—of Art, of Law, of Morals [*der Sitten*], of Religion, of Science.
All the activity of Spirit has only this object—the becoming conscious
of this union, *i.e.*, of its own Freedom. Among the forms of this conscious union *Religion* occupies the highest position. In it, Spirit . . . becomes conscious of the Absolute Spirit [*wird der existierende, der weltliche
Geist sich des absoluten Geistes bewußt*]. . . . The second form of the union
of the objective and the subjective is *Art*. This advances farther into the
realm of the actual and sensuous than Religion. . . . But the True is the
object not only of conception and feeling, as in Religion—and of intuition, as in Art—but also of the thinking faculty; and this gives us the
third form of the union in question—*Philosophy*. This is consequently
the highest, freest, and wisest phase. . . .
The actual State is animated by this spirit, in all its particular affairs—
its Wars, Institutions, etc. But man must also attain a conscious realization of this his Spirit and essential nature, and of his original identity
with it. For we said that morality is the identity of the *subjective* or *personal* with the *universal* will. (*PH*, 47, 49, 50)

This sequence of passages illustrates with particular intensity the
infrastructure that will make conceptually possible a volume that goes
on to superimpose the histories of the East, Greece, Rome, and Germany on each other. The state is an objective manifestation of the interstice between subjectivity and objectivity, whose *subjective* counterparts include morality and religion. This fusion between the outside

and the inside is presented not as an uneasy social contract but as a foundation of organized human activity, a sine qua non for cultural manifestations. Given this union, which in *The Philosophy of History* Hegel leaves intact in a charmed circle of unquestioning, the various collective institutions of politics, religion, and art can be henceforth schematized according to such factors as abstraction, practicality, and the degree of public or private involvement. The Church and the Law, for example, may be regarded as moments of each other, or rather as products of a series of variables implanted into the discourse by Hegel. But if first religion, and then art and philosophy, the latter occupying the critical position, can be moments in Spirit's awareness of itself as it manifests itself in the world, there is nothing to preclude the incorporation of entities designated "ancient Egypt," or "revolutionary France," or "modern Germany" in a parallel configuration, one whose operating principle continues to be a certain expansionistic superimposition. It is in this sense that the Roman world can be grounded in a subjective license that epitomized the corruption of classical Greek culture (*PH*, 279), or that the diffusion of Germanic culture, the self-certainty that this cultural sphere gains for itself through externalization, coincides with the self-discovering innovation of the New World (*PH*, 341).

The Philosophy of History, as it pursues the Sun of History from East to West, is rich with factual details and curiosities. A certain anthropological flair and distance surround the inclusion of such bits of information as the moral responsibility of the father for the performance of subsequent generations in the Chinese family and state or the number of Chinese functionaries (*PH*, 122–25), and the function of various elements in the Indian caste system (*PH*, 143–48). *The Philosophy of History* exists as a certain climax in Hegel's fascination with the facts, in his concrete relation to his material, in his demonstration of a tangible grasp. The curiosities assimilated into the text of *The Philosophy of History* constitute an anthropological tribute exacted from the cultures incorporated into the System, souvenirs gathered on a speculative voyage. We learn, for instance, by how many years the Chinese, Egyptian, Assyrian, and Indian traditions anticipated Christ; the Chinese laws concerning the son's mourning a deceased father; the number of Chinese written characters; the population of India and the height of the Himalayas; the differences between various grades of Yogis; and a plot summary of the "Nala" episode of the *Mahabharata* (see *PH*, 116, 121–22, 135, 143, 149, 151). The grand sweep from East to West endows this work with a storybook quality. It serves as a precedent for adventure books continuing even into this writer's lifetime, such as Richard Halliburton's *Books of Marvels*.

The curiosities of society, art, and even geology furnish a diversion, an amusement animating what might otherwise be construed as the "dry" subject matter of history. They also serve to obscure and camouflage the conceptual machinery whose elements and operations we have begun to explore. Without such anthropological wall coverings, the spaces delineated by the machine might appear too stark, too confining. Each successive stage of schematization allows for additional certainty. The diverse historical stages and points on the globe become increasingly reducible to a shorthand. As it moves closer to its culmination, the course of History lends itself more easily to summaries and summations:

> In summing up the constituents of the *Greek Spirit*, we find its fundamental characteristic [*Grundbestimmung*] to be, that the freedom of Spirit is conditioned by [*bedingt*] and has an essential relation to some stimulus supplied by Nature. . . . This phase of Spirit is the medium [*die Mitte*] between the loss of individuality on the part of man (such as we observe in the Asiatic principle, in which the Spiritual and Divine exist only under a Natural form), and Infinite Subjectivity as pure certainty of itself [*reiner Gewißheit ihrer selbst*]—the position that the Ego is the ground of all that can lay claim to substantial existence. The Greek Spirit as the medium between these two, begins with Nature, but transforms it into a mere form of its (Spirit's) own existence; Spirituality [*Geistigkeit*] is therefore not yet absolutely free; not yet absolutely *self*-produced—is not yet self-stimulation. . . . This stamps the Greek character as that of *Individuality conditioned by Beauty* [*zur schönen Individualität*], which is produced by Spirit, transforming the merely Natural into an expression of its own being. The activity of Spirit does not yet possess the material and organ of expression, but needs the excitement of Nature and the matter which Nature supplies: it is not free, self-determining Spirituality, but mere naturalness formed to Spirituality—Spiritual Individuality. The Greek Spirit is the plastic artist [*der plastische Künstler*], forming the stone into a work of art. In this forma-

tive process the stone does not remain mere stone—the form being only superinduced from without; but it is made an expression [*Ausdruck*] of the Spiritual, even contrary to its nature, and thus *trans*formed [*umgebildet*]. (*PH*, 238–39)

This passage hinges on two parallel processes of self-reflexivity taking place in Spirit and history. As the Greek character evolves toward its optimal freedom, Greek art advances, though haltingly, toward the self-sufficiency of the imagination as the setting for aesthetic production.[8] The limit of the Greek imagination in this regard is its continued reliance on the "excitement of Nature and the matter which Nature supplies." So sensitive, however, is the temperament of the Greeks to natural beauty, so gifted are the Greeks at effecting syntheses, that their historical moment determines future crowning points in artistic production despite this too-tangible connection to nature.

The raw materials for the Greek syntheses effected in this passage—between "loss of individuality" and "Infinite Subjectivity," between nature and culture and freedom and despotism—derive from previous and less successful crystallizations in the course of history. These earlier attempts were located in Asia. The Chinese relinquished their individuality to the emperor, as a conceptual as well as a political force (*PH*, 123, 127–28, 130–31, 136, 147), while the Hindus retreated into an arbitrary and all-encompassing state of Subjectivity from the severe social stratification and, occasionally, the physical torture that they inflicted upon themselves (*PH*, 148–49, 156–58, 161–63). The Greeks are successful, in part owing to their acuities and in part because of their ability to circumvent and transcend the mistakes made prior to them in history.

Yet history is at all times a drama, situated on a *stage*. More as a construct than as a people, the Greeks effect syntheses of dazzling complexity. For all this sophistication, however, historical speculation is not resistant to typecasting. On the contrary, typecasting is at the same time the product, privilege, and mechanism of Hegelian historical

8. For the notion of the infrastructure, as well as a sense of the parallelism between developments in art and history, I am entirely indebted to the work of Rodolphe Gasché. See Gasché, *The Tain of the Mirror: Derrida and the Philosophy of Reflection* (Cambridge, Mass., 1986), 144, 147, 149, 152, 155–57, 172, 174–75.

thought. In terms of the historical theater at hand, the Chinese are faceless pawns united in vast, almost-inconceivable undertakings (Kafka's "The Great Wall of China" owes something to this scenario), while the Indians are kept back from the progress of history by masochism and unbridled sensuality. A more positive role fortunately falls to the Greeks. Their individuality, more vibrant than that of the Asiatics, is conditioned by beauty; their conceptual capability fits them out to be transformational and generative artists.

Hegel thus launches nineteenth-century historiography on an ambitious program of annexation by superimposition. Deriving from a self-created nation, the culture of the United States could lull itself into a certainty about its own origins inaccessible to its timeless counterparts in Eurasia. It has been briefly suggested above why the nascent culture of the United States, with certain illusions of eternal newness and its own brand of messianism, would be particularly susceptible to this type of schematization. Precisely because of the recordability of its origins, the United States has been obsessed, well into its history, with its foundations and groundings. The practices and techniques of superimposition, as Hegel perfected them, are indispensable in accounting for the compositional principles and narrative strategies underlying a broad range of American artifacts from novels (Hawthorne's *The Marble Faun*) to poems (*The Cantos of Ezra Pound*) to films (D. W. Griffith's *Intolerance*), not to mention the Declaration of Independence.

The *historical novel* may well constitute the most direct literary manifestation of the Hegelian historiography, and in the American scene, its influence may extend well beyond the novelistic sphere. My selecting a non-American example, Alexandre Dumas' *Count of Monte Cristo*, emphasizes that American writers turned to Europe not only for conceptual models of history but also for precedents of a literary genre in which their historical concerns could be registered. Dumas' vast novel reconciles the fictive present in which it is written with the political upheavals following the French Revolution through the "lifetime events" experienced by its central character, Edmond Dantès. Spatially, the island of Monte Cristo is the base of Dantès' operations and the location of his secret treasury where he redeems, economically as well as spiritually, the treachery that ruins his fortunes; geographically, Monte Cristo is situated at a crossroads of History. It is a primordial outpost of European culture, a place from which the Light of the Orient first fell upon Europe and from which, in the interest of imperialism, Europe can retrospectively annex its source.

It is on Monte Cristo that Dantès locates his patrimony from his spiritual and adoptive father, Abbé Faria. This theologian and political prisoner also supplies Dantès' "life" and the novel with their moral payoff, their ontotheological horizon: "attendre et espérer," "wait and hope"—but for what? Initially, Dantès surely waits for (and actively plans) a settling of accounts, a worldly revenge, but also a rewarding of the decent and faithful folks whom he has encountered. Dantès divides his time between his marginal, near-Eurasian base of operations and the capitals of Europe, above all Paris and Rome (the cultural and theological centers). Through the latest innovations in ship-design and communications (*e.g.*, the telegraph), Dantès is able to function as a kind of nautical jet-setter, appearing now in Paris, now in Marseille (the "origin" of France in ancient Rome), now in Rome, seemingly without delay. Dantès' wealth, his technological facility, and his "team" of allies, including Haydée, his Greek-Turkish consort, facilitate the structure of a "double life," in which Dantès joins the Parisian society, where he encounters his betrayers at later and wealthier moments of their lives, and in which he secretly plots his revenge. The novel's moral allegory, a progression from revenge to forgiveness and redemption, is the sequential correlative to the vacillation between "public" and "secret" lives. Dantès' awakening to the possibilities of forgiveness and moral restraint is tantamount, in his "life," to the manifestation of Spirit in History. *The Count of Monte Cristo* is thus a historical novel in the philosophical, as well as the narratological, sense of the word.

As in the Hegelian historiography, the implementation of a conceptual gridwork—in this case, consisting of geographical and moral elements applied to specific events in political and technological histories—affords a broad, almost intoxicated freedom in the annexation of fictive episodes. In one sense, these branchings of plot (in today's parlance, *spinoffs*) serve the same function as the factual curiosities that Hegel incorporates into his *Philosophy of History:* they obscure a structural machinery, seemingly *limit* its success. Within this context, Dumas is free to cook up a bewildering menu of plots, crimes, and mechanisms of revenge, ranging from poisonings to financial intrigues to staged infanticides. Dumas enlivens his central character's moral education by means of a certain narrative *jouissance* in the varieties of perversity. The titillating variations of evil in this novel are as much motivated by its status as an entertainment medium as *The Philosophy of History* is constrained to account for curiosities in keeping with *its* pretensions to be encyclopedic.

I turn to Dumas' *Count of Monte Cristo* as an instance (almost a truism) of its genre, the historical novel—a genre mediating between the Hegelian speculations on history and certain important American literary productions. This novel is, of course, only one of its "type," within which each example is, on its own terms, unique. Its choice within the present essay is not entirely haphazard, however, since with its freewheeling spinning out of events and certain of its specific scenes, such as the Roman carnival, it was almost certainly important to the Nathaniel Hawthorne of *The Marble Faun*, a pivotal American adaptation of the Hegelian historiography. I have elsewhere argued that this novel would do no less than graft the culture of an emerging United States upon the trunkline of European and classical cultures.[9]

In the case of *The Marble Faun*, Rome is situated at the catastrophic crossroads of history and geography.[10] Hawthorne dispatches two aspiring American artists there, for professional training and to survey the origins of their culture. One of these is a stodgy male sculptor, and the other a painter and copyist who embodies, as the narrative amply informs us, the Spirit and aesthetics of Wordsworth's Lucy Gray. As the Americans Kenyon and Hilda approach the European sources of their culture, however, they become increasingly alienated from the enterprise of artistic production. This is owing to their involvement in an affair of Nietzschean moral indeterminacy, the murder of a menacing male figure committed by their European friends and companions, Donatello and Miriam. Donatello and Miriam are as representative of their European nationalities as Kenyon and Hilda are of theirs. Donatello belongs to the last generation of an ancient but weakblooded Italian aristocracy. Miriam is a pan-European mongrel, a blend of several possible national and religious "stocks." In different ways, she and Donatello both are emblematic of the deep groundlessness of European culture, of the submersion and indeterminacy of its historical

9. See Henry Sussman, "*The Marble Faun* and the Space of American Letters," in *Demarcating the Disciplines: Philosophy, Literature, Art*, ed. Samuel Weber, Glyph Textual Studies, n.s., I (Minneapolis, 1986), 129–52.

10. Joseph Riddel has written convincingly on the centrality of Rome to nineteenth-century American thought and letters, specifically with regard to Nathaniel Hawthorne and Henry Adams. See Riddel, "Reading America/American Readers," in *Modern Language Notes*, XCIX (September, 1984), 903–27.

origins. The novel, in its insistence on sanctioned play between "fact" and fancy, even suggests that Donatello's "line" extends as far back as the Pelasgian creation myth.

Donatello and Miriam cast over the parapet of the Capitoline Hill a menacing character known as the Model, who, like Donatello himself, seems to exist in two time frames, one immediate and one of venerable origins. Within the fictive context of the novel, this murder is as inevitable as the Model's evil and shame are timeless. Hawthorne's Europeans are left with the task of facing and cleaning up the mess of moral undecidability, the Manichean struggle between good and evil. The yet-unformed Americans look on. They assist at the struggle as spectators, only in the most farfetched sense as accomplices. Still, they do not emerge from the melodrama unfazed: even for having been exposed to the pestilence of indeterminate moral and historical consciousness they must sacrifice, in the sense of the minister at the conclusion of Hegel's "Unhappy Consciousness," their work and their pleasure—their art, in the name of the purity of future American culture.

In order to implement this study, Hawthorne devises a historical framework whose design is hardly unfamiliar to the student of Hegelian historiography. By allusion and setting, he superimposes four historical moments of importance to the story "on top" of each other: the timeless time of ancient myth, when Donatello-as-faun disported freely; early Church history, when the contemporary Model served as a monk; the Romantic era in Britain, from which Hilda as a modern-day Lucy Gray derives; and the fictive "present" of the novel. Not only do these moments qualify certain aspects of the characters, but they also comment on the options confronting an emergent American culture. Romanticism remains the prevalent conceptual and thematic repository for literary invention. Ancient myth is the cultural foundation or substratum in which Hawthorne, following the Goethe of *Faust* and in the name of an American readership, would like to secure a foothold. Byzantine as the appearance of the early Church in this novel may seem, it forms the backdrop for the theological soul-searching (and shopping) in which Hilda engages. Hilda's flirtation with the Church, the allure that a universal theological institution (and historical ideology) holds for her, cannot be entirely irrelevant to the theological choices available to the novel's public.

The historical arc that Hawthorne feels constrained to incorporate into his novel is, of course, considerably longer than the period encompassed by the experience of Dantès in *The Count of Monte Cristo*. (The latter novel's historical moment is slightly extended by the inclusion of the aged revolutionary M. Noirtier.) Yet Dantès' "life" fuses together the several generations encompassed by Dumas' novel (extending from the Revolution through Napoleonic time into the relative stability of the 1830s) no less ably than Hawthorne's historically ambiguous characters, Donatello and the Model, "fuse" the fictive "present" to, respectively, classical antiquity and the early Church. Although Kenyon's rediscovery of Hilda amid the revelry of the Roman Carnival at the end of *The Marble Faun* ends the romance in an atmosphere of healthy (and wholesome) humor, the historical framework in which Hawthorne retrospectively aligns three time frames behind the fictive setting of the novel endows its conclusions and values with the force and necessity of a historical syllogism. Griffith, in appropriating ancient Egypt, the French Revolution, and the American Civil War as the backdrops for the contemporary drama of *Intolerance*, engages in a quite similar form of historiographic parallelism and synchronicity.

Nothing could seem more remote from such schematic works than *The Cantos of Ezra Pound*, and yet, I would argue, Pound devotes considerable attention in this work to Homer, Provence, Renaissance Italy, China, and the period *entre deux guerres* in implementing some of the same historiographic strategies as did Hawthorne and Griffith.[11] At the heart of an enterprise running through many, if not all, of the *Cantos* is the reinstatement of the cultural values prevailing at certain of the pristine and seminal moments of world-cultural fecundity. History, for Pound, is a never-ending fluctuation between cultural purity and adulteration. He defends his privileged historical moments, artifacts, and characters with the same oedipal fascination with which his *Cantos* "record" the steamy love scenes between Circe and Odysseus. Jews, women, usurers, homosexuals, and war-profiteers, on the other hand, constitute a corrupting force periodically obliterating the major achievements of culture—a culture constituted by masculine restraint and purity.[12]

11. For a fuller discussion of the historiography governing *The Cantos of Ezra Pound*, see Henry Sussman, *High Resolution: Critical Theory and the Problem of Literacy* (New York, 1988), 115–96.

12. Kathryne V. Lindberg, in her theoretically informed recent work on Pound, draws our attention to the "spermatic economy," based on Pound's reading of Rémy de Gourmont, pervading his work. See Lindberg, *Reading Pound Reading: Modernism After Nietzsche* (New York, 1987), 149–50, 153–54, 175–81.

From the outset of his career, Pound endows poetry with the capacity to distill, preserve, and discharge into the "present" the vitality of privileged moments throughout the history of culture. "The Flame," a poem from *Personae* (1908, 1909, 1910), hovers more around the image of jewels and precious stones than that of pyrotechnics. The beryl, chrysoprase, sapphire, opal, and pearl of the poem function as "time's seed corn," as transtemporal batteries, shifters, and catalysts of poetic energy, or, with Pound's overarching economic scenario, of solvent cultural currency. The value of gems, the "flame" of their luster, can only be calculated in cultural terms.

The diversity and distance of the cultural theaters that Pound assembles in the *Cantos* is as jarring and open-ended as the spatial arrangement that he devised for the lines that compose these texts. Within the modernist *bricolage* of the *Cantos*, ancient Greece and China, Renaissance Provence and Italy, revolutionary and contemporary America somehow manage to coexist, even to cast interesting illumination upon each other. How is this possible? Largely, I would argue, by virtue of ongoing fluctuations within the stock market of cultural value. Pound's exemplary political leaders promote literature and the arts, lower taxes, and renounce their own privileges and those of their class. Language is a cultural capital to be kept pristine and invested wisely. Usury is not merely an economic practice; it is the very adulteration of artistic values and language. The sacred shrines along Pound's cultural itinerary—the Tempio in Rimini, Saint Trophîme in Arles, and Saint Hilaire in Poitiers—derive from moments of aesthetic and sociopolitical modesty, proportion, and fervor. War-profiteers, bankers, and eunuchs continually pervert and obscure this sense of value.

The *Cantos* thus constitute an intricate economy in their own right as they address the processes of the political economy. They operate in part as a superimpositional economy within whose parameters the political and sexual rivalries between the Medicis and Malatestas can foreshadow the tragedy of World War I; the enlightened moments in Chinese imperial history can serve as models for the issues pondered by John Adams and Thomas Jefferson; the intertwined adventures of Dionysus, Odysseus, and the troubadours can prefigure the overwhelming sexual ambivalences addressed by the major modernists— Proust, Joyce, Stein, and Woolf, as well as Pound. If the *Cantos* are free to act out a certain spatial and allusive promiscuity, this is in part owing to an exportable matrix of value placing (potentially) all times and cultural theaters in communication with each other. In a certain sense, then, Hegel is Ezra Pound—disguised as Sloppy Joe.

I conclude, then, with the assertion that Hegel taught American writing much of what it knows about history; he taught it the cybernetic program as well as the progression and direction of history. Hegel formed a dynamic link between the exegetical imperialism of Christianity and an epistemology that functioned according to structural grids. The combination was nothing short of deadly for nineteenth-century nations striving to realize their destinies, and no nationality could be more receptive to such a scheme than one that could point to its origin and could weigh its options in so deliberate a fashion. The historical fulcrum of Pound's *Cantos* is indeed a moment late in the eighteenth century when Adams and Jefferson carefully reviewed the legal history of England and the imperial traditions of Austria, France, and Italy in order to decide the founding *moment* of American culture. Although a fascinating historical study situates the bridgehead of Hegelian influence on the United States in Ohio,[13] it may be well argued that Hegelian attitudes and operations did much to structure the ground rules according to which an emergent American culture assessed its origins, potential, and destiny.

13. See Loyd David Easton, *Hegel's First American Followers: The Ohio Hegelians* (Athens, Ohio, 1966), 1–27.

# Thresholds of the Sign
## Reflections on "American" Poetics

· · · · · · · · · · · · · · · · · · ·

*Joseph N. Riddel*

> Remember, Falcon-Ace,
> Thou hast there in thy wrist a Sanskrit charge
> To conjugate infinity's dim marge—
> Anew . . . !
> > —Hart Crane, *The Bridge*

> I too knitted the knot of contrariety
> > —Walt Whitman, "Crossing Brooklyn Ferry"

> the poet turns the world to glass
> > —Ralph Waldo Emerson, "The Poet"

We are all, unsuspectingly or not, Hegelians under the skin, even the so-called poststructural theorist, according to one of the most eminent of that genre.[1] For despite the poststructural or postmodern fracture of the Book and the Symbol, there would be no site for the parasites of contemporary theory without the "great Hegelian formulas," as Whitman called them, those large schemas for totalizing thought that organize and institutionalize intellectual life and at the same time offer the possibility of innovative and individual contretemps. But what kind of Hegelian or counter-Hegelian might we be, what kind of narrativist or counter-narrativist of the imagination? What kind of "Nietzsche in Basel" or "Lenin by the lake," to recall Wallace Stevens' lines from "Description without Place," might our modernist poets, or even we their "critics," assume as personae in order to read this Hegelianism, this modernity?

---

1. See Paul de Man, "Sign and Symbol in Hegel's *Aesthetics,*" *Critical Inquiry,* VIII (Summer, 1982), 761–75.

The notion of "Hegel in America" must appear a very arbitrary one, just as the idea of an "American" thought or the unity of our national consciousness is virtually unthinkable, especially in the context of an intellectual history that can refer confidently to the differences and oppositions of "German" and "French" thought, or employ such notions as those of a national or nativist language, or even of a certain kind of language that is the ground of a discipline. I am referring, of course, to the claims, virtually unchallenged from Kant to Heidegger, that German is the natural language of philosophy, and French only one of its noncognitive branches, of aesthetics, erotics, play. In this history, "America," as Hegel himself forecast, is out of the game. "America," he proclaimed, in the Introduction to *The Philosophy of History*, is the beyond of history, some future site of history that is, at the same time, other than any history played out in Europe, the West: "It is a land of desire for all those who are weary of the historical lumberroom of old Europe"; as the "Land of the Future," it is "only an echo of the Old World" up to the present moment, the nineteenth century, which marks an end of history; and thus it stands beyond History with a capital *H* and is of no regard for Philosophy, since Philosophy's concern is with "neither past nor future" but with Reason's or Mind's destiny.[2]

"America" was, is, the kind of potentially "new" idea that Emerson and later Whitman tended to imagine and inscribe within the power of an act, we may say "writing," that would in turn invent an astonishingly new "America." And Whitman—if not Emerson, who showed little or no knowledge of Hegel—claimed to find the key to the new, the idea of democracy, in what little of the German he read, which he knew from Frederic H. Hedge's selections from *The Philosophy of History* and the essay "Who Thinks Abstractly?" in his anthology, *Prose Writers of Germany* (1847). In Whitman's view, based on a most limited series of Hegelian texts, these "formulas" manifest the broadest and most comprehensive expression of the democratic self as power, though, as we will see, in his poems there are ever-intensifying glimpses of this self's limit and undoing. Without examining too closely Hegel's mode of articulating individual (finite) and collective consciousness in the metaphors of "family romance" or genealogy, Whitman was

2. G. W. F. Hegel, *The Philosophy of History*, trans. J. Sibree (1899; rpr. New York, 1956), 86–87.

quick to grasp in the general systematics of "Hegelian formulas" the notion of an interplay between force and form, act and idea, that would allow the "poet of the modern" to overcome his belatedness, and his bad conscience, and reclaim his agency, his inventive potency—or in other words, to "make it new" in repetition.

Out of this appropriation of the Hegelian Idea, and in the name of the democratic, the poet could refashion a genetic myth in the name of "America" and the "Me-myself." His "Poem," as literal corpus of the self, would be at once the Book and the agent of history, the actualization of force and the advent of the modern—in sum, what Pound would call "ideas into action." Thus Whitman in a sense inaugurates the rewriting of genetic myths as myths of originary displacement, beginning again. And this partial reading, or inevitable misreading, of Hegel makes the Whitmanesque poem/poetic into a trope of the very mythogemes and mythothemes it has itself originarily, as it were, re-*fashioned* (redressed) out of philosophy or philosophemes. That is, the Whitman mythos, the figure of the "self embodied and the body as cosmos," becomes, in the tropological fashioning of the poem, a notion of consciousness as symbol, but a symbol that repeatedly undoes itself in the history of its becoming. The figure a poem makes foreshadows its own undoing or self-overcoming. A poem/figure, after Whitman's "fashion," a poem of the future, a democratic poem, can neither "be" nor "mean." It can only "do."

Whitman's "democratic" poetics is forcefully examined for its political implications in another essay in this collection.[3] I would like to concentrate here on what is at stake in his claim for a poem of the future for which there is no present poem, only a pre-figuration, as it were. We might recall that as late as *Democratic Vistas* he was calling for this poem of the future, this realized democracy that was not yet realized, even in his own sublime prefigurations, or "Leaves" of the book. The poem of the future, that is, could only appear in a poem anterior to it, a poem in the act of inventing it, and thus a poem of history that was autogenetic. In American poetics, from Emerson to Wallace Stevens and beyond, this poem would be like a "giant on the horizon" ("A Primitive Like an Orb") and "patron of origins," and thus a revisionary figure of the sublime. It is as if every poet had to invent "America" as "future" anew and prefigure it as a trope. Like Emerson's horizonal

3. See Kathryne V. Lindberg's essay elsewhere in this text.

"literature" in the essay "Circles," which gives us purchase in our "hodiernal circle" in order to see further circles, this poem would also forecast, or throw forward. This poem would be some new kind of sublime, not an awesome and uncognizable figuration that heralds the universal by marking its own limit or blinding the "transparent eyeball," but a figure marking its own ultimate sublation and death. For while Hegel's theory of art anticipates a future in which the Spirit overcomes its phenomenal fate, or philosophy displaces poetry, the "American" (and democratic) poem seems to imagine its sacrifice as the sacrifice of the father to his own second coming or second childhood—a kind of genealogical auto-production in which the figure tropes itself, prefigures by disfiguring, and thus marks itself as the origin of representation and not the presentation of origin. As Stevens writes of contradiction in "Connoisseur of Chaos," the poem will offer "Pages of illustrations," but the "luster" will be its own artful performance or tropology. Much like an essay.

In his essay "Circles," Emerson sets out to amplify, or indeed supplement, the titular figure that he calls the "highest emblem in the cipher of the world," the figure of metaphysics, ontotheology, of God, but also of figure itself: "emblem" and "cipher." And the inquiry, if it is that, or elaboration soon turns up a problematic. The figure Emerson addresses has already been drawn, or redrawn, in a poem that serves as epigraph. It is Emerson's poem, his particular signature or "emblem" of a totality he has already overwritten while underwriting it as the "highest." The circle is not one cipher among others; it cannot be reduced or partitioned, yet it is also a part, a synecdoche, of the whole, and a part of a part, an emblem of the "eye" and of the "I." The "eye" forms the first circle, just as an "I" or finite consciousness may "form" the first poem, the Idea's emblem. For if the circle, as Emerson cites Saint Augustine's adage of the form "whose center was everywhere and its circumference nowhere," is an emblem, and the eye both one of its manifestations and its genesis, then the origin is always already a trope. "A new genesis were here," as the poem/epigraph puts it—the poem being Emerson's own composition that forms the textual genesis of his essay, a work in turn originating itself out of the Augustine text.

    The essay, then, stages its own production as an act of reading, as a "circular and compensatory" troping of the circle's "copious sense" into a yet-larger sense. This decentering of origin by repetition, of the first by the second, of center by circumference or "horizon," marks an Emersonian displacement of "perfection" (the "Unattainable") by "power." For many readers of Emerson, this is the first act or gesture of a new humanism, of positioning the "central man." But in its displacement of Nature (symbol of God in his phenomena) by man ("eye," "I"), or the proper by the figural, man appears as the name of his generic act. He appears as trope, a center precipitated upon the horizon, outside of our "hodiernal circle," and the new center is named the poet, a son replacing the father. The poet/son is like the philosopher, a reader and troper of a pre-text: "Aristotle platonized"; man not only "realizes" but "adds," like the various actors—poets, lovers, and so on—of Wallace Stevens' "A Primitive Like an Orb" who constantly rewrite the "giant on the horizon" by a kind of tropological supplementation.

Emerson thus nominates himself, both as poet and as "literature" itself, as an "experimenter" that projects by "quotation." To recall both an earlier essay, *Nature*, and a later one, "Quotation and Originality," both of which I have commented on at length elsewhere, we might note that this positioning of literature and maker on the "verge," or horizon, anticipates or repeats in a curious way the structure of the family romance of Hegel that Derrida reads in *Glas*. Just as language, posing as a system of natural signs, sublates the thing, "in the sign, the signifier (exterior) is sublated [*relevé*] by signification, by the signified sense (ideal), the *Bedeutung*, the concept. The concept sublates the sign which sublates the thing. The signified sublates the signifier which sublates the referent."[4] This produces what Derrida calls a "dialectophage," or murder of the sign, a destruction of natural language: "Natural language bears and touches in itself the sign of death," and its cadaver is resurrected in the concept (Philosophy), just as the son must be sacrificed (murdered) in Spirit's fulfillment of its *telos* and, by extension, poetry must experience its death in the service of philosophy.[5]

But Emerson's (almost) parody of Hegel, his mimicry of this "dialectophage," becomes a strategic intervention allowing poetry to displace philosophy, and the son the father. Poetry does not annul philosophy but resurrects itself by quotation, reinscribing the "idea" in the

4. Jacques Derrida, *Glas* (Paris, 1974), 15, left column. (My translation.)
5. This Hegelian role of art and literature is reversed in Nietzsche, according to Paul de Man, just as the relation of, and distinction between, the two discourses is put in question and marked as an aporia throughout poststructural discourses. See de Man, *Allegories of Reading* (New Haven, Conn., 1979), 119–31.

"act," the sign as both signified and signifier in the trope's turning, its circle. The "eye/I" becomes the horizonal position literally in its turn.

Literature's belatedness becomes a strange earliness. One might read into this a kind of allegory of what American literature might be, as originary quotation. Whitman's advertisements for himself are only indices to the thematic redundancy of claiming originality while at the same time regretting that the original and yet "modern" poem has still to be written. In *Democratic Vistas*, for example, long after the almost virginal appearance of "Song of Myself" has issued in revisions and elaboration of a developing *Leaves*, the Bard still announces that we are only on the verge of the truly modern and democratic poem. And like Emerson's verge, its figure remains the tropologically embodied "I," the "eye" in and out of the body, the referent sublated in the sign and the sign (corporeal signifier) as the provisional sign for, and "wound" of, the "idea."

This is the figure of Emerson's *Nature*, the notoriously overdetermined "transparent eyeball" that is misread, I believe, as a simple emblem of unmediated vision. Because Emerson situates his figure not at a transcendental center but in a "bare common" or even "in the woods" or upon a "bare ground" or "wilderness"—that is, a horizonal landscape that it organizes as "part and particle of God"—the self is effaced in the emblem of the "eye." This poet's "eye" and "I" are figural, synecdochal, "part and particle," a reading borne out in the essay's conclusion, which evokes the figure of man as a "god in ruins" and the poet as self-redemptive man. The poem, the poetic "I," includes "both history and prophet." It repairs the axial law that should align "vision" and "things," that law which has become a "ruin or blank" for contemporary man. Disunited within himself, suffering from an "opaque" eye rather than transparency, man has become like Hegel's finite consciousness. But in the poem it remains possible to "behold the real higher law" once again, even though the poem remains figural, historical as well as prophetic.

The "new center," Emerson had written in *Nature*, is prospective, the "verge of today," not an origin but a "patron of origin" as in Stevens' poem, and thus pre-original. The "concentrum" of the poem is a figural prophecy of a unity to be, but as Stevens' poem reads it, the poem is a "fated eccentricity." The "giant" of writing is overdetermined, a "skeleton of the ether," and a figure "ever changing." As "tenacious particle," it is a synecdoche, but only of some possible and futural "central poem." The "patron" on the "horizon" centers the origin eccentrically in its tropological maneuvers, revealing how each rewriting is a reading of an earlier figure as if it were later; and the anticipation of a later figure inscribes both past and future within itself, its double writing, just as Stevens' poem may be said to read the eccentric and prophetic role that Emerson makes the poem play in his essay.

Stevens' poem allows us to read Emerson's positioning of the poem, of figural language, on the "verge" as a situating of trope at the "new center," just as Whitman would read the Emersonian prophecy of the poem/figure as a self-engendering (and even auto-inseminating) trope. It is what Whitman celebrates as "Nature without check with original energy," a nature centered in the corporeal "I" that celebrates itself and sings itself. Celebrating and singing the self ("oneself"), however, is not a simple notion, and its conditions would produce some extreme transformations, from "Song of Myself" to the "Sea Drift" poems, that can tell us something about the economy of self-reflective perform-ances. Quite simply, to celebrate oneself requires the conditions of un-doing an old self with each utterance that adds to or enlarges the self, so that the self in saying "I" falls victim to the conditions of unfolding that Hegel engages when he examines what is entailed in the "I" saying "I." "With the twirl of my tongue I encompass worlds and volumes of worlds," Whitman writes in "Song of Myself," but like Melville in *Moby Dick*, to encompass old "volumes" is to quote a nature and be trans-formed in it.

We might recall Paul de Man's analysis of the Hegelian utterance "When I say I." According to de Man, it leads to yet another kind of utterance: "I cannot say I."[6] The ironic rigor of de Man's reading can-not be summarized here, but it is necessary to point out that he begins this reading by tying Hegel's ontology to his aesthetics, specifically to his distinction between sign and symbol, and by arguing that contrary to familiar notions, Hegel's apparent privileging of the "symbol" over the "sign" leads to a problematical impasse, or aporia, in his efforts to write the history of consciousness. De Man's startling linkage of aes-thetics and history turns on Hegel's contradictory notion of the sign's arbitrariness and phenomenality, its degradation on the one hand and its freedom from determination, or its "free" function, on the other, in

6. De Man, "Sign and Symbol," 768.

contrast to the symbol's phenomenal inscription as a signified. Out of this apparent, but not symmetrical, contradiction, de Man notices and remarks on Hegel's double stress on the "I" as sign and sign-producing—that is, on the nature and the stature of the "grammatical subject" that realizes itself with a certain predicative freedom. Just as the symbol is at once reified and determined in perception, the percep-tual "I" would be entombed in its body or phenomena; but the gram-matical "I," in its saying or performance, *would be*, in a certain sense, *free* even of its own determinations. Like Emerson's over-celebrated fig-ure of "Man Thinking," the Hegelian "I" or grammatical subject lives at risk of its freedom.

Now, one hesitates to pull back from the abstractive formulas of a Hegel, which move between stable concepts and performative over-determination, to poetic performances upon such already overwrought figures as the tropic "I." First, as Hegel notices, the characteristic of thought, of thinking as manifest in sign, is abstraction, or increasing abstraction—repetition as generalization. Thus the "I" as grammatical subject is a generalized/generalizing "I" and not the reference to an essential or privative subject; an "I," therefore, that stands for all selves in relation to the other. "The philosophical I," writes de Man, and we might add here the poetic "I," the "I" that speaks "volumes," "is not only self-effacing, as Aristotle demanded, in the sense of being humble and inconspicuous, it is also self-effacing in the much more radical sense that the position of the I, which is the condition for thought, implies its eradication . . . as the undoing, the erasure of any relation-ship, logical or otherwise, that could be conceived between what the I is and what it says it is."[7] This "I" that says/thinks is a sign rather than a symbol and can be represented only by a linguistic position. Perhaps the most startling formulation of its position is Charles Sanders Peirce's apothegmic declaration that "man is a sign," at once representation and interpretation. We should not forget what this irresistible self-efface-ment meant for Emerson and for Whitman, threatened as they were by the role thrust upon them as "representative men" in a democratic world where all representations were equal and anonymous, like He-gel's "abstract generality."

As soon as Whitman conceives (almost literally) himself as dem-ocratic poet speaking "volumes of worlds," he must confront the end of

7. *Ibid.*, 768–69.

any dream of transparency or reflexive identity. The poet in his free-dom was subject to the velocity of change, of self-effacement, which also involved effacing those worlds he had encompassed, nature or other texts, in order to translate and sublate them. While every poet finds himself already inscribed in the "printed and bound book," he must speak yet other volumes. For "He most honors my style who learns under it to destroy the teacher," a sentiment echoed nearly a century later in Williams' *Paterson*, a poem dedicated to effacing the Europeanized or Western subject, the father (Pater) language, in order to free the son to father a New World language.

The problem, however, is not the inevitability of this succession or displacement, this genealogy, but its ever-increasing speed, what Whitman calls its velocity. The velocities of change overwhelm self-reflection and accentuate its eccentricity or liminality, its representa-tions, that is, the disfigurement and death of the self transacted in the subject's thinking. There is perhaps no more vivid a figure of the dis-placed middle of American poetics than the one that organizes the scene of self-reading in Whitman's "As I Ebb'd with the Ocean of Life," one of the two canonical "Sea Drift" poems and first titled "Bardic Symbols." The poem's scene is, to echo Emerson, a verge, a liminal ebbing of the "electric self" who discovers that his very act of creation, of writing, is a death—but death in a strange and unfamilial sense. First, there is no scene of instruction here, no handing of the mantle from father to son; nor even a scene of displacement. Rather, we are witness to a massive undoing of any such genealogical drama of telic violence. Second, the poem graphically portrays writing as an act of reflective effacement (the poet walking upon the "shores I know . . . seeking types" but finding no self-representations) that annuls his es-sential or symbolic nature. Reflection upon these driftworks reveals no origin either of them, as natural objects, or of the poetic self. Like the hieroglyphic bones of Hart Crane's "At Melville's Tomb," these obscure signs cannot be read as the poet wishes: that is, as reflections or repre-sentations of himself. They are neither synecdochal nor symbolic, but graphic signs (like Crane's "livid hieroglyphs") provoking interpreta-tion, demanding to be read. The poet discovers himself as only another of the pieces of detritus, as a reader reading. Nothing is a type or be-longs to a typological order; nothing reflects its origin or reveals direc-tion, neither "sands" (and one remembers Blake's figure) nor "dead leaves" (possibly Whitman's own poetic leavings). In sum, what one might hope to be a readable, or symbolic, world is effaced. There is no revelation, and the face of things, resisting a reading, interfering with self-reflection, becomes the sign of the self's undoing, its death. The poet's acts of reflection, of thought, entail his own effacement. The returning objects or signs compose a dirge of his own thinking/reading. It is as if all the poems of the world pass before his eyes, drift up in his memory, but from what direction?

And the question of direction, of *telos*, is crucial, since all questions of the future seem questions of direction. But drift, as we know, is a "modern" problem in which the innuendo of teleology is subject to redundancy and overdetermination. With this gesture, and others in the "Sea Drift" poems, Whitman annuls once and for all the illusion of a symbolic or reflexive world, and makes indelible the flaws or marks of contradiction that had been so artfully (rhetorically) concealed in Emerson's false dialectic of the way one might build a "house" or American genealogy out of driftworks or quotations. Just as Poe in "The Fall of the House of Usher" made us gaze upon the "barely perceptible fissure" that turns to nightmare the dream of an American genealogy, and by extension, the possibility of an "American poetics," Whitman must submit his own translative poem to a deconstruction that turns out to be a commentary on its difficulties in catching the drift of what has come before his eyes.

These signs are not symbols and will not reflect him. Instead, he repeats them in a kind of reading. There is a similar scene in the other canonical "Sea Drift" poem, "Out of the Cradle Endlessly Rocking," in which the divided "I" of the poet serves as a kind of "translating" song, hearing and interpreting a division, a "he-bird" and "she-bird" who can be united only as a "thousand warbling echoes" that might be gleaned in the utterance of the former. But the utterance of the "he-bird" is only heard as echoes because of the silence or absence of the former, that is, of "death," the name of absence that is also the "word." The "word" includes, inscribes death, but no longer in the presence-absence, self-other opposition; and the poem develops in terms of, in the regard of, a self who in translating this scene is translated by it. The fate of the poet, the subject, the translator lies in the time, the tempo, of his reading translation. Whitman writes on the verge of the modern, of the modern as verge. Its theme, as Henry Adams knew, was speed or velocity, turning or trope rather than representation. In Emerson's terms, it will be not the figure of "representative Man" so

much as "Man Thinking," and for Whitman it will mandate an effacement of the self in the body or death.

Whitman had discovered in "Song of Myself" that even to sing
and celebrate the self was to augment and enlarge it, to increase the
body's mass so as to encompass the "en-masse." But this growing sublimity tended not to regulate the axiological and analogical relation between finite and universal consciousness, or between the natural and
transcendental, with Emersonian transparency. The scene of translation performed in "Out of the Cradle" and "As I Ebb'd" would have to
reflect on the obdurate figure of the body/poem that undoes all such
hopes for the "word" and for the possibility of anthropocentric literature. If Whitman begins by evoking something like Kant's figure of the
sublime colossus in the *Critique of Judgment*, in which the human body
and language regulate what Wallace Stevens calls the "effects of analogy," the movement between natural and transcendental, he will have
to conclude with a rather more despairing vision of vision, in which
the figure of the sublime obscures the sun with its shadow. In Whitman, music signifies the law of nature's order, just as the poem as music
orders and catalogs the manifold and multitudes. The words or drifts
of the later poems, which are no less revisionary translations of the
earlier, disperse the celebrated man/center and precipitate it upon the
horizon: as in "On the Beach at Night Alone," the "clef" (of "I think a
thought of the clef of the universes and of the future") is both break
and dividing musical notation or sign. While the poet still desires to
enclose the "vast similitudes" in the "All" of his utterance, while he
wants not only to declare but to regulate the purpose and direction of
nature, as center dispatched to the verge or margin this "I" (which no
longer sees) can speak only as one of the fragments or atoms that proceed in "motley procession" ("After the Sea-Ship").

Man is no longer the measure, nor the poem an adequate place or
agent. To recall the Derridean reading of Kant in "Parergon," the figure
of the poem is no longer an adequate presentation of the unpresentable
but, more importantly, must reflect the inadequacy of itself as presentation ("the inadequation of the presentation to itself").[8] The poem no
longer serves as bridge and symbol but rather announces the strange
effects of another economy (what Derrida examines as the "economi-

8. See Jacques Derrida, *The Truth in Painting*, trans. Geoff Bennington and Ian
McLeod (Chicago, 1987), 144.

mesis" of aesthetics, of taste, of repetition, in Kant; and the undoing of the "family romance" or genealogical order in Hegel). The poem/ word/"I" on the shore/margin/horizon can only reflect on itself, its marginality. Yet, decentered and eccentric, the poem does reflect the contradictions of self-reflection. Like the detritus washing up on the sands in "As I Ebb'd," old poems and figures return and are turned in the new poem's reflections, revealing that these new reflections are echoes, like the "thousand warbling echoes" of the poet's song in "Out of the Cradle." These echoes reveal that this song, which is a "translation," bears within itself the word *death*. The "word" is at once death and the "word death." It has become a sign, but a thinking or grammatical sign marking the destiny of the "I."

It is within this scene that Whitman begins to rethink the idea of "America" or the great democratic poem as a poem always already horizonal, a future-present, and hence inadequate presentation. This poem, then, will be adequate, but only "ages hence," and then only in the writings of "recorders" who take instruction from present inscriptions: "I will tell you what to say of me" (see both "Recorders Ages Hence" and "Inscriptions"). Present poems offer a "profound loss of reception" ("Song of the Open Road") but, like Peirce's sign, inscribe the necessity of their own interpretation. The American poet is fated to write this poem endlessly, like Stevens in "A Postcard from the Volcano," musing upon the fate of reading in the hands of "Children picking up our bones." That Whitman chooses to enact this scene of reading/instruction as a scene of death within poems like "As I Ebb'd" indicates his apprehension over the major problematics of the "modern."

This may help explain why American writers in general, and in particular those who were so preoccupied not only with personal identity but with the task of impersonally re-presenting the nation, of engendering a national identity and language, found that literature was a better instrument for thinking than was philosophy. Literature could mark the strategies of *making*, of invention and self-invention as prospective more than self-reflective. Having no history or tradition to determine representation, the American poet would be enslaved to a false "patron of origins" unless s/he could make the last first, the repetition originary, and the act of recording a translation. The modern poem, then, or Emerson's threshold "literature," would have to function with the prospective force of trope, rather than reveal the imminence of symbol. An American poetics of the sublime could be, not the sublime in the old sense, as Stevens recorded in the first canto of "Esthétique du Mal," making "sure of the most correct catastrophe," but a "sublime" revealing the undoing of the "book" of the sublime. This poem will mime its own undoing and translation. I have described this effect elsewhere, particularly in regard to the writing of Hart Crane and William Carlos Williams, as the "poetics of failure," a phrase which does not mean aesthetic failure or failure of perfection but, on the contrary, implies the poem's rigorous questioning of "perfection," closure, and totalization.[9] It is thus a rejection of the very poem as symbol the poet sets out to realize.

Crane, indeed, is an exceptional case of the "modernist" crisis that one can find in poets as different as Stevens and Pound—exceptional perhaps only in the anxiety he evidences over the indirectness of language and thus the motives for metaphor. While Pound and so-called objectivist poetics in general found the Image (its aesthetic, phenomenal, and even "natural" status) preferable to the "symbol" and indeed prior to it, and found in symbolism a move away from the precision and historicity of originary poetic language, and while Stevens revels in the productive irony of a "world of words" spun out of the "act of the mind," Crane seems almost paralyzed by the double-bind of the poem that remains a cryptic symbol. Compare his famous (or infamous) claims for the "logic of metaphor" and his argument that the poet generates a new "single word" out of some alembic of the words at his disposal with, on the one hand, Pound's argument, following Fenollosa's notes, that all poetic language is metaphoric or translative, transferential, thus natural, or, on the other hand, Stevens' insistence upon a "fictive" reality, a "realm of resemblance" that we recognize to be fictive and thus a human construct, cultural and not natural. The question of the "word," of what experimental modernism heralded as the "revolution of the word," always arises in the place that Derrida calls the "tain" of the mirror, the position of reflection. It is situated at precisely the "point" (Derrida would emphasize the French double sense of the noun position and the adverbial negation, not exact oppo-

9. See my early, and very different, essay on Crane, "Hart Crane's Poetics of Failure," *ELH*, XXXIII (December, 1966), 473–96; and also Chapter Five, "The Poetics of Failure," in Riddel, *The Inverted Bell: Modernism and the Counterpoetics of William Carlos Williams* (Baton Rouge, 1974). Also *cf.* Murray Krieger, *Theory of Criticism* (Baltimore, 1976), 220–22.

sites) where the poet/poem is forced to reflect upon itself. The point, that point, is what is called "modernism."

What attracts us to Crane, then, is not his anxious and essentially sublimated preoccupation with the aesthetic symbol, but the effects of his trying to produce it and thus the effects of his reflections upon the status and stature of the "word"—the erection of the "word," as in "The Broken Tower," and its undoing in the "tolling" (as in the Derridean "*glas*") of the "broken" poem. It is a question, as the poem phrases it, not of cognition but of the "cognate":

> My word I poured. But was it cognate, scored
> Of that tribunal monarch of the air
> Whose thigh embronzes earth, strikes crystal Word
> In wounds pledged once to hope—cleft to despair?

The tolling and mourning of the "word," its cleft and clef, and thus its flawed nature, situates it in that middle place that Kant saw for the aesthetic, where it is not cognitive but might be a fulcrum or bridge between phenomenal and noumenal. Crane's "word" reverberates the questionable nature of the Word incarnate, of the poem as disfigured and fallen body—of the poem as fallen erection that is no longer central. The poem undoes itself in self-mourning. Again, as in Whitman, the musical clef and the cleft of writing mingle to disturb the meditation of the poem/word upon itself, leaving the body of the Word, the poet's body, in fragments.

The poet's eye, his emblem of the "visionary company of love," is now drawn to that which does not exactly reflect him or mediate between finite and universal consciousness. He cannot decide whether the poem as bridge is himself as symbol or a technical construct, a sign. He cannot read himself. This reinscription (probably unconscious) of Hegel's notion of the symbol and the sublime into the problematics of modernism begins to reflect modernism's undoing at its so-called origins. Hegel's writing already predicated the "turn" toward language. First, recall the famous definition of the "symbol" in his lectures on aesthetics, the symbol as a unity divided within itself, at once prior to the "sign" but also of the sign, a kind of sublation of the sign, yet grounded literally, or at least phenomenally, in the sign.[10] This symbol

---

10. G. W. F. Hegel, *Aesthetics: Lectures on Fine Art*, trans. T. M. Knox (2 vols.; Oxford, 1975), I, 303ff.

is, as de Man observed, a synecdoche; but as part of a whole, the universal, it is also an arbitrary part or kind of radical fragment. It is thus a kind of synecdoche of synecdoche.

Symbolic art, as Hegel subsequently argues, must inevitably be involved in the question of the symbol's sublimity, of its being unreadable because it is the "beginning of art" or the "threshold of art," belonging to the East, yet prima facie a sign and a mark of that death necessary for the transit of spirit through the West. Taking up the Kantian distinction between beautiful and sublime in the *Critique of Judgment*, Hegel extrapolates the Kantian effort to situate (the figure of) man—and, thus, as we have seen, "consciousness" or the "I"—into a notion of the sign's freedom or action, the movement toward law and generalization manifest in the grammatical "I" and thus through the sign's self-nullification. The sign is both repetitive (it submits to an "inner obedience") and resistant (it manifests a "stubbornness against the law"), giving it, as we will see, a critical as well as aesthetic status.

What Hegel calls, in a chapter title, the "Conscious Symbolism of the Comparative Art Form" (378ff.) evidences the peculiar role of sublimity and symbolism, in which one must consider the symbol both as work and working, thing and act. For "conscious symbolism" (and it serves Hegel as a kind of name for modernism, or at least for the "threshold" of the modern, though it belongs to ancient, glyphic art or writing) marks its difference from "unconscious symbolism" in its marked *"non-correspondence"* or "separation" of "meaning, explicitly known in its inwardness, and the concrete appearance divided therefrom." This "separation" and hierarchization of meaning and particularity, of the universal and its representation, is the irreducible signature of the sublime and cannot be repaired. In the "subjective activity of the poet," the relation of the two is always characterized as a "more or less accidental concatenation," so that the figure of the sublime always appears as a "cognate spiritual meaning" in which the marks of separation and degradation can never be effaced; and thus the "determinate or restricted meaning" (the phenomenal representation) comes to displace the priority of the Absolute (the "concept," the "content"). In terms of the earlier distinction between the sign and the symbol, which is also prima facie a sign, the particularity (or negativity of the concept) of the work, its figurality, is at once de-privileged and reinscribed in its priority. Its fallenness, its historicity, its didacticism becomes a kind of ironic firstness, as a Peircean might say.

The recalcitrance of the "symbolic" is essentially for Hegel the limits of language, marking the unbridgeable abyss between figure and concept. But it also centralizes the marginality of the abyss whose figure is the bridge, figure itself. At once natural and spiritual, or an uncertain conjunction of the two, the "symbolic and comparative art-form" never quite overcomes the duality of separation and conjunction that signifies the historical economy of the West. Hegel's literary or art history, which is also an allegory of the "history" of Spirit, unfolds dialectically from East to West, and from the symbolic to the classical to the romantic, but always in terms of the ratio between ideal "content" and phenomenal "form." Spirit is repeatedly drawn through the beautiful (the material and sensuous) and never quite manages to escape the drag of its objectivity. In its sublime and sublimated stages, Spirit's symbolic form can only hint at the subjective overcoming or the sublative moment in which its determinations and yet its freedom (as sign) is returned to itself. Thus the history that also unfolds from the many to one, from pantheism to monotheism, and from representation to expression, even finally from the tentative balances and unity of form-content in classical art to the death of the naturalized spirit and finite consciousness in the romantic, can only be seen as an arc of the circle, the negation of negativity. For the romantic can never quite throw off the face of this negation (the prima facie beauty and health of the classical sign), this tragic mask of death as the mother of beauty, and thus reveal the ugly contingency, the phenomenality of degradation that Spirit must pass through. Hegel calls this the "genuine phoenix-life of spirit," which includes forms of its dissolution—like Poe's forms of the grotesque and the arabesque.

However formulated, this Hegelian "art" history can never extract the concept from its figuration (and disfiguration). Philosophy, as he says, always has its Good Friday, but it is reflected in the religious revelations of the romantic art-form that never finally sublates, overcomes, or transcends its representations, however effectively it outlives and effaces the "graven images" of pantheism with its visage of the divine man. If the Hegelian story brings us to the "threshold" of the Spirit's return, its turn toward and into itself "through the finite consciousness and its grammatical tendency toward generalization," it also brings us to an impasse or impassable horizon, the "modern," where the old crisis of "symbolic and comparative art-form," the symbol as sublime sign, is redoubled. The return of the symbol as construct, as technical or unnatural erection, reintroduces the question of representation and negation in terms of a new thematic, of dynamism and power rather than genealogy, so that the determining phenomenality of the figural form, of language, is reinscribed as problematical. In other words, Hegel brings us through self-reflection to the impasses of reflection upon reflection, to what Derrida calls the chiasmatic moment of dissemination.

The problematic status of art, of the poem as conscious symbol, fills the entire history of the West, like a bridge, and cannot be effaced or repressed by the expressive dis-figurations of the romantic. Modernism, in the guises of romantic art, rehearses that history in the drama of art's displacement of religion. But this ensures that the "work" of this art-form will appear not as a representation or expression of spirit or even of the idea of man, but as a technical construction signifying the idea of the natural/organic. Hegel's romantic pathos anticipates its modernist deconstruction, in which the technical erection not only represents the organic, the idea of nature, but serves as its pseudo-origin. Just as in the later Heidegger, where the bridge does not so much provide transit over the abyss as it defines the form of the abyss, otherwise formless, the symbol in Hegel, which is also irreducibly a sign, indicates in its repetitive nature the priority and originarity of figurality.

For modernism, the metaphor of performance and action, what Stevens called the "poem of the act of the mind" and Pound named in the dynamics of the moving "Image," later "Vortex," displaces the immanence of the symbol in a manner that can only reveal that the symbol is always already a symbol of the symbol or of the sublime. What Lyotard calls the modernist sublime, or modernism as a poetics of the sublime, subsists in the Janus-faced symbol that averts reflection, that resists self-reflection. The "act" of the modern poem is less reflexive, and genetic, than it is a productive act of self-reading. In its attempt to legitimate itself, to reify itself as symbol, the poem tropes itself or produces a set (a tropological series) of effects, of quotations, like those that Pound discovered in Malatesta's "post-bag" (or the "rag-bag" with which he began an early version of Canto II) or Tempio; or even like the "Thesaurus" of Canto IV, which remains the genetic source that will conclude in the acknowledged "incoherence" of the "palimpsest" of Canto CXVI, which asks who will "read" it, or who, in the Peircean sense, will mark its necessity as "interpretant" sign. The Stevensian "and yet[s]" of his "never-ending meditation" in "An Ordinary Evening in New Haven" compose another rhetorical version, and a different kind of poetry perhaps, of this modernist confrontation with what Williams called the "edge" of the image, the glyphic and graphic sign, the poem as a "word" that marks its limit, its own margin.

Hart Crane's poetry might seem to offer, as we have noted, an exception (a "sublime" one) to this paradoxically affirmative and productive celebration of the modernist Image as glyph or graphic resistance to self-reflexivity. His "logic of metaphor" and his confrontation with the "livid hieroglyphics" ("At Melville's Tomb") posed by all old texts, in this particular case with the "American" versions or reinscriptions and, thus, "readings" of a past that cannot be its origin, might provide us with a scene of modernism. His attempt to write an "American" or literary "epic" in *The Bridge*, to engender, as he claimed for the "logic of metaphor," a poem that would be a "new word" that the reader would re-cognize when he "left it" or, presumably, finished with his reading-interpretation, might very well provide us with what Heidegger might call the technical impasses of modernism.

   In his effort to appropriate and then reverse the very dynamics that have replaced the unitary force of the *logos*, Crane is forced to redraft a poetics of the margin or the sublime, of the symbolic as a "failure," into a poetics of what Henry Adams called the "dynamo." One way of following out what Crane asserts as the uncanny "logic of metaphor," his phrase for the poem as "new word," might be an exploration of his misreading of a text that had an inordinate if perverse effect on early American modernism—Spengler's *Decline of the West*. But this cannot be done as a history of ideas, of nihilism, in the manner of many studies of poetic derivation from philosophy. Indeed, Crane's and Eliot's opposed uses of Spengler's metaphysical narrative (more Hegelian than Nietzschean, one might argue) is in itself one of the curious instances of (mis-)interpretative violence within modernism: Crane's forced optimism set against Eliot's echoes of Spengler's pessimistic critique of the modern. Eliot, of course, accepted what Spengler described as decline and authored a move to redeem this plight of spiritual history; in this he repeats Hegel's ontotheology even as he rejects romanticism. Crane, on the other hand, chose to misread or trope declination, to skew it, to produce ascesis, as it were. Recent studies of Crane, most significantly John Irwin's study of the uses of perspectivism in the paneling of *The Bridge*'s unfolding structure, have enforced this Cranian reading of Spengler's negative theology. Irwin reveals the haunting and even perverse function of perspective in any aesthetics that is centered upon the economy of specularity, for perspective is clearly (a strange word here) a notion of resistance and power, as in Nietzsche, an interpretative effort to preserve an individual or communal entity and thus a historical act.[11]

At stake in Crane's anti-Eliot reading of Spengler, as Irwin speculates, is a problem of the sublime, of *trans*lating the eternal into a history that represents it as spectacle. It is a problem of the image and of the imaginative, and of the "marge" that must be negotiated in any act of translation—like that of Michelangelo's translation of biblical revelation into spatial narrative or Crane's retranslation of "history" and its perspectives (including the literary texts of "America") back into some *verbum res* of the poem. Irwin focuses on the task of the translation assumed by Michelangelo, Botticelli, and Cosimo Rosselli in his Sistine narrative, a problem of perspectivity in recounting a narrative cycle within the spatial enclosures of a single room (the task of sanctification along with that of closing an enclosure). In Spengler's narrative, the artist is a Faustian figure willing to lose himself in accumulation of power, and he marks in a certain way the modernist's logical conclusion of post-classical culture.

Irwin recounts Spengler's argument for a cultural history derived from a history of art that has to engage the question of temporality in spatial terms, and the efforts of artists to find, between the classical figure of the naked human body and the modernist or Faustian world of polyphonic music, some "third dimension" or resolution of the space-time dilemma. He argues that Crane, under the influence of Spengler, is motivated to think out the modern poet's dilemma in terms of this space-time, visual art–polyphonic music dialectic, with the poet cast in the role of Faustian subject whose perspective of individual will centralizes without resolving the struggle. It is my contention that Crane is or becomes less a Spenglerean than he appears, and simply because he has to confront all the problems of self-reflexive ordering, and thus of the symbol, opened up by Hegel and aggravated by Nietzsche. We find it worked out in Crane's attempt to resolve the po-

11. John T. Irwin, "Foreshadowing and Foreshortening: The Prophetic Vision of Origins in Hart Crane's *The Bridge*," *Word & Image*, I (July–September, 1985), 288–312. For Nietzsche on "perspectivism," see *The Will to Power*, trans. Walter Kaufmann (New York, 1967), p. 149, Sec. 259.

sition of the poetic self, the poem, and the word, or poetic language in general.

This is the condition of Crane's *Bridge*, both figure and poem. The poet aspires to reify its title, and thus the poem, as genetic figure—the bridge, and hence the abyss it covers, as origin and end—while at the same time affirming its priority to either origin or end. As *logos*, or new word, it reveals itself in the poet's gaze as only a trope at the threshold. It reveals the trope of the center to be only a technical construction, a "Paradigm" of the center on the horizon, which like the figure of the colossus in Kant can never quite be read by the one who conceived it as "Paradigm" or "Verb." And the abyss it bridges (ocean or oceanic force; river or entropic manifestation of that force's unilinear and irreversible direction that the poet desires to see flowing back into itself) becomes a "threshold" center, precipitating the poet as reader into its "shadow." This is the complicated and problematic issue of poetic "space" Crane encounters in trying to conceive the poem as new word.

Crane's figure of the bridge, then, is not an immanent figure but a graphic one, one to which he gives names derived from language—the Bridge as both noun and verb, subject and predicate. It does not organize within itself the moment of spirit's self-reflection or return but motivates the poet's acts of reading, his efforts to find hints of the transcendental in the signs of a history that have flowed under and across it, through it, and are perhaps sublated in it, as in proper names and metonyms. The "bridge" as symbol is also a sign of chiasmatic crossings that everywhere mark the limit of vision in the sublimity of representation. And the poet, who wants to find himself reflected in this "Verb," finds himself, as finite consciousness, initially exiled from it. And further, neither he nor it is at the center.

Let us try to follow the historical logic of Crane's installation of the "bridge," his attempt to resurrect from the erection the power of its conception. First, Brooklyn Bridge is a modern technical miracle, a product not of mechanics but of dynamics, and thus it signifies a new spatial organization of time, a new sense of bridging. Second, Crane conceives it as a metonymy for the position of America in world history, as the place of the dream of opening up again a closed history of the West, of restoring the circle beyond the old teleological dream of manifest destiny. Connecting the lost Atlantis with Cathay, the bridge as symbol also doubles for the American continent as phenomenal connective or spirit's historical state of sublation. Yet the continent also bears within its geography a double mark of history: transcontinental railroad and macadam highway ("From Far Rockaway to Golden Gate") cross in one direction the movement of another river, the Mississippi, just as the Bridge crosses the East River, which links oceanic force with continental mass. The Bridge, then, is not a fixed and sublime symbol but a master trope, turning under the poet's gaze like the enigma of a threshold that has occulted the transcendental. The Bridge is not stable but turning, as the poet sees it, not a Virgin but a Dynamo "of the fury fused," as Henry Adams had put it.

Crane's poem, however, takes its representative model not from the material Bridge but from the modern graphic design of Joseph Stella that is an undoing of representation, or a representation of dynamics, of troping; for Stella's painting is a nonperspectival rendering of Roebling's dynamic (and Hegelian) idea of the dialectical bridge.[12] Wherever the poet as finite consciousness turns he must confront the enigma of a turning stability. He is drawn to the Bridge as (if he were) a part of it, seeking his reflection in it. But all he discovers is that the Bridge is refractive rather than reflective. As paradigm it will not be conjugated under his control but marks the abyss between figure and any possible transcendental. The Bridge as poem/symbol is not only part (arc) rather than whole (circle), it is not simply unreadable, but it signifies further the aberrations of the poet's desire to master it, to translate it (the "word") as other in his image ("new word"). The Bridge as figure tropes the poet, transforms him into an abyss, and marks his anonymity as a pariah. Like Whitman's democratic self, or Emily Dickinson's diminished self, he becomes everybody and nobody, reflected in and by everything, and reflecting nothing.

Crane's poet becomes the poem/Bridge, then, in a disincarnation of the "word," being consumed by his work: he is at once self-consumed and consumed by the other. Simple sublation is suspended, and the self is disseminated, like the atoms of a democratic nation, in every direction, to be gathered up into nuclei or multicenters that sug-

---

12. The designer of Brooklyn Bridge, John Roebling, was, as scholars have shown, a follower of Hegel, and he conceived of its structure in dialectical terms. Crane, who happened to occupy Roebling's apartment near the bridge after the designer's death, thought of Roebling as a genius-visionary who had resolved the phenomenological problem of translating vision into spatial form. See Alan Trachtenberg, *Brooklyn Bridge: Fact and Symbol* (2nd ed.; Chicago, 1979).

gest a new sense of history. America is not a mythos or a history of repetition, any more than one can find in it, as Eliot sought and thought he found in Judeo-Christian history and in pagan mythology, a pattern that legitimated and reified the circle. Crane's poet, precipitated beneath the arc of the circle, finds himself turning within its turnings (see the proem), reading that which curves back upon itself not as past but as some kind of future anterior. The future consumes him, consumes the past. Just as Columbus was consumed by an anticipated discovery he could not possess, and was possessed by it even as he tried to name it in borrowed (proper) names, so Melville, Whitman, Dickinson, Isadora Duncan, and Poe, among others, have been consumed, only to reappear in the misty figurations of their culture's history as the ignored spokes(wo)men of that culture, metonyms of a culture that exiles them. In *The Bridge*, they compose a metonymic history of the true but suppressed representatives of the history, because their representations interdict the idea of America's continuity with the West. As performers, they signify America's decentered and decentering role—the role of exile—in the history of the West (ontotheology).

Crane's poem confesses, in a sense, that the only America it can envision is nothing-more than what was originally nothing-other than a represented vision, a re-presentation that precedes the ideal it represents. The re-presentation preceded any presentation, as the threshold preceded not the future but the past. The Bridge as structure and thing is celebrated, in a most exclamatory poem, as "Vision of the Voyage." But the act of vision, percept as perspect, or the bringing of vision to legibility, is revealed throughout as an act of reading/interpreting and projecting an earlier text. Yet the reading is not determined by the earlier idea or its representation. Thus, Columbus' journals of his voyage or even Whitman's exhausted account of manifest destiny in "Passage to India," which are some of the matter of Crane's poem and America's textuality—that is, all these figures of the voyage as return—turn out to be little more than attempts to understand the conditions of voyaging or transport itself. The central problematic of the poem, in short, is the poem—language, metaphor, bridging, transport. The attempt in all such narratives to celebrate the means of transportation and, at the same time, to occlude them, to herald the possibility of unmediated vision, turns upon itself to re-mark the problematics of the voyage. As in Whitman's poem the points of connection are all, as it were, man-made (the Suez Canal, the transatlantic cable, the transcontinental railroad, crossing discontinuities such as oceans and land-masses from east to west to confirm the "continuity of American poetry"), Crane's poem features the deferral points and the problematic media of transport. Within the poem itself, these points are its own metaphors.

Trying to induce an "American" dream or vision, the poet is consumed by it. He is disfigured by his own figurations, just as Columbus was, or Poe; or decapitated, like Isadora Duncan, like the figure of Poe the poet envisions in the section entitled "The Tunnel." The poem signifies this in its modes of transportation, moving from the sailing ship of Columbus, endangered by the sea that "tests the word," to the modern conveyances whose speed and dynamics mark the vitality and the entropy of the present, both of which signify the capitalist ravishment forewarned in the "Ave Maria" section. Consumption and self-consumption, then, are the economic themes extended to language and used to characterize the risk of the poet who must be sacrificed to his vision: he is the one through whom the vision is to be delivered. He himself, the pariah, is the language, to echo H. D.'s line in *Helen in Egypt*.

*The Bridge*, then, is a quest poem, to recall Harold Bloom's generic category for romanticism, and a part of the "American sublime," but it is a quest undone by the conditions of the modern sublime. At every step or point, the poet finds himself marginalized or exiled in his own language when he is forced to recognize the incommensurability of his language to his dream and can only present, as Lyotard defines the modern, "the fact that the unpresentable exists."[13] He can only reflect on his own technical expertise. The sublime "takes place," writes Lyotard, "when the imagination fails to present an object which might, if only in principle, come to match a concept." Crane's poet can only present his own heroic failure as a repetition of a historical succession of failures. But the failure of the "return," of language's stubborn incommensurability, can itself be turned, in an uncanny way, into an affirmation of the future present enacted in the poet's own performance.

13. Jean-François Lyotard, *The Postmodern Condition: A Report on Knowledge*, trans. Geoff Bennington and Brian Massumi (Minneapolis, 1984), 78. See also Paul de Man, "Hegel on the Sublime," in *Displacement: Derrida and After*, ed. Mark Krupnick (Bloomington, Ind., 1983), 144: "The moment Hegel calls sublime is the moment of radical and definitive separation between the order of discourse and the order of the sacred."

Thus Crane must reject enabling myths such as the "return," or such quest motifs as those Eliot appropriates from mythology and Pound from literature—any nostalgic turn toward powerful ancestors that are either sustaining (say, Tiresias) or threatening—and live out the anxiety of influence as an influence of the future. For what lies in the future, on the horizon, is always the cryptic "word." It has replaced all origins, and it both beckons and threatens. It is at once his other and his fate, his destiny. It marks his ultimate and present disfiguration, this divided word. It is like the "flashing scene" or non-origin that draws the crowd in the proem toward the movie, compels the suicide to leap from the Bridge, or sends its dynamic energy (its sunlight) "down Wall, from girder into street." This future-present "word" is no longer the singularity of the *logos*, or of the symbol, and even the synecdochic bridge can only serve as emblem, holding the poet in its shadow and compelling him into new language games in order to catch its dangerous vibrancy.

The emblem, however, shares one thing with the ancient's conscious symbol, as Hegel would have it. It is a kind of sphinx whose riddle is not exactly to be interpreted or divined in a manner that would reflect man to himself. Rather, the emblem compels a dynamics of reading. It is dynamics, the unrepresentable, itself, the ever-changing "word." The Bridge emblematizes history (and "America") in its figuration and asks the poet not to solve its riddle but to repeatedly tell a story about it. That is the fate and destiny of all American writers. "What cunning neighbors history has in fine!" Crane exclaims in the "Quaker Hill" section, where he contemplates the former sacred space of the word now converted into a commercial hotel. This space is under "lease," is mortgaged, its antique "seal" materialized. It is no longer a home or meeting place (canny) but an uncanny place of dalliance and distraction. The artist's burden is always to restore its signification: "Shoulder the curse of sundered parentage." But he soon discovers that it was not a seal hiding the secrets of some immanent and now-lost plenitude but the sign of a genealogical fracture that preceded origins. America was always already sundered, and the poet's heritage is derived from mortgaged texts. Every sign of the past reveals this genealogical fracture; America is not simply a quotation, but a quotation of a quotation. Every new poem, then, is something more than a repetition of the past. It is also necessarily a quotation of the act or performance of turning away; it is a troping.

Unlike Spengler's Faustian artist, who manifests his lust for the infinite in his commitment to perspectivism, Crane finds perspective blinding: "Perspective never withers from their eyes," he writes of those who occupy the *unheimlich* space of the "New Avalon Hotel." They are blind to the sublime as to their own desires. Only the artist contemplates the infinite, but in an ironic mode of its impossibility. Isadora Duncan's utterance serves as epigraph to "Quaker Hill," renouncing the infinite in terms more applicable to Stevens' claim that the truest belief is to believe in a fiction that is known not to be true: "I see only the ideal. But no ideals have ever been fully successful on this earth." That would include the sublime figure the artist makes, his or her performance, and conscious symbols.

Every manifest form of the ideal, then, every symbol bears the mark of artifice, reveals a *technê*. None is "fully successful." The symbol bears within itself at once the hint of a lost natural plenitude and an indication that even nature, or the phenomenon, is only a mechanical representation. The incompatibility of the natural and the artificial in every symbolic performance paralyzes the poet, since he must read its double character. He cannot make the other reflect him; nor can he possess an other's representation. The burden he "shoulder[s]" is not the history of the past but the production of a history, a genetic poem that will unfold some representation of the future.

*The Bridge* is above all a made poem, not a visionary revelation. It dramatizes vision as a perspectival (in the Nietzschean sense) scene of reading or interpretation in which the reader finds himself, as it were, transfixed in the gaze of the symbol he is producing. For in reading the figure in translating it, or translating its translative power, he is undone and "exiled." The Bridge/symbol is a perspectival focus or concentration that defines the crowd as it defines the abyss, and the anonymous "pariah" cannot find anything but his anonymity in its turning. The Bridge has become the active agent or subject, holding the poet in thrall. The "crowd" hastening toward the "cinema" negates both the space of Plato's cave and Hegel's pit of memory; and the Bridge, which should organize space, opens it to the accidents of history's indirection. The Bridge, then, as both "harp and altar, of the fury fused" and "terrific threshold of the prophet's pledge," reflects only the poet's exile in his language. If it is an "unfractioned idiom, immaculate sigh of stars," it is an oxymoron. The Bridge is that which should signify at once the unity of city, country, and world history, but instead it signifies (not only to the poet) his double exile, his inability to command its perspective. It signifies to him the condition of all historical restlessness, what Nietzsche called, in referring to the modern situation of being beyond metaphysics or the Platonic-Hegelian nostalgia, being homeless: "The City's fiery parcels all undone, / Already snow submerges an iron year."

Given to the poet as his language and his future, the Bridge, which he calls "threshold of the prophet's pledge," is asked by the poet to "lend a myth to God." But like every capitalist obligation, that which lends exacts some interest. The poem opens into a strange economy. To ask the symbol to "lend a myth" is to apostrophize and to appeal to one's language to produce. It is to apostrophize the medium. And that is where the poem concludes, in an attempt to reify the genetic figure as center, noun as verb:

> [a] Choir, translating time
> Into what multitudinous Verb the suns
> And synergy of waters ever fuse, recast
> In myriad syllables.

Here, the Bridge as symbol/poem is also invoked as "index" and as "one arc synoptic of all tides below," but the "pervasive Paradigm" everywhere redoubles itself as "myriad syllables" in a kind of uncanny dissemination. "Synergy" proves to be the key and the problem, for Crane treats the Bridge as a conscious symbol, virtually a modern "pyramid" and hieroglyph, and at the same time as a trope, subject to its temporal and historical destiny, or better, the nondestiny of entropy.

The concluding "Atlantis" section no more resolves the problem than the introductory "Proem" managed to reify the "curveship." If the Bridge is "synoptic" and an "index," it is no less a limit, and it is the marking of this limit, as both a threat and a force, that occupies the "history" inscribed in the poem between "Ave Maria" and "The Tunnel." If America is both *word* and *bridge*, she is also a "threshold" to her own self-consumption. Of "sundered parentage," and without a past, she shoulders the destiny of Hegel's future, which will be a different and presently inconceivable form.[14] Crane's sublime lies in his effort to conceive this inconceivable, to represent the unpresentable, as

---

14. *Cf.* Hegel's remarks about America as a "future" and different "history" in the passage quoted earlier and cited in *n*2.

a kind of auto-insemination. From the beginning of "Ave Maria," which is a restaging of the section of Columbus' journal dealing with his anxiety over delivering the word of his discovery, Crane's theme is not the immanent nature of a virgin land but the risk and limit of any representation of such a plenitude. He cannot preserve the "immaculate sigh" of the word that at every turn reveals its divided face as well as its self-consuming force.

Like Lévi-Strauss in *Tristes Tropiques*, recording the alienation his historical sense brings to a mythic and timeless culture, Crane retells Columbus' account as a moment of disfiguration and exploitation that forces the visionary to revise his own mode of revelation. That is, his own language is put at risk. Like Williams' *In the American Grain*, though to different purpose, Crane emphasizes the true danger of quest as the danger of the return, and thus the danger to the "word" (along with the quester who embodies it). Like Williams, Crane treats the discovery as an act of misnaming—Columbus thinks he has found "The Chan's great continent," or "Cathay"—but his essential concern is with possibly failing to communicate that discovery. So he places a written record of his discovery in a cask (Crane mistakenly writes *casque*, or military headgear) and sets it afloat on the stormy ocean: "For here between two worlds, another harsh, / This third, of water, tests the word." The "word" is always "between" and at risk, because it is an "incognizable Word / Of Eden and the enchained sepulchre," thus a "parable of man" and a prayer. Crane finds Columbus' Logos, his Christian vision, already inscribed in the mast of his ship, the figure of the cross; for ship, as well as "casque," bears the "word" and is tested. The ship, as well as its captain, is the "word" as metaphor, not the "incognizable Word."

Each section of *The Bridge* renews and repeats this questioning of the word as the medium of communication, of that which is always already "between." Whether bridge or ship, whether macadam highway stretching from "Far Rockaway to Golden Gate" in the "Van Winkle" section or the subway of "The Tunnel," Crane's figure of the poet/quester as word incarnate is always a double of the Bridge/figure that consumes him in the "Proem" and "Atlantis." But it is a strange, disfigured double, a double with a difference. Whereas sailing ship, highway, and river signify a continuity of nature or a natural bridge, the continent is also marked by another kind of communications system and thus another kind of history—one might say a telecommunications system: the "telegraphic night" of "The River" that marks the age of "iron dealt cleavage"; or the vortex carved out by the Falcon Ace's crashing plane in "Cape Hatteras" that ends in "dispersion" and "debris." The latter both binds the modern poet hand-in-hand with Walt Whitman and cleaves them, like the difference between a natural and a dynamic language, the language of "tribal morn" ("The Dance") and "Open Road" ("Cape Hatteras") with and against the language of the "arrant page" ("Quaker Hill") or the "Refractions of the thousand theaters, faces" that connect "Times Square to Columbus Circle" in the performative and decapitating speed of "The Tunnel."[15]

Indeed, one can read *The Bridge* as a record of this denaturalization of the word, as in the movement from Maquokeeta's dance to that of the stripper grinding out dull repetitions to jazz in "National Winter Garden." That is, one can read it as a repetition of the decline of the West within America's attenuated history, or within the genealogy of the American visionary poet from Columbus and Whitman to the modern. Yet, as we have seen, Whitman recognized his own situation as modern; and Crane's poem dramatizes Whitman's situation as caught

---

15. See Michel Serres, "Turner Translates Carnot," in *Hermes: Literature, Science, Philosophy*, ed. Josué Harari and David Bell (Baltimore, 1982), 54–62. This is one of several essays in this collection of Serres' writings that deal with the rupture or break between mechanics and thermodynamics. Serres calls Turner, the artist, the "first true genius of thermodynamics" (57) and discusses in detail Turner's representation of a moment in which the stochastic replaces the formal, as when the steamship replaced the sailing vessel, or when that which moved in continuity with what was considered natural force was displaced by a transformational energy that converted form into something else: "From Garrard to Turner, the path is very simple. It is the same path that runs from Lagrange to Carnot, from simple machines to steam engines, from mechanics to thermodynamics—by way of the Industrial Revolution. Wind and water were tamed in diagrams. One simply needed to know geometry or to know how to draw. Matter was dominated by form. With fire, everything changes, even water and wind" (56). Almost every modernist of the early twentieth century had to respond to this new time and nontelic history, from Henry Adams on. But as Serres indicates, earlier artists like Turner, without a cognitive grasp of the new science (but perhaps with an "education" of the kind that perturbed Adams), sensed and represented the same perturbation. This would include Melville, whom Serres cites in his essay, but also, as I have noted elsewhere, Emerson, and of course Poe and the Whitman I have dealt with earlier in this essay. The problem for criticism, both then and now, is how to account for change or transformation in old words, or how to account for the "new word" in old words. As Charles Olson put it in his poem "The Kingfishers," in the (post)modern world, "What does not change / is the will to change"—so that Heraclitus' notion of change is itself a changing concept. In the modern/postmodern era, this concept of change even changes the sense of "concept" and its representations. And so forth. We are in the "time" of the "trans-." The subject, the translator lies in the time, the tempo, of his reading translation.

"between two worlds" as surely as is Columbus' "word." It is not, then, as if the natural threshold of Cape Hatteras is suddenly victimized and displaced by the dynamic one signified by the Wright brothers' craft. The two have always already been entangled the one in the other, not as antithetical notions of reality, but as two interpretations of history. As in Henry Adams' "history," they mark an originary discontinuity that did not simply occur in the middle of the nineteenth century, falling nicely between tradition and modernity; and Whitman's poetry, as Crane celebrates it in "Cape Hatteras," already inscribes the Virgin and the Dynamo, "*Panis Angelicus*" and "Falcon Ace." They mark a discontinuity as indelibly as the "barely perceptible fissure" in Usher's House, a legacy left for each poet to shoulder.

In contemplating his own inheritance, therefore, the modern must rely as inevitably as did Columbus and Whitman upon an old idiom to name the new. Crane resisted the pessimism of Spengler's and Eliot's crisis of the modern and sought in the violence, speed, and unrepresentable nature of modern energy, in thermodynamics and telecommunications, a kind of synergy or unity of heterogeneity and dispersal. But his task remained as impossible as was Poe's in *Eureka* or "Usher," to cover over or bridge the abyss that had opened up beneath equivocal alternatives. The old names would work only as catachreses, marking their own artifice or technical appropriation. They would have to be made into conscious symbols, but in a new and different sense. And they would not be readable except as some kind of future anterior, to borrow Lyotard's notion.

Translating Whitman's "prophetic script" into a "Sanskrit charge," then, Crane re-marks figural language in spatial terms that undo the dream of closed space. He produces "abysmal cupolas of space" ("Cape Hatteras") and a new notion of history. But by embracing the dynamic within the natural, by finding the natural sublated in the dynamic, Crane gives himself up as modern poet/poem/word to the disfigurement and displacement of Poe ("The Tunnel") or the marginality of Duncan, Dickinson, and Melville in a capitalist culture. He pulls the "Umbilical" of the modern poet's genealogy and memory and writes a new history of the "word" without destiny or destination, repeating Whitman's call for the modern democratic poem that is still to be written and posted. He returns vision to the graphic nonrepresentation of its own failure of representation, and thus, as de Man would say, to the extreme conditions of Hegel's sublime. He submits future poetry to the fate of a dynamic entropy that will not sustain the individual self or finite consciousness—to "One Song, one Bridge of Fire" that is heterogeneous and "Whispers antiphonal in azure swing." The figure on the horizon turns slowly in the wind, but it is not an aeolian harp or romantic symbol (or self) any longer. It is a bridge of an other kind and without a proper name.

# Hegel and the Dialectics of American Literary Historiography
## From Parrington to Trilling and Beyond

*Gregory S. Jay*

> Instead of writing history, we are always beating our brains to discover how history ought to be written.
>
> —Hegel, *The Philosophy of History*

## AMERICAN DIALECTICS

The assertion of Hegel's importance for an understanding of American literary criticism and historiography should come as no surprise. Hegel's thesis that the "History of the world is none other than the progress of the consciousness of Freedom" underlies most standard theories of American literature, though in its appearance one must see that the "History of the World is not the theatre of happiness."[1] The correspondences between Hegel's philosophy of history, with its emphasis on self-consciousness, and American literary histories stem in part from their common beginnings. Both rewrite the legacy of Christian historiography, especially in regard to the immanence of Providence, the dialectic of good and evil, and the salvational teleology governing the unfolding of individual and national destinies. Both recast Protestant pietism and millennialism through the mediation of Enlightenment epistemology, the political revolutions in France and America, and the quarrel of idealism with materialism in the age of science, capitalism, and urban industrial development. In this latter regard, Hegel's theory of history will come down to future generations most often through its Marxist revision. In the United States, the thematics and

---

1. G. W. F. Hegel, *The Philosophy of History*, trans. J. Sibree (1899; rpr. New York, 1956), 19, 26.

dialectics of literary historiography will privilege the terms of Puritanism, transcendentalism, and romanticism, though these too belong to a cultural tradition in which Hegel remains a central figure.

The modern use of dialectical terms in American literary historiography often lapses into static contradictions, having lost faith in the teleology of Spirit and exhibiting little of the philosophical or cultural rigor of Hegel's dialectical speculation. The result is a dehistoricizing of dialectic and a separation of the aesthetic from the psychological, the philosophical, and the political. Dialectic reverts to schemas of binary opposition, and aesthetics takes refuge in formalism. As we shall see, the work of Lionel Trilling played a crucial role in the formal and psychological redefinition of dialectic. Mark Krupnick and Russell Reising have recently argued that Trilling emptied dialectic of its original force and, as part of his reaction to Marxism, offered instead a formula for stasis, equilibrium, and tragic impotence.[2] This reaction was not Trilling's alone, and he stands as the epitome of the dehistoricizing criticism that came in the wake of the 1930s, despite his effort to use literary commentary to criticize contemporary culture. Although this account of Trilling contains much truth, it overlooks the dialectic between self-consciousness and writing that continued to play an important part in his work up through his chapter on Hegel in *Sincerity and Authenticity* (1972). This dialectic may be the most truly Hegelian quality of Trilling's work, and one of interest to criticism today, since it involves a recurrent resistance to writing by a self that nevertheless repeatedly recognized the representational status of consciousness and the subject. Trilling's repression of literary theory was representative of much of the humanist scholarship in his time (and in current resistances to theory), but his essays and books also demonstrate the dialectical return of writing despite (or because of) every effort to negate it.

Here I need briefly clarify my understanding of Derrida's critique of the repression of "writing" and its significance to the project of my essay. "Writing" (or *écriture* or textuality) does not simply refer to literal acts of inscription, representation, and dissemination, though it indeed encompasses them. This is why charges of formalism, reductionism, and ahistoricism made against Derrida usually miss the mark, for his speculations on the general economy of "writing" entail a rupture of

2. See Mark Krupnick, *Lionel Trilling and the Fate of Cultural Criticism* (Evanston, Ill., 1986), 156–59, and Russell Reising, *The Unusable Past: Theory and the Study of American Literature* (New York, 1986), 93–107.

form's domination and a transgression of the meaning usually in charge of history. "Writing" is a kind of catachretic metaphor for the labors of *technê* in Heidegger's sense—for the processes and institutions that make presence and meaning come into appearance and, hence, into being. In a discussion of how Heidegger's thought on *technê* influences deconstruction's program for cultural criticism, Derrida argues that

> an essential affinity ties together objective knowledge, the principle of reason, and a certain metaphysical determination of the relation to truth. We can no longer—and this is finally what Heidegger recalls and calls on us to think through—we can no longer dissociate the principle of reason from the very idea of technology in the realm of their modernity. . . . The concept of information or informatization is the most general operator here. It integrates the basic to the oriented, the purely rational to the technical, thus bearing witness to that original intermingling of the metaphysical and the technical. . . . Delivery in German is *Zustellung*, a word that also applies, as Heidegger points out, to the delivery of mail. . . . Computer technology, data banks, artificial intelligence, translating machines, and so forth, all these are constructed on the basis of that instrumental determination of a calculable language. Information does not inform merely by delivering an information content, it gives form. . . . It installs man in a form that permits him to ensure his mastery on earth and beyond.[3]

As I have argued elsewhere, Derrida's attack on the logocentric idealism that effaces the labor of "writing" extends and corrects Marx's critique of how ideology posits truths as divine and natural while obscuring how these truths come into being historically, materially, and in the service of various powers.[4] Where Derrida's critique differs is in his resistance to any simple reversal that would posit history or politics or material conditions as the true essences or originary causal determinants of discursive forms or cultural systems. Such a reversal would only reinstall metaphysics elsewhere and once more succumb to a forgetting of the *technê* (necessarily historical) informing the concepts of historicism, materialism, or politics.

3. See Jacques Derrida, "The Principle of Reason: The University in the Eyes of Its Pupils," *Diacritics*, XIII (Fall, 1983), 12–14.

4. See Gregory Jay, "Values and Deconstructions: Derrida, Saussure, Marx," *Cultural Critique*, VIII (Winter, 1987–88), 153–96.

When I pinpoint a specific version of the repression of writing in Trilling's (or others') theorizing, then, it is not because I wish to reestablish art's autonomy or to depict literature as a synchronic system independent of diachronic, material, and contingent determinants. These latter are not only always already at *play* in the system of meaning; the system of meaning functions by (logocentrically) representing this play so as to posit, organize, and reproduce certain values. It is in this process that history takes place and that the indeterminate and interminable economy between synchronic and diachronic acquires a local habitation and a name. The repression of writing occurs as a symptom of an occlusion of cultural *technê* in general, and so to open the question of writing is to broach the possibility of a deconstruction of a historically specific articulation of values and their material (re)production in culture. Let me say, however, that the potential for cultural criticism inherent in deconstruction has not been widely realized in most of the projects of Derrida and his followers, who have preferred to continue their theorizing in the domains of the histories of philosophy and literary theory. In and of itself this containment is neither exemplary nor heinous; it only marks the occasion of future projects that will risk the translation—which is to say the necessary misreading and misappropriation—of deconstruction as work switches to another site.

Trilling's encounter with Hegel must be understood as part of a tradition in American literary historiography dating back at least to Van Wyck Brooks and Vernon Parrington. In their canonical collection, *Theories of American Literature*, Donald Kartiganer and Malcolm Griffith entitle the first section "American Literature as Dialectic," and it is Trilling's *Liberal Imagination* that provides their epigraph:

> A culture is not a flow, nor even a confluence; the form of its existence
> is struggle, or at least debate—it is nothing if not a dialectic. And in
> any culture there are likely to be certain artists who contain a large part
> of the dialectic within themselves, their meaning and power lying in
> their contradictions; they contain within themselves, it may be said,
> the very essence of the culture, and the sign of this is that they do not
> submit to serve the ends of any one ideological group or tendency. It is
> a significant circumstance of American culture, and one which is sus-
> ceptible of explanation, that an unusually large proportion of its
> notable writers of the nineteenth century were such repositories of the

dialectic of their times—they contained both the yes and the no of their culture, and by that token they were prophetic of the future.[5]

Reacting against Parrington's neo-Marxist account of American literary history as the dialectic of liberal and conservative, Trilling self-consciously used the diction of Hegel and Marx to make Hawthorne and Henry James into the forerunners of the infinite dialectical complexity of the modernist mind. This philosophy of literary history casts the writer in the role of Spirit, as a self-consciousness that lives and transcends the contradictions of the national experience. This psychological Hegelianism locates the struggle for unity in the individual self, in contrast to the social resolution emphasized by Marx and other proponents of the historical dialectic, including the American Marxists of the 1930s from whom Trilling parted company. It is also akin to the psychological aestheticism that the New Criticism will advance.

Kartiganer and Griffith follow Trilling's lead in narrating the story of American literature and its historiography as a series of binary oppositions leading to unavoidable tragedy. Their introductory comments highlight a loose but recognizable concept of dialectic in the work of such critics as Brooks, Perry Miller, Richard Chase, A. N. Kaul, Leo Marx, Richard Poirier, R. W. B. Lewis, and Roy Harvey Pearce. The "common practice" of such critics, they note, "has been to discuss American life and literature in terms of tension and polarity, to view our culture as essentially an expression of radical oppositions." These "unreconciled forces" receive various names in different versions, including "the New World vs. the Old, America vs. Europe, liberal vs. conservative, agrarian vs. technological, the individual vs. the community, the private imagination vs. cultural convention—ultimately man, or Man, vs. all the apparatus, natural and civilized, which make up his splendid if necessarily resistant environment."[6] Students of Hegel will rightly object that this list confuses mere opposition with the highly specific structure of necessary negation that characterizes

---

5. Lionel Trilling, *The Liberal Imagination: Essays on Literature and Society* (Oxford, 1981). Trilling's critique of Parrington first appeared as "Parrington, Mr. Smith and Reality," a review of Bernard Smith's neo-Marxist *Forces in American Criticism* (*Partisan Review*, VII [January–February, 1940], 24–40). This passage on culture as dialectic was added during revision for the book.

6. Donald M. Kartiganer and Malcolm Griffith, eds., *Theories of American Literature* (New York, 1972), 28, hereinafter cited parenthetically in the text by page number.

Hegelian dialectics. Certain terms associated with the New Criticism, such as *tension* and *polarity*, become the abstracted metaphors for terms that in their original context had considerable philosophical, historical, and political weight.

In tracing the sources of the American "tendency toward dialectical thinking" back to German romanticism, Kartiganer and Griffith never mention Hegel (much less Marx or even Parrington). Rather it is the "Kantian recognition of the split between mind and world" that they cite. "Through subjectivism," they explain, "through imagination and art, man could recognize all those antinomies that blocked a rational approach to knowledge, and yet embrace them in an imaginative structure enabling the human mind to survive in what might very well be an actual chaos" (28). Here one detects the aesthetic Kantianism advocated by René Wellek and Cleanth Brooks and underlying much of the New Criticism. The experience of chaos and disunity is defined as a psychological problem that can be resolved through aesthetic and perceptual devices, rather than as a response to material, social, or political circumstances whose alteration might allow the "human mind to survive." Kartiganer and Griffith go on to nationalize the achievement of harmony and order out of tension and opposition: it is a capacity of the "European mind," while in America the dialectic yields no synthesis. Echoing Richard Chase, they define the Americanness of American literature as a willingness to live in irreconcilable contradictions, as "a perpetual argument of persistently antithetical positions" (29). A tale of eternal conflict replaces the historically specific experiences that inform it. Moreover, the psychological and aesthetic emphases, especially as the latter privilege vision or perception over the mediation and negation of writing, indicate that the enervation of dialectic in "tension" or "opposition" also involves a fundamental resistance to the temporality and history of representation.

A quite different account of dialectic, and of its role in history and cultural works, can be produced by a look back to Hegel's texts. Stated briefly, the dialectic of Hegel's *Philosophy of History* presents the realization of the Idea in space as Nature, in time as Spirit. These realizations necessarily entail the self-negation or self-differencing of the Idea as it seeks its potential through the materiality of spatial and temporal existence. (This differing from itself of the Idea in its materialization will, of course, later spur deconstructive allegories of writing that subvert the metaphysical claims of representation.) The end of

the dialectic is self-subsistence, unity, and freedom from external determination. For Hegel, the dialectic of materialism and idealism is
guided by the teleology in which Spirit achieves Freedom through History. Thus temporality as mere sequence becomes the time of a narrative, the story of the emergence of the self-consciousness of Spirit. The
dialectical stages of self-consciousness in history, moreover, directly entail political consequences as Spirit seeks to realize its potential as Freedom, moving from merely individual liberties to the organic unity of
necessity and will when the Spirit of the People and the State conjoin
at history's end. Hegel's speculative political anthropology declares that
for the Orientals "one is free"—the despot; for the Greeks and Romans, "some are free"—the ruling class; for us moderns, beginning
with the Germanic peoples, "man, as man, is free."[7] The sequence of
political institutions reflects the stages of this dialectic, wherein freedom becomes the end (in both senses) of the world-historical process.
Aesthetic, political, psychological, and philosophical oppositions are
reconciled when contradiction is read as an internal negation requiring
the revision of the terms and institutions themselves.

Hegel places America beyond this dialectical sequence, however,
because in his version of the frontier thesis America's abundant geographical space combines with the absence of Old World institutions
to eliminate the political contradictions necessary for the development
of a Culture and Spirit of Freedom. Freedom in nature is primitive,
"for a real State and a real Government arise only after a distinction of
classes has arisen. . . . America is therefore the land of the future,
where, in the ages that lie before us, the burden of the World's History
shall reveal itself."[8] The dialectics of American literary historiography
are usually cast in terms of the thematics of freedom and are often
reduced to a particular impasse in the relation of the individual to the
powers of social, cultural, or political determination. This relation,
moreover, bears directly on how such concepts as "freedom," "nature,"
and the "individual" itself are defined. Now the conclusion that an
irreconcilable split separates matter from spirit, man from nature, or
the self from society was anathema to Hegel, who saw such dualisms
as catastrophic notions inherited from Rousseau's romanticism. In Hegel's view there is no "state of Nature" in which "mankind at large are

7. Hegel, *Philosophy of History*, 18.
8. *Ibid.*, 85–86.

in the possession of their natural rights with the unconstrained exercise and enjoyment of their freedom":

> The perpetually recurring misapprehension of Freedom consists in regarding that term only in its *formal*, subjective sense, abstracted from its essential objects and aims; thus a constraint put upon impulse, desire, passion—pertaining to the particular individual as such—a limitation of caprice and self-will is regarded as a fettering of Freedom. We should on the contrary look upon such limitation as the indispensable proviso of emancipation. Society and the State are the very conditions in which Freedom is realized.[9]

For Hegel, freedom apart from society and the state, or nature conceived as original freedom, was an anthropological fiction and a logical impossibility. Only in the narrative of the historical dialectic by which practice seeks to achieve the Idea, and thus Freedom, does the individual come to the Truth of Self-Consciousness and of its Being.

The self's rejection of society, culture, and the determinations of history, on the other hand, is recounted by American literary historians as the salient (and quite un-Hegelian) truth of American literature, from Trilling and Fiedler to Poirier and Sacvan Bercovitch. In such mythologies an eighteenth-century individualist liberalism persists, propped oddly by a romantic metaphysics of nature, perception, intuition, and expression. The judgment of irreconcilability masks an a priori definition of nature, liberty, and the soul as existing somehow outside the determinations of culture, society, and language. One must also underscore that this metaphysics entails a resistance to, or repression of, writing, to textuality in the general sense, so that the self's anxiety toward society is also an anxious self-consciousness of "the death of the author." At the level of politics this metaphysics disrupts the practical dialectic of idea and realization that informs social change; at the level of hermeneutics it forecloses the text around binarisms rather than reading the historical and representational contradictions that produce them. Freedom is thus doomed by metaphysics to be always already a paradise lost, and history to be of no use to the writing—or the making—of the future. While Hegel (and Marx) argue that "Society and the State are the very conditions in which Freedom is

---

9. *Ibid.*, 41.

realized," the antinomian Liberal Mind sees itself as the "opposing self," ideally "beyond culture," and thus ultimately uninterested in altering the conditions of the State. Formal and aesthetic scenarios effect a state of organic psychological or artistic harmony in which the Idea realizes its potential for Freedom through symbolic representations.

Hegel himself, of course, had begun the *Phenomenology* with a critique of Kant, intuitionism, and aestheticism. He mocks the neo-Kantian philosophies of immediate intuition that, in the work of Jacobi and Fichte and others, would so influence New England transcendentalism. The antinomy between empiricism and idealism had not been resolved by Kant; rather, he left the opposition between consciousness and the thing-in-itself intact. The result, writes Hegel, was a renewed enthusiasm for the sublime, for an "immediate knowledge of the Absolute, religion, or being," which is the "opposite of the form of the Notion." Hegel describes the predicament of philosophy in terms that will be repeated for the next 150 years:

> Spirit has not only lost its essential life; it is also conscious of this loss, and of the finitude that is its own content. Turning away from the empty husks, and confessing that it lies in wickedness, it reviles itself for so doing, and now demands from philosophy, not so much *knowledge* of what *is*, as the recovery through its agency of that lost sense of solid and substantial being. Philosophy is to meet this need, not by opening up the fast-locked nature of substance, and raising this to self-consciousness, not by bringing consciousness out of its chaos back to an order based on thought, nor to the simplicity of the Notion, but rather by running together what thought has put asunder, by suppressing the differentiations of the Notion and restoring the *feeling* of essential being: in short, by providing edification rather than insight. The 'beautiful', the 'holy', the 'eternal', 'religion', and 'love' are the bait required to arouse the desire to bite; not the Notion, but ecstasy, not the cold march of necessity in the thing itself, but the ferment of enthusiasm, these are supposed to be what sustains and continually extends the wealth of substance.[10]

Hegel's commitment to the labor of the negative, to "the differentiations of the Notion," would in theory distinguish his dialectic

10. G. W. F. Hegel, *Phenomenology of Spirit*, trans. A. V. Miller (Oxford, 1977), 4–5.

from the stale antinomies or dogmatical choices posited by philosophy's stalemate between mind and matter, idealism and empiricism. His *Aufhebung* or synthesis would be not a suppression of differences but their activation and preservation in real achieved harmonies. Thus there is doubtless a Hegelian strain in even the vulgar dialectics of American literary historiography and criticism, which posit themselves against the absolutisms of scientific and political representations. But when Derrida argues that Hegel is the last philosopher of the book and the first philosopher of writing, he means to trace an *other* labor of the negative in Hegel that does not contribute to the profit of the Notion. The concepts of truth, speech, presence, time, space, memory, consciousness, and the state in Hegel can only be posited through the simultaneous deployment and repression of representation. In giving philosophy over to the "differentiations of the Notion," Hegel opens up the textuality of ontological and epistemological terms and so becomes the first philosopher of writing, of a writing without end, of speculative representation without object or foundation. Yet in continually closing up these differences into metaphysical concepts, Hegel remains the last philosopher of presence, totality, truth, the mind, and the book. Indeed, the difference between a dialectical Hegelianism constrained by harmony and a disseminated Hegelianism without reserve is difficult, if not impossible, to read. That difference or undecidability, however, may be the "same" one that haunts the dialectics of American literary historiography, in which the commitment to irreconcilable contradictions seems also, at another level, to perpetuate certain fixed and metaphysical oppositions. In each case, the history *of* writing spurs a reflection upon it that both activates the differentiations of ideological notions *and* attempts to erase representations of temporality through various figures that transcend them.

"Americanness" has itself served as precisely one such figure, used to order and foreclose the differences of American literary history into a narrative that almost parodies the *Phenomenology*, as in each successive stage of its experience the "American mind" posits and negates itself in ever more complex realizations of its Spirit. In this process the spectacle of differentiation or radical opposition masks a drama of exclusion as well, this time of such "empirical" others as Indians, women, and blacks. The absorption of American tensions and polarities into a series of psychological conflicts implicitly sets up a model in which a single homogeneous consciousness becomes the reality of America—

a consciousness most distinctly white, male, and usually middle- or upper-class. Speaking of the tropes of the millennium and the "New Jerusalem" in American literary historiography, Houston Baker speculates that a "secularized Hegelian version of the framework implied by traditional American history would claim that the American *Volksgeist* represents the final form of absolute Spirit on its path through history. . . . Similarly, the world triumph of an absolute literary creativity finds its ground properly prepared in the evolutionary labors of American writers." This narrative, argues Baker, requires an original exclusion of the deportation and slavery that made Armageddon, rather than the New Jerusalem, the figure for American history in Afro-American discourse. Baker also analyzes how the black's "scene of writing," in which instruction in the master's language both empowers and reenslaves the writer, makes any forgetting of representation impossible and dooms any unitary account of American literary evolution. In this context Henry Louis Gates, Jr., has discussed Hegel's racism and the effects of the master/slave dialectic on images of writing in Afro-American literature. Judith Fetterley, Nina Baym, and many other feminist critics have demonstrated as well the unsuitability of canonical accounts of American literary history when it comes to women writers.[11] The differences of black or female experience and textuality interrupt the metaphysical sublimation of the American writer's conflicts and leave decipherable marks that cannot be located within the opposition. While there is some danger that the empiricism enabling such critiques will again repress textuality and fall back on essentialized concepts of race or class or gender, it is equally possible that these critiques will open up the history of writing in America by exposing the false dialectics, metaphysical readings, and cultural agendas that have governed our literary histories. One cannot promulgate a model in which figuration determines politics, or in which material interests determine figuration: rather, the economy regulating the exchanges between figuration and reference, meaning and determination, will have to be charted in a given case without recourse to metaphysics

---

11. Houston Baker, *Blues, Ideology, and Afro-American Literature* (Chicago, 1984), 20; Henry Louis Gates, Jr., *Figures in Black: Words, Signs, and the "Racial" Self* (New York, 1987), 19–21; Nina Baym, "Melodramas of Beset Manhood: How Theories of American Fiction Exclude Women Authors," in *The New Feminist Criticism*, ed. Elaine Showalter (New York, 1985), 63–80; Judith Fetterley, *Provisions: A Reader from Nineteenth Century American Women* (Bloomington, Ind., 1985).

and with a methodological self-reflexivity that mitigates the ideological values of the critical project itself.

## HEGEL AND THE LIBERAL MIND

The influence and uses of Hegel in American literary historiography have been long-standing and various, direct and indirect, and this essay means only to sketch a part of the story. In doing so it lapses partially into historicism of an undeconstructed kind by locating the (mis)-reading of Hegel within the frame of the quarrel between an American Marxism and American New Criticism, as if the complexities here were locally determined rather than inherent in the problems and representational issues at stake. This historical schema, moreover, slides over the question of actual influence, since few of the critics under discussion (other than Trilling) actually read Hegel with any seriousness. On the first count, I would respond that I mean to suggest, not that the Marxism/New Criticism debate determined the reception of Hegel, or vice versa, but that this debate and that reception belong to a single "history" whose place, character, and importance we have yet to read. On the second count, I would say that the structures of conception and writing that I trace and describe here belong to a "history" that cannot be limited to the notions of authorship, intention, and influence, though these no doubt have their local appearances there. One can only gesture vaguely toward the whole body of post-structuralist thought to justify such a mode of historical reading. A diagram of Hegel's American place must be multidimensional, then, partly because of his double role as a source of ideas for American writers and a source of themes and analytical methods for theorists of American literature. Beyond this still-rather-empirical complexity lies the horizon in which the texts of Hegel and those of America (literary, historical, theoretical) participate in the "same" general economy of representations concerning "history" and "literature."

The direct influence of Hegel on the generation of New England transcendentalists appears to have been minimal.[12] A standard account

---

12. For background, see René Wellek, "Emerson and German Philosophy," in his *Confrontations: Studies in the Intellectual and Literary Relations between Germany, England, and the United States during the Nineteenth Century* (Princeton, 1965), 187–212.

by one of the younger participants, O. B. Frothingham, dwells at length on Kant, Fichte, and Jacobi but dismisses Hegel. In 1876, Frothingham writes that Hegel's speculation "was scarcely known thirty-five years ago, and if it had been, would have possessed little charm for idealists of the New England stamp." Frothingham's influential chapters on the German roots of American transcendentalism stress the development of idealism out of the quarrels between realism and nominalism, spiritualism and materialism, and portray the philosophies of faith, intuition, and "sublime egoism" in Jacobi and Fichte as the true sources of New England transcendentalism. In Kant as well he finds a pietistical individualism that recovers moral and ethical duty as the practical consequence of the vision of pure reason. (This will be important in regard to the social and political reformism so central to New England transcendentalism.) In Hegel, by contrast, Frothingham finds a conservative and counterrevolutionary philosopher who had "struck hands with church and state in Prussia." Frothingham speaks caustically of the subordination to authority he finds in Hegel's system, for it clashes with the radical Protestant and antinomian strains of New England transcendentalism. Frothingham's one-dimensional attack makes no mention of dialectic or the labor of the negative. Unlike the Emerson of the "Divinity School Address," Hegel "was more orthodox than the orthodox; he gave the theologians new explanations of their own dogmas, and supplied them with arguments against their own foes. . . . The ideal elements in Hegel's system were appropriated by Christianity, and were employed against liberty and progress." Whatever the merit of this reading of Hegel, it helps explain the absence of much reference to him in contemporary documents of transcendentalism, as well as in subsequent movements in American intellectual history. (There was, of course, a flourishing Hegelian school in St. Louis during the late nineteenth century, but American philosophy took a pragmatic and analytic turn and forgot Hegel until the recent revival of Continental speculation.)[13] Frothingham's reading suggests that one should ask whether modern Hegelian interpretations of transcendentalism or America's literary history supported the antinomian spirit or "were employed against liberty and progress."

13. Octavius Brooks Frothingham, *Transcendentalism in New England: A History* (New York, 1959), 43, 44, 45. The main reference work detailing the impact of German philosophy on American writers is Henry A. Pochmann, *German Culture in America, 1600–1900* (Madison, Wis., 1957).

Obviously the American destiny of Hegel cannot be separated from readings of Hegel's politics and from his perceived usefulness for programs of American cultural or social reform. In Europe it was Marx, however, who played the key part in addressing Hegel's legacy, representing his own work as the rehistoricization and materialist correction of Hegel's dialectical system. Much of the modern revival of Hegel in France, in fact, is attributed to the Marxist commentary offered in Alexandre Kojève's lectures delivered from 1933 to 1939 at the Ecole des Hautes Etudes and collected in *Introduction to the Reading of Hegel*, which had a profound influence on phenomenology, structuralism, and deconstruction.[14] (It should be noted, however, that Kojève himself drew upon Husserl and Heidegger extensively.) In the United States of the latter nineteenth century, the impact of Marx was relatively minimal, especially among literary intellectuals and critics. Henry Adams wistfully wrote that he should have been a Marxist, but his disillusionment with dialectics of consciousness, evolution, and progress, along with his lingering ties to the ancien régime, foreclosed that option. More important than the discourses of Marxism was the continuing development of an American liberalism that borrowed themes from European socialist thought. The specific events of American historical experience—the conquest of the native land, the absence of monarchical and feudal relations, the establishment of slavery, the rapid industrialization of production, the domination of representative government by commercial interests, the heterogeneous mass culture derived from disparate European and Asian sources—created a particular crisis of capitalism and its social formation by the end of the century.

In the Progressive movement, this crisis was addressed by a return to Jeffersonianism—a doomed reaction to the emergent hegemony of urban factory life and the steady decline of the economic and political power of small-town and agricultural America. The dialectical terms, then, that appear in the literary criticism of Brooks and Parrington, the founders of modern American literary historiography, come out of this era. As in writings from the period of transcendentalism, the Hegelian strain in the work of Brooks and Parrington was modulated through theories of individual consciousness, social reform, and

14. Alexandre Kojève, *Introduction to the Reading of Hegel: Lectures on the Phenomenology of Spirit*, trans. James H. Nichols, Jr., ed. Allan Bloom (1969; rpr. Ithaca, N.Y., 1980).

of the shape of history itself. Kartiganer and Griffith quote at length from Brooks's 1915 manifesto, *America's Coming of Age*, which recasts the conflict between idealism and materialism as the tragic flaw of American culture. In a phrase that will in turn give Parrington the title for his own study, Brooks writes that "from the beginning we find two main currents in the American mind running side by side but rarely mingling." On the one hand is the spiritualism and transcendentalism running from Edwards to Emerson and beyond; on the other is the "catchpenny opportunism" and mercantile pragmatism running from Benjamin Franklin to the Gilded Age and into "the atmosphere of contemporary business life." [15]

The work of differentiation and self-negation *within* bourgeois criticism turns into an opposition *between* antinomies as Brooks's backward glance projects American cultural history as an eternal recurrence of binary opposition. Brooks's famous essay "On Creating a Usable Past" will then be able to narrate the contemporary appearance of Progressive critical consciousness as the necessary resolution of the quarrel between idealism and materialism that has shaped American life. This places the writer—creative or critical—in the position of embodying this knowledge and this consciousness at the "end" of American history. At the same time, the labor of creating, of writing, a past to ground the consciousness of the present inevitably subverts the authority of the present claim to knowledge and once more entangles consciousness in the temporality/textuality that engenders it. The psychologization of contradiction increases throughout Brooks's career until he suffers a nervous breakdown—while trying to write a study of Emerson. Spiritualism and organicism will emerge as the prevailing discourses in his massive literary history, *Makers and Finders: A History of the Writer in America, 1800–1915*. As its five volumes appeared between 1936 and 1952, however, Brooks's novelistic portraits of the spiritual lives of writers in particularized historical locales proved unsatisfactory to materialists and formalists. Marxist criticism had already insisted on a strictly economic rereading of the dialectic in American literature, and New Criticism had already begun to produce a formalist redaction of it as well.

Parrington's place in this genealogy is central, though Kartiganer

15. The quotations are from Van Wyck Brooks, *America's Coming of Age* (New York, 1915), 9–10.

and Griffith never mention his name. His three-volume study, *Main Currents in American Thought* (1927–1930), was arguably the most influential work of American literary historiography produced in the modern period. It narrated the story of America, from the Puritans to the robber barons, as an unfolding dialectic of pointedly political proportions. His famous statement in the foreword to the first volume establishes the dichotomies: "The point of view from which I have endeavored to evaluate the materials is liberal rather than conservative, Jeffersonian rather than Federalistic; and very likely in my search I have found what I went forth to find." Parrington sought a past usable for the purposes of bolstering the cause of the Progressive movement as it faced the new economic and political challenges of the 1920s. The Liberal Mind becomes the hero of Parrington's *Bildungsroman* as it does successive battle with reactionary Puritan theologians, mercantile Federalists, and the various spokesmen of conservatism he aligns with the rise of capitalism and industrialism in the nineteenth century. (Parrington's original title was *The Democratic Spirit in American Literature*.) Transcendentalism will be but one of the major moments of the Liberal Mind that Parrington celebrates. An evolutionary philosophy of spirit imbues his conviction that "to enter once more into the spirit of those fine old idealisms and to learn that the promise of the future has lain always in the keeping of liberal minds that were never discouraged from their dreams, is scarcely a profitless undertaking."[16]

While Parrington's flaws are well known, it is less often observed that he was a subtle practitioner of dialectical thought, both in handling the relation of representation to modes of production and in describing the necessary negation of idealism by material conditions, and vice versa. Parrington's opening summary of transcendentalism avowedly borrows Frothingham's schematic opposition of idealism and materialism, only to later abandon Frothingham's emphasis on the primacy of intuitionism and spiritualism. Instead he delineates the determining dialectic of transcendentalism and social or cultural criticism:

16. Vernon L. Parrington, *The Colonial Mind, 1620–1800* (New York, 1927), vii, xiii, Vol. I of Parrington, *Main Currents in American Thought*, 3 vols. On the politics of Parrington's historiography, especially the contradiction between his Populist and Marxist tendencies, see Richard Hofstadter, *The Progressive Historians: Turner, Beard, Parrington* (New York, 1968), 349–436. See also Peter Bellis, "Vernon Parrington," in *Modern American Critics, 1920–1955*, ed. Gregory S. Jay, Dictionary of Literary Biography, LXII (Detroit, 1988), 210–20.

Communing with the ideal rarely begets complacency; the actual seems poor and mean in comparison with the potential. Hence the transcendentalists, willingly or not, were searching critics of their generation. . . . In the midst of a boastful materialism, shot through with cant and hypocrisy and every insincerity, fat and slothful in all higher things, the critic proposed to try the magic of sincerity, to apply the test of spiritual values to the material forces and mechanical philosophies of the times. His very life must embody criticism; his every act and word must pronounce judgment on the barren and flatulent gods served by his countrymen. . . . Here was a revolutionary business indeed, that the critic was proposing to himself; and the calm serenity with which he set about it was disconcerting.[17]

This last remark on the revolutionary business of the critic was, as Parrington might admit, a bit of self-projection. Still, whereas Van Wyck Brooks's schema followed Frothingham's in displaying idealism and materialism as tragic antagonists of a timeless quarrel, Parrington's narrative revivifies the power of idealism and refurbishes its reputation as an agency of cultural criticism. The language of a logical or dialectical historical progression is heard in his *begets, hence,* and reiterated *must.* Materialism calls forth its own negation in idealism, which out of this origin is compelled to negate materialism in turn. Historical determinism subtly corresponds to the will of the spirit in shaping the calling of the critic.

Hegel's description of world-historical individuals, such as Caesar, sheds some light on Parrington's figuration of Emerson:

It was not, then, his private gain merely, but an unconscious impulse that occasioned the accomplishment of that for which the time was ripe. Such are all great historical men—whose own particular aims involve those large issues which are the will of the World-Spirit. They may be called Heroes, inasmuch as they have derived their purposes and their vocation, not from the calm, regular course of things, sanc-

---

17. Vernon L. Parrington, *The Romantic Revolution in America, 1800–1860* (New York, 1927), 377, 379, Vol. II of Parrington, *Main Currents in American Thought,* 3 vols. Parrington's position has been convincingly developed in Anne C. Rose's definitive study, *Transcendentalism as a Social Movement, 1830–1850* (New Haven, Conn., 1981).

tioned by the existing order; but from a concealed fount—one which
has not attained to phenomenal, present existence—from that inner
Spirit, still hidden beneath the surface, which, impinging on the outer
world as on a shell, bursts it in pieces, because it is another kernel than
that which belonged to the shell in question.[18]

The world-historical individual is *not* the determined emanation of material cultural circumstances, *not* the representative man or spirit of a
particular age. Instead his inner spirit belongs organically to another
development, and his bursting forth is from a kernel of the Idea quite
different from the origin from which the shell of mundane history
springs. The inner Idea that determines the Hero is none other than
Freedom, which is why his relation to circumstance is one of resistance, negation, and the will to power. In the case of Caesar, who is
only a man of action and not a philosopher, the world-historical individual is an agency but not an instance of Self-Consciousness. Emerson's antinomian self-reliance moves him closer to the philosopher's
achievement, though his effort to realize the freedom of his self-
knowledge brings him once more into dialectical conflict with materiality, experience, and fate.

   In taking seriously the economic and political registers of "materialism" in transcendentalist discourse, and in emphasizing the involvement of the transcendentalists in various oppositional social movements, Parrington's history is a salutary reminder of much that was
obscured by the formal, symbolic, and psychological readings of the
"American Renaissance" that prospered after 1940. Parrington's portrait shows Emerson as a hero driven by dialectic into becoming the
conscience of the nation and the natural heir of Jefferson. After survey-
ing Emerson's views on democracy, commerce, and the state, Parrington's chapter becomes even more self-reflexive in the admission that
Emerson "rejected the economic interpretation of politics," though as
"a child of the romantic revolution he understood quite clearly how the
waves of humanitarian aspiration broke on the reefs of property rights,
how economic forces were in league against the ideal republic."[19] This
admission made, Parrington proceeds to argue that while Emerson
could not "accept the theory of economic determinism," his essay "Pol-

18. Hegel, *Philosophy of History*, 30.
19. Parrington, *Romantic Revolution in America*, 387.

itics" deals at length with the "philosophy of property" and its contemporary effects.

"Politics" is the only Emerson essay quoted in any substance during Parrington's chapter on Emerson. (He does quote the journals frequently.) Of course it is the "property" and "material" of Emerson's writing—namely, his styles and forms of representation—that Parrington himself fails to discuss in formulating the economics of Emerson's transcendentalism. *Main Currents* had begun by rejecting "belletristic" literary history (a reference to Barret Wendell), and here the repression of writing in the service of a profitable allegory of critical conscience yields a caricature of Emerson's work. While Parrington can cite Emerson, he can't read him. The resistance to "economic determinism" turns out also to be an allegory of the resistance to textuality as "Emerson" is separated from his writing and made into a figure in Parrington's story of the Liberal Mind. Emerson, as Harold Bloom has reminded us, worried much about how representation determined the fate of the subject and conditioned his experience. The dialectic of individual and society in transcendentalist discourse should not be separated from the dialectic of the subject and the text, for both such oppositions are engineered by the same metaphysical strategy and result in similar repressions of writing and history. In Parrington's chapter on Emerson this becomes clear as Parrington avoids the return to individualism and the primacy of the soul in Emerson's discourse, bravely ending instead with his opposition to slavery and his action on behalf of "justice, truth, righteousness." Emerson's liberalism, like his philosophy of authorship, rejected determinism in basing reformation on the original power of the independent soul of virtue and self-reliance. When treated thematically, this move produces a very nondialectical conceptual opposition of determining circumstance and liberated selfhood, which runs throughout Emerson's prose and many commentaries on it. Parrington's recourse to such a thematic reading truncates the dialectic of Emerson's style and reduces him to the figure of the liberator, a strategy that evades rather than negates (in the Hegelian sense) the material conditions of literary or social production.

Thus the materialism of late nineteenth-century America assures the doom and alienation of the Liberal Mind, and the heir to Jefferson and Emerson becomes Henry Adams, if not Parrington himself. Yet even here Parrington appears ready with a new dialectical turn. The defeat of transcendentalism will set the stage for the critical realism of

a new middle-class ideology that might, as Brooks had dreamed, formulate an internal, and hence transformative, critique of late nine-
teenth- and early twentieth-century America. *The Romantic Revolution
in America* ends with this prophecy:

> In the world of Jay Cooke and Commodore Vanderbilt, the transcen-
> dental dream was as hopelessly a lost cause as the plantation
> dream. . . . A new age had come and other dreams—the age and the
> dreams of a middle-class sovereignty, that was busily surveying the
> fields of its future conquests. From the crude and vast romanticisms of
> that vigorous sovereignty emerged eventually a spirit of realistic criti-
> cism, seeking to evaluate the worth of this new America, and discover
> if possible other philosophies to take the place of those which had gone
> down in the fierce battles of the Civil War. What form this critical spirit
> assumed, and what replies it returned to the strident challenge of the
> time, are questions not to be answered here.[20]

Parrington did not live to furnish the answers. His unfinished
third volume appeared posthumously, an ironic twist for a literary history so teleologically conceived as the evolution of the Liberal Mind
toward its present regenerative fulfillment. The Pulitzer Prize accorded
Parrington signaled the acceptance of his economic emphases as the
1920s ended, while the individualism and liberal politics of his narrative assured a warm reception from most literary intellectuals. Parrington's fate in the 1930s, however, belied his prophecy. Marxism took up
the mantle of the waning Progressive movement and won the allegiance
of the dominant portion of the literary and intellectual left in America.
From their standpoint, Parrington's work, while grounded in the concepts of economic production and class struggle, remained insufficiently materialist. On the other hand, the rise of literary theory and
the beginnings of the New Criticism would bury Parrington's work
with the observation that it was a history of everything but the literary.
The victory of this latter movement came with the publication in 1941
of F. O. Matthiessen's *American Renaissance*, which begins by explicitly
appropriating the democratic political nationalism of Brooks and Parrington and then subordinating it to the new concern with language,
style, and tragic vision. While Matthiessen's effort to remember writing

20. *Ibid.*, 465.

often yields salutary results, his work is finally undone by an allegiance to T. S. Eliot's logocentric nostalgia for language that would unite the word with the Word. (Matthiessen, of course, had written first on Eliot, and the latter's postlapsarian thesis concerning the "dissociation of sensibility" underwrites the theoretical program of *American Renaissance.*)

The turn against the liberal tradition in American literary historiography was also signaled by the rise of Perry Miller, who set out to save the Puritans from the castigations of Brooks and Parrington. (Brooks had punningly entitled his 1908 study of America *The Wine of the Puritans.*) In 1940, Miller published "From Edwards to Emerson," a polemical piece of revisionary historiography in which the genealogy traced by Brooks and Parrington is put to different uses. Miller writes as American literary Marxism and the Progressive school are under seige, and his purpose is to show the insufficiently dialectical character of economic determinism. He mocks the consensus in "contemporary criticism" that believes that "ideas are born in time and place, that they spring from specific environments, that they express the force of societies and classes, that they are generated by power relations."[21] He

---

21. Perry Miller, "From Edwards to Emerson," in *Theories,* ed. Kartiganer and Griffith, 326, hereinafter cited parenthetically in the text as *Theories.* The essay also appears in Miller's *Errand into the Wilderness* (Cambridge, Mass., 1956). It first appeared in the *New England Quarterly* in December, 1940.

This essay is one of two by Miller included by Kartiganer and Griffith. (He is the only critic so honored.) Their volume reprints his "Errand into the Wilderness" as its prologue. This canonizing move is motivated, one surmises, by the nationalism and teleological dialectics of Miller's historical vision, which must have been welcome in the 1950s. He dwells, in New Critical fashion, on the "ambiguity" of the word *errand,* its "double meaning." The nation, on the one hand, is like an "errand boy" or a husband who "must run an errand for his wife"; on the other hand, it is like "the runner of the errand [who] is working for himself" (*Theories,* 12). Historical fulfillment and national identity become the achievement of a self-reliant male consciousness who embodies God's will in his own Spirit. The dialectic between obedience and creative will repeats those between Europe and America, tradition and the individual talent, and—prefiguring Leslie Fiedler—woman and man. As the dialectical ambiguity oscillates to emasculate the will of the Puritan, the "problem of his identity" is psychologized. Rather than a conflict with "stones, storms, and Indians," it becomes a search for the new American mission. Having emptied the native land of its inhabitants and natural integrity, and having imagined the blankness of their own social context, the Puritans "were left alone with America," wondering if they were men enough for the job. There is a trace here of Parrington's complaint that "our literary historians have labored under too heavy a handicap of the genteel tradition—to borrow Professor Santayana's happy phrase—to enter sympathetically into a world of masculine intellects and material struggles" (*Colonial Mind,* xii).

disparages the presentist perspective in which "Emerson becomes most vivid to us when he is inscribing his pungent remarks upon the depression of 1837, and Thoreau in his grim comments upon the American blitzkrieg against Mexico" (*Theories*, 325). Admitting that transcendentalism was a response to "commercial times," Miller strongly objects to accounts (such as Frothingham's) that trace the origins of its philosophy to European or Asian sources. Was theirs not a "natural reaction" for "descendents of Puritans and Quakers" (*Theories*, 328)? Miller tacitly rejects Parrington's version of the historical dialectic as a quarrel between various imported liberalisms and conservatisms. Instead he finds the essence of the dialectic within the single structure of Puritan consciousness and theology itself: "At the core of the theology there was an indestructible element which was mystical, and a feeling for the universe which was almost pantheistic; but there was also a social code demanding obedience to external law, a code to which good people voluntarily conformed and to which bad people should be made to conform" (*Theories*, 331).

The dialectical historiography running through Miller's two-volume *New England Mind* is evident here: the internal contradiction between the spiritual core and the rational shell of Puritanism determines the stages from Edwards to Emerson. Miller finds himself writing a history of ideas, and he must stop to admit that "I am as guilty as Emerson himself if I treat ideas as a self-contained rhetoric, forgetting that they are, as we are now discovering, weapons, the weapons of classes and interests, a masquerade of power relations" (*Theories*, 337). Yet he immediately drops this politico-critical rhetoric in arguing that Emerson and Fuller led careers that disobeyed the laws of economic determinism, which should have made them the spokespersons for "respectable, prosperous, middle-class Boston and Cambridge" (*Theories*, 339). Miller's argument sets up as a straw man a very undialectical notion of economic determinism; in this regard it is less sophisticated than Parrington's observation of how transcendentalist social criticism grew out of its idealism. Miller cannot rejoin the history of ideas with the history of economics, since he is committed to seeing ideas as the representations of willing subjects rather than as parts of an always already material signifying practice. His own position as an antagonist to Marxist historiography and as an apologist for nationalist mythologizing also dictates a reimposed binarism of idealism and materialism; otherwise he would have to undertake a more unsettling reflection on the economic, political, and historical determinants of his own thoughts as a spokesman for respectable, prosperous Boston and America.

Matthiessen's and Miller's arguments were enabled in part by the major turn against Parrington and against Marxism in the career of Lionel Trilling.[22] In his 1940 essay "Parrington, Mr. Smith, and Reality," which would later be revised to open *The Liberal Imagination*, Trilling argued that the Left view of literature, history, and politics offered a simplistic mind-*vs.*-reality dualism. While acknowledging Parrington's preeminence and the importance of "his informing idea of the economic and social determination of thought," Trilling attacks the mimetic fallacy that structures Parrington's way of relating aesthetics and politics. Trilling's Parrington believes that "reality" is "one and immutable," "wholly external," an object that the artist reflects by constructing an artifact that corresponds to it. "It does not occur to Parrington," he writes, "that there is any other relation possible between the artist and reality than this passage of reality through the transparent artist."[23] Like others, Trilling finds that Parrington's rejection of the "belletristic" amounts to a refusal of mediation—of writing itself. Yet Trilling's formula again erases writing by making the mind of the artist (rather than language itself) the agency of negation and mediation. Trilling's future interest in Hegel's *Phenomenology* is forecast here by the decidedly psychological bent of his own aesthetics, in which the mind-*vs.*-reality dualism becomes a largely psychological dialectic.

Passing over Parrington's "most cherished heroes, Jefferson and Emerson," Trilling defends Hawthorne's "questioning of the naïve and often eccentric faiths of the transcendental reformers." Trilling praises the realism of the "man who could raise those brilliant and serious doubts about the nature and possibility of moral perfection, the man who could keep himself aloof from the 'Yankee reality' and who could dissent from the orthodoxies of dissent and tell us so much about the nature of moral zeal."[24] In the original essay, the example given is *The Blithedale Romance;* its excision in the book version allows Trilling's sen-

22. See Gregory S. Jay, "Lionel Trilling," in *Modern American Critics*, ed. Jay, 267–89. A few passages of the present essay first appeared there in different form.
23. Trilling, *The Liberal Imagination*, 4–5.
24. *Ibid.*, 8–9. Trilling expands these points influentially in "Hawthorne in Our Time," in Trilling, *Beyond Culture: Essays on Literature and Learning* (Oxford, 1980), 155–80.

tence to fall in general terms on the leftists and dissenters of the 1930s. It is at this point that he also adds the passage on culture as dialectic and the artist as the consciousness of social contradictions quoted by Kartiganer and Griffith. As with Parrington, Trilling's description of the artist appears to be a sketch of the critic's situation and vocation as well, here of the modernist critic confronting the end of the Liberal dream.

In the Preface to *The Liberal Imagination*, Trilling describes the "paradox" afflicting the mind of the modern liberal critics and artists. While liberalism begins in the emotional imagination of "variousness and possibility" in life, the "organization" of liberalism as a political or cultural ideology inevitably (if unconsciously) imposes limitations. In Hegelian terms, the realization of the Idea in practice negates its original form (the Idea of Freedom), and thus provokes the dialectical criticism of "naïve and eccentric reformers" by the Hawthornes and the Trillings. In his deep suspicion of liberalism's hope "to organize the elements of life in a rational way," Trilling displays the same Populist resistance to the institutions of government and society that Parrington had felt. The modernist "tragic vision" in the wake of liberalism's paradoxes and failures is the rather banal view that "the world is a complex and unexpected and terrible place which is not always to be understood by the mind as we use it in our everyday tasks." The special cognitive virtue of the literary, according to Trilling, is its dialectical power to reopen the complexities foreclosed by ideologies. Trilling's version of Cleanth Brooks's thesis, in "The Language of Paradox," that contradiction is the essence of the literary, appears here to unite literary, psychological, and moral theory.[25]

> The job of criticism would seem to be, then, to recall liberalism to its first essential imagination of variousness and possibility, which implies

---

25. Cleanth Brooks, "The Language of Paradox," in Brooks, *The Well Wrought Urn: Studies in the Structure of Poetry* (New York, 1947), 3–21. For Brooks, "the language of poetry is the language of paradox," so that while "the tendency of science is necessarily to stabilize terms, to freeze them into strict denotations; the poet's tendency is by contrast disruptive" (3, 9). In "Wordsworth and the Paradox of the Imagination," Brooks explains that these disruptive "ambiguities" and "contradictions" spur the work of the "synthesizing imagination," so that poet and reader unite in a single act of aesthetic cognition superior to the referential discourse of science or the propositional discourses of religion, morals, or politics (147). The similarities between *The Liberal Imagination* and *The Well Wrought Urn* deserve extended reflection.

the awareness of complexity and difficulty. To the carrying out of the job of criticizing the liberal imagination, literature has a unique relevance, not merely because so much of modern literature has explicitly directed itself upon politics, but more importantly because literature is the human activity that takes the fullest and most precise account of variousness, possibility, complexity, and difficulty.[26]

Trilling posits his literary theory as more dialectical, more attuned to difference, than that of the Left's dogmatists, so that one might see here a strong return to the labor of the negative in writing. On the other hand, tropes such as the "imagination" and "awareness" restore a Kantian or aesthetic psychology to the position of a center of consciousness that can contain "the fullest and most precise account" of contradiction, thus recuperating the "differentiations of the Notion" in a spiritual and timeless, rather than materialist and historical, narrative.

There are few explicit references to Hegel in *The Liberal Imagination*. In "Freud and Literature," Trilling mentions the enthusiasm of Hegel and Marx for Diderot's *Rameau's Nephew* in a passage that serves as the germ for *Sincerity and Authenticity*.[27] Clearly, Trilling turned to Freud as well as Hegel during the 1940s and 1950s in order to find a model for the psychological dialectics he wished to substitute for what he saw as the mind-*vs.*-matter dualisms in Marxism and liberalism. Hegel's presence, however, looms larger than Freud's in the volume's final essay, "The Meaning of a Literary Idea." The literary idea is not a referential reflection or a timeless proposition. Rather, "the very form of a literary work" is "a developing series of statements": "Dialectic, in this sense, is just another word for form, and has for its purpose, in philosophy or in art, the leading of the mind to some conclusion." But "in our culture," argues Trilling, "ideas tend to deteriorate into ideol-

---

26. Trilling, *The Liberal Imagination*, xv.

27. It can be surmised that Trilling's reading of Hegel began in the late 1930s as a result of his friendship and team-teaching with historian Jacques Barzun at Columbia, where their colloquium on modern culture included *Rameau's Nephew*. In 1943, Barzun dedicated *Romanticism and the Modern Ego* (1943; rpr. New York, 1947) to Trilling. In a note on Hegel, Barzun confesses guilt for the "vulgar error" of previously representing Hegel as "a Prussianizer *à outrance*" and as a source of modern fascism. Against the "recurrent epidemics of anti-Hegelianism" he prescribes an "inoculation" of "reading or re-reading" *The Philosophy of Right* and the *Phenomenology* in order to clarify the meaning of *The Philosophy of History*. Apparently Trilling undertook the treatment, though in translation.

ogy," which explains the hostility toward ideas on the part of even the most sensitive readers and critical theorists. Some of these, like Wellek and Austin Warren, respond to ideological reading by turning to "purely aesthetic values." Here Trilling parts company with the New Criticism in insisting that the dialectic of literary ideas can have "the authority, the cogency, the completeness, the brilliance, the *hardness* of systematic thought." In support, he quotes from the Introduction to *The Philosophy of History*, in which Hegel states that "grammar, in its extended and consistent form, is the work of thought, which makes its categories distinctly visible therein."[28] In the coming decades, Trilling will increasingly adapt the teleology of historical self-consciousness in Hegel to his own diagnoses of the modern spirit and its literature, though he mutes the millennialism of Hegel and the revolutionary hope of Marx with the "tragic" stoicism he finds in Freud. Hegel's recognition that the form of grammar coincides with the work of thought implies an inseparability of consciousness and language that will be exploited by deconstructive readers of Hegel. The consequences of this inseparability, however, will produce as many ambivalences in Trilling's texts as they do in Hegel's.

## TRILLING AND THE SUBJECT OF HEGEL

As a theorist of literary history, Trilling was principally concerned with describing the character and qualities of modernism. He was specifically interested in developing moral and psychological accounts that would complement or displace the aesthetic and political readings of modernism offered by New Critics and Marxists. This view of modernism would be American insofar as the "tragic" complexity of contemporary ethical and cognitive problems was a direct result of the rise and fall of the Liberal Mind and its literature. The individualist strain in American cultural politics, which had produced the ambivalence in Parrington between a desire for the reform of institutions and a desire for freedom from all determination, yields in Trilling the idea of the "opposing self." This subject will also significantly be a troping of the Marxist economic explanation of "alienation" and thus not surprisingly

28. Trilling, *The Liberal Imagination*, 266, 269, 272; the quotation from Hegel appears in *Philosophy of History*, 62.

involve a return to Hegel's thinking on the topic, specifically in the chapter "Self-Alienated Spirit. Culture" in the *Phenomenology*.

In the 1955 Preface to *The Opposing Self*, Trilling defines the "distinguishing characteristic" of the modern self as "its intense and adverse imagination of the culture in which it has its being." He deliberately substitutes *culture* for *society* in order to extend the dialectic to the individual's relation to the entire range of a tradition's legacies—textual, psychological, moral, material, and institutional. Drawing on Freud as well as Marx, Trilling theorizes the "indignant perception" of the modernist as a view turned toward the "unconscious portion of culture." The specter of determination, the haunting figure that threatens the self's freedom, does not simply inhabit the machinery of external institutions or historical formations, but lives within every aspect of culture, as well as within the self or subjectivity as such. "Men began to recognize the existence of prisons that were not built of stone, nor even of social restrictions and economic disabilities," he writes. Leaning on Freud's notion of the superego as internalized social determination, Trilling describes how the "newly conceived coercive force required of each prisoner that he sign his own *lettre de cachet*, for it had established its prisons in the family life, in the professions, in the image of respectability, in the ideas of faith and duty, in (so the poets said) the very language itself."[29]

The metaphor of the *lettre de cachet* and the final reference to "language itself" (however parenthetically modified) are enormously suggestive. They imply that the dialectic of the subject is inextricably a matter of language and of writing, and that the historical process is itself carried on within the legacies, practices, and institutions of textuality. The prison house of language, one might say, is glimpsed here by Trilling as the agency of coercive determination that everywhere impinges on the self's freedom. Cultural history cannot be separated from writing, and hence the substitution of *culture* for *society* effectively acts here as a remembering of representation, if not a return of the repressed. To play on Hegel, "history ought to be written" rather than theorized as a referent whose ontology lies outside of language. Any attempt to use writing as a technique for overcoming determination and thus achieving a dialectical transcendence or Hegelian *Aufhebung* is doomed from the start; each new letter is a re-mark of history, materi-

29. Lionel Trilling, Preface to *The Opposing Self* (Oxford, 1980), n.p.

ality, contingency, and otherness. The struggle to achieve subjectivity or freedom through language can only produce more letters, further disseminating the "differentiations of the Notion" and entangling the Spirit in the historical matter of textuality. The *lettre de cachet*, if you will, must be purloined from the cultural archive, and the authority of its signatory becomes undecidable. Who signs for freedom? The letter or the spirit? History or the subject? Writing or desire? Determination or chance? In French, not only is the *cachet* a seal, stamp, or character, it is also the sign of genius and of achieved subjective expression: *son style a un cachet particulier.* The stamp that seals writing's difference, says the dictionary, also marks the *lettre de cachet* as an "arbitrary warrant of imprisonment."[30] The plight of the modern self is that of a desire for freedom that nevertheless cannot forget its determination by writing, or that may even suspect the determination of this desire and this dialectic by "language itself."

Trilling wrote in the Preface to *The Opposing Self* that the "best account of the strange, bitter, dramatic relation between the modern self and the modern culture is that which Hegel gives in the fourth part of his *Philosophy of History.*" Trilling uses Hegel to set Marx back on his feet by arguing that Hegel's discussion of "alienation" centered on psychological, moral, and aesthetic phenomena (rather than politics or economics). But in Hegel's chapter on alienation in the *Phenomenology*, the forces of state power and of wealth are explicitly incorporated into a dialectic of consciousness (thus sparking Marx's argument for a dialectic of historical materialism). Trilling's version of alienation, like the tragic vision spoken of so frequently by American critics in the period after the 1930s, constitutes a teleological dialectic "which the modern self contrives as a means for the fulfillment of its destiny" in a pain the self incurs as a "device of self-realization." This self-realization requires rendering judgments on the quality rather than the fact of an act: "Not merely the deed itself, [Hegel] said, is now submitted to judgment, but also the personal quality of the doer of the deed. It has become not merely a question of whether the action conforms to the appropriate

30. *The New Cassell's French Dictionary*, entry on *cachet*. Of the many texts of Jacques Derrida bearing on these metaphorics, one might begin with *The Post Card: From Socrates to Freud and Beyond*, trans. Alan Bass (Chicago, 1986). My entire analysis, naturally, depends upon Derrida's incessant encounter with Hegel and the question of writing, as exemplified in "The Pit and the Pyramid: Introduction to Hegel's Semiology," in Derrida, *Margins of Philosophy*, trans. Alan Bass (Chicago, 1982), 69–108.

principle or maxim of morality, but also of the manner in which it is performed, of what it implies about the entire nature, the *being*, of the agent." In other words, style is the man.

Hegel's text becomes a pretext in Trilling for affirming the ontological reality of the "performed" self, the written subject, who thus recovers from the inauthenticity of repetition and the impotence or errancy of action. Hence Hegel "brought together the moral and the aesthetic judgment" and "made the aesthetic the criterion of the moral." Trilling remedies the threatened disappearance of the modern self, intimated by the passage on the *lettre de cachet*, by postulating in this paragraph an ontological and referential determination of writing by selfhood. Whereas the fact or "deed," the mark of writing, may be the work of cultural history, the manner or stylus "implies" "the entire nature, the *being*, of the agent." Style is freedom, choice, and responsibility, and Trilling can thus theorize the cohesion of the moral and the aesthetic judgment. To do this, he must smuggle back into the equation a binary opposition between "deed" and "manner," "act" and "quality," history and writing, which his own previous argument has rendered groundless. The liberation of the free aesthetic/moral subject from the determinations of history is accomplished by an a priori fiat that arbitrarily establishes the very differences that are supposed to be determined later by the deliberations of judgment. Needless to say, the political consequences of separating the judgment of deeds from the judgment of their quality are enormous, especially in an era when the destiny of the Liberal Mind led it to contemplations of Auschwitz and Hiroshima.

The essays of *The Opposing Self* chart the "duality" or "dialectic" of "spirit and matter," "form and force," art and common fact in various writers. Each of the analyses, as is typical with Trilling, becomes an opportunity to address contemporary quarrels in criticism and culture, here the fate of individuality, politics, and literature in the post–World War II era of middle-class normalcy. The only Americans included are Henry James and William Dean Howells. The quite extraordinary essay on Howells and his style is pervasively Hegelian in its terms and argument. Trilling characterizes Howells' bourgeois mind as an "unhappy consciousness," and he seeks to redeem Howells for our interest by seeing the dialectic between "the conditioned" and "life as pure spirit" in his work. The distinction between act and quality that Trilling finds in Hegel is here utilized to restore respect for the "way of life, of quality of being" represented by Howells. The mundane world of Howells should not be judged aesthetically but rather celebrated as "social witness" and "loving wonder at the fact that persons of the most mediocre sort somehow manage to make a society." Trilling offers this democratic humanism as a counter to the "revolutionary" Marxists who condescend to Howells' "genteel" critique of capitalism; Trilling sympathetically situates Howells' allegiance to the ordinary within a tradition stretching back to Wordsworth, whose gentility and orthodoxy are rehabilitated by a similar argument elsewhere in the volume. Howells' place in the American canon, moreover, is assured by the assertion that a Hegelian dialectic is peculiar to the nation's history: "From one point of view, no people has ever had so intense an idea of the relationship of spirit to its material circumstances as we in America now have. . . . Yet it is to be seen that those conditions to which we do respond are the ones which we ourselves make, or over which we have control, which is to say conditions as they are virtually spirit, as they deny the idea of *the conditioned.* Somewhere in our mental constitution is the demand for life as pure spirit."[31] This demand, says Trilling, informs the views of those Americans who find hope in the dream of a Communist society in which the conditioning determinations of materiality wither away with the ascendancy of the people's spirit. Howells' insistence on mundane matters offers a corrective, as it reminds us that "much in our dull daily lives really does make a significant part of man's tragic career on earth." In contrast,

> when we yield to our contemporary impulse to enlarge all experience, to involve it as soon as possible in history, myth, and the oneness of spirit—an impulse with which, I ought to say, I have considerable sympathy—we are in danger of making experience merely typical, formal, and *representative,* and thus of losing one term of the dialectic that goes on between spirit and the conditioned, which is, I suppose, what we mean when we speak of man's tragic fate. We lose, that is to say, the actuality of the conditioned, the literality of matter, the peculiar authenticity and authority of the merely denotative.[32]

The cunning of Trilling's dialectic may leave the reader a bit confused at this point. Hegel's terminology led us to expect Howells to

31. Trilling, *The Opposing Self,* 79.
32. *Ibid.,* 82.

emerge as the embodiment of the oneness of the Bourgeois Mind, which will find its historical destiny in the 1950s return to normalcy. And indeed he does so appear, though at the cost of his freedom. Trilling turns away from the typical, the formal, and the representational in an effort to recover the "authenticity" of material life and of the "merely denotative." This would appear to be a nostalgia for a life outside of language and *its* conditioning powers, for a life beyond culture. Yet Trilling quickly insists that to lose these material facts is to lose the facts of spirit, for the conditioning forces of actuality are none other than the cultural forms made by men themselves in the practice of their ideas. What one recovers through Howells, then, as through Arnold or Wordsworth, is not a natural material world outside language or beyond culture; rather it is an argument for the value of the cultural tradition inhering in the mundane quality of life lived by the middle-class bourgeoisie. Trilling's unease with the formal radicalism of modern literature coincides here with his distrust of modernism's attack on the spirit of the middle class. Where the opposing self had once found authenticity in expressing its alienation from the bourgeoisie, it now becomes authentic in adopting an adversary relation to the culture of modernism and the politics of the Left.

The cultural and political turmoil of the 1960s severely tested Trilling as he struggled to understand the alienation of the New Left and the attack on humanism coming from European critical theory, which was using Hegel in ways Trilling had not anticipated. The result was *Sincerity and Authenticity*, a speculative discussion of the dialectic informing the development of the modern self since the Renaissance. Like Trilling's previous volumes, it traced the conflict between the socialized personality and the autonomous individual, though now with references to Raymond Williams, Claude Lévi-Strauss, Lucien Goldmann, Walter Benjamin, Nathalie Sarraute, Michel Foucault, and Jacques Lacan. Although Trilling will continue to resist a purely structural approach to selfhood (whether economic, linguistic, or psychoanalytic), fearing that it weights the case too far in the direction of determinism, he nevertheless shows a capacity to balance notions of the will and its artistic forms with a deep understanding of the history and ideological mechanisms that inform them, and his recourse to Marx here is more explicit—and sympathetic—than it had been since the 1930s. It is Hegel, however, who provides Trilling with the fundamental terms of his argument and who is the subject of the key chapter, "The Honest Soul and the Disintegrated Consciousness." Hegel's world-historical dialectic will enable Trilling to universalize the American quest for freedom and selfhood, and so to negate American literature and modernism in a dialectic that would contain and surpass them.

In the manner of Williams and Foucault, Trilling undertakes an archaeology of *sincerity* and *authenticity* as terms of moral consciousness and forms of textual representation, beginning with Polonius' "To thine own self be true" and ending with R. D. Laing's advocacy of madness as an authentic rejoinder to the reigning culture's insanity. *Sincerity* may be defined as "the avoidance of being false to any man through being true to one's own self." Sincerity is social, moral, even theatrical, and it is this latter quality that dooms it to its modern devaluation, since we are quick to see the incongruence between feeling and avowal. Iago's "honesty" is the foil to Polonius' sincerity, itself enmeshed in a dubious and self-serving rhetoric. For Trilling, the breakdown of any cultural consensus of moral values makes sincerity almost impossible, for there is no faith in the public creed to which the self subscribes: "Which is not to say that the moral temper of our time sets no store by the avoidance of falsehood to others, only that it does not figure as the defining purpose of being true to one's own self." The gap between the self and its representations can no longer be closed by protestations of sincerity: "In short, we play the role of being ourselves, we sincerely act the part of the sincere person, with the result that a judgment may be passed upon our sincerity that it is not authentic." The cult of authenticity, which informs the sublime, romanticism, and much of the modernist avant-garde, arises as a reaction against the consciousness of "dissimulation," which is often associated with the artifices of culture. "Society" appears, argues Trilling, when culture becomes the primary audience for the self's definition, displacing God and the monarchy. Citing the invention of mirrors by the Venetians, as well as Lacan's thesis on the "mirror stage," Trilling sees that the "individual" comes into being as the subject of representation. The example is Rousseau, but the lesson is for all modernity: "His conception of his private and uniquely interesting individuality, together with his impulse to reveal his self, to demonstrate that in it which is to be admired and trusted, are, we may believe, his response to the newly available sense of an audience, of that public which society created."[33]

33. Lionel Trilling, *Sincerity and Authenticity* (Cambridge, Mass., 1972), 9, 11, 25, hereinafter cited parenthetically in the text as *SA*.

In his chapter on Hegel, Trilling returns to the remarks on Diderot's *Rameau's Nephew* that appear in the *Phenomenology*'s section on the "self-estranged" (or self-alienated) spirit in culture. Hegel here tracks the dialectic in its historical guise, as the forms that self-consciousness passes through in its relation to culture as state power, culture as wealth, and culture as language. Both state power and wealth are the products of alienation, while language is simultaneously the enactment and transcendence of self-estrangement. The feudal monarch receives the estranged selfhood of his vassals in the form of obedience, so that ultimately he can say, "L'Etat c'est moi." The wealth received by the nobility in turn represents their alienated essence, only now in the form of a thing. The nobility of service passes dialectically into base cynicism and the language of flattery, while wealth passes from the representation of noble being into the representation of the self's estranged essence. The witty and satirical talk that pervades this culture expresses its alienation in the form of wit—of a negativity that cynically gives voice to the hollowness of the culture and its dependence on power, servitude, and hypocrisy. Diderot's dialogue of the *philosophe* with Rameau's mimic nephew captures, for Hegel, the dialectic overturning of eighteenth-century culture and portends its revolutionary transcendence.

In his commentary on this section of the *Phenomenology*, Jean Hyppolite (seeing partly through Marx's eyes) stresses Hegel's allusions to the stages of French aristocracy and its lacerated end in the Revolution, a background reinforced by the citations of Diderot.[34] Revolution is the inevitable result of this torn consciousness; like Rameau's nephew, the spirit in revolt speaks the language of demystification, at once disintegrating the pretensions of the cultural world and, in its own self-condemnation, achieving a transcendence (or *Aufhebung*) of its alienation by returning to itself in the language of laceration. The spirit knows itself as alienation and thus returns to itself, preparing the way for a new set of dialectical phases (of faith and intellect) as self-consciousness pursues a world of absolute freedom beyond *this* world of culture and alienation.

Language in the form of speech, Hegel insists, has an essential role throughout these dialectical reversals. In speech, self-consciousness comes into existence as "something for others" (as state power and

---

34. Jean Hyppolite, *Genesis and Structure of Hegel's "Phenomenology of Spirit,"* trans. Samuel Cherniak and John Heckman (Evanston, Ill., 1974), 376–426.

wealth had been the representation of self for others). But whereas in "every other mode of expression" the self "is absorbed in some concrete actuality," in speech it attains transcendence through a grammatical *Aufhebung* that cancels and preserves its existence:

> Language . . . alone expresses the "I," the "I" itself. This *real* existence of the "I" is, *qua* real existence, an objectivity which has in it the true nature of the "I." The "I" is this particular "I"—but equally the *universal* "I"; its manifesting is also at once the externalization and vanishing of *this* particular "I," and as a result the "I" remains in its universality. The "I" that utters itself is "*heard*" or "*perceived*"; it is an infection in which it has immediately passed into unity with those for whom it is a real existence, and is a universal self-consciousness.[35]

The content of the "I," however, may be negative, as in the "witty talk" of those like the nephew who give voice to this alienated "I." But "only as self-consciousness in revolt is it aware of its own disrupted state, and in thus knowing it has immediately risen above it." All moral and cultural content is negated: "The positive object is merely the *pure 'I' itself*, and the disrupted consciousness *in itself* this pure self-identity of self-consciousness that has returned to itself."[36] This dialectic will yield either the left Hegelianism of Marx and Lukács, in which the masses are identified as the "I" of history, or the Right Hegelianism of much of modernism, in which the alienated "I" engages in a ceaseless revolt against culture. Hyppolite comments that the "decent soul of the philosopher cannot adapt itself to such a perpetual reversal of values. Indeed, Hegel too often tries to evade the consequences and the logic of his own dialectic."[37] Such an evasion will mark Trilling's text as well. There the "I"'s entanglement in language and representation promises no accession to absolute freedom but only a further determination and disintegration of the will. Rather than being taken as the proper target of negation, culture for Trilling becomes the possibility of a sincere or authentic "I," though this once more, dialectically, costs the "I" its freedom.

According to Trilling, Diderot presents us with an honest and

---

35. Hegel, *Phenomenology*, 308–309. This phenomenology of speech as the privileged mode of self-conscious truth in language is subjected by Derrida to deconstruction, most pertinently in his *Speech and Phenomena*, trans. David B. Allison (Evanston, Ill., 1973).

36. Hegel, *Phenomenology*, 321.

37. Hippolyte, *Genesis and Structure*, 413.

sincere *Moi* who confronts in the nephew an alienated figure whose "social being" is "a mere histrionic representation." "Mimetic skill" is the "essence of his being" as he apes all the social roles: "There you have my pantomime; it's about the same as the flatterer's, the courtier's, the footman's, and the beggar's" (*SA*, 31). The modernity of the nephew, however, lies in the truth of his pantomime as it exhibits the inauthenticity at the heart of the theater that is society. He becomes an image of the anti-hero and of the self Trilling elsewhere celebrates: "he figures not only as an actual person but also as an aspect of humanity itself, as the liberty that we wish to believe is inherent in the human spirit, in its energy of effort and its limitless contradictions" (*SA*, 32). This leads immediately to the Hegelian Spirit, whose power of negation is the dark but authentic experience producing cultural criticism and self-knowledge. While we harbor our nostalgia for "the archaic noble vision of life" embodied by Diderot's *Moi* or Austen's "idyllic" England, no such life without negation is open to us. Instead there is only "culture," Hegel's (and Arnold's) *Bildung*, an "exigent spiritual enterprise" in which self-negation and social transformation are caught up in interminable dialectics. Art itself, which requires representation and thus the confining dictates of a social audience, corrupts the self with its theatrical seductions. "Literature is an accomplice in the social betrayal," and thus the move within art to defy the bourgeois audience, after Nietzsche, with a Dionysian assault upon its very conventions. "The astonishing performance" of the pantomime, quoted with such delight by Hegel, "proposes the idea which Nietzsche was to articulate a century later, that man's true metaphysical destiny expresses itself not in morality but in art." As if drawing back from the postmodern implications of his argument, Trilling turns again to Austen's *Mansfield Park*, where the condemnation of "amateur theatricals" recalls us to the dream of a life of sincerity beyond representation (*SA*, 33).

Trilling's hostility to Hegel's reading of *Rameau's Nephew* turns on his assertion that Hegel sides completely with the revolt of the nephew and loses sight of the value of the nobility of Diderot's *Moi*. Explicating the stages of the dialectic of alienation in Hegel's chapter, Trilling describes how the noble passes from obedience and identification with the state into the language of flattery, baseness, and an assertion of freedom:

> Between the intentions of the base self and its avowals there is no congruence. But the base self, exactly because it is not under the control of

the noble ethos, has won at least a degree of autonomy and has thereby fulfilled the nature of Spirit. In refusing its obedient service to the state power and to wealth it has lost its wholeness; its selfhood is 'disintegrated'; the self is 'alienated' from itself. But because it has detached itself from imposed conditions, Hegel says that it has made a step in progress. . . . The 'honesty' of Diderot/*Moi*, which evokes Hegel's impatient scorn, consists in his wholeness of self, in the directness and consistency of his relation to things, and in his submission to a traditional morality. Diderot/*Moi* does not exemplify the urge of Spirit to escape from the conditions which circumscribe it and to enter into an existence which will be determined by itself alone. (*SA*, 38–39)

Diderot/*Moi* sounds suspiciously like William Dean Howells, and Hegel appears to be father to the countercultural radicals of the 1960s who lacerated the self-consciousness of Columbia University. Trilling disparagingly quotes Hegel's conclusion to the chapter, in which "self-consciousness in revolt" leads to the dialectical return of self-identity. Trilling's resistance to representation is the reverse side of his desire to restrain the labor of the negative: both language and cultural self-consciousness in Hegel threaten to unleash a history of differentiation that will not submit to any "traditional morality." In contrast, the figure of Matthew Arnold presides over the conviction in Trilling (and in T. S. Eliot) that the antidote of tradition should be prescribed for the disease of self-consciousness.

*Sincerity and Authenticity* brings the story of Hegel and American literary historiography full circle. The dialectical schema that had begun in Hegel as a world-historical phenomenon became nationalized in the context of American critical writing, adapted and made specific to the destiny of the nation. Trilling's return to Hegel projects American dialectics back onto the scene of the history of the Self in the West, as one can see in those few passages that touch upon American writers. A later chapter discusses Emerson's *English Traits* and repeats the tired cliché that "the American self can be taken to be a microcosm of American society, which has notably lacked the solidity and intractability of English society." The dialectic of material determinism and spiritual freedom, or of writing and the self, passes through the dialectic of "Tradition and the Individual Talent" to become a national opposition: "The Hegelian terms I touched on earlier bear upon the difference between the two nations [England and America]. Americans, we might say—D. H. Lawrence did in effect say it fifty years ago—had moved into that historical stage of Spirit which produces the 'disintegrated' or 'alienated' consciousness." Emerson's warm response to English traits "must" be ascribed to "the archaic intractability of the English social organization: the English sincerity depends upon the English class structure" (*SA*, 113–14). Back in America one would only find Melville writing *The Confidence Man* or Huck and Jim fighting to retain their sincerity in the face of the King and the Duke and all of society's masquerades. (Trilling later mentions Melville's "Bartleby the Scrivener" as evidencing the total inauthenticity of the social world.) Trilling's reference to Lawrence clearly indicates that this account falls within the mainstream of American literary histories that have taken up Hegelian dialectics as their themes, from Matthiessen and Chase through Fiedler and Poirier.

But Trilling cannot long remain content with sincerity. The power of the negative remains a function inherent in cultural history per se, so that any recourse to a tradition will entail some dialectic with anarchy (or the indeterminate "differentiations of the Notion"). He takes up Marx's rewriting of Hegel's notion of "alienation," specifically in Marx's 1844 manuscripts. Trilling likes the humanism of *this* Marx and the pathos with which he expresses man's loss of his authenticity. What Trilling doesn't like is the economic determinism that stipulates that "money, in short, is the principle of the inauthentic in human existence" (*SA*, 124). In this observation, Marx is being truer to Diderot and Hegel than is Trilling, since the dialectic of wealth and self-consciousness forms an essential ingredient in *Rameau's Nephew.* (As Trilling knows, Marx sent Engels a copy of Diderot's book with an enthusiastic note.) For Trilling, inauthenticity is rather the condition of social existence as such, for in society the self exists and has freedom only by virtue of the pantomime of representation, the agreement to participate in the spectacle of a tradition's script. The worlds of Diderot, Austen, and Arnold give birth to the alienated practices of Stendhal, Joyce, and Conrad. Hegel and American literary history bequeathed to Trilling the search for an authenticity that would not be conditioned by the social, and in his final chapter on Freud he imagines he has found it, though the tale is every bit as tragic as Ahab's or Huck's or Gatsby's.

"The Authentic Unconscious" offers a version of Freud as a resolving figure of the dialectics that haunt Trilling. He notes the decline of narrative in contemporary literature and ties it to the death of the past for the modern deracinated self: "It bears upon the extreme attenuation of the authority of literary culture, upon the growing indifference to its traditional pedagogy; the hero, the exemplary figure, does not exist without a sharp and positive beginning; the hero is his history from his significant birth to his significant death" (*SA*, 139). Trilling's "hero" is the self, whose birth and death his volume traces. The word *hero* rings hollow in the late 1960s, since it requires either a shared communal goal or a radical belief in the power of the individual. As structuralist terminology suggests, the heroic self is now replaced by the "subject," an entity who always functions within and is defined by a system from which there is no "beyond." Trilling recognizes this lesson in his defense of Freud against Sartre, when he points out that the theory of the superego, especially as its implications are spelled out in *Civilization and Its Discontents*, lodges the culture within the self, and vice versa, so that the self is always doomed to perform for a symbolic father or social audience that has been internally incorporated: "The virtually resistless power of this principle of inauthenticity is the informing idea of Freud's mature social theory" (*SA*, 150). Freud's book "may be thought to stand like a lion in the path of all hopes of achieving happiness through the radical revision of social life" (*SA*, 151).

The argument now takes some surprising turns as Trilling seeks to capture for Freud the mantle of the authentic consciousness. Unlike a rational conscience, the superego institutes a "largely gratuitous" and harsh sense of guilt, felt not for a deed done but for the repressed wish of "aggression against a sacrosanct person, originally the father" (*SA*, 152). While the superego makes civilization possible, the price is "deplorable irrationality and cruelty." Moreover, "although it was to serve the needs of civilization that the superego was installed in its disciplinary office, its actual behaviour was not dictated by those needs; the movement of the superego from rational pragmatic authority to gratuitous cruel tyranny was wholly autonomous" (*SA*, 154). Thus the superego achieves that autonomy the self dreamed of, an authenticity that as "a given of biology" becomes a force not susceptible to social reform or corruption. The superego is beyond culture. Freud has postulated a "flagrant inauthenticity" within the self: "Man's existence in civilization is represented as being decisively conditioned by a psychic entity which, under the mask of a concern with social peace and union, carries on a ceaseless aggression to no purpose save the enhancement of its own power." Power, not spirit, appears as the teleology of self-consciousness. Ironically, this irrational fate becomes the origin of man's authentic will, the necessity or Ananke that inspires his oppositional being in a world where cosmic and theological absolutes have expired: "Freud, in insisting upon the essential immitigability of the human condition as determined by the nature of the mind, had the intention of sustaining the authenticity of human existence that formerly had been ratified by God" (*SA*, 156). What Trilling once called the "tragic" appears here as the irreconcilable dialectic of will and negation, something that goes on within the self and within society, not simply in the adversarial relation between them. The separation of the superego from its function as representative of society removes the conflict from history, makes it mythic and universal, and so restores a vision of primal essences liberated from the pantomimes to which human existence seems otherwise doomed.

American literary histories since the 1970s have taken a quite un-Hegelian turn. The speculative terms and narratives dominating works from Brooks and Parrington through Trilling are now subject to critique, either by poststructuralists who elaborate deconstructions of Hegelian thematics or by feminists, Afro-Americanists, and New Historicists who reject the totalizing cultural and political psychology of the previous models. It would take another essay entirely to analyze these developments in light of current rereadings of Hegel. Suffice it to say here, by way of prospect, that the current antinomy between the literary and the historical in much critical writing has its correspondence to the opposition of writing and being in Hegel. Poststructuralist readings of Hegel call us back to remember the work of representation in this text, and so to defer the transcendence or *Aufhebung* his dialectics recurrently posit. Derrida's notion of *différance*, along with his other inconceivable "concepts," maneuvers to displace dialectics with a power of the negative that no *Aufhebung* can account for. *Différance* reactivates and reinscribes the terms of dialectical opposition in ways that recover their "history," though history is now thought beyond the categorical opposition of representation and reality. Much of the current return to history in American criticism has failed to attend to the relevance of this lesson, offering versions of the historical that are quite conventional in their assumptions of what the historical *is* or how and where it might take place. Trilling's agon with Hegel should mark the death of the subject of literary history, in each sense of the phrase. Efforts to move past the antinomies of his criticism, and of the tradition he belonged to, require a thinking of the dialectic of the literary and the historical that does not subordinate itself to the tale of the freedom of consciousness. It can only be historical, and political, if it remembers that history is a way of being that cannot simply be referred to. Our responsibility is rather to rewrite it, though it cost us our "I"'s in the process.

# II READING THEORETICALLY

# Early American Antigone

· · · · · · · · · · · · · · · · ·

*Mitchell Breitwieser*

Puritan and Hegelian thought grow from a common problem: given that Protestantism has defined negation as an essential motion of true spirit, how can Protestantism be put to the task of legitimating a sociolegal order, since such legitimation requires specific positive codes, norms, and precepts rather than a devout contemplation of the evanescence of codes? Despite important historical and theoretical differences—notably the insuperable segregation between the saved and the damned maintained in Puritan predestinarianism—the crucial energy of both Puritan and Hegelian thought is generated by the challenge of a Protestantism seeking to enter politics without losing its intrinsic character. Thus, though there are compelling resonances between Hegel's philosophy and the social theory of the romantic and imperial periods of American history from Jackson through Wilson, that philosophy also strongly recalls the major issues of seventeenth-century New England social theory. According to Richard F. Lovelace, Cotton Mather was in his later years contemplating German Pietism as a specimen of the sort of socialized spirituality he felt New England was forgetting, and Mary Fulbrook and Lawrence Dickey have suggested lines of common concern between early British Puritanism and the Pietist Lutheranism of areas such as the Old-Württemberg of Hegel's youth.[1] The "delay," as it were, may be attributed to the different rates of national political unification, which kept German Protestantism from the opportunity to apply itself directly to social administration until the mid-eighteenth century, and then only in certain zones. Thus whereas

1. Richard F. Lovelace, *The American Pietism of Cotton Mather: Origins of American Evangelicalism* (Grand Rapids, Mich., 1979); Mary Fulbrook, *Piety and Politics: Religion and the Rise of Absolutism in England, Württemburg and Prussia* (Cambridge, Eng., 1987); Lawrence Dickey, *Hegel: Religion, Economics and the Politics of Spirit, 1770–1807* (Cambridge, Eng., 1987).

Anglo-American philosophy during the second half of the century pur-
veys the moderate pragmatist tranquillities of Hutcheson, Hume, and
Scottish common sense, German philosophy during the same period
grapples with the Calvinist turmoil around the force of the negative;
and whereas Kant attempted to resolve the quandary in his first critique by debarring the absolute from representation (save figuratively,
in the aesthetic, according to the third critique), Hegel commenced his
work as a demonstration of the manner in which the Protestant "abro-
gation of externality" can pass into an explicit political culture without
crucial self-loss—a demonstration, in fact, he hoped, of the inferiority
of spirituality that holds itself back from articulation for fear it will lose
the purity it enjoys when it remains *in potentia*.

I am contending, not that Hegel's Germany and Puritan New
England were substantially or essentially identical, only that they share
certain important ideological features and that Hegel's manner of argument offers perspectives that the writings of the American Puritans
as a whole do not. By virtue of his decision to impersonate dramatically
the *voices*, or specific local rationalities, of the social forms annulled in
the march of history toward the *ecclesia-polis*, Hegel imagines the cogency of alternate social formations, sometimes, to follow from Henry
Sussman's argument, to the detriment of the credibility of what he
seeks to view as progression rather than as repression or suppression.[2]
Such a dramatic staging of the ascent of Protestant politics offers insights absent from the stark binarism of Puritan rhetoric—internal ap-
preciations of the antagonist as a form of reason rather than as an
inchoate hostility to be assailed without hesitation, recognition, or self-
critique. Hegel's staging of historical conflict offers, or at least permits,
an understanding of the lines of tension and relation between the Protestant whole and the distinct socialities it bears in its midst, rather than

2. Henry Sussman, *The Hegelian Aftermath: Readings in Hegel, Kierkegaard, Freud,
Proust, and James* (Baltimore, 1982). Sussman is for the most part concerned with the first
half of the *Phenomenology of Spirit*, whereas my argument in this essay concentrates on the
reading of *Antigone* that begins the second half. Consequently, he focuses on questions of
a less directly social nature and sees "a world whose only principles are indeterminacy
and linguistic copulation" as the major source of inner resistance to Hegel's design,
whereas I will emphasize a specifically social form of resistance. Despite this difference,
I agree with Sussman's general judgment that "Hegel may place his forced twists and
leanings at the service of a smooth-running machine of logic and abstraction, but the
blunt force involved in this application points in the direction of another, less domesticated realm" (2)—though, of course, Antigone's threat to Creon originates in a more
domesticated realm.

labeling such distinct bodies outbreaks of chaotic declension as a means of interdicting communication and its transformative power, a power Puritanism could only see as loss of focus. In this essay, I will use Hegel's rather divided and even tormented or guilt-ridden view of one such imagined opponent, Antigone, as a paradigm for the theoretical challenge to Puritanism developed in the course of Anne Bradstreet's poetic career.

*Antigone* is of interest to Hegel because it depicts political life as a struggle over representation, specifically over the power to control the proper manner of remembering the dead, an issue that had been of great importance for Protestantism since Luther first objected to the way mourning was theologized in the sale of indulgences and in the doctrine of purgatory itself. If the stresses Hegel puts on the text of *Antigone* (and the meanings he projects into it) carry his reading of the play away from Greek society, they do so in order to allegorize a confrontation endemic to Protestantism; if Hegel's Creon is in several aspects not Sophocles' Creon, this transmutation of Sophocles' intention is performed in order to present a Creon gripped by the problems of a Protestant sovereign.[3] To this end, Hegel imagines a Creon eager to control representation, to legitimate the postwar Theban regime he heads by engaging in legend-manufacture, vaunting the civic heroism of Eteocles and denouncing the noxious infamy of Polyneices in order to promote a socially accepted genealogy of virtue to which he is the remaining heir. As Hegel remarks, this ideological labor is extremely problem-fraught, given the rival brothers' tenuous claims to sole possession of the throne and the consequent difficulty of seeing either one as a hero. Creon's legends are precarious, and he is nervous but at the same time aware of the tremendous power of exemplification, one of the central topics of the *Phenomenology*, as Derrida contends.[4] Creon risks raising the question of the brothers' relative political merits, even insists on the question, because if he can persuade the citizens to accept a general veneration of Eteocles (and a vilification of Polyneices), he

3. G. W. F. Hegel, "The Ethical World. Human and Divine Law: Man and Woman," in Hegel, *Phenomenology of Spirit*, trans. A. V. Miller (Oxford, 1977), Sec. C. (BB.) VI. A. a. I will footnote this chapter only when I use specific quotations from it. My argument draws most heavily on paragraphs 449–52, 455, 460, and 462–63.

4. Jacques Derrida, *Glas*, trans. John P. Leavey, Jr., and Richard Rand (Lincoln, Neb., 1986), throughout, but pp. 29–30 especially, in the left columns. I became aware of the theoretical importance of the topic of exemplification through conversations with, and essays by, Jonathan Elmer and David Lloyd.

will have devised a putatively dialectical ideology that can move between an abstract notion of right (defense of the city as a source of virtue in the absence of a clear claim to the throne) and the memory of concrete experience. The example declares that the personal singularities of the brothers are only vehicles or vessels bearing their standings with respect to virtue; exemplification negates or annuls this extrinsic singularity in order to preserve in unobstructed form what is declared to have been the essence of their personal being. The example in this way implies that the negation of at least a portion of experience is an expression *of* experience rather than a simple external opposite such as Kant's categorical imperative. The example lays claim to being an immanent representation, an articulation of what is posited as the gist of a social whole and not just as an aggressive individual participant within a diverse community. If the battle between the brothers allegorizes the damage that ensues from attempting to unify a heterogeneous society under a single head (an issue of great concern in Hegel's Germany, as in seventeenth-century England), Creon's labor proves to be, not a reconsideration of the project of forcible unification, but a search for a more sophisticated tool, *Aufhebung* in place of war—a search that will be seriously compromised by Antigone's insistence that Creon's way is an extension of the recent war rather than a way of making peace.

Antigone's defense of the right and duty of mourning emerges for Hegel as the most radical possible challenge to exemplification per se (by *radical* I mean "at the root," rather than "from the Left"). Throughout the subsequent analysis of social history in the *Phenomenology*, Hegel will see struggle lying between competing orders of exemplification, such as between the Christian saint and the Roman patriot, because Creon's origination of collective spirit has established exemplification as the axiom of political conflict. But unlike later antithetical figures, Antigone does not stand for a counter-exemplification—her argument is not that Polyneices was the true hero, or that both brothers were heroes. Rather, according to Hegel, her allegiance in mourning is to the singular "personalities" of the two brothers, to a full memory that includes those aspects of the dead that the example would annul or declare extrinsic to what is posited as the lesson each has to offer. From the vantage of mourning, the discrimination among and the hierarchization of the traits of the dead amount to an opportunistic meddlesomeness, a reduction rather than a refinement or enhancement of memory. For mourning, the social dialectic of the example is an episode of repressive violence—of semiotic war—instead of adequate and satisfying transumption.

Antigone thus refuses to comply out of respect for what is unassimilable by Creon's rhetorical order (but not by representation itself). She becomes for him an area of darkness in the midst of his lucidity, and Hegel often joins his voice to Creon's, calling her *nature*, an underground, a primordiality. But the Hegel who thus naturalizes Antigone is the Hegel concerned with the progress of the book toward its denouement in the moral state—an impatient Hegel eager to get on because lingering will endanger the project, and the danger here is precisely Hegel's own hesitations about the necessity of branding Antigone a form of natural obscurity. As Derrida argues, the truly unassimilable force in this chapter is the entropic tendency of matter, which manifests itself in the decay of Polyneices' body or its consumption by birds and beasts of prey, and in the concomitant danger that he might be forgotten. Antigone's task, as Derrida summarizes it, is to represent "pure singularity: neither the empiric individual that death destroys, decomposes, analyzes, nor the rational universality of the citizen, of the living subject."[5] Both Creon and Antigone oppose such oblivion, Creon with condemnatory exemplification—Polyneices should be remembered as being unworthy of the basic respect of burial, remembered as being unworthy of remembrance, which is not the same as being forgotten—and Antigone with the homage of mourning, symbolized by the dirt with which she seeks to cover the corpse, an homage that does not avail itself of canons of civic value. Both of them, therefore, are engaged in ethical work, purposive activity guided by a sense of obligation and directed against a resistance. However much the "progressive" Hegel depicts the contest between Creon and Antigone as a duel between reason and nature in order to set a tone of regrettable necessity, another Hegel sees the scene in its complexity as a confrontation between two conflicting ethical teleologies, both directed against the resistance of nature and the added resistance of the other. If Antigone represents a darkness within Creon's ethics—seems to him like nature in being repellent to his project—she is not alien to ethics as such. This is perhaps why Derrida's search for Hegel's final horror, an *X* that will not yield to consciousness, leads his argument away from

5. *Ibid.*, 143, and throughout the left columns in the book.

attending to the theoretical contest between Antigone and Creon, toward the carrion.

But though Creon and Antigone both represent ethical orders, there is a dissymmetry in their conflict that was not present in the battle between Eteocles and Polyneices. Creon begins with a superpersonal type—hero or traitor—and fits the person to the type. The possible ends are determined in the beginning, and subtle portraiture would only dilute the bluntly homiletic representation he seeks. Antigone, however, apprehends primarily the surviving ego's ruination, the self as crater, and must construct in slow memory a portrait of Polyneices that is adequate to her extensive experience of her brother. Such a portrait would honor Polyneices by preserving him, translating him from the shame of being unable to control the exhibition and corruption of his body, a labor begun in the attempted burial, which does not remove him from thought but on the contrary covers his unbounded shame with what Hegel calls an assertion of the "right of consciousness." And, in so honoring Polyneices, she restores herself, not by recovering wholeness, but by transferring the place-that-was-Polyneices from being a ruination of representation to being an object of representation. The area of zero or space left by Polyneices' departure is not closed in post-mourning subjectivity, but neither is it an impassable obstacle to the capacity to form representations and engage in purposive living. The labor of mourning, like the labor of the slave earlier in the *Phenomenology*, is neither sudden nor supreme, but rather abject and gradual, a point on which Hegel foreshadows Freud.[6] Working on an inscrutable schedule, mourning is a summoning of numerous memory bits, each of which adds to, deepens, and challenges the representation of the dead the mourner has constructed to this point, compelling revisions to the image—revisions that frequently feel similar to what Lacan calls second deaths, repetitions of the first loss rather than labor exerted against it. But if the memories assault the image, so too does

6. Sigmund Freud, "Mourning and Melancholia," in Freud, *Complete Works*, trans. James Strachey (24 vols.; London, 1953–66), XIV, 239–58, especially 236. My reading of Hegel is heavily influenced by Jacques Lacan's fusion of the Hegelian and Freudian theories of mourning in "L'éclat d'Antigone," in Lacan, *L'éthique de la psychanalyse* (Paris, 1986), 285–333, Vol. VII of *Le séminaire*, 21 vols., and by Stuart Schneiderman, *Jacques Lacan: The Death of an Intellectual Hero* (Cambridge, Mass., 1983). See also Jacques Lacan, "Desire and the Interpretation of Desire in *Hamlet*," trans. James Hulbert, in *Literature and Psychoanalysis: The Question of Reading: Otherwise*, No. 55–56 of *Yale French Studies* (1977), 11–52.

the image challenge the memories, stripping away what were the emotions that dominated the remembered moment in order to reconstrue the moment as significant anecdote, as incremental contribution to the emerging notion of who Polyneices was for her. And what more complete image could there be than that made from the memorial archive of the family member, who remembers even when he or she fails to be uniformly fond, given that mournful memory incessantly interrogates what sentiment might direct one to remember, and given that desire and love are operating under a stern injunction that Hegel calls divine and Lacan calls the law of the unconscious, an injunction to take account of what was rather than of what the mourner might otherwise want to have been the case. In this scheme, the family member's power of objectification is not compromised by fondness but guided by an extensive knowledge that interferes with expedient simplicities such as Creon's exemplifications: the family member guards and ensures the truth of the dead, in hope that the dead will be known to have been. Antigone's labor is thus in a sense also a process of exemplification, a search to mark out how her moments of having experienced her brother were examples of what she is coming to define as what he was, again, for her; but not a specification of how Polyneices was an example of a superpersonal ideological type. Polyneices is for her the end, not the means, of a teleological hermeneutic.

Her labor differs from Creon's, therefore, in four ways: 1) the representation that it seeks does not relinquish the person as its telos; 2) though the question Antigone seeks to answer—who was he?—is posed at the outset, the answer sought is generated in the process of inquiry rather than selected from a repertoire of possibilities that predated the question and governed the inquiry; 3) the image and the moments that are to exemplify it undergo reciprocal dialectical transformation, but Creon's image subdues the moment to its demand; and 4) whereas Creon's image is immediately ready, Antigone's is, at the time of her death, only begun, its date of completion unpredictable, had she lived. Her defiance of Creon, therefore, can only state that his representation is simple and factitious but cannot at this point propose a nonexistent alternative.

Hegel finds it important that Antigone's defiance is a response to Creon's initiative in prohibiting the burial, not an independently chosen course. The prewar society Hegel imagines was ethical and harmonious but not unified around a single notion. Rather, it was ethically heterogeneous, its contradictions latent, not brought to crisis, but also not resolved. Creon's prohibition of alternate or nonaligned sociality is consequently for Hegel a dialectically productive project, and his desire for a single social ethic informing the whole of social life becomes a first draft for what Hegel hopes history will accomplish, the adequate and transumptive monologization of society under the sunlight of reason. Creon's first draft of *Sittlichkeit*, however, though it is the origin of the idea, is nevertheless preliminary and prefigurative, and therefore partial, because it is repressive and exclusionary; it is not preservative with respect to all the elements of spiritual worth present in the initial social array: its cancellations yield a partial and restricted field, rather than a *summa* purged of inconsequentialities. In approaching such a judgment against Creon, Hegel postulates that were it not for Creon's oppression, the ethic of political exemplification and the familial ethic of mourning would have been simply adjacent, alongside each other, perhaps with relations of communicative exchange. By prohibiting the burial, Hegel contends, Creon creates Antigone's defiance as a politically articulate antithesis instead of leaving it as some other happening elsewhere in the city or just outside its walls.

Sophocles suggests several reasons for Creon's anxious and jealous prohibition: he is perhaps a less forceful figure than were the brothers, or fears that he will be perceived as such; he lacks a pedigree as clear as theirs, not being one of Oedipus' sons (hence his emphasis on patriotism rather than lineage as the essence of political virtue); or, perhaps, he fears that the fact of Antigone's rebellion, rather than its specific character as mourning, will reveal him as a man bested by a woman. No matter which or what combination of these motives drives him, however, until the last moments of the play he sees Antigone as a specimen of stubborn and irrational intransigence, not as the proponent of an ethic. Hegel also assumes Creon's blindness to Antigone's commitment but constructs a non-Sophoclean explanation for Creon's intensity. The incidental dividend of the war, Hegel contends, was Creon's discovery of its power to cancel the separate lives of relatively autonomous bodies within the polis in order to make their energies available to the urgent cause: war inaugurates society unified under the idea. Hegel suggests that Creon is so entranced by this by-product of group self-preservation that he seeks to perpetuate it. He is, in a kind of dark version of William James's "moral equivalent of war," striving to prolong into peacetime the consolidating force of crisis. For Creon, therefore, adjacent energy is lost energy: allegiances such as Antigone's mourning are not simply other actions in addition to patriotism but episodes of hoarding or squandering, a sequestering or wasting of affective funds he feels should properly be at his disposal for investment in the unified future.

Hegel's Creon is thus less a weakling and a despot than a state theorist who anticipates Freud's theses on civilization and sublimation—the perception of society as a quantitatively limited supply of energy that, if prevented from following its diverse innate courses, will flow as one toward the higher cause, though remaining prone to jump its bounds and dissolve the whole should vigilance relax. But the theory of sociolibidinal economic sublimation that Hegel projects onto Creon's thought differs from Freud's: Creon seeks, not to annul and absorb *eros* directly, but to annul and absorb the mourning that arises from an *eros* destroyed by another source (though he eventually becomes the primary destroyer as well as the ideological parasite). Since mourning is an attempt to sublimate partial memories into a comprehensive image of the dead one, Creon is seeking to sublimate a labor of sublimation, not a simple, primary, intact love. The contest between Creon and Antigone, therefore, is not between a direct desire and a repressed desire returning in the form of social identification, but between two uses of memory to respond to the fact of death.[7] The sublimation and the sublimated are much closer to phenomenological iso-

7. In "Mourning and Melancholia," Freud argues that melancholia (or depression) results from a derangement of mourning. His argument that this derangement originates in a certain fixated or intransigent incorporation of the dead seems to me to invite supplementation by Hegel's theory: if mourning ceases prematurely because of an incorporation of an image of the dead advanced by a scheme of social exemplarity, it becomes melancholia. The missing factor in Freud's theory is a consideration of the preemptive intrusion of ideology into the course of mourning. In his Introduction to the work of Nicolas Abraham and Maria Torok, Derrida claims that for Freud, mourning accomplishes an *introjection* of the dead whereas melancholia is stalled by having *incorporated* the dead: introjection brings the image of the dead into full assimilation with the self, but incorporation assimilates the dead as an alien presence, a *crypt* in the midst of the self with which the self does not communicate. This distinction is useful but does not seem to me complete. In the case of the sort of prolonged and intimate contact that exists between family members, the dead does not need to be introjected into the self because that self is in large measure already determined by the history of the relation—the task is not to bring the dead in but to convert the dead from being an element of life *taken for granted* to being an object of representation, to being an inner image with which the self can communicate to the limit of all the messages that memory proposes. Derrida's, Abraham's, and Torok's concept of melancholia and incorporation might therefore also be enriched by a consideration of ideological intrusion into mourning: if the mourner takes in an image of the dead that *seems* adequate but that in fact only *simulates* the dead, then that image will not communicate adequately with memory but will remain as an en-

morphism in Hegel's theory than they are in Freud's. Hence the allure of Creon's way, as it registers in Ismene's and Haemon's hesitations: they do not have to forgive or accept Creon's extinction of love (again, at first), because the deaths of the brothers were not his deed—he is only a fellow survivor; and the representation of the dead that Creon offers, were it to prove satisfying, were he to prove solicitous as well as innocent, would be a welcome gift, because it would bring a prompt completion to what would otherwise be the painful and prolonged course of mourning. Exemplification seems to offer the benefit of mourning without the full cost, and only Antigone's apparently stubborn, willful, ungrateful insistence that the two orders of memory are distinct, that exemplification *mimics or simulates* mourning instead of advancing it, can reveal Creon as other than magnanimous, thereby provoking him to tip his hand, to reveal the hermeneutic violence implicit in the reductive simplicity of the example by allowing it to come into the open as the political violence he wreaks on Antigone. Although exemplification thus shows itself as a structurally necessary insensitivity to mourning's complex care, it represents itself to mourning as generosity, offers itself as a sufficient surrogate that spares the mourner her renewals of pain, offers itself as Christ, and thus establishes its credentials by an appeal to desire, not by a command to suppress desire, and reveals itself as force only after a careful critique has rebuffed its generosity.[8]

---

crypted alien body, like the apple embedded in Gregor Samsa's flesh in Kafka's *Metamorphosis*, a flesh rendered insectivorid by its unrepresenting alienation from what it surrounds (Jacques Derrida, "*Fors:* The Anglish Words of Nicolas Abraham and Maria Torok," trans. Barbara Johnson, in Nicolas Abraham and Maria Torok, *The Wolf Man's Magic Word*, trans. Nicholas Rand [Minneapolis, 1986], xiv–xxi).

8. Most theories of ideology assume the agency of a direct inculcation of fear—fear of criminal punishment, ostracism, guilt, shame, and so on. But an ideology that sublimates mourning puts the feared thing—death—outside itself and thus can appear in the form of benign desirability, as in Reagan's speech after the *Challenger* disaster, which constructed the exemplarity of the victims in such a way as to fortify a national commitment to the renewed militarization of space *so that their deaths would not have been in vain*. On October 2, 1988, Rick Hauck, commander of the first manned space mission after the disaster, responded to Reagan's speech in a manner that displayed a full comprehension of the technique of sublimating mourning through emulative exemplification: "Today, up here where the blue sky turns to black, we can say at long last, to Dick, Mike, Judy, to Ron and El, and to Christa and Greg: Dear friends, we have resumed the journey that we promised to continue for you; dear friends, your loss has meant that we could confidently begin anew; dear friends, your spirit and your dream are still alive in our hearts" (San Francisco *Chronicle*, October 3, 1988, Sec. A, pp. 1, 18). Hauck implies that the *Challenger* mission was *Christic* (Christa); the debility of the O-rings was a lurking danger or dark necessity that the earlier mission brought forward and thereby purged,

It is not quite correct to contend that Hegel's Creon wishes to eliminate mourning. Rather, he wishes for sorrow to commence, for the mourner to feel the vastness of her affliction, then to allow that feeling to flow over into the coffer he prepares for it: sublimation is not hostile to, but in fact depends upon, the energy over which it hopes to preside; it is hostile only to certain contrary directions in which the energy might flow. The autonomy of mourning, therefore, lies not in its force of emotionality but rather in its ethical—that is, rational, dialectical, and teleological—channeling of emotion toward the composition of a representation of the dead in his or her singularity. Mourning is consequently a work of consciousness and not of nature. But, Hegel argues, Creon's suppression makes mourning into something that resembles nature—melancholia. By burying Antigone, Creon exiles the inevitable obligation she stands for from the city, even from the surface of the earth, commits it (he hopes) to oblivion, to a deep and unbreachable privatization and exclusion from public discourse that will leave exemplification as the sole standing order of remembrance. Antigone, however, is buried alive, which for Hegel means that Creon cannot eliminate an *Antigone effect* from the polis but can only transform that effect from a dialogical ethical contestant into a mute virulent contagion that haunts public logic without respite or relief—a new historical player, the specter that shadows the end of Sophocles' play in the rapidly burgeoning sequence of new griefs that march inexorably toward Creon's own house and heart. *Now* he understands what mourning was—but too late, because it is that no longer, because he has transformed it into an area of vindictive darkness impenetrable by, and unresponsive to, any ethical lucidity.[9] Rather than dialogue between his

---

enabling a confident new beginning; that this is how we are to remember them, as those who died for us; and the proper form of remembrance is emulation of what are designated as their values, which ensures that *they are not really dead—only the vehicle has dropped away*. It now appears that NASA suppressed evidence that the *Challenger* victims may have survived for some minutes after the explosion, a horrifying possibility that would tend to impede an easy passage into symbolicity. Although he does not discuss mournfulness, Stuart Hall quite persuasively engages the question of desirable ideology in "The Toad in the Garden: Thatcherism among the Theorists," in *Marxism and the Interpretation of Culture*, ed. Cary Nelson and Lawrence Grossberg (Urbana, Ill., 1988), 58–73.

    9. Hegel's theory supplements the explanation of the connection between simulative ideology and intransigent unresponsiveness in Jean Baudrillard, *In the Shadow of the Silent Majorities . . . or the End of the Social*, trans. Paul Foss, Paul Patton, and John Johnston (New York, 1983): "The mass absorbs all the social energy, but no longer refracts it. It absorbs every sign and every meaning, but no longer reflects them. It absorbs all messages and digests them. For every question put to it, it sends back a tautological and

project and another, there is now only his project and a vindictive, relentless force of adulterating resistance, irony:

> Since the community only gets an existence through its interference with the happiness of the Family, and by dissolving [individual] self-consciousness into the universal, it creates for itself in what it suppresses and what is at the same time essential to it an internal enemy—womankind in general. Womankind, the everlasting irony [in the life] of the community—changes by intrigue the universal end of the government into a private end, transforms its universal activity into the work of some particular individual, and perverts the universal property of the state into a possession and ornament for the family.[10]

Hegel's essentializing equation (mourning = ironic perversion = nature = woman) is not at this point in his argument a retraction of his earlier view of mourning as a human and ethical act, because the equation of woman as mourning as irrationality is Creon's creation, the result of his violence, a demonization of women and mourning and not their phenomenologically original condition. Once it is posited that the community can exist only by interfering with the family, that a community that is not universal and totalized is not a community at all, then any perception of individuals as anything other than the state's universal property will necessarily seem cloyed, frivolous, and perverted. As with the American Puritans, anything even simply alongside the errand is a force of declension. With the ascendancy of such reasoning to full power at the end of *Antigone*, all who spoke for mourning are gone, so the undone work manifests itself only as the sociosemiological terrorism of vindictive deformation, odd slants of black light

---

circular response. It never participates. Inundated by flows or tests, it *forms a mass or earth*" (28). Baudrillard acknowledges the connection between this nonparticipation and Hegel's description of melancholia, but he shows little interest in the etiology of melancholia when describing what melancholia is a deranged form *of:* "There would thus be a fantastic irony about 'matter,' and every object of science, just as there is a fantastic irony about the masses in their muteness, or in their statistical discourse so conforming to the questions put to them, akin to the eternal irony of femininity of which Hegel speaks—the irony of a false fidelity, of an excessive fidelity to the law, an ultimately impenetrable simulation of passivity and obedience, and which annuls in return the law governing them, in accordance with the immortal example of the Soldier Schweick" (33; the quotation from Hegel to which Baudrillard refers appears in my text shortly after this note).
    10. Hegel, *Phenomenology of Spirit*, 288. Brackets are the translator's.

that introduce unaccountable fractures into meaning but no longer issue from a discernible ethical source. But though the passage is not a
contradiction of earlier statements when it calls mourning and women
nature, its tone does turn toward Creon in vaunting his premises and
in a certain misogynist horrification. Whatever one Hegel thought
about the ethics of mourning and its demonization is here usurped by
what another Hegel considers necessary in order to move on with the
historical mission of the universal community that Creon has initiated,
an eagerness that mandates a repression of the knowledge of repression,
a hiding of evidence to make the dead seem to have been satisfied and
to have grown irritated with the petty intransigence of women. To be
sure, this second Hegel promises that there will be a moral state that
accounts for, or makes reparation to, the ironic underground, that sublimates without ironic residue; but insofar as the reader is asked to wait
patiently, insofar as a reunion between Antigone's vehement ghost and
a Creon enhanced and edified by his progression through history is not
yet, the resentment of melancholia is presently unappeased, and all the
second Hegel can do is perform uncomfortable closures that fail to sat-
isfy precisely because they transcend by a force of anxious denial rather
than by the sovereign competence of *Aufhebung*, failing to appease a
remainder that Hegel has himself brought forward. When Hegel returns to Antigone in *The Philosophy of Right*, this tonal duplicity will
have been almost entirely remedied by a scrupulous avoidance of the
topic of mourning.[11]

   As an origin destroyed to commence collective spirit's march toward the moral state, Antigone's mourning poses certain problems for
the Hegelian system. The prewar harmony, according to Hegel, was
ethically heterogeneous: it depended on inner disparities remaining latent or demotic, in the form of *both/and* rather than *either/or*. The reconstruction after the war, however, brings disparity into the open by its
contrast with the preceding unity and thereby instigates the work of
mediatory unification, which will replace harmony on a higher level.
But the events of the play—which constrain Hegel precisely because
he knows that he feels himself responding to them so strongly—lead
to questions about the inevitability of seeing disparity as contradiction
instead of as what Paul Zweig calls "a broad miscellaneous esthetic":

11. G. W. F. Hegel, *The Philosophy of Right*, trans. T. M. Knox (Oxford, 1952), 105–
22.

Creon forces disparity into contradiction in pursuit of his desire to preside over a unity with nothing outside itself, so the contradiction that seems to call for the arrival of social unification turns out to have been precipitated by the desire for social unification, a monomania-induced circularity that seriously compromises Hegel's assertion of the necessity and inevitability of the progression.[12] Creon produces conditions he calls crises and then uses them as a mandate, a ploy that suggests it might have been otherwise: the harmony of ethical heterogeneity is not intrinsically or dialectically flawed (as is sense-certainty), not in itself in need of remedial supplementation from above, only vulnerable to the insurgent and intransigent exclusivism of one of its members, the semiosis of the legend. Mourning, therefore, does not fail because of some inadequate theorization that calls for transcendental reformulation but is only defeated, and not even completely. Not a form of naïve satisfaction oblivious to the negative, mourning is an activity of careful reciprocal mediation between representing subject (the mourner) and represented object (the dead) and is thus more dialectical than exemplification, which fits the object to a category ordained before the object is engaged—a procedure Hegel elsewhere calls bad infinitization, the night in which all cows are black. The initial existence and demonized survival of mourning therefore haunt the founding act of the *Phenomenology*'s history of the collective subject, exposing it to view as a form of diminishment and self-aggrandizing repression rather than of dialectical enhancement or improvement. The existence of mourning challenges the core of Hegelian politics: its wishful longing that misery be an edifying passage to a higher stage. Would that it were so; but is such a supposition adequate to what is the case, or is it a flight into a disastrous imagination of remedy?

Hegel's reading of Sophocles is quite revisionary, highlighting some features of the play and overlooking others, extending faint suggestions, at several points adding ideas that are not present in the text; and so too is my reading of Hegel's reading. As he wishes to use *Antigone* as an allegory to reveal certain problems at the foundation of the idea of the moral state, so I wish to use his reading of *Antigone* as a paradigm in order to sketch three points about Puritanism: first, the political importance of typological exemplarism in American Puritan social

12. Paul Zweig, *Walt Whitman: The Making of a Poet* (New York, 1984), 8.

thought; second, the utility of a sublimated mournfulness to the project of Puritan exemplification; and third, the power of a certain kind of lyric moment to shine a rare light into Puritanism's central ideological endeavor.

Puritan studies have for some time now recognized the central importance of typology, the exercise of perceiving persons and events in terms not of their singularity but of abstract spiritual types recurring through history. Puritanism challenged Augustine's belief that sacred history stopped with Christ and asserted its extension into the present. The Protestant critique of Catholic allegorism, in which the concrete vehicle seemed too easily to evaporate into abstraction, resulted not in what we would now see as a realism but in a historical scheme that searched for abstraction realized or actualized in present circumstances: the abstract was concrete; it relinquished its nervous celibacy and organized the world. At its most intense moments, according to Sacvan Bercovitch, American Puritanism postulated that the present instance of the type was not merely a recurrence but the purest and least encumbered actualization of the abstraction, so that history amounted to a series of imperfect adumbrations. In the dual movement that also underlies Hegel's historicism, the past announces and legitimates the present, and the present renders explicit the hidden meaning of the past.[13]

The sophistication and complexity of the typological connections developed by Puritan writers, especially Edward Taylor, have been taken as evidence that the American Puritans did not oppose or fail to feel the power of poetic figurality as such, but instead set bounds within which the operation of figurality was not only permissible but desirable, though Taylor's concealment of his verse reveals the anxiety attendant upon setting and maintaining the border of permissibility.[14] The fear of poetry's slipping into unregulated areas reveals that for the Puritans themselves there was an *outside-of-the-type*, which, though it could be labeled sin or error, was nonetheless a real factor in signification and had considerable force. Responding to this Puritan fear of, or worry over, its other, literary criticism that moves beyond describing the internal structure of typology seems to encounter repeatedly the

13. Sacvan Bercovitch, *The Puritan Origins of the American Self* (New Haven, Conn., 1975).

14. *Cf.* Karen Rowe, *Saint and Singer: Edward Taylor's Typology and the Poetics of Meditation* (Cambridge, Eng., 1986).

question of segments of experience to which the type (but not representation as such) is inadequate. Unwilling to avail themselves of the Puritan thesis that such an apparent experience of the real is merely an illusion produced by sin, twentieth-century critics have clustered in three groups. First, an aesthetic historicism has claimed that the type seems to us to be a coercive representation of reality because we inhabit a wholly different notion of mimesis that we naïvely project back, faulting the type for failing to address our view of what is real. In its most contemporary expression, this stance reappears as American Foucaultianism, with a similarly dismissive contention that the contemporary reader's identificatory involvement with books from periods other than his or her own is a naïve obstacle to be surpassed on the way to a scientific historicism. The antinomy to this new historicism is a new pragmatism that claims that identificatory involvement is the only possibility, that reading cannot even be said to exercise a reductive force against the text because there is no text except insofar as it is construed in its readings. The perfect symmetry of these positions, stressing the impotence and omnipotence of the reader's identification, suggests that they are partners in a system designed to appear to exhaust the field of possibility—to repress the notion of interchange between reader and text, of identification gratified but also blocked, the reader changed by the encounter with the blockage, then returning for a different kind of identification, in a cycle whose repetition is not necessarily terminable. The mutual exclusivity of the two poles in the antinomy seems to sterilize the possibility of reading as dialectical education, a process with several points of resemblance to mourning. Second, the post-Coleridgian Christian existentialism of New Criticism admits the existence of a countervailing experience of the real in Puritan society but sees it as the chaos of physical and social incoherence, which the type opposes with the clarifying redemptiveness of the symbol: the discord between the type and experience is, precisely, the type's intrinsic virtue. Third, a post-sixties social criticism addressing ethnic and gender issues sees the type as a form of ideological slander, deploying images such as those of the Diabolical Indian or Licentious Woman, the Virtuous Savage or compliant Domestic Goodwife, to repress the idea that the other can be extratypoligical and still be a coherent subject—conscious, composed, social, even if not assimilated to Puritanism's restricted view of sociality. Puritanism's uncontained other does not exist, because it is an anachronistic retrojection; or it is redeemed by the type; or it is repressed by the type.[15]

I do not want to adjudicate the relative merits of these critical positions here (because each has descriptive utility according to the text at hand); instead, I want to point out the regularity with which the question of the type raises the question of the inadequation or antithesis between the type and some X. The recurrence of this question in critical studies of Puritanism indicates the intentional structure of the type and its crucial function as a manner of addressing experience by annulling and then absorbing alternate representations of the real. Typology takes up a concrete experience of a person (including oneself), thing, or event, highlights a trait that reveals the referent's participation in a preordained and historically repetitive category, and then declares the referent's other traits (those which might make the referent's emblematicalness seem partial, unimportant, secondary, or derived) to be inconsequential for determining the referent's state of being—at best, pleasantly ornamental; at worst, a blurring or obfuscation of the true. Thus, typology is antithetical not to experience per se but to those aspects of experience that do not confirm it: representation that concerns itself with the other-than-exemplary is lost in the woods, wilderness being for Puritanism an emblem for what is outside emblematicalness; the type annuls wilderness thought in order to edify it, to teach the soul the path for which it has been searching. The discord criticism feels between the type and experience, therefore, results not from the type's unreality or lack of concreteness, its falsehood, but from its insistence on exclusivity and totality, on being the whole story, the only path through the forest of memory. The negational abstraction of the

---

15. My typology of critics of typology is, like Creon's scheme of embodied virtue, exaggerated and reductive: individual critical works mix the three stances and assert by way of tone and emphasis rather than by polemical announcement. For a sample of position 1, see Cecilia Tichi, "Spiritual Biography and the 'Lord's Remembrancers,'" in *The American Puritan Imagination: Essays in Revaluation*, ed. Sacvan Bercovitch (Cambridge, Eng., 1974), 56–76. In an essay in the same volume, after several concessive gestures to position 3, David Minter, echoing the last page of *The Great Gatsby*, concludes with position 2 (see p. 55). Or see Mason I. Lowance, Jr., *The Language of Canaan: Metaphor and Symbol in New England from the Puritans to the Transcendentalists* (Cambridge, Mass., 1980), 295. For a systematic statement of position 3, see Ann Kibbey, *The Interpretation of Material Shapes in Puritanism: A Study of Rhetoric, Prejudice and Violence* (Cambridge, Eng., 1986), which fuses ethnohistory, women's studies, and literary theory to mark out an important new area in Early American studies.

type does not accept the status of being one order of mimesis among others in a socially heterogeneous amalgam but rather insists on its status as representation's final instance, with all the other modes either arrayed in proper subordination below it or improperly straying into forgetfulness, the autonomy of error. If the type were not intentionally antithetical in this manner, it would subside into being a mere member of a heteroglossic array. Because it is intentionally antithetical to the other ways of formulating experience, typology can bid for the sovereign power to be a Protestant version of Plato's science of sciences, to acquire the capacity to assemble discourse into a centered whole, and thereby to accomplish the dream Puritanism extracted from the Tudors, the Stuarts, and the fledgling British bourgeoisie—the creation of a homogeneous social space, but in the case of Puritanism, grounded on manifested spirit rather than on sheer political power, staged personal charisma, or a developed commodity market.

The type, then, mobilizes the Protestant politics of *Aufhebung*, negating not experience but alternate modes for representing experience, preserving what is declared to have been the unconscious essence of each, the ligaments of their connection with truth. The unrest with which literary criticism returns to the question of an experience resistant to typification, therefore, broaches the problem of anti-, non-, or counter-ideology, the problem that vexes Hegel's Creon, who, though he proposes martial and civic, rather than theological, exemplars, nonetheless seems to me to be Hegel's most heartfelt portrait of the discontents of those who preside over the type—and fear that the divine may lie on the side of mourning. When read through Hegel's reading of *Antigone*, the three modes of viewing typology assume positions in a dialectical dramatic structure: insofar as aesthetic history holds that there is no real outside the type for Puritanism, it sees a Creon who has succeeded in extinguishing alternate activity; insofar as it shows that the type has an effective expressivity, it reveals typology's allure as a simulated shortcut for mourning; insofar as the New Critical view posits the antithesis as a darkness, it not only recapitulates Creon's blindness to the coherence of any project except his own, but also correctly discerns the derangement inflicted by the repression of the other. Social criticism's assertion that the other has an intentional structure of its own brings us closest to Antigone's view but often swerves into simplicities of counter-exemplification—especially the exemplum of

Innocent Victim—that render its challenge more like an argument over whether Eteocles or Polyneices was the hero, rather than developing a deep critique of the means by which its opponent's historically triumphant machine works. Such criticism fails, therefore, to apprehend the acute subtlety of stances such as Anne Bradstreet's.

Criticism's inquiry into the dialectical negativity of Puritan typologism follows almost inevitably from the work of Perry Miller, whose allegiance to post-Kierkegaardian negative theology led him away from what was in his time the prevailing view of Puritanism as a static body of dogmatic affect and into the dialectical energetics that he called the marrow of Puritan divinity.[16] According to Miller, the critics with whom he disagreed failed to perceive Puritanism's resolute devotion to Calvin's unknown god. A presence manifested as inscrutable force, known by its turbulent impact on cognition and signification, this god demanded a fealty that in practical consequence resulted in taking all explicit formulations of truth to be flawed and inadequate, however useful for regulating the conduct of ordinary life. God is an interruption of sense. In New England, however, pressed upon by the urgencies of social administration, the Puritans allowed such provisional formulations, sanctioned by the idea of the Covenant, to multiply, to receive considerable emphasis, and to absorb the Puritans' attention so fully that they came to be taken as sufficient articulations of spirit despite lingering perfunctory obeisances to Calvin's abandoned legacy. Thus a figure such as Winthrop is for Miller a melancholy figure, a beautiful soul compelled by his concern for the world to betray his vision; and those critics who associate the marrow of Puritanism with the surrounding bone—the body of ecclesio-social dogma—mistake a nobly tragic adulteration of the thing for the thing itself. The true Puritans, for Miller, are those such as Williams and Edwards who sought to stem or arrest the decline into rationalization and earned exile as payment for their fidelity.

The problem with Miller's argument is that he uses a Kierke-

16. Miller's position is most succinctly stated in "The Marrow of Puritan Divinity," in Miller, *Errand into the Wilderness* (Cambridge, Mass., 1956), 48–98. On Miller's relation to negative theology, see Donald Weber, Introduction to *Jonathan Edwards*, by Perry Miller (Amherst, Mass., 1981), v–xxix. On Miller's challenge to what was the dominant view of Puritanism, see Russel L. Reising, *The Unusable Past: Theory and the Study of American Literature* (New York, 1986), 53–57.

gaardian dialectic to appraise a Hegelian dialectic but often presents the former as if it were the dominant Puritan dialectic. This mingling of appraisal with analytic paraphrase creates certain confusions, for instance in his analysis of declension after the first generation: whereas Puritans such as Increase Mather see declension as a falling-off from the first generation's adequate codification of spirit, Miller sees such codification as itself a falling-off. Miller is therefore wrong, but only at those moments when he represents his thought as a synopsis of mainline American Puritanism rather than as an evaluation from the perspective of a stern but sympathetic critique.

If we fail to make this distinction, we will also fail to understand Puritanism's characteristic attitude toward the type, its Creonism. For Miller, typology's socially regulative intention would reveal it as an expedient device peripherally appended to the fear and trembling that was the marrow, and thus not distinguishable *on theological grounds* from all other such homiletic encodings of eupraxis. Miller's supreme negative would result in a liberal tolerance when it came to distinguishing among definitions of good society, a tolerance that sprang from an indifference toward such lower things. But the American Puritans did not practice liberal tolerance, because for them the negative lay *between*, not above, lesser and greater notions of sociality. The negative was a cancellation of false discourse preparing the way for the sufficient articulation of the true, not a thoroughgoing evacuation of homily, maxim, and example as such. Again, I am neither questioning nor affirming Miller's powerful and lifelong explanation of what he found of value and pathos in Puritanism; rather, I am distinguishing what he found of value in Puritanism from the central attitudes of the Puritan establishment, which did not see the type as a falling-back from the pristine into a recurrence of the excessive literality of the British past but saw the negation of the Church of England as a preliminary moment of the passage into the splendid lucidity of the type and of the holy society it imaged. This distinction is important for our understanding of those who felt the pressure of the type against their mental and discursive representations of their own experience: they did not feel themselves confronted by an order of representation that was confessedly as provisional as their own, equidistant from an unknown god; on the contrary, Puritan exemplarism presented itself to them as the pipe through which the Word arrived, as an order of representation that was their truth, a truth they would acknowledge could they only relinquish their weak eyesight and sickly loves.[17] Extratypological defenses of experience were rare feats, not logical consequences of an epistemologically and semiologically humble concession of the shortcomings of all paradigms. This is why there are so few of them in the literary archive, and why discourse such as that of Anne Hutchinson exists only in court transcripts.

For Puritan theory, then, negation was a passage from inferior wisdom to the perfection illustrated in the type, rather than the ultimate moment of the dialectic. This understanding of the negative is most explicitly represented in Puritan meditations on death, which used mortality as an emblem for the passage into emblematicalness. One's own death, of course, whether immediately or at the last judgment, whether with body intact or not, was a refining event, the shedding of obfuscatory biographical detail in order to reveal the life's stark truth—Elect or Damned?[18] At the ultimate moment, God will not dally with subtle representations, which he will dismiss as evasions and prevarications. More useful, though, for Puritanism's social ambition was the contemplation of the deaths of others, which was made into an occasion for determining their status with respect to exemplarity. In this, Puritanism returns to the Protestant origin: Luther's Ninety-five Theses assailed not just the profiteering motive behind Tetzel's indulgences but also their easing of the purchaser's discomfort at the thought of his own or others' deaths, their reassuring implication that the negative could be placated by something less than a total and meticulous

17. Puritan writers from Winthrop through Cotton Mather took careful note of reports that Anne Hutchinson and her friend Mary Dyer conceived deformed fetuses, and they suggested points of resemblance between the details of the deformity and the tenets of the heresies that these women had entertained before and during the pregnancies. The fetuses, therefore, were emblems of the two women's invisible spiritual states; their bodies told an exemplary truth that their mouths were laboring to disguise; but the truth will out. Cf. Thomas Weld, Preface to *A Short Story of the Rise, reign, and ruine of the Antinomians, Familists & Libertines*, by John Winthrop, in *The Antinomian Controversy, 1636–1638*, ed. David D. Hall (Middlebury, Conn., 1968), 214–15: *"for look as she had vented mishapen opinions, so she must bring forth deformed monsters; and as about 30. Opinions in number, so many monsters; and as those were publike, and not in a corner mentioned, so this is now come to be knowne and famous over all these Churches, and a great part of the world."* This intrusion of divinely composed exemplification, *"as clearly as if he had pointed with his finger,"* must have gratified Weld, Winthrop, and others, in part because the Antinomians had denied that the emulation of examples was of any worth to the soul: *"Error 6: The example of Christs life, is not a patterne according to which men ought to act"* (220).

18. Cf. Michael Wigglesworth's vindictive delight in binaristic clarification at the bar of final judgment in *The Day of Doom*.

reform of the self—personal singularity is the only adequate sacrifice; money is like Cain's vegetables.

The hermeneutic of the type dominates New England biography in the seventeenth century as it had dominated the medieval saints' lives, testing the life against a grid of abstract categories.[19] But the Protestant pressure for actualized types, for a passage out of celibate allegorism by surrounding abstraction with an ambience of concretion and specificity, risked the real to a much greater extent than did the more hermetic saints' lives and thereby embroiled biography in an environment where stray or dissonant constructions were more likely almost endemic. Puritan rhetoric, therefore, required an image of tremendous force to discredit its competitors, an image of death that could avail itself of deepest fears and sorrows to prop up the credibility of an ingenious argumentative circle: the exemplary life worthy of praise was characterized as an unflagging allegiance to higher things and by an indifference to the selfish distractions of personal or other nonspiritualized love. The survivor's intensity of grief, therefore, which was affixed to the singularity of the dead person, turned out to be an infidelity to the gist of what was lovable about the dead person. True remembrance, true mourning, would be an emulation of the exemplarity of the dead and would entail a relinquishing of selfish grief, a feat that would become less difficult once the survivor accepted the contention that his emulation of what is postulated as the essence of the dead in fact preserves the dead. Nothing has died: only the extrinsic vehicle of the virtuous trait, itself inconsequential except as a means of making virtue manifest to enfeebled visions, has dropped away, its mission completed; henceforth, discourse and emulation will replace the dead person as vehicles for what the dead person was. In the manner delineated in Hegel's theory of sublimation, love is not jeopardized directly by the pressure to sublimate. Rather, the almost unimaginably regular arrivals of seventeenth-century American death—epidemic, childbirth, starvation, war—yielded an incessant call for grieving, a torrent of loose energy that ideology then diverted from its intrinsic course toward intense identifications with the values it proposes. This diversion succeeds not primarily because *it* is intimidating but because *death* is intimidating, because it claims not to negate desire but to negate the negation of desire *post haste*, to supply a vantage or Pisgah from which to see that

19. *Cf*. Bercovitch, *Puritan Origins*, 1–34.

all that is of worth survives here, not just in heaven, through concrete activity in service to the *ecclesia-polis*, that only what is of *no matter* drops away. Puritanism bridges mournfulness and the state by way of a desirably repressive sublimation of the mournful response to the undesirably repressive force death exerts against desire. Mourning is not a thing one desires to do, though it does eventuate in a personally credible restoration of the ability to desire—a bridge that is Puritanism's major bequest to American psychopolitics, however much the values exemplified may change. From Whitman's direction of elegiac teleology toward the assertion that "there never was death but it led forward life" to the addresses in the wake of the Challenger disaster, grief has been one of the major resources of consensus formation.[20]

And grief has therefore been one of the major grounds of contest in American renegade or recusant literature, from Ishmael at Mapple's sermon, later rescued by the mournful Rachel; through Emerson's sharply tortured "Experience" and Dickinson's verse;[21] in Huckleberry Finn's lonely thanatos and the implacable derision Twain aims at the sentimental ennoblement Emmeline Grangerford's odes confer on the brutality of the feud; in the anomalous sad wonder of *The Country of the Pointed Firs*, to Marilynne Robinson's *Housekeeping* and Toni Morrison's *Beloved*. If such works are predominantly, but not exclusively, produced by women, this may be the result of a domestic ideology that assigns stereotyped mourning to women in a gender division of labor but thereby inadvertently risks an opening of the critical potential of a

20. On representations of death, funeral sermons, and funerary practices in American Puritan society, see Bercovitch, *Puritan Origins*, 6; Gordon E. Geddes, *Welcome Joy: Death in Puritan New England* (Ann Arbor, Mich., 1981); David E. Stannard, *The Puritan Way of Death: A Study in Religion, Culture, and Social Change* (Oxford, 1977); David H. Watters, *"With Bodilie Eyes": Eschatological Themes in Puritan Literature and Gravestone Art* (Ann Arbor, Mich., 1981), Allan I. Ludwig, *Graven Images: New England Stonecarving and its Symbols, 1650–1815* (Middletown, Conn., 1966); and Ronald A. Bosco, ed., *New England Funeral Sermons* (Delmar, N.Y., 1978), Vol. IV of Bosco, ed., *The Puritan Sermon in America, 1630–1750*, 4 vols. (Bosco's introduction is quite shrewd). In a recent work on Melville and mourning in antebellum America, Neal L. Tolchin identified the centrality of a blocking and channeling of mourning in genteel culture and the consequent production of an underground melancholia (*Mourning, Gender and Creativity in the Art of Herman Melville* [New Haven, Conn., 1988]). Tolchin's extensive and perspicacious investigation of Melville's America suggests to me that sentimentalism is a reappearance of the Puritan sublimation of mourning, promoting quite different social values but availing itself of Puritanism's legacy of social technique.

21. Cf. Sharon Cameron, "Representing Grief: Emerson's 'Experience,'" *Representations*, No. 15 (Summer, 1986), 15–41.

mournfulness not tamed by exemplarity: being confined to an area, as Hegel argued in his investigation of the consciousness of the Slave, one is more apt to find the circumscribed terrain's secret places than is the Master who simply looks at the map.[22] In such works, there is no quick passage from grief to sublimated identification with socially stipulated values, but there is an insistence on the ethical and emotionally necessary task of a prolonged and painful construction of the dead in what was experienced as its complexity. Such arts of memory are not specimens of sentimental antiquarianism, though they involve sentiment, but instead preventions of melancholia, the mute remainder of the obligation left after sublimation has taken what it needs. Characteristically, American grieving literature does not simply rebuff ideology, because it feels the deep and seemingly salvific allure of the circle of emulation, but rather postpones it, reducing it to the status of a possible future for the text's present tense, quarantines that future, so that the present of the literary act is protected as a place for engaging the work of mourning. To borrow Heidegger's phrase, the grieving text occupies the anomalous or mutant temporality of no-more/not-yet, the sheer experience of what Nietzsche called "time and its it was." Instead of positing a contrary exemplarity, it aims its criticality at the central operational premises of exemplification. Thus, the grieving text drags its heels, procrastinates in the face of a looming future, and avoids getting caught up in the velocity of a rhetoric nervously aware that the mourner might realize that the exemplary image of the dead is at best an allegory, a personification of a catachresis, rather than a full representation; at best, a crude foreshadowing of what the mourner seeks to construct. If this nonexemplarity does not oppose ideological projects

22. Cf. "Independence and dependence of self-consciousness: Lordship and Bondage," in Hegel, *Phenomenology of Spirit*, 111–19, and Alexandre Kojève's revisionary explication in *Introduction to the Reading of Hegel: Lectures on the Phenomenology of Spirit*, trans. James H. Nichols, Jr., ed. Allan Bloom (New York, 1969). See also Georg Lukács, *History and Class Consciousness: Studies in Marxist Dialectics*, trans. Rodney Livingstone (Cambridge, Mass., 1971), 83–222. Hegel, Kojève, and Lukács argue, not that those consigned to the slave position are better off, but that they are more likely loci of insight because they are denied participation in fantasias of mastery as well as basic social and material rights. In the consignment of stereotyped mourning to women, the purpose is presumably to effect a specular localization in one gender of the powerlessness that mourning necessarily implies, so that the other gender can enjoy a deluded feel of final competence. The slave's lucidity is, however, not inevitable, because exclusion can prompt an intensely energetic quest to secure mastery or access to the heavenly heart of whiteness, as in *The Great Gatsby* or in *Native Son* before Bigger's imprisonment.

with the force of a clear stance or course of action, its hesitations are nonetheless significant because they call into question fundamental means of clarification: nonexemplarity insists that there was a real that was other than what is said to have been and thereby preserves the possibility of subsequent counter-exemplifications where there would otherwise only have been, on the one hand, an order of exemplification seemingly coterminous with life itself and, on the other hand, the aimless, ironic, incessantly retributive fury of melancholia, as in Gilman's "The Yellow Wallpaper."

Grieving literature thus unveils the anxiety subtending much of the precipitous velocity of American society, a velocity inaugurated in part by the Puritan funeral sermon, which mentions grief and the singularity of the dead very briefly, as it must, to conjure the energy it seeks to use, then makes haste to exemplification, a more loquacious, leisurely, and expansive cataloging of the virtues displayed during the life just ceased. A similar hastiness pervades the funeral sermon's major generic ally, the poetic elegy, the most common sort of poem in seventeenth-century New England. The linguistic stylization of the elegy mimics death by interrupting prose discourse, signaling the transcendence that is the poem's concern—a meticulously explained transcendence whose emulability is enhanced by the poem's metrical memorizability, its capacity to remain etched in thought despite the vicissitudes of subsequent attention.[23] Poetry's power to break from the currents of the prosaic and to leave a durable mark vanquishes quotidian discourses, which are to disappear without significant remainder, like the body of the dead. The formal and rhetorical devices of the sermon and the poem speed representation to a high plateau, an elevated city, a site of carefully extricated contemplation in the pure sun of wisdom.

My intention here is not to explicate Anne Bradstreet's work at length (which has been done quite well) but instead to outline its importance as one of the founding episodes of American mournful literature.[24] Bradstreet's early poetry, collected in the first edition of *The Tenth Muse Lately Sprung Up in America* (1650), is not Puritan in either

23. I am here drawing on an as-yet-unpublished essay by Eva Cherniavsky, "Night Pollution and the Floods of Confession in Michael Wigglesworth's Diary."

24. See Anne Stanford, *Anne Bradstreet: The Worldly Puritan* (New York, 1974), Wendy Martin, *An American Triptych: Anne Bradstreet, Emily Dickinson, Adrienne Rich* (Chapel Hill, N.C., 1984), Anne Stanford and Pattie Cowell, eds., *Critical Essays on Anne Bradstreet* (Boston, 1983), and Adrienne Rich, Foreword to *The Works of Anne Bradstreet*, ed. Jeannine Hensley (Cambridge, Mass., 1967), ix–xxi.

matter or manner, but it is markedly exemplaristic. The bulk of the volume is taken up by her "Quaternions" ("The Four Elements," "The Four Humours," "The Four Seasons," "The Four Ages of Man," and "The Four Monarchies"), the first four of which use Renaissance "characters" or allegorical types as dramatis personae in various quarrels concerning their relative excellences that were to have added up to an encyclopedic schematic representation of the sum of human and natural phenomena—not to be taken as science but to be admired for its inclusive virtuosity. The poem reduces concrete phenomena to the instances of either one of the types or one of the quarrels, and thus promotes itself as (to use Baudrillard's term) a total simulation, a Renaissance compendium, a poetic replacement for the world.[25] A catalog of abstract personified attributes deployed across a three-dimensional and geometrically symmetrical armature with all the diagonals accounted for, the poems of "The Quaternions" assimilate reality to a rigorous scheme, though the components of the scheme were secular personae such as Choler rather than Puritan types such as the Reprobate Woman Writer. The verse, however non- or anti-Puritan and however consequently threatening to Puritan representation's aspiration to exclusivity, bids to compete with Puritanism (as well as with other poetic encyclopedias such as du Bartas' *Week of Creation*) on its own terms of transcendent mimesis, vies with Puritanism to be an equally (or more) imaginative (if not virtuous) feat of abstraction without significant unprocessed remainder. Bradstreet hoped that success in this encyclopedic venture would render her exemplary, again, not in Puritan terms, but as a member of a canon, a model poet such as she saw Spenser and du Bartas to be, a splended specimen of the energetic poetic traits she found outlined in Sidney's *Defence of Poesy*. Affiliating herself with the only conception of achievement available in her cultural repertoire that had the prestige and legitimation necessary to rival or at least stand alongside Puritanism, a conception of discursive performance that seemed to offer greater range to her imagination and a greater tolerance for her gender, Bradstreet expected that the more completely she demonstrated her prowess at composing a system of explanatory "characters," the more thoroughly she would show herself

25. Jean Baudrillard, *Simulations*, trans. Paul Foss, Paul Patton, and Philip Beitchman (New York, 1983), especially 83–92, on the Renaissance aesthetic of the counterfeit. See Michel Beaujour, "Genus Universum," *Glyph: Textual Studies*, VII (1980), 15–31, on the theoretical axioms of Renaissance encyclopedias.

to be the Sidneyan Poet, rather than the often sick, melancholy, and helpless being who speaks in the various short lyrics that were written during this period but were for the most part excluded from the first volume. And she seems to have succeeded, though the laudatory remarks of figures such as Nathaniel Ward and Cotton Mather are etched with anxiety, perhaps because her rather dour father, Thomas Dudley, sometime governor of Massachusetts who was remembered in large measure for having been considered too strict by John Winthrop, found poetic composition morally permissible, having himself apparently composed a poem entitled "The Four Corners of the World" (since lost).[26] This "first Bradstreet," then, is attempting to hold Puritan mimesis at a distance, to clear a space of uninfected thought, to legitimate an order of composition not coordinated with her society's dominant moral significations; but her device for performing this sequestration mimics what it resists in its sovereign indifference toward the singularities of the real, in its commitment to escaping by outdoing.

Such a definition of achievement is as inclined toward exclusivity and as disinclined to mutuality and heterogeneous two-way exchange as is the Puritan doctrine of *sola scriptura*. Although Bradstreet's voice continually mediates among the aggressive voices of the characters within the universe she controls, mediation between this universe and others is unlikely. If the mark of the Poet's achievement is ultimate comprehensiveness and mimetic finality, how can there be several poetic encyclopedias? There could only be either a not-yet-decided contest or a victor whose example demotes the others to being more-or-less inferior prefigurations of, or afterwords to, the one. The inevitable propulsion of her idea of sufficient achievement toward exclusivity seems to have worried her to an increasing degree as her career developed, as she perceived her axioms moving toward their ineluctable consequences. The fifth "Quaternion," "The Four Monarchies," itself a violation of the shapely "four by four" she had initially projected, relinquishes the compositional principles she had observed in its predecessors: none of the monarchies has a clear character distinct from the other three; and none of them, therefore, is amenable to personifica-

26. See Augustine Jones, *The Life and Work of Thomas Dudley, the Second Governor of Massachusetts* (Boston, 1900), and Elizabeth Wade White's thorough and insightful biography, *Anne Bradstreet: The Tenth Muse* (New York, 1971). The values expressed by Sidney seemed to Bradstreet to be more respectful of the example of Elizabeth I than did Puritanism.

tion, to voicing its superiority over the rest.[27] Rather than a dialogic mediation of speaking emblems within the work, "The Four Monarchies" is a meandering annal of history as incessant, violent tyranny, a work that draws cynicism from Raleigh's *History of the World* and echoes tonally with the weary despair of Jacobean revenge tragedy and the seventeenth-century *Trauerspiel*.[28] Strung together by the parataxis of the list rather than by a tight plan, "The Four Monarchies" is an unfinishable and wrecked poem, not because Bradstreet's talent or interest flags, but because she has come across the role of exclusivistic ambition in wrecking the world. The ambition that propelled the first four "Quaternions" has been almost entirely expurgated from Bradstreet's motivation to reappear as an object of representation—the supreme and splendid homicides, the insatiable and uncontrollable acquisitiveness of figures such as Alexander or Semiramis with her four-gated city (an allegory for Bradstreet's own quadrilaterals, the formidable space she had sought to protect against the force of external encroachment but now perceived as not different in kind from the encroachment). Her critique of Puritan exclusivism has been transformed into a critique of exclusivism per se, of its proclivity toward hermeneutic if not actual violence—into a perception that such desire results not in the temple or palace of the whole but in continually unbalanced reciprocities of senseless force, in history as concussion. Each of the monarchies—Assyrian, Persian, Greek, and Roman—like all the tyrants that make them up, equals no more than the current redundant avatar in a sequence of sterilizations; history is reduced to the repetition of wreckage, and the only transitions the poem can manage are on the order of "and then there was . . ." Most importantly, the poem holds out little promise that the arrival of Christianity, Protestantism, or Congregationalism will redeem history.[29]

This depressed vision—depressed by the dwindled but lingering

27. It might at first seem that the Sidneyan emphasis on personal achievement was even more exclusionary than was Puritanism, because it precluded the idea of a collective subject of sovereign representation. However, Bradstreet's knowledge of the sorts of division that arose within Puritanism after it moved past its early oppositional solidarity—the arguments between Winthrop and Dudley, the Antinomian crisis, the English Civil War—and American Puritanism's dependence on acts of exclusion (such as the antifeminism whose force she felt) to rejuvenate a sensation of collective subjectivity would have revealed Puritanism's equally strong proclivity toward egoistic atomization.

28. See Walter Benjamin, *The Origin of German Tragic Drama*, trans. John Osborne (London, 1977).

29. We can only speculate about whether Bradstreet's poem alludes to Fifth Monarchism, a splinter group to the left of Congregationalism, which held that Cromwell's

allure of the tyrants—arises from Bradstreet's perception that her defense of poetry was complicit in the demand she was defending against, and it calls for a new ground on which to mark off an unassimilated space. A matter of dismay as it gains expression in "The Four Monarchies," the transformation of secular exemplarism from a mode of ambition into an object of scrutiny may arise from her internal pursuit of the logic of her desire, perhaps from news of political violence such as the Antinomian debacle, the English Civil War, or the Thirty Years War, perhaps from personal traumas such as the death of her father, or from meditation and event intertwined.[30] Whatever the source, the poems written after the publication of the first edition are in the main markedly briefer (though she continues to work at the manuscript of "The Four Monarchies" and to revise earlier poems), less taken with the ingenious construction of impersonal personae, and more preoccupied with moral theology where their predecessors had played with the secular psychology of humoral character.

Bradstreet criticism seems to me to be about evenly divided on the question of whether the later poems are devout or ironically satirical with respect to Puritan moralism, a division that suggests that interrogating them for an unequivocal stance regarding such morality may be a misguided means of approach. In one of her few theological allegories, "A Dialogue Between the Flesh and the Spirit," before commencing the verbal duel between the two voices, Bradstreet presents a nonallegorical voice—presumably her own, Bradstreet as concrete person rather than president of the work—as she who overheard the dialogue and locates itself "on the banks of the lacrim flood."[31] If Flesh and Spirit represent two ways of rendering experience lucid to abstraction, the quiet initial voice positions itself between these paradigms, on the location of grief: the unabashed hedonism of Flesh is no longer cogent because Flesh is rather brashly oblivious to the streaks that failure and death put through life; the easy transcendentality of Spirit is not fully compelling because its harsh and insulting dismissals of other-than-transcendent love are too easy and oblivious—Spirit slides too rapidly and opportunistically from love's precariousness to a denunci-

---

commonwealth, like the Church of England, was a lingering trace of the Roman monarchy, and that Christ's Fifth Monarchy was still to come. See Christopher Hill, *The World Turned Upside Down: Radical Ideas During the English Revolution* (New York, 1975), and Bernard Capp, *The Fifth Monarchy Men: A Study in Seventeenth-Century Millenarianism* (London, 1972).

30. This possibility was suggested to me by Wendy Martin.

31. Hensley, ed., *Works of Anne Bradstreet*, 215–18.

ation of its odiousness. Spirit's view has allure, because it suggests both that what is lost need not be mourned since it was not worth loving to begin with and that future restrictions of affection will transfer love to higher things that are more durable if not vastly more qualitatively desirable. However, this allure is not sufficient for the tone of the poem, an unrest that lingers between the dead and an exemplary representation of the dead that is a possible, but not an inevitable, outcome for the poem's present tense. Bradstreet thus constitutes the anomalous time of the grieving voice, of a subjectivity that might become exemplary before it has become so, a time of waiting and a pre-Puritanism, Puritanism's human material, a complex field in which exemplification is not the master voice but a contestant, an option under consideration.

Bradstreet's elegiac verse, then, is engaged in setting out the conditions exemplification must meet to gain allegiance.[32] To this end, the poem is composed as an act of concrete mournful memory, exploring the overdetermination and manifold reality of the lost in order to set the terms for an adequate hermeneutic, what it would have to tally with to establish its credibility and to avail itself of the energy it desires. Bradstreet was fully aware of the generic specifications of the Puritan elegy: her poem written after the death of Dorothy Dudley, her mother, though heartfelt and showing more stylistic competence than is usual in such poems, where an overingenious attenuation often prevails, is a simple list of abstract attributes defining the pious wife and mother and an assertion that the mother will be best remembered as someone who met all the criteria. But her other late elegies reverse the direction of demand: the mourner no longer fits memory to generic requirements but now requires genre to demonstrate its suitability to what is remembered. Such poems are not moral and generic but are

32. For an opposed view, see Timothy Sweet, "Gender, Genre, and Subjectivity in Anne Bradstreet's Early Elegies," *Early American Literature*, XXIII (1988), 152–74. For Sweet, the early poems represent a vigorous attempt to constitute an unprecedented female writing subject, whereas "most of her later poems are written from within a discourse of domesticity and display an acceptance of the 'woman's place' " (168). Consequently, "while these poems are good of their kind, they are comfortable and unproblematic in terms of their acceptance of the gender system" (169). This vision of Bradstreet's career as a falling away from, rather than a further refinement of, the vigor of the early challenge seems to me wrong. Sweet defends the early verse by accepting a certain early/late//either/or and then reversing the commonplace critical valuation of the late. I would prefer to see the late as a dialectical development from the early that maintains the vigor of the early in a more profound register: *genuine expression*, though a heavily laden term with a checkered ideological career, is not therefore necessarily without worth.

about morality and genre. They do not conclude whether exemplification will or will not pass the test, because in the raw freshness of new
loss the work of mournful memory is only commenced, and exemplification has to wait until its test has been prepared. Bradstreet's elegies
therefore contest Puritanism, not with equally lucid and sufficient abstractions, but with the strength of a confusion, an allegiance to remains, and an insistence that the dialectic prove its claim to annul nothing of merit, to preserve the sum of what is worth remembering.

By putting typology on probation, Bradstreet composes an archi-
val memory of an extra-exemplary experience that actually existed
(contrary to the claim, made by aesthetic or Foucaultian history, that
Puritans simply saw in types). Furthermore, this experience is not automatically in need of redemption by the imaginative triumphalism of
Puritan ideology; Bradstreet does not permit the thought of the transient to slide into a moral representation of chaos.[33] The radicalism of
her constitution of a real in the poem of mourning does not put her *to
the left of* Puritanism in a counter-ideology such as Familism or Anti-
nomianism—this is not a defense of Polyneices' political virtue. But by
representing a real in the poem of mourning, Bradstreet puts exemplification on trial and asserts the existence of a piece of complex sociality—between the mourner and the dead—that a counter-ideology
would require in order to have something to correspond to, though it
would be subject in turn to a similar test of adequacy. Bradstreet's challenge is therefore not purely a resort to irony, the force of deformation
that Hegel associates with melancholia, with mourning forestalled and
preempted. Her challenge has a positive content, if not a stance or
thesis, and consequently it is not condemned to being a marauding
vacuity. Furthermore, it would not be entirely individualistic or private, though it is lyric, because the composition of the poem is an exemplary act of anti-exemplarism, a well-plotted and edifying example
of how one might mourn that does not mandate form, content, or pace,
a public acknowledgement and legitimation of the right and necessity
of mourning.[34]

Bradstreet's boldest defense of mourning is, I think, "Some

33. *Cf.* Martin, *An American Triptych*, 46: "For [Bradstreet], an attachment to earthly
existence is vain only because it does not last."
34. On the compatibility between lyric voice and social criticism, see Abdul
JanMohamed, Preface to *Salutes and Censors*, by Dennis Brutus (Trenton, N.J., forthcom-
ing).

Verses Upon the Burning of Our House, July 10, 1666," because the lost object of love is here a thing rather than a person.[35] Disengagement from the lost thus seems easier, and the pressure to view lingering attachment as a senseless willfulness is correspondingly greater: the physical structure cannot be viewed as a bearer of virtue, affection cannot surreptitiously love the real under the cover of rendering homage to its exemplarity, and grief is less focused because a house is replaceable whereas a person is not. But, Bradstreet will argue, not *this* house: another house will duplicate this one's function as shelter, but not the load of life and family memory this one bears. Just as with, for instance, a dead grandchild, the notion of either heavenly or mundane replaceability presumes fungibility, which in turn presumes the essential equality of the lost with something else under the sign of a categorial being, essentially a repudiation of its singularity. The doctrine of compensatory consolation promises a surrogate that, though not unwelcome, is not equal to what is lost, and the doctrine therefore must be supplemented with a systemic derision of what remains unduplicated in the surrogate. The poem struggles to hold at bay this derision.

Bradstreet begins with an episode of fright, the intrusion of vacuum into a world that had shortly before been *replete:*

> In silent night when rest I took
> For sorrow near I did not look
> I wakened was with thund'ring noise
> And piteous shrieks of dreadful voice.
> That fearful cry of "Fire!" and "Fire!"
> Let no man know is my desire.
> I, starting up, the light did spy,
> And to my God my heart did cry
> To strengthen me in my distress
> And not to leave me succourless.
> Then, coming out, beheld a space
> The flame consume my dwelling place.

She dramatically reconstructs the emotional density of the time of the blow, the heart pointing back to what it is rapidly learning is no more and forward to some imaginable redemption that will negate the event's

---

35. Hensley, ed., *Works of Anne Bradstreet*, 292–93.

negativity and restore whatever plenitude she felt upon going to sleep: what was "dwelling"? and what could "succor" possibly be? The desire that the disaster *not be*, or that it prove to be of little consequence, moves the voice onward, off the thought of the loss, into a homiletic rationalization that displays the mechanistic sententiousness of the orthodox Puritan elegy:

> And when I could no longer look,
> I blest his name that gave and took,
> That laid my goods now in the dust.
> Yea, so it was, and so 'twas just.
> It was his own, it was not mine,
> Far be it that I should repine.
> He might of all justly bereft
> But yet sufficient for us left.

She enters this zone of dogma not simply from a sense of ought or from a fear of tempting renewed disaster by complaining but also from desire, because dogma will lay the event to rest, restore the sensations of regularity and trust that are part of an experience of home, remake living into an unruffled surface—obviate the need for "repining." But the heart's other vector, pointed toward the lost, is not appeased. The inertly repetitive recitation of maxims indexes the presence of an unconvinced segment of herself that needs preaching to, a segment that returns to voice in the ambiguity of the last couplet's verb: he *did* leave us something that is sufficient (religious consolations); or he *might* have left us something that was sufficient (a large part of the house unburned) but chose *not to do so* and destroyed it all. The ambiguity turns precisely on the unanswered question, what *suffices*?

The tonally subtle resentment expressed in the second option brings forward an antithetical voice that proceeds to do what shortly before had been declared unnecessary—repine:

> When by the ruins oft I past
> My sorrowing eyes aside did cast,
> And here and there the places spy
> Where oft I sat and long did lie:
> Here stood that trunk, and there that chest,
> There lay the store I counted best.

> My pleasant things in ashes lie,
> And them behold no more shall I.

The day after the disaster and the days after that, Bradstreet tours the ruins, her eyes turned aside, looking away from theological renderings of the event in order to permit the progression of pangs that will at some future point culminate in a sufficient representation of the life for which the house had been a rich vehicle. (Among the pangs may have been the thought of the loss of the manuscript of an extended version of "The Four Monarchies," perhaps referred to in the phrase "the store I counted best.")

But this intervening time is the time of the ghost, the time of memory reaching an intensity that seems to equal presence only to collide with the knowledge of absence. The sheer pain of this prolonged series of alternating phantasmal gratifications and disturbances by fact threatens to extend into an infinite future, replaying rather than tempering the first agony. The pain thus prompts her to a renewed desire to terminate mourning, this time with blunt negatives instead of rationalizing aphorisms:

> Under thy roof no guest shall sit,
> Nor at thy table eat a bit.
> No pleasant tale shall e'er be told,
> Nor things recounted done of old.
> No candle e'er shall shine in thee,
> Nor bridegroom's voice e'er heard shall be.
> In silence ever shalt thou lie,
> Adieu, Adieu, all's vanity.

The harsh dismissiveness of the last clause bespeaks her desire to close the book on mourning, to clarify and so to be able to disregard the event, to go on to some life governed by something besides pertinacious memory. But the overinsistent iteration of the negatives (like the *no more* of "Lycidas" and the *nevermore* of "The Raven"), the incipiently idolatrous apostrophe both to the house and to the part of her that is with the house, the obvious love for the personal past that is our only real possession (despite the predatory alienability that is exemplification's founding premise), and the emphasis on transience rather than

moral demerit all keep faith with the insistence of mourning in the face
of the desire to escape.

Escape, therefore, will require a more formidable and yahwistic
means of dismissal:

> Then straight I 'gin my heart to chide,
> And did thy wealth on earth abide?
> Didst fix thy hope on mold'ring dust?
> The arm of flesh didst make thy trust?
> Raise up thy thoughts above the sky
> That dunghill mists away may fly.

The reduction of the lost to dung, an imaginative preemption of the
obliviating power of physical decay, readies the stage for a view of adequate substitutability:

> Thou hast a house on high erect,
> Framed by that mighty Architect,
> With glory richly furnished,
> Stands permanent though this be fled.
> It's purchased and paid for too
> By Him who hath enough to do.
> A price so vast as is unknown
> yet by His gift is made thine own;
> There's wealth enough, I need no more,
> Farewell, my pelf, farewell my store.
> The world no longer let me love,
> My hope and treasure lies above.

In a maximal typological act, the loss of the house is likened to Christ's
relinquishing of his body, an utter agony but an utterly necessary agony that purges the true of its encumbering vehicle in order to show it
in its pristine state. When the type invades the dialogue between the
antitheses of feeling, mourning becomes synonymous with a regret that
would have hidden Christ from humanity, letting history go its way
without a beacon. Mourning becomes a profoundly unconscionable in-
gratitude and a monumental selfishness—a threat to the revelation of
being. The objects to which it clings are "pelf," stolen goods, fetishes.

But they are also "store," a concrete transcript of personal history, of her life as it was rather than as a rationalized echo with an ancient misery. The replacement of "pelf" by "store" recalls mourning from its inhumation in the crypt to which the type assigns it, signifying in a packed word her procedure of having composed a manner of living, and helping to instigate the task of now patiently closing up or putting away that life. The familial is thus still present to memory, not under the Puritan conceptions of domestic virtuous economy and their various relations of authority and subordination, but as a mode of the social and the human with modest intrinsic dignity requiring hermeneutic respect and sophistication from any candidate that would seek to represent the extent and meaning of the loss. If the familial life recalled in mourning does not assail the theocratic state's adjunct image of the patriarchal authoritarian family with an equally complete ideological reconceptualization of the family, mourning at least remembers that there is something else, that ideology and sociality are not isomorphic.

Bradstreet's protection of the memory of a social reality against the encroachments of aspirants to ontologization results, in "Contemplations," in a thoroughgoing critique of exemplarity.[36] Several natural and human entities are proposed as emblems for divine might, only to be exposed as frail and partial things in contrast with an intrasigently mysterious force that scores all things with their brevity. The process of contemplation, therefore, is a matter of considering possible types but then realizing that they are products of fancy or of human figuration rather than of a figurality that a covenant god built into the order of things. Bradstreet's career thus comes round to a version of Miller's negative theology, to a centralization of awe, but with an important difference: instead of an accent on the ways in which divinity is sullied by attempts to embody it in rational vehicles, the consequence of awe for Bradstreet is that the real is released from the task of being vehicular—riddled by mortalities without relief or appeal, but pervaded by numerous incomparable aesthetic and emotional singularities, such as the strikingly direct erotic love she expresses in her poems for her husband, which operate at such a level of intensity as to render both Simon Bradstreet's public exemplarity (Husband, Father, Governor) and Puritan conceptions of the proprieties of marital service and subordination *beside the point.*[37]

36. *Ibid.*, 204.
37. *Ibid.*, 261–62, 265–66.

"Authority without wisdom," Bradstreet wrote in one of the meditations she composed for her children, "is like a heavy axe without an edge: fitter to bruise than to polish."[38] This homily expresses succinctly the vision her literary development reached, the demand that the representations of experience upon which power bases itself be wise, that is, adequate to the real, however desirable it might be to accept without question. If such skepticism fails to present a coherently defined challenge, this failure perhaps results less from timidity than from what Bradstreet had come to see at the end of the aspiration to transcendental representativity—not an inclusive and pacifying sunlight but either the incoherence of uncommunicating ambitions or the forced coherence of a supremacist social epistemology. In order to impede movement along these disastrous trajectories, Bradstreet sought to preserve an area of the real, not a zone free of ideological determinations or fully informed by a lucid alternative to Puritan domination, but an aggregate of experience recalled at a pitch that precludes the ability to subsume it, that recalls what was, which is hard to do even if you can remember how to do it.

38. *Ibid.*, 274.

# Romance and the Prose of the World
## Hegelian Reflections on Hawthorne and America

• • • • • • • • • • • • • • • • • • •

*Joseph G. Kronick*

Commentators from Alexis de Tocqueville to Henry James have described America as a prosaic nation, a characteristic that, according to James, leads to the production of a second-rate literature—romance. James is not alone in associating prosaism with romance; Hegel maintains that "a romance in the modern sense of the word presupposes a world already prosaically ordered."[1] For Hegel and, as we will see, for James, romance is a compensation for a world bereft of the historical richness necessary for art. Critics have since argued that romance is the exemplary American genre, one whose self-reflexive form calls attention to its own mode of representation.[2] American literature has been particularly receptive to theories of reflexivity because the questions of

1. G. W. F. Hegel, *Aesthetics: Lectures on Fine Art*, trans. T. M. Knox (2 vols.; Oxford, 1975), II, 1092, hereinafter cited in the text as *HA*. The following abbreviations will be used for citations of Hegel's works: *FK—Faith and Knowledge: The Reflective Philosophy of Subjectivity*, trans. and ed. Walter Cerf and H. S. Harris (Albany, N.Y., 1977); *Logic—Hegel's Logic, Being Part One of the Encyclopedia of the Philosophical Sciences*, trans. William Wallace (1873; rpr. Oxford, 1975); *LPR—Lectures on the Philosophy of Religion*, trans. R. F. Brown, P. C. Hodgson, and J. M. Stewart, and ed. Peter C. Hodgson (3 vols.; Berkeley, 1984–87); *LWH—Lectures on the Philosophy of World History. Introduction: Reason in History*, trans. H. B. Nisbet (Cambridge, Eng., 1975); *PM—Philosophy of Mind, Being Part Three of the Encyclopedia of the Philosophical Sciences*, trans. William Wallace, *Zusätze*, trans. A. V. Miller (Oxford, 1971); *PR—Philosophy of Right*, trans. T. M. Knox (1952; rpr. Oxford, 1967); *PS—Phenomenology of Spirit*, trans. A. V. Miller (Oxford, 1977).

2. For representative arguments for the self-reflexivity of romance, see Charles Feidelson, Jr., *Symbolism and American Literature* (Chicago, 1953), Richard Poirier, *A World Elsewhere: The Place of Style in American Literature* (London, 1967), and Richard H. Brodhead, *Hawthorne, Melville and the Novel* (Chicago, 1976). Despite the critiques of formalism in the wake of post-structuralism, theories of self-reflexivity still dominate discussions of American fiction. See John Irwin, *American Hieroglyphics: The Symbol of the Egyptian Hieroglyphics in the American Renaissance* (New Haven, Conn., 1980). I do not wish to imply that all these authors' arguments are the same nor that they are in any way to be denigrated for their emphasis on the literariness of Romantic fiction.

national identity and the past have led to the ideology of a self-created and self-sustaining nation. "American" literature, according to this tradition, is a self-engendered work that is at once object and concept, or the text that bears within itself the marks of its own production. We might say that the self-reflexive text mirrors (the representation of) the idea of America as a self-created nation.

Modernist theories of self-reflection, such as T. S. Eliot's concept of the autotelic text, or the work that refers to nothing outside itself, provided the impetus for characterizing American literature as nonreferential and self-reflexive.[3] This coupling of nonreferentiality with self-reflexivity indicates the confusion of referentiality with representation. Reference is properly understood as deixis, or the act of pointing or indicating in words. Emile Benveniste has shown that rather than provide a foundation for referentiality, deixis reveals that indicators, such as *I* and *you* or *here* and *now*, refer not to any object or reality in space and time but to the unique instance of the utterance that contains them. Deixis deprives language not only of the hard tangibility of reference but also of its self-referential capacity, since discourse is always dependent on what is outside it—there would be no reason to indicate or refer if language contained the object of reference.[4]

This confusion of referentiality and representation, we can conclude, forms the basis of ideology. "What we call ideology," writes Paul de Man, "is precisely the confusion of linguistic with natural reality, of reference with phenomenalism."[5] When this confusion takes the form of the self-reflection, the belief in language's ability to render what is outside it is replaced by the belief it can render what is internal to it: consciousness. If we are to address the problems of representation and ideology, we must begin by reassessing the proximity of the concept of literature, with its roots in aesthetics, to a philosophy of reflection. We can begin such a critique of what we may call the aesthetic ideology of reflection by turning to Hegel's concept of the prosaic world. Hegel

3. See T. S. Eliot, "The Function of Criticism," in Eliot, *Selected Essays* (New York, 1950), 12–22.

4. Emile Benveniste, *Problems in General Linguistics*, trans. Mary Elizabeth Meek (Coral Gables, Fla., 1971), 218. For a valuable study applying Benveniste's linguistic studies to literature, see Wlad Godzich and Jeffrey Kittay, *The Emergence of Prose: An Essay on Prosaics* (Minneapolis, 1987), 18–22. Also see Paul de Man's brief discussion of Hegel and deixis in "Hypogram and Inscription," in de Man, *The Resistance to Theory* (Minneapolis, 1986), 41–42.

5. See the title essay in de Man, *Resistance to Theory*, 25.

conceived of the prosaic in four ways: 1) as the historical stage when society is organized in a hierarchical fashion according to universal law; 2) as the world bereft of God; 3) as the opposition between subjective inner life and external reality; 4) as a mode of language that frees thought from sensuous form. Hegel's notion of prosaism is contradictory: on the one hand, the prosaic world is one of banal particularity—the world abandoned by God; on the other hand, it is a world in which the idea is realized in the state, and art, consequently, takes the trivial form of romance. Hegel denigrates romance as a form of allegory, wherein the linkage between the idea and its material form is totally arbitrary, but he praises prose as the vehicle of thought for precisely the same reasons. Prose gives philosophy its mastery over matter. Despite Hegel's dismissal of allegory, he is, in fact, hospitable to a theory of allegory we have come to associate with Walter Benjamin and de Man. But Hegel does not call it allegory; he calls it philosophy. By locating his concept of the prosaic world in his theory of the sign, we can shift the ground of literary representation from aesthetics, which is always ideological, to a nonreflexive grammatical relation. This shift would allow the possibility of initiating a critique of aesthetic ideology.

Whereas a reading of romance as either a subjective or symbolic genre tries to reconcile thought with material form, a Hegelian reading of the kind I have just sketched will reveal that a critical difference emerges that forever postpones just such an aesthetic penetration of thought in the phenomenon. We can locate this difference by tracing in Hegel's works the concept of *Darstellung*, a word that means not only "presentation" but also "exposition," "staging," and "portrayal."[6] The staging of the Idea concerns Hegel from his early critical works on Kant and romantic philosophy through the *Phenomenology* to the late lectures on fine art, where we find that the aesthetic concept of the prosaic world, a nonproblematic world in which universal law and maxim have been actualized, comes into existence along with a nonaesthetic art—romance, which is a purely grammatical linking of idea and form rather than a sensory manifestation of the idea in the phenomenon. Romance, then, signals the end of art as the sensory manifestation of the idea.

But Hegel's statement, in his Introduction to *Aesthetics*, that art is

6. My discussion of *Darstellung* is indebted to Philippe Lacoue-Labarthe and Jean-Luc Nancy, *The Literary Absolute: The Theory of Literature in German Romanticism*, trans. Philip Barnard and Cheryl Lester (Buffalo, N.Y., 1988), especially 31–36.

a thing of the past does not simply mean that art has come to an end; for if art is but one of the forms taken by self-consciousness (the other forms being religion and the state), then the romantic art form, wherein the concept is freed from the concrete, will be seen to be identical with criticism and, as such, the supplement of the state. For in the world of prose, the state is the reproduction of aesthetic reflection, and when the state is aestheticized, art becomes problematic. Georg Lukács says as much in his 1962 Preface to *Theory of the Novel:* "the 'world of prose,' as he [Hegel] aesthetically defines this condition, is one in which the spirit has attained itself both in thought and in social and state praxis. Thus art becomes problematic precisely because reality has become non-problematic." The idea of the aesthetic state may resemble Schiller's *On the Aesthetic Education of Man*, but it is notable chiefly for its distance from "The Oldest Systematic Program of German Idealism," a manuscript discovered in 1917 by Franz Rosenzweig, who also gave it the present title, and variously attributed to Hegel, Schelling, and Hölderlin. (H. S. Harris argues for Hegel's authorship and dates it 1796.) The younger Hegel with his enthusiasm for Hellenic civilization might have subscribed to the statement that "there is no idea of the *state* because the state is something *mechanical*, just as little as there is an idea of a machine. . . . Only that which is the object of *freedom* is called *idea*."[7] But the relation of the idea to the machine is reversed in *The Philosophy of Right* (1821), in which we find there is an idea of the state but not of art, because art *is* something mechanical (*PR*, 54). The transformation of the state into an aesthetic work signals that art has been replaced by romance. Whereas classical art reflected the Greek world (and for Hegel, Greek art alone is art), romance does not reflect the modern capitalist world of bourgeois individualism and private property but stands in a nonreflexive and critical relationship that I will call, after Hegel, prosaism.

By setting Hegel and Hawthorne on the same stage, we can begin to determine the extent to which reflexivity dominates our concept of an American literature and our critical practices as well.[8] To do so, we

7. Georg Lukács, *The Theory of the Novel: A Historico-Philosophical Essay on the Forms of Great Epic Literature*, trans. Anna Bostock (Cambridge, Mass., 1971), 17; "The Oldest Systematic Program of German Idealism," in *Philosophy of German Idealism*, trans. Diana I. Behler, ed. Ernst Behler (New York, 1987), 161. For a critical assessment of the controversy surrounding the authorship, see H. S. Harris, *Hegel's Development: Towards the Sunlight, 1770–1801* (Oxford, 1972), 249–57.

8. For an implicitly Hegelian analysis of desire, see Edgar A. Dryden, *Nathaniel Hawthorne: The Poetics of Enchantment* (Ithaca, N.Y., 1977). For explicit treatments of

must read Hawthorne as theorist. Our reading of Hawthorne's prefaces will, however, be mediated by a reading of Hegel on the exposition of the Idea in art and property. The place of Hegel in American literature is not necessarily a historical one but a theoretical one. By turning to Hegel, we can address the interlacing of the representation of the idea (of America) with aesthetics.

The problem of reflection is philosophy's attempt to secure a self-foundation.[9] Defined thus, reflection may seem far removed from so unphilosophical a writer as Hawthorne, but insofar as the incipient modernism of nineteenth-century American fiction is said to lie in its self-reflexivity, then this fiction may be considered within the Kantian problematic of self-presentation. Hawthorne's prefaces have played the crucial role in guiding critics toward a self-reflexive theory of the romance. His concern in the prefaces, however, is not with the object of imitation—a supposition that has directed most critics to speak of romance as an allegorical and subjective genre—but with the presentation of the idea. This in turn involves a theory of allegory that always posits a difference between meaning and understanding, and thus resembles Hegel's concept of reflection. In reflection, thought displaces the object; what we perceive is a product of our own thought. This means that in reading, if we apply to it what Hegel writes about reflection in the lesser *Logic*, the translation of sense into consciousness occurs by way of a representation that inserts itself in place of what the sense is supposed to be.[10] The difference posited by reflection uncovers the purely grammatical nature of romance; consequently, self-representation and self-reflection cannot be realized.

As long as interpretations of Hawthorne thematize the metaphors

---

Hegel and Hawthorne, see John Carlos Rowe, "The Internal Conflict of Romantic Narrative: Hegel's *Phenomenology* and Hawthorne's *The Scarlet Letter*," *Modern Language Notes*, XCV (1980), 1203–31, and Evan Carton, *The Rhetoric of American Romance: Dialectic and Identity in Emerson, Dickinson, Poe, and Hawthorne* (Baltimore, 1985).

9. The critical literature on self-reflexivity is extensive, and one could not do better than to start with Rodolphe Gasché, *The Tain of the Mirror: Derrida and the Philosophy of Reflection* (Cambridge, Mass., 1986). My discussion of reflection owes much to his analysis. Derrida's "The Double Session" is particularly important to discussions of the problem of reflection in literature. See Jacques Derrida, *Dissemination*, trans. Barbara Johnson (Chicago, 1981), 173–285. See also Lacoue-Labarthe and Nancy, *The Literary Absolute*, Lacoue-Labarthe and Nancy, "Le dialogue des genres," *Poetique*, XXI (1974), 149–75, and in the same issue, see Lacoue-Labarthe, "L'imprésentable," 53–95.

10. In addition to *Logic*, 163, see Hegel's discussion of reflection and hermeneutics in *LPR*, I, 123.

of reflection or engage in a hermeneutic that seeks a signified, they remain within a metaphysical concept of mimesis. Hawthorne's bracketing of the real or actual as not being an object of his fictions by no means makes romance a nonmimetic genre. If romance is read as a self-destructive presentation of its own fictional premises, then it conforms to the tradition wherein mimesis is the presentation of being. Reading would be the thematization of that which lies within the play of signifiers; that is, reading raises the unthought or natural given to the level of the articulation of consciousness.[11]

We indeed find in Hawthorne's prefaces that the reflexive gesture of a self-reading thematizes the narrative proper. And the narrative, in turn, functions as the critique of the preface. In other words, a chiasmatic structure determines the relation between the prefaces and the narratives. We can say not only that the prefaces thematize the problem of representation in terms of the ensuing narrative but that the romances are the critique of the theoretical principles of the prefaces. The parallels between the autobiographical preface, "The Custom-House," and the story of Hester have been frequently noted by readers of *The Scarlet Letter*. In *The House of the Seven Gables*, property functions as a trope common to preface and narrative, and a similar role is played by copying in *The Marble Faun* and by theater in *The Blithedale Romance*. In his prefaces, Hawthorne defines the genre of romance and performs a self-reading that can be called the critical exposition of the text's process of representation. The narratives, in turn, are a reading of the prefaces as romance, the grammatical linking of subject and predicate.

The doubling of the narrative as criticism is nowhere more evident than in *The Blithedale Romance*, which is already a critique of the romance of the Brook Farm experiment. In describing himself as the "Chorus in a classic play, which seems to be set aloof from the possibility of personal concernment," Coverdale repeats Hawthorne's gesture in the preface, where he explains that he has chosen Brook Farm as his model "merely to establish a theatre, a little removed from the highway of ordinary travel, where the creatures of his brain may play their phantasmagorical antics, without exposing them to too close a comparison with the actual events of real lives."[12] The theater meta-

11. See Gasché's discussion of thematization in *The Tain of the Mirror*, 264.

12. Nathaniel Hawthorne, *The Blithedale Romance and Fanshawe* (Columbus, Ohio, 1964), 97, 1, Vol. III of William Charvat, Roy Harvey Pearce, and Claude Simpson, eds., *The Centenary Edition of the Works of Nathaniel Hawthorne*, 19 vols. to date, hereinafter

phors stress Brook Farm's removal from ordinary life, just as Coverdale's metaphors express his desire to extricate himself from the affairs of Blithedale.

The symmetry between Coverdale's role as narrator and Hawthorne's self-presentation in the preface has not gone unnoticed. Hawthorne's preface presents the text as a self-reflexive system of referents. He suggests his romance conveys "the inner truth and spirit," but not the "outward narrative," of Brook Farm. Coverdale also confesses to be truer to the spirit of what he witnesses than to outward circumstances. Following a dissection of Hollingsworth's character, Coverdale confesses, "I am perfectly aware that the above statement is exaggerated, in the attempt to make it adequate. . . . The paragraph may remain, however, for its truth and its exaggeration, as strongly expressive of the tendencies which were really operative in Hollingsworth, and as exemplifying the kind of error into which my mode of observation was calculated to lead me" (*BR*, 71). His errors of perception become a part of the narrative and function not only as the critique or dissolution of the romantic project of Blithedale but also as a self-critique that undoes the historical narrative. Coverdale's "mode of observation" is hard to distinguish from Hawthorne's. The difference lies within their respective frames: as the narrator within the play, Coverdale is guilty of distorting what is staged before his eyes; Hawthorne's theater frees him from the demands of verisimilitude.

The thematics of the theater, veils, and the duplicity of perception play as important a role in the preface as they do in the narrative. The self-reflexive unity is enhanced by Hawthorne's calling Brook Farm "the most romantic episode of his own life—essentially a daydream, and yet a fact—and thus offering an available foothold between fiction and reality" (*BR*, 2). The tension between realistic fiction and romance involves the text in a reflexive model of mimesis. Hawthorne both invites comparison to recent events and declares his freedom from the constraints of accuracy. He goes on to say that in Europe, the romancer has the privilege of not putting his work "exactly side by side with nature," but in America, "there is as yet no such Faery Land, so like the real world, that, in a suitable remoteness, one cannot tell the

---

cited parenthetically in text as *BR*. The following abbreviations will be used for citations from Hawthorne's novels in *The Centenary Edition*: *HSG—The House of the Seven Gables* (Columbus, Ohio, 1965), Vol. II; *MF—The Marble Faun* (Columbus, Ohio, 1968), Vol. IV; *SL—The Scarlet Letter* (Columbus, Ohio, 1962), Vol. I.

difference." In absence of this fictive world, "the beings of imagination are compelled to show themselves in the same category as actually living mortals; a necessity that generally renders the paint and pasteboard of their composition but too painfully discernible." Hawthorne uncovers an important paradox: the Faery Land of the European writer is so far removed from reality that it has the power of the real, whereas the mimetic works of American writers so closely resemble the prosaic world that they seem mere appearance. Hawthorne's theater is not unlike Pirandello's.

Hawthorne is not simply arguing for a place for literature in a vulgar society that has no interest in art. In allegorizing the prosaic world, the romancer transforms experience into what Hegel calls, in a discussion of historical writing, "reports for the faculty of representation" (*LWH*, 15). When Hawthorne speaks of having "availed himself of his actual reminiscences" to give an air of reality to his "fancy-sketch," he draws upon a textualized history: Brook Farm, a thoroughly prosaic community, is already an allegory. Only by turning to a romantic experience can he escape the confines of the novel and create a work whose "paint and pasteboard" cannot be discerned. The allegorical life has greater claims to mimetic illusion than does naturalistic representation. Hawthorne here defines romance as an imitative genre—its subject is itself a romance.

The self-reflexive structure of *The Blithedale Romance* rests upon this doubling of the narrative by the preface. When critics read the text as an example of ironic self-consciousness, they only elaborate what is already claimed in the preface. Hawthorne prepares for Coverdale's metaphors to mirror or duplicate his own. The motif is not unlike that of "The Custom-House," where Hawthorne's account of his relation as writer to his ancestors and the community parallels Hester's situation as the Puritans' Other, which she embodies both as adulteress and artist. Furthermore, if language worked the way it is described in theories of reflection, the choice of such historically embedded subjects as Puritan Boston and Brook Farm would only strengthen the dialectical fusion of consciousness and history.

The power of this reflexive structure is overwhelming: the contemporary reader of Hawthorne mirrors the very self-conscious construction of meaning by a narrator who himself mirrors the author's preface. The text performs its own speculative reading, or we can say it thematizes its own self-reading. A reflexive reading involves a projection of one's own meaning upon the text. But Coverdale's self-critical remarks about his analysis of Hollingsworth indicate that his reflection is raised to the level of the speculative: it includes its own negation as part of its truth. Any reading of *The Blithedale Romance* is somehow tautological—it repeats what the text says but does so in an abstract language about irony and tropes. Even a misreading of the text repeats the very act of perception performed by Coverdale. If interpretation is to escape tautology, it must take the meaning of the text *as* something other than what it says, and this analogical reading in which difference and identity together form a totality is ideally the temporal horizon that embraces past, present, and future. The meaning of the text is what lies before the reader and what the reader is always trying to catch up to.

Yet if all readings of Hawthorne had repeated the thematics laid out in the preface, they would be superfluous, a mere repetition of what the text says. Criticism would be the reproduction of the work. In his critical doubling of the narrative, Hawthorne is very close to Friedrich Schlegel, in whose work Lacoue-Labarthe and Nancy find the beginnings of criticism. Criticism is neither a supplement nor a parasite; it "originates" the work of art: "it is not because there is art that there is criticism . . . on the contrary, it is the romantics, and not Hegel, who in this aspect did no more than follow them, who first found art to be a thing *of the past* [que l'art est chose *passée*]; rather, it is only insofar as there will be a criticism that there will be an art, an altogether different art."[13] Criticism stands before literature: before criticism there was writing, but not art. Criticism not only faces literature but precedes literature insofar as it determines what is literature. Schlegel speaks of a need for a literary form—the novel (*der Roman*)— that will be the object of his criticism. Consequently, he speaks of what the novel will be, but having spoken of the novel to come, he finds it before him in such works as *Don Quixote* and *Tristram Shandy*. If as Schlegel says, "a theory of the novel would have to be itself a novel," then his *Dialogue on Poetry* is a novel and *Don Quixote* is its theory.[14] The

13. Lacoue-Labarthe and Nancy, *The Literary Absolute*, 117.
14. Friedrich Schlegel, *Dialogue on Poetry and Literary Aphorisms*, trans. and ed. Ernst Behler and Roman Struc (University Park, Penn., 1968), 102. My discussion of the problem of priority in the relation of criticism to literature is indebted to the opening section of Jacques Derrida, *The Post Card: From Socrates to Freud and Beyond*, trans. Alan Bass (Chicago, 1987), 1–256.

novel comes into being as a critical literature, or a second re-production
of the narrative as theory and theory as narrative.

Many of the problems related to questions of narrative and an "American" literature can be clarified by a return to the efforts of romantic
theorists to overcome the Kantian crisis of presentation (*Darstellung*) or
the question of the adequation between concept and appearance. When
we remind ourselves that the value of reflection lies in its being both
method and foundation, we discover that philosophy is confronted by
the inability to present itself, since, according to Hegel, it is unable to
overcome the separation between thinking and being. Art promises to
reconcile matter and idea, but insofar as it is tied to material form, art
remains for Hegel an inferior mode of consciousness; consequently, he
praises prose as the vehicle of thought, which separates him from Kant
and romantic aesthetics.

Kant's solution to the difficulty of establishing the identity of concepts of the understanding and empirical intuitions led him to formulate the schema, which applies the categories—pure concepts of the
understanding—to appearances. As is well known, Kant's recognition
of the dualism inherent in the distinction between noumena and phenomena led him to attempt a completion of his critical philosophy in
aesthetics. He introduced the schema in the *Critique of Pure Reason* and
returns to it in the discussion of hypotyposis in the *Critique of Judgment*.
Hypotyposis is "a sketch, an outline, a draft of a book, a model or
pattern." The Latin translation of the term is *exhibitio*, and the German
is *Darstellung*, the rendering of a concept in terms of sense.[15] When
Kant returns to schemata in the third *Critique*, he distinguishes symbolic hypotyposis, in which "there is a concept which only reason can
think and to which no sensible intuition can be adequate," from schematic hypotyposis, in which the intuition corresponding to a concept
of the understanding is given a priori. Kant goes on, however, to attack
the misconception that has led some logicians "to speak of the *symbolical*
mode of presentation as if it were opposed to the *intuitive*, for the symbolical is only a mode of the intuitive." Both schematic and symbolical
modes of representation are hypotyposis, *Darstellung*, presentation.
Schemata contain direct, symbols indirect, "presentations of the con-

cept." (Symbols operate through analogy.) In preserving intuition for symbols, Kant introduces, only to denigrate, "*characterizations* or designations of concepts by accompanying sensible signs which contain nothing belonging to the intuition of the object and only serve as a means for reproducing the concepts."[16] Characterization is inimical to art because it leaves intuition behind. It designates and does not present; therefore, characterization is not aesthetic—that is, it does not apply an intuition to a concept. It is simply a mnemonic device for recalling concepts. Characterization anticipates Hegel's remark that names have nothing to do with intuition (*PM*, 212). Schematic and symbolic hypotyposes resemble the symbol and sign respectively. Hegel's revision of Kant is to praise precisely that form of language that Kant considers the least certain vehicle of knowledge.

The influence of Kantianism, particularly as it had been reformulated by Coleridge, upon Anglo-American criticism has meant that literary representation has been conceived within epistemological terms and that reflection has been the constitutive notion of American literature. And because Kantian reflection is dualistic—that is, consciousness stands over and against being—the resolution between the rational and the empirical was envisaged in the presentation of the beautiful. Literature would thus be a form of knowledge higher than that of philosophy, because it is the sensory manifestation of the idea.

Aesthetics is the locus of romantic ideology, for in the problematic of *Darstellung*, we have the ordering of the phenomenal realm by the conceptual. Hegel recognized this in the philosophies of Kant, Jacobi, and Fichte, as well as in the religious point of view of Protestantism and, as we shall see, in the prosaic world of romance. In other words, romantic ideology is prosaism. The division of concepts from intuition leads to the desire to externalize that which can be felt but not made an object of cognition. The "struggle of subjective beauty" to verbally represent the inner world leads to the denigration of the objective, a feature common to discussions of romance (see *FK*, 57). As the presentation of the Idea, *Darstellung* embodies the ideal of mimesis. Thus, the beautiful is idealism itself, and any talk of literature as the reflective operation in which the Other is appropriated for the subject in the form of a representation can be identified as ideology, for the

16. Immanuel Kant, *Critique of Judgment*, trans. J. H. Bernard (New York, 1951), 197. Kant introduces the schematism in *Critique of Pure Reason*, trans. Norman Kemp Smith (New York, 1929), 180–87.

power of reflection is said to lie in its overcoming of difference by reflecting the Other back into the subject to form a totality. When this occurs, natural reality is taken to be equivalent to language.

But if the aesthetic principles governing literary criticism are Kantian, the thematics of interpretation are Hegelian in their emphasis on the dialectics of desire. When the relation of form and content, or concept and phenomenon, is given a historical and experiential basis in the periodization of the symbolic, classical, and romantic art forms, and when these historical stages are seen as the manifestation of the stages of consciousness, then we are approaching a Hegelian philosophy of art. A structural system unfolds wherein literary form is linked to historical epochs through the mediation of consciousness. When this is tied to the subject of the "Americanness" of our literature, then we have a system wherein subject matter is thoroughly imbued with historical consciousness, and the problem of form is resolved by the introduction of an argument that conflates the semiological with phenomenological consciousness. In the critical literature on Hawthorne, this has meant that romance is said to resolve the problem of both form and content. A tradition has developed that has presented romance as the uniquely American form of the novel.

Romance is the privileged genre in American literary criticism because it provides, through self-reflexivity, a formal solution to the problem of history. The idea of history is itself the idea of representation, for history always poses itself as the problem of the embodiment of the Idea, whether this Idea be that of national identity, economic systems, or an original literature; hence, whenever the American writer speculates on the idea of history, he or she raises the question of genre. Emerson's opening lament in *Nature*—"Our age is retrospective. It builds the sepulchres of the fathers. It writes biographies, histories, and criticism"[17]—signals what Hegel calls a reflective world: lacking the "living experience" of a "past age and its life," we are left "with a reflective world, i.e. with a *past* stage in the spirit, interests, and culture of the society in question, [we at once feel] the need for a *present*. The present [is] not [to be found] in history; [it arises out of] the insights of the understanding, the subjective activity of the mind itself" (*LWH*,

---

17. Ralph Waldo Emerson, *Nature, Addresses, and Lectures*, ed. Robert E. Spiller and Alfred R. Ferguson (Cambridge, Mass., 1971), 7, Vol. I of Joseph Slater and Douglas Emory Wilson, eds., *The Collected Works of Ralph Waldo Emerson*, 4 vols. to date. All citations from Emerson are from this text.

19). In this form of reflective history, which Hegel calls pragmatic history, meaning lies in the teleological working out of the concept or the actualization of reason in the state. These reflections belong to the present, but when this stage is reached, we are in the prosaic world where art is a thing of the past—that is, when the concept is realized in the state, acting has replaced telling.

The displacement of art by action should not be confused with a commonplace opposition between theory and practice. As long as political action is seen as the realization of thought, it is an aesthetic concept. Emerson admits as much when he closes *Nature* with the Orphic fable of the creation as the emanation of man. He translates his theory of language—"the whole of nature is a metaphor of the human mind"— into allegory. His theory of language promises to reconstitute the unity of thought and nature, but Emerson confesses that "words are finite organs of the infinite mind. They cannot cover the dimensions of what is in truth." But Emerson does not leave the aesthetic, in Kant's sense, when he writes, "An action is the perfection and publication of thought," for he still looks upon the sensuous as the presentation of the idea. But insofar as allegory is a comparative art form that dissolves the union of thought and sensuous form, Emerson's fable is the narrative of the unraveling of his symbolic theory of language. The transparent eyeball is not the symbol of a transcendental subject but the "empty *form* of subjectivity" (*HA*, I, 399)—"I am nothing; I see all"—that presupposes a prosaic world where neither sensuous form nor content expresses the inwardness of the writer. In other words, Emerson's fable is an allegory of the freedom of discourse from the body. Prose is the vehicle of thought.

The Hegelian concept of prose, however, is anything but idealistic, in the sense that the absolute Idea is taken to be free from materiality. Quite the contrary, prose is materialistic to the extent that it is free from the idealism tying thought to speech and concept to intuition. Thus, Hegel argues that thinking can take place in prose alone because "poetic creation and formation is a reconciliation in the form of a *real* phenomenon itself" (*HA*, II, 976). For Hegel, poetry is confined by nature and probability and, consequently, is an inadequate medium for history: "in historical situations the play of chance is revealed, the breach between what is inherently substantive and the relativity of single events and occurrences. . . . These in this prose have far more things that are extraordinary and eccentric than those miracles of poetry which must always keep within the limits of what is universally valid" (*HA*, II, 988). The prosaic cleavage between the universal and the material indicates that romance is prosaic to the extent that it is free from intuition and gives to the phenomenon "a signification foreign to it" (*PM*, 212). In other words, prose makes use of signs only, whereas poetry is symbolic.

In a prosaically ordered world the "universal is present in law and maxim" and no longer is "one with the sense and freedom" (*HA*, I, 10). Thus, art is replaced by romance, which seeks to regain "for poetry the right it had lost, so far as this is possible" (*HA*, II, 1092). It is in the context of a discussion of representation in the prosaic world that Hegel makes his famous announcement: "art, considered in its highest vocation, is and remains for us a thing of the past" (*HA*, I, 11). Art "is the freedom of intellectual reflection," and as such, it reconciles thought and sensuous being and brings before us the truly actual—that which has being in and for itself. But art is not the highest mode of truth because it is bound by form to a specific content. Art for Hegel is ultimately classical art, where form and content are unified, and it comes to an end with Christianity, which is not "friendly to sense." In the romantic world, art no longer fulfills the spiritual need of a society where "thought and reflection have spread their wings above fine art," for the universal is now present in the state. The artist cannot extricate himself from the "world of reflection," a world in which the present is found no longer in history but in the subjective activity of the mind. Consequently, art "has lost for us genuine truth and life, and has rather been transferred into our ideas. . . . What is now aroused in us by works of art is not just immediate enjoyment but our judgments also" (*HA*, I, 11). Art is now subjected to consideration of its content and "means of presentation." For Hegel, art's mode of appearance is on the order of *Darstellung* or *Scheinen* (showing forth) rather than *Vorstellung* (representation), which is an intellectual mode of appearance on the order of signs.[18] When art submits to philosophy, its union of idea and sensuous form dissolves; criticism has taken the place of creation.

When the artist "stands within a world of reflection," he is in a world of afterthoughts or a world that deals with thoughts as thoughts

18. See Charles Taylor's discussion of *Darstellung* and *Scheinen* in *Hegel* (Cambridge, Eng., 1975), 472.

(*Logic*, 4). Since "philosophy may be said to do nothing but transform conceptions [*Vorstellung*] into thoughts [*Gedanken*]," philosophy may be said to translate picture-images into thinking. Art has reached its "highest vocation" when it no longer presents the idea in its concrete immediacy, since the idea would be limited by the concrete, but presents the idea as reflection, a mediating activity that introduces difference in the presentation of the object.

Classical art leaves the idea in its immediate concrete form, but the aim of philosophy, which "is often represented as the ascertainment of the essence of things," is to show things "to be mediated by, or based upon, something else. The immediate Being of things is thus conceived under the image of a rind or curtain behind which the Essence lies hidden" (*Logic*, 163). To discover the essence of things or "the real constitution of the object," reflection is required. Reflection comes of the desire "to get behind the surface," to distinguish Essence from Being. "Hence, the phenomenon becomes double, it splits into inside and outside, into force and its manifestation, into cause and effect" (*Logic*, 33). The split engendered by reflection is the necessary alteration that transforms the material object into the idea. Whatever is "presented in sensation, perception, or conception [*Vorstellung*]" must be altered for its true nature to be discovered (*Logic*, 34). Art is a thing of the past, not because it has been superseded by philosophy, but because as the material inscription of the idea, the content is forgotten. When Being and Essence stand in a relation to one another as does a curtain to the hidden stage, then Essence is mediated by the material sign that hides it. If classical art belongs to the order of *Darstellung*, or the material manifestation of the idea, then romantic art is devoid of images and has "to do with signs only" (see *PM*, 212–13). We can conclude that romance, prose, and philosophy constitute a discourse of signs, or *Vorstellung* rather than *Darstellung*.

Romantic art resembles what Kant dismisses in his section on hypotyposis as characterization. Consequently, the art form that materially manifests thought is prose, which is on the order of the sign or memory and, therefore, is not aesthetic or beautiful. In the sign, "the meaning is not only explicitly known but is expressly posited as different from the external way in which it is represented." The relation between meaning and concrete shape "becomes a more or less accidental concatenation produced by the subjective activity of the poet, by the immersion of his spirit in an external existent, by his wit and his invention in general" (*HA*, I, 378). The material is the slave to wit. When we are in the realm where the material inscription of thought takes a purely mechanical form and the relation between meaning and shape is that of master and servant, we are in the world of prose and, as we will see, the world of property: "In the slave, prose begins, and so this entire species is prosaic too" (*HA*, I, 387). Hegel refers to Aesop and the fable, a form that he derides, along with parable and allegory, as trivial art.

In allegory, the subject is an abstract universal, an "empty *form* of subjectivity"; therefore, it is "to be called a subject only, as it were, in a grammatical sense" (*HA*, I, 399). De Man writes of this passage, "Allegories are the most distinctly linguistic (as opposed to phenomenal) of categories, namely grammar."[19] We might add that allegories, as linguistic categories, do not confuse linguistic phenomenon with natural phenomenon; they are, in de Man's work, nonideological or the critique of ideology. Prose is a nonaesthetic mode of discourse that fails to achieve the level of *Darstellung*, and so it is the romantic art form that is the end of art. There is no need for art in a prosaic world since prose has come to diffuse itself through all life, and all existence falls equally under this mode of discourse.

The prose of the world is allegory, the "separation of subject and predicate, universal from particular" (*HA*, I, 399). With this "prosaic universality . . . art has nothing to do" (*HA*, I, 400). It is what Hawthorne condemns in the Puritan typological reading of the scarlet letter and in Catholic ritual throughout *The Marble Faun*. The letter negates Hester's being as individual and makes her the sign of adultery, an abstract concept of sin, and, as such, a universal. But now Hester only possesses the infinite; she lacks finite individuality because history is voided—all events are transformed into the infinite text of divine history as it is revealed in the letter. When the preacher takes her as the text for his sermon and points to her and calls her "the figure, the body, the reality of sin" (79), he gives her being and deprives her of it. The letter is the absence of being. In Hegelian terms, her natural existence is annihilated as she is given a purely spiritual meaning.

Despite his prejudices, Hawthorne, like Hegel, finds Catholicism more favorable to art than Protestantism because the former depends

---

19. Paul de Man, "Sign and Symbol in Hegel's *Aesthetics*," *Critical Inquiry*, VIII (Summer, 1982), 775.

more upon the material manifestation of spirit and the latter scorns the sacred art of the Church. Emerson, however, finds in Catholicism an implicit link with romance—the complete mastery of the idea over the form. He writes to Margaret Fuller of a visit to a Catholic service in Baltimore: "This morning I went to the Cathedral to hear mass with much content. It is so dignified to come where the priest is nothing, & the people nothing, and an idea for once excludes these impertinences. . . . We understand so well the joyful adhesion of the Winkelmans & Tiecks & Schlegels; just as we seize with joy the fine romance & toss the learned Heeren out of the window; unhappily with the same sigh as belongs to the romance 'Ah! that one word of it were true.' "[20] Although Emerson is as dismissive of Catholicism as he is of romantic fiction, the shrewd recognition of the appeal of the universal idea to the German romantics echoes Hegel's accusation that the outcome of romantic irony is a search for the "bad infinite"—that is, an abstract universal.

In romance, allegory, and irony, the form is completely subordinated to the meaning; the idea is master over material. But if prose is the discourse of the slave, then a reversal is inevitable, for the idea cannot find adequate embodiment in the form, just as the master does not find in the slave consciousness-in-itself. Therefore, as the slave by virtue of his labor "rids himself of his attachment to natural existence" and comes to be master, prose frees itself from the idea by inscribing it as a thing of the past.[21] Finally, as the split between the essential and the contingent is embodied in the unhappy consciousness, Hegel gives a basis in consciousness to the historical, religious, and aesthetic categories of prose.

20. Ralph L. Rusk, ed., *The Letters of Ralph Waldo Emerson* (6 vols.; New York, 1939), III, 116.

21. The quotation is from *PS*, 117. *Cf.* de Man, "Sign and Symbol": "[Art] is of the past to the extent that it materially inscribes, and thus forever forgets, its ideal content" (773–74). De Man's argument here and in "Hegel on the Sublime" (in *Displacement: Derrida and After*, ed. Mark Krupnick [Bloomington, Ind., 1983], 139–53) concerns the relation of material inscription to Hegel's two concepts of memory, *Erinnerung*, an inner recollection and gathering of experience, and *Gedächtnis*, rote memorization. In the latter essay, de Man concludes, "To the extent that art is aesthetic, it is also prosaic—as learning by rote is prosaic compared to the depth of recollection." I have been arguing that the Hegelian idea of the prosaic is closer to philosophy, as Hegel conceives it, than to aesthetics. My essay owes a great deal to de Man's work on Hegel, but my concern is not with the relation of rhetoric to cognition but with the relation between aesthetics and the philosophy of reflection.

This union of history, aesthetics, and consciousness finds expression in the prosaism of nineteenth-century America, an age that saw not only the emergence of national identity but also the identification of the American with the middle class—and it is this middle class that provided the audience for fiction. If romance signals the existence of a prosaic world, then nineteenth-century America was, by all accounts, the proper setting for romance. Tocqueville found little in American democracy conducive for poetry: "Having deprived poetry of the past, equality also takes away part of the present." But the most theoretical condemnation of American prosaism can be found in Henry James's 1879 book on Hawthorne, in which he locates the origins of romance in the spectacle. Without the culture and history of the "European spectacle," the writer lacked the substantial content required of the novel; in the United States, "life was not in the least spectacular." Hawthorne argues in the Preface to *The Marble Faun* that such a fund of history and manners is needed for the romance, but he would concur with James's suggestion that romance is to provide such a spectacle: "There was therefore, among the cultivated classes, much relish for the utterances of a writer who would help one to take a picturesque view of one's internal possibilities, and to find in the landscape of the soul all sorts of fine sunrise and moonlight effects." [22]

James's allusion to the moonlight passage in "The Custom-House" links the motif of specularity to the discourse of signs. James uses *spectacle* in the sense of a fanciful image or thought, but the Latin *speculatio*, together with *contemplatio*, translates the Greek *theoria*. And though James writes, "He was not a man with a literary theory; he was guiltless of a system, and I am not sure that he had ever heard of Realism," Hawthorne's romances are themselves the speculative presentation or staging of self-representation. Reflection is a mirroring of the object—that is, a presentation of both the object and the cognition of the object. When the object is the mind, we have a mirroring of the mirror, a mirroring of the object and the mirroring subject. [23] Romance, according to a self-reflexive theory, is the privileged genre of romanti-

22. Alexis de Tocqueville, *Democracy in America*, trans. George Lawrence, ed. J. P. Mayer (Garden City, N.Y., 1969), 484; Henry James, *Hawthorne*, in *Literary Criticism: Essays on Literature, American Writers, English Writers*, ed. Leon Edel and Mark Wilson (New York, 1984), 351, 383.

23. James, *Hawthorne*, 321; Gasché, *The Tain of the Mirror*, 20.

cism, since it fulfills the romantic philosophy of overcoming Kantian dualism by reuniting thought and being in the speculum of fiction.

We might say that for Hawthorne, tropes of speculation, such as that of the mirror, allegorize speculation itself in an attempt to reconstitute the unity of American life. America is the realization of the Hegelian "world of prose." The split between a subjective inner world and quotidian reality is the very condition for romance. The power of the antinomies governing American historiography lies in their promise of giving the American subject—that is, the subjectivity of the American—access to itself. The history of the formation of the American character is a history of self-representation, one that incorporates the Other as the same, at least in potential if willing to adopt the principles of capitalism, as Holgrave proves to be when he marries Phoebe and inherits the Pyncheon fortune.

Sacvan Bercovitch's *American Jeremiad* presents a convincing argument that among the New England Puritans the jeremiad provided a fund of themes, metaphors, and symbols to foster and sustain a myth of homogeneous identity that helped America to define itself in cultural and historical terms. The cohesiveness of the Puritan vision of a divinely directed history was transferred to the rest of America. The Puritan rhetoric of the errand into the wilderness joined with the Revolution's promise of a future made present to produce a "*cultural*, not a national, myth of consensus." These forces provided for the relatively easy adoption of capitalism, the denial of the past, and the conformist spirit wherein the realities of class, ethnicity, and religion could be suppressed in the name of an identity—"American"—that had superseded such ties. In other words, *American* meant middle-class culture.[24]

When we keep in mind how much this self-representation is predicated on Old World eschatology and mercantilism, then the self-reflexive gesture of accounting for history in terms of ritual, myth, and symbols repeats the very script set down by the historical subject. In other words, the tendency to produce cultural or literary histories according to the paradigm of the New World repeats the very narratives they purport to analyze. The most fruitful of American historiography may well be studies of historical consciousness. We can say after Hegel, "Our culture is such that all events are at once recorded and trans-

24. Sacvan Bercovitch, *The American Jeremiad* (Madison, Wis., 1978), 158, 154–55.

formed directly into historical representations [*Berichte für die Vorstel-lung* (literally, 'reports for the faculty of representation')]" (*LWH*, 15).

It is out of the prosaic world of an emergent capitalist America that Hawthorne seeks to regain for poetry the subjective realm of the Idea, or the unity of concept and experience, but as he consistently acknowledges, the ground for the Idea remains the prosaic world. The struggle to wrest a domain for art from a mercantile society is central to "The Custom-House"; Hawthorne can write only if he is freed from his dependency on a government sinecure. Economics also plays an important role in *The Blithedale Romance*, since much of the action turns upon Hollingsworth's efforts to raise money for his scheme for prison reform and upon Old Moodie's transferring his fortune from Zenobia to Priscilla.

At Brook Farm itself, the plan for social and intellectual growth and equality was based on ownership of property. Brook Farm, Anne Rose tells us, "was organized as a joint stock company." The integrity of the individual, according to the farm's organizers, "required private property for its material support." The Brook Farm experiment imposed a capitalist system of organization on an agrarian principle of labor, but it was indeed romantic to the extent that it attempted to overcome the division of the classes that had become of greater concern to Boston and its environs since the craft tradition had declined and the concentration of capital within trades had meant the beginning of the formation of a working class. In addition, the period between 1837 and 1843 saw widespread bankruptcy and high unemployment. During this depression, labor agitation disappeared, a sign of the centralization of capital into fewer hands and the surplus of available laborers. The introduction of a modern capitalist economy also came at a time when the homogeneity of provincial Boston was breaking up not only because of increased mobility provided by good roads, canals, railroads, and steamships, but also because of the economic reorganization of the Unitarian churches, which now sold or rented pews, thus instituting an economic division among the worshipers and ending the practice of promoting contact between the classes.[25]

25. Anne C. Rose, *Transcendentalism as a Social Movement, 1830–1850* (New Haven, Conn., 1981), 135. I am indebted to Rose's account of the economic and social background for Boston and Brook Farm, 9–10. For an analysis of the changing economic conditions in Salem, see Robert Doherty, *Society and Power: Five New England Towns, 1800–1860* (Amherst, Mass., 1977).

Coverdale exposes the pretensions of Brook Farm to found a classless society when he remarks that the whole program is founded upon the economic independence of its members who mingle with the laboring classes by choice only because they know they can always return to their bourgeois world. Despite their respect for labor as contributing to the health and welfare of both the individual and society, the founders of Brook Farm valued labor only insofar as it contributed to the maintenance of private property upon which the integrity of the self depended. It was designed more for the benefit of the shareholder than for the laboring class.

The relation of property to representation receives its fullest treatment in *The House of the Seven Gables*. Walter Michaels argues that the nonrepresentational mode of romance expresses a desire to render self and property secure from "the violence of mimetic representation," whereas the novel is the mirror of capitalist appropriation of property. Romance would free the claim to property from the world of business. Michaels sums up Hawthorne's strategy in romance: "Where representations are unrealities produced by mirrors, the romance represents nothing; thus romance is not a compensation for the coldness of American life, but in opposition to its terrible vitality."[26] Michaels' argument is persuasive, but one can go a step further and conclude that rather than representing nothing, romance represents the very dissolution of what the claim to property is founded upon—the inalienable self. Rather than possess a fear of capitalism and an anachronistic belief in the inalienable self, Hawthorne represents romance as a speculative genre—his tropes and narrative mirror romance's process of exposition. Hawthorne's romance is anything but nostalgic for an inalienable right to self and property; instead, it is a critique of the false belief in mimetic representation that governs realism and capitalist ideology. Michaels reaches a contrary conclusion because he not only defines the novel as a mimetic genre and romance as nonrepresentational—and thus constructs a reflective theory of representation, a theory Hegel criticized in *Faith and Knowledge*—but he also follows Locke's theory of property, which was based on nature, rather than Hegel's, which was based on *Darstellung*.

Property rights of any sort in *The House of the Seven Gables* are

26. Walter Benn Michaels, "Romance and Real Estate," *Raritan*, II (Winter, 1983), 70, 73, 77.

governed by the principles of narrative representation. To possess property is to stamp the will upon matter and so render it recognizable for others as mine: "When I grasp a thing or form it, this also means in the last resort that I mark it, and mark it for others, in order to exclude them and show that I have put my will into the thing" (*PR*, 239). Hawthorne makes such a claim to property in "laying out a street that infringes upon nobody's private rights" (*HSG*, 3).

The principle governing property is *Darstellung*, the presentation and staging of the will. Property, according to Hegel, is the phenomenal materialization of freedom, and as such, it transforms nature from a symbol into a sign: "The notion of the mark . . . is that the thing does not count as the thing which it is but as what it is supposed to signify" (*PR*, 239).[27] When nature exists in itself, it is pure externality. Man, on the other hand, is self-consciousness and cannot be external to himself. This is why consciousness, unlike property, is inalienable. In property, man can externalize self-consciousness as the concrete idea, whereas mere nature remains abstractly external because it cannot think the concept of its externality. The mark signals that nature is to be regarded not as the thing that it is but as the Other—its abstract externality and pure being have been negated.

To "make a thing, I give to it a predicate, 'mine,' which must appear in it in an external form and must not simply remain in my inner will" (*PR*, 237). And precisely because this mark, this "mine," is an external indicator, its materiality signals the erasure of interiority. Hegel writes, "What I only mean or suppose is mine: it belongs to me—this particular individual. But language expresses nothing but universality; and so I cannot say what I merely mean. And the unutterable—feeling or sensation—far from being the highest truth, is the most unimportant and untrue. . . . [W]hen I say 'I,' I mean my single self to the exclusion of all others; but what I *say*, viz. 'I,' is just every 'I,' which in like manner excludes all others from itself" (*Logic*, 31).

The distinction between *meinen* (with its pun on *mein*) and *sagen* lies in the difference between the sensible and thought. Language, as "the work of thought," outflanks the sensible, thought's other, and is both "that other and itself." When we seek to indicate a "here" and "now," or an "I" or "mine," we discover that the very foundation for all

27. Hegel's discussion of the mark bears a strikingly close resemblance to Walter Benjamin's discussion of the Baroque allegorist in *The Origin of German Tragic Drama*, trans. John Osborne (London, 1977).

indication or pointing is unsettled; instead of referentiality being grounded in either external or subjective referents, it proceeds from language itself. When, in the case of property, the mark is said to establish something as mine, this thing is something negative, the other of my will, a "representative" of it only (see *PR*, 49). The "mine" is a nonreferential sign that carries meaning only in the instance of discourse where one says the word *mine*. The present instance constituting the reference to the object is internal to language. But the speaker's presence is an event in time; in other words, subjective presence is internal to language, and all reference proceeds from the inaugural act of indication wherein language refers to itself. To mark something as mine is to inscribe it materially or to forget the ideal content of the "mine" and the grammatical foundation of the subject. Mimetic fiction can be said to be such a forgetting, for it would attach consciousness to nature and thereby transform a purely external world into a "human" world—that is, a world in which nature is possessed as property.

Allegory dissolves the right to property insofar as it reveals the predicate to be unattached to the subject. The mark, the sign that something is mine, may be said to produce the subject insofar as in taking possession of property the will is actualized. Because a mark is a sign, it manifests that property is a grammatical, as opposed to an aesthetic, principle. Property rights thus come to resemble allegory and *Vorstellung*. Like allegory, the mark rests upon the necessity that its abstract content be recognized. For there to be "congruity between subjectivity and the abstract meaning . . . the allegorical being must make subjectivity so hollow that all specific individuality vanishes from it." Having pointed out the instability of the predicative power of "I is I" in an analysis of Section 20 of the lesser *Logic*, de Man remarks, "What the allegory narrates is, therefore, in Hegel's own words, 'the separation or disarticulation of subject from predicate.' "[28]

Unlike property, the "goods" or "characteristics" that constitute the "private personality and the universal essence of my self-consciousness are inalienable and my right to them is imprescriptible," but they can be assigned away when they are externalized in superstition, slavery, encumbrances on property, and disqualification from holding property (*PR*, 52–53, 55). Women's self-consciousness is alien-

---

28. De Man, "Sign and Symbol," 775. The quotation from Hegel appears in *HA*, I, 399.

able not only because women are barred from holding property but because they are, for Hawthorne and Hegel, devoid of interiority. Hester may be introspective, but unlike Dimmesdale, she lacks the philosophical idea that constitutes interiority: Dimmesdale's *A* is the product of thought and stands for *Art*; Hester's is an empty universal and stands for *Abstract*. The self proves to be as alienable as property. As Michaels points out, Alice Pyncheon's self is purchased by Matthew Maule: she is exchanged by her father for the lost documents that give the Pyncheons title to the Eastern territories.[29] We can add that Hawthorne prefigures Maule's appropriation of Alice Pyncheon in the Venetian artist's portrait of her, which is preserved in a private residence in England "not on account of any associations with the original, but for its value as a picture" (*HSG*, 201). Alice is a commodity—her portrait's value is as much economic as it is aesthetic. And her transformation into a commodity is underlined by the portrait being mentioned when she is summoned to appear before Maule. Moreover, both her portrait and her father's betrayal of her form a pattern consistent with Hawthorne's work—women are equated with alienable exteriority.

In *The Scarlet Letter*, the theme of woman's exteriority is allegorized in the letter, which is the sign of Hester's sin, as is Pearl, whom Hester dresses to resemble the letter in order to reinforce the union of sensuous form and spirit; but the *A* does not give Hester to herself in the sense of allowing the fusion of outer and inner being: "It had the effect of a spell, taking her out of the ordinary relations with humanity, and inclosing her in a sphere by herself" (*SL*, 54). Hester represents for Hawthorne the problematic of *Darstellung*. She is one of those "who speculate the most boldly" but do not act. "The thought suffices them, without investing itself in the flesh and blood of action." It is only in Pearl's education that her "thought had something to wreak itself upon" (*SL*, 164–65). Hester's consciousness is alienable, since she possesses it in the abstract universality of the *A*, which signals the empty subjectivity of pure thought. The *A*, moreover, is appropriated by the marketplace in the form of Hester's embroidery, her feminine art, as Hawthorne calls it. Her labors produce a purely ornamental commodity whose only value lies in its distinguishing "individuals dignified by rank or wealth" from the "plebeian order." Anyone who purchases

29. Michaels, "Romance and Real Estate," 83, 87.

Hester's art appropriates her otherness and thus comes to confirm social divisions and the order of divine retribution.

The marketplace of letters first appears in "The Custom-House." Hawthorne refers to his pecuniary motives for accepting the sinecure that he hoped would free him to write, but the only thing his name appears on is the merchandise that comes through his office. When he discovers Surveyor Pue's documents, Hawthorne imagines the ghost urging him to make the story public and telling him " 'the profit shall be all your own. . . . But, I charge you . . . give to your predecessor's memory the credit which will be rightfully its due' " (*SL*, 33–34). By giving credit, he will profit in return. And so once he is "decapitated," he makes "an investment in ink, paper, and steel-pen" and is a literary man once more (*SL*, 43). Having invested in the tools of his trade, Hawthorne can turn a profit on a borrowed story and, in turn, extend to the broker (for Pue cannot be called an author) credit for having provided the fund justifying Hawthorne's capital expenditure.

Hawthorne presents himself in the role of copyist here and in the other prefaces. The theme of copying is more pronounced in *The Marble Faun*, where Hawthorne not only acknowledges having stolen works by living sculptors to supply material for Kenyon, his fictional artist, but also characterizes the American artist as copyist. Miriam goes so far as to tell Kenyon that "you sculptors are, of necessity, the greatest plagiarists in the world" not because they copy live models but because the art of sculpture "has wrought itself out, and come fairly to an end" (*MF*, 124). In fact, Kenyon works in plaster, and he leaves it to an underclass of artisans to realize his ideas in marble: "His creative power has wrought it with a word." (Hawthorne's allusion to Genesis echoes Hegel's preeminent example of the prosaic: " 'And God said, Let there be light, and there was light.' . . . [T]hus light is degraded to the rank of a word" [*LPR*, II, 188].) Hawthorne offers some reflections on the sculptor's freedom from the "drudgery of actual performance" and finally denies him any credit for his work: "They are not his work, but that of some nameless machine in human shape" (*MF*, 115). Because the reproduction of the work lies in the hands of the laborer, it no longer belongs to Kenyon. He has alienated his creation. Nevertheless, the work cannot be said to be fully possessed by his artisans, because they copy a mere externality and not the idea. The laborers transform nature by imposing, not their will on it, but that of an alien consciousness. This scene in *The Marble Faun* stages the master-slave dialectic, wherein through work the slave frees himself from his attachment to natural existence and becomes master (*PS*, 117–18).

Hilda is the other copyist in the romance. Having left America for Italy, she has lost whatever impulse she had for originality and now devotes herself to copying the masters. Her reverence for "these wonderful men" is so deep that she subordinates herself to them and so "became a copyist." Hilda, it would seem, is a slave to the masters in a nearly literal sense. But whereas Kenyon is ultimately dependent upon his laborers to actualize his creation—to fix it in external form and give it determinate being—Hilda's method of copying a portion of a painting "in which the spirit and essence of the picture culminated . . . enabled [her] to execute what the great Master had conceived in his imagination, but had not so perfectly succeeded in putting upon canvas" (*MF*, 58–59).

Here and in the description of Kenyon's studio, Hawthorne suggests that copying is a higher achievement than originality, since it is of a purely mechanical nature and free from the picture-making capacity of imagination. In fact, he calls Hilda an "exquisitely effective piece of mechanism" who helps the dead achieve "his ideal." Hilda is a machine that copies not the external form of the work but the idea of the Master, just as the laborers are machines that translate Kenyon's word into art. By "sacrificing" herself, she chooses "to be the handmaiden of those old magicians." Hawthorne concludes that Hilda's loss of originality is a gift: as a painter in her own right, she would have given us "pretty fancies of snow and moonlight, the counterpart, in picture, of so many feminine achievements in literature" (*MF*, 61). It is both sacrifice and gift, and therefore remarkably close to Hegel's master-slave dialectic and Georges Bataille's reading of it.[30] Hilda's sacrifice is a pure negation that transforms desire into the purely material form of the work. As desire held in check, work holds death in reserve by turning the negative into something determinate (*PS*, 118). Rather than produce "feminine" art, she produces funerary monuments for male artists. But this repression of the feminine is not complete; "pretty fancies of snow and moonlight" may very well be said to describe Hawthorne's own tales. Moreover, the dark heroines of Hawthorne's fiction—Hes-

30. Georges Bataille, "Hegel, la mort et le sacrifice," *Deucalion*, V (October, 1955), 21–43.

ter, Zenobia, and Miriam—are all figures for the artist who must be destroyed to allow the male narrative voice to emerge.

Insofar as Hilda's work is the external form of the Master's thought, her work is a product of mechanical memory and is itself "memory *qua* memory . . . the merely *external* mode, or merely *existential* aspect of thought" (*PM*, 223). In the *Philosophy of Right*, Hegel says that in

> works of art, the form, which makes an image of the thought in an external material, is a thing [*als Ding*] so much the property of the producing individual that a copy of it is essentially the product of the original producer's [*der eigenen*] intellectual [*geistigen*] and technical skill. In a literary work, the form, through which it is an external thing [*Sache*], is *of a mechanical kind*, just as it is in the invention of a technical device—in the former, because the thought is presented only in a series of isolated abstract *signs*, not in concrete illustrations; in the latter, because it has an altogether mechanical content—, and the manner and way of producing such things as things belongs to the usual dexterities. (*PR*, 54)[31]

The original producer's claim over any copy lies in his/her being the source of the idea. Hegel here seems to be referring to the plastic arts of sculpture and painting, because he suggests there is a union of form and content. Kenyon does not truly possess his creation, since he lacks the technical skill of sculpting in marble. But neither technical skill nor thought, in the sense of *Darstellung*, is necessary for literature, because the purely technical or mechanical aspect of copying is indistinguishable from the object that is being copied; the relation between thought and matter is as mechanical in the "original" creation as it is in the copy. Writing is a purely mechanical activity governed by *Gedächtnis*, the faculty that "has always to do with signs only" (*PM*, 213).

Hawthorne's account of the arts is an allegory of writing—it narrates the abolition of the distinction between meaning and name. The object that Hilda deals with is not "an image derived from an intuition," to quote Hegel, "it has rather to do with an object which is the product of intelligence itself" (*PM*, 220). Since we know our thoughts only by words, words are "an inward externality." When intelligence receives into itself the word, "it takes on the nature of a *thing* and to

---

31. The translation is by Bainard Cowan.

such a degree that subjectivity, in its distinction from the thing, becomes quite empty, a mindless container of words, that is, a mechanical memory" (*PM*, 221). Intelligence is a machine that recalls words; it is the "inwardizing representation," which makes intelligence "the mere *being*, the universal space of names as such, i.e. of meaningless words" (*PM*, 221–22). Words no longer are the material manifestation of thought but are thought itself as the reproduction of a purely external and material script. Hilda's copies are just such a pure externality. Because the masters never fully realize their ideas, Hilda does not copy the external form; she copies the idea, and in doing so, she deposits the thought in its material form. Thus, she renders such perfect copies, because they do not proceed from the image to thought, as would a mere reproduction of the surface. Hilda is a figure for mechanical memory.

As a purely external embodiment of thought, romance remains the allegorical undoing of the foundation of the inalienable self in property. Just as property is founded on the importing of a foreign signification to a sensuous material, the foundations of self and property rest in the aesthetic principle of representation, or the presentation of thought in matter. But if we follow Hegel's analysis of allegory, then we find that aesthetics is the ideology of bourgeois individualism and that allegory is the critical dissolution of mimesis and, consequently, of the link between consciousness and nature. The desire for an inalienable self is a flight not from capitalism and realism but to capitalism and mimesis insofar as mimesis or imitation is confused with referentiality. Whenever realistic fiction is spoken of as a mirror to the world, the critic has confused mimesis with referentiality—language cannot imitate anything but language.[32] Referentiality in either case proceeds from language. If the mark, as a representation of my will, belongs to nature, and nature as thought in-itself or pure externality becomes for-itself or time, then nature is mine by virtue of my endowing it with consciousness. But as the relation between property and the will is mediated by the mark, ownership is "a more or less accidental concatenation produced by the subjective activity of the poet, by the immersion of his spirit in an external existence" (*HA*, I, 378). I quote once more from the section on the comparative art form to draw attention

32. See Gérard Genette, *Figures of Literary Discourse*, trans. Alan Sheridan (New York, 1982), 132.

to the extension of the prosaic world through the realms of art, religion, and politics.

The Hegelian world of prose is both the mundane world bereft of spirit and the unproblematic world where the idea is realized in the state. Nineteenth-century America seems to have embodied these two contradictory meanings. As the flourishing of a capitalist society purportedly free from the deeply rooted class structures of Europe that produced a series of revolutions, America, in the eyes of commentators from Tocqueville to Pound, was not a place for poetry. This version of the prosaic world finds its expression in those critics who either argue for romance as an alternative world or look to both romance and the novel as the ideological reflections of society. Hegelian prosaism finds its shape in the nonaesthetic mode of allegory and its purely abstract and mechanical linking of form and idea. This side of prosaism can be seen as the critical identity of the work as an infinitely repeatable text, but as this identity rests in allegory, it is a synthesis of meaning and name, or what Hegel calls the "fundamental desideratum of language" (*PM*, 217); in other words, it is a purely mechanical exteriority. The aesthetic is an ideological phenomenon that signals the forgetting of this purely mechanical linking of interiority and exteriority. It is the aesthetic, therefore, that allows us not only to read literature as the phenomenalization of the idea but also to link consciousness to history. The aesthetic and prosaism exist in a chiasmatic relation wherein the latter is the suppressed trace of the former.

If we return to our earlier discussion of the critical characterization of romance in America, we find that the originality of American fiction lies in a self-reflexive totalizing of consciousness and nature or the rational and irrational. Hegel determined the relation to the Other or the irrational through negation; hence, thought thinks the negative and thereby incorporates it. In those critics who have disclosed how American writers demystify the metaphysics of a pure origin, the transgression of the self-reflexive unity occurs within this discourse and, therefore, affirms it. Transgression is a negative knowledge. The Emerson who declares that "every man is a quotation" or the Pound who speaks of the "American habit of quotation" shakes the founding principles of the American Adam only to elevate repetition into the principle of an "American" originality. Emerson exemplifies the American mode of literary production—copying as creative reading. American literature belongs not to post-modernism; it is post-art. American literature has always been for us a thing of the past. It is and always has been a critical literature; that is, the subject of American literature is its exposition, performance, staging, presentation—its *Darstellung*. But *Darstellung* is undermined by *Vorstellung*. Art always occupies a central place in Hawthorne's romances, whether it be thematized in Hester's embroidery and Coverdale's fondness for metaphors drawn from the theater or whether it be represented by Holgrave's daguerreotypes and the artwork of Kenyon, Miriam, and Hilda.

Reflexivity has been the major theme in Hawthorne criticism, but reflexivity is just an effect of the chiasmatic relation between aesthetics and prosaism. Every reading is of necessity a doubling of the text, splitting it into an inside and an outside. What is presented in sensation must be altered in order for the passage from sensation to thought to take place. But this reflective division of the object into ideal content and phenomenal appearance is possible only by virtue of what Derrida calls "erasure": "Finitude then becomes infinitude according to a non-Hegelian identity: through an interruption that suspends the equation between the mark and meaning."[33]

In his essay on Mallarmé's "Mimique," Derrida writes that the mark determining textuality can account for the totalizing power of a reflexive reading only if the "graphic 'affinities,' " the marks within a signifying chain, are erased: "Thematicism necessarily leaves out of account the formal, phonic, or graphic 'affinities' that do not have the shape of a word, the calm unity of the verbal sign."[34] But what would a nonthematic reading be? Such a reading would first of all not be an account of how tropes or themes undercut the ostensible argument or object of representation; it would be closer to an account of how representation takes place, but even then the text would be read as the mirroring of its own mode of production. Finally, it would not reside solely in the denial of a transcendental signified or a truth value in the text. The question then remains, can there be a nonthematic reading of a literary text?—which is as much as to say, can there be a reading of a text that is other than Hegelian? We locate in Hegel's concept of property the economy of *Darstellung*: the exteriorization of will, or the idea, must always be a differentiating of exterior and interior, a disarticulation of subject from predicate that permits the pure transparency

33. Derrida, *Dissemination*, 253.
34. *Ibid.*, 255.

that makes reading, or the recognition of the other's will, possible. This economy is governed by allegory, which conveys its own mode of thematization, but the graphic remains; the spacings that constitute the signifying chain are suppressed.

We discover that Hawthorne—and the same could be shown of Melville, Emerson, Dickinson, *et al.*—shares the essential traits of romanticism with Hegel's philosophy. To produce a deconstructive—that is to say, a nonreflexive—reading of Hawthorne would be a doubling of the commentary, a reading that remembers in a non-Hegelian way the purely grammatical character of signification, the nonidentity of meaning and name, and turns the prosaic world into a critical one.

# Romancing the Stone
## Melville's Critique of Ideology in *Pierre*

· · · · · · · · · · · · · · · · · ·

*John Carlos Rowe*

The founders of Rome . . . —Romulus and Remus—are, according to
the tradition, themselves freebooters—represented as from their earliest
days thrust out from the Family, and as having grown up in a state of
isolation from family affection. . . .

The immoral active severity of the Romans in this private side of
character necessarily finds its counterpart in the passive severity of
their political union. For the severity which the Roman experienced
from the State he was compensated by a severity, identical in nature,
which he was allowed to indulge towards his family—a servant on the
one side, a despot on the other.

—Hegel, *The Philosophy of History*

In his Introduction to the 1949 Hendricks House edition of *Pierre*,
Henry A. Murray criticizes Melville for not providing a clearer cultural
motivation for Pierre's alienation: "Melville does not present us with a
pertinent spectacle or analysis of American society, nor does he state
explicitly what forces of the culture are so inimical to his spirit that he
and his hero are driven to condemn it *in toto*. . . . This hiatus in emotional logic is one of the outstanding structural defects of the novel."[1]
Murray very clearly identifies a central problem that has caused both
contemporary reviewers and twentieth-century scholars to judge *Pierre*
as Melville's most incoherent work. What little explicit commentary
Melville gives the reader about social issues appears in those chapters
set in New York, after Pierre has crossed his Rubicon and rebelled
against his family. Indeed, what Murray terms "this hiatus in emotional
logic" applies equally well to the customary division critics make be-

1. Henry A. Murray, Introduction to *Pierre, or The Ambiguities*, by Herman Melville (New York, 1949), xcvi.

tween the pastoralism of the domestic romance at Saddle-Meadows and the surrealism of the episodes in the city. Instead of offering us the naturalist's microscopic examination of urban corruption, Melville focuses on Pierre's efforts to write his "infernal book." Instead of the pastoral romance of Saddle-Meadows giving way to the gritty realism of New York, we find pastoralism transformed into a metafictional romance in which virtually every urban experience relates to Pierre's problem of artistic creation. The social issues in *Pierre* thus appear to be forgotten as Melville shifts his attention from the domestic conflicts at Saddle-Meadows to Pierre's artistic problems in the city.

Yet this problem may well be a consequence of our critical methods rather than an inherent defect in the work's composition and structure. This is not to say that *Pierre* is an unacknowledged masterpiece. Quite the contrary, the novel is full of difficulties that I shall not try to resolve, intending as I do instead to use them to clarify Melville's contempt for "the man of letters" and thus for himself. Melville's wicked critique of authorship is not, however, simply a symptom of madness or uncontrolled ranting. His indictment of idealist philosophy and literary practice, especially focused on the Transcendentalists, is coherent and profound, because it recognizes how powerfully such abstractions would serve the political purposes of the new American ruling classes. At the same time, he could find no acceptable alternative to this complicity of the author with those more powerful authorities whom Melville judged to have ruined the republican dream from the beginning. Intricately worked out in the very novelistic form Melville had come to detest, his critique of ideology in *Pierre* remains a testament to the limits of literature as a force for political reform. In *Pierre*, Melville bids farewell to the literary forms of romance and the novel neither because he had lost control of them nor because he had lost control of his own life, unless we understand that life to be inseparable from his conception of his vocation as an author. What he recognizes instead is how powerfully these forms contribute to the social forces of domination they so often claim to contest. The argument of *Pierre* is thus *too* coherent and *too* convincing to result in any other conclusion than that Literature is the enemy.

Above all, it is literature's inclination to make its fantasy credible that troubles Melville, because he recognizes this tendency toward "fictional realization" as comparable to the work of ideology in naturalizing otherwise arbitrary social fictions. Among the many literary forms, romance and novel tend particularly to accomplish this work of naturalization by way of characters and dramatic situations that substitute interpersonal psychologies for more complex social and economic forces. In *Pierre*, Melville focuses on family relations both at Saddle-Meadows and in New York because he recognizes that the family is the institution through which the dramatic social changes of Jacksonian America would be rendered acceptable and normal. And it is the family as the focus of the fiction of manners—whether it be the sentimental romance or the "novel of social manners"—that had such a powerful influence on Melville's readers. As a primarily bourgeois form, the nineteenth-century novel of social manners quite obviously helped legitimate its middle-class readers and their values, often by ruthlessly criticizing aristocratic pretensions. Insofar as bourgeois values are identified with democratic sentiments, the novel became the primary literary form of urban and industrial America. It is, of course, quite conventional to notice how the novel of social manners from Jane Austen to Henry James concentrates on the specific social functions of a fictional family. More often than not, the family's class identification governs other mimetic criteria, even in writers, like Trollope and James, for whom bourgeois values are considered necessary to the well-ordered state. Even so, it is surprising how often literary critics treat such family relations in phenomenological and psychological terms. By personalizing characters and dramatizing interpersonal conflicts, novelists tempt readers to identify with characters in ways that encourage the use of psychological and phenomenological terms to understand the narrative functions of characters. One consequence of this critical inclination is the relative neglect of the social and political significance of family relations in fiction. In short, the form of the novel and the reader-competence it constructs often work contrary to the larger class significance that "character" and "the family" are supposed to convey.

Social historians traditionally have had as much difficulty studying the social functions of the family as literary scholars have had. Whereas literary critics tend to treat fictional families in psychological terms, social historians have relied on demographic statistics and other empirical data that do not adequately reflect the family as a form of social behavior. As Mark Poster has written, "While quantitative demographic studies are needed, they cannot provide historians with a concept of the family that can pose the important questions and render the family intelligible in premodern and modern Europe."[2] Only recently have works like Philippe Ariès' *Centuries of Childhood: A Social History of Family Life* and Jacques Donzelot's *The Policing of Families* begun to combine psychological and traditional sociological approaches to the family in order to understand the particular mediatory function played by families in the relation of individual behavior to communal practices.[3]

The rediscovery of the family by the social historian has interesting consequences for the literary critic. Literary critics interested in the political functions of artistic forms should find theoretical suggestions in the work of those social historians who have begun to write the "social psychology" of the family as a historical institution. The analogy between the family and art is not merely coincidental; both employ discursive practices that explicitly combine public and private terms and values. Both the family and the artistic work are representational forms that must address the bases for their actual and nominal authorities (parent and author), the origins and ends of such authority (biology and genius; history and tradition), and the status of those subject to such authorities (children and readers).

I have suggested that Melville's concentration on family relations and artistic creation in the two major movements of *Pierre* has encouraged critics like Murray to consider Melville's often strident social criticism to be unjustified or inexplicable. I want to argue that Melville's social criticism in *Pierre* is focused primarily on the social psychologies of the nineteenth-century family and Romantic theories of art. I want to demonstrate not merely how the family and art serve different social purposes, which are often disguised by the naturalness and privacy of the family and the idealism of art, but also how the family and art participate with each other in maintaining a nineteenth-century American politics of self-reliance.

The social history of the nineteenth-century American family is one of the principal concerns of Michael Paul Rogin's *Subversive Genealogy: The Politics and Art of Herman Melville.* In its attention to the socioeconomic impact of Jacksonian America on the family, Rogin's study

2. Mark Poster, *Critical Theory of the Family* (London, 1978), 144.
3. Philippe Ariès, *Centuries of Childhood: A Social History of Family Life,* trans. R. Baldick (New York, 1965); Jacques Donzelot, *The Policing of Families,* trans. Robert Hurley (New York, 1979).

gives historical specificity to Eric Sundquist's psychoanalytical approach to the question of nineteenth-century literary authority, so often figured in metaphors of paternity, in *Home as Found*. Both critics pay special attention to *Pierre* as Melville's defensive autobiography. *Pierre* is both Melville's willful rebellion against the aristocratic pretensions of his mother's family, the Gansevoorts, and the fictional confession of his failure to live up to his aristocratic ancestry. Characterizing himself in *Pierre* as a dilettante and literary dabbler, Melville also associates himself with Pierre's unsuccessful efforts to champion those characters exploited by the Glendinnings: the illegitimate Isabel, the vanishing Indian, the black slaves kept by Pierre's ancestors. Rogin calls *Pierre* a "bourgeois family nightmare" that employs Pierre's initiation into urban life to explore the crisis of the family occasioned by the rapid industrialization of Jacksonian America: "The adolescent male, coming of sexual age, symbolized the disruptive forces at work in Jacksonian America. Poised to break free from his family of origin, sexually and in his working life, he was the locus for Jacksonian anxieties about the disruption of the preindustrial family. The chaste woman . . . was society's agent to discipline him."[4]

The great transformation of America from an agrarian to an industrial economy in the first half of the nineteenth century brought with it the customary problems associated with industrial production: the alienation of the laborer from both the finished product and the control of his own labor, the growing division between the workplace and the home, and the migration of workers from rural towns to unfamiliar cities. It is commonplace to speak of the social consequences of the capitalist economy that began to govern American production in this period, but American capitalism did much more than merely establish the economic determinants for social changes. Ideology may be defined as the collective effect of different discursive practices designed to naturalize or normalize new social practices and working relations. In the simplest Marxist terms, this naturalization is accomplished by means of an apparently "free" exchange of labor-power for wages, whereby the disruptive and alienating owners and workers would appear to be part of a larger democratic process. Much of Marx's attention in *Capital* concerns just how this apparently "free" exchange between

4. Michael Paul Rogin, *Subversive Genealogy: The Politics and Art of Herman Melville* (New York, 1983), 165; Eric Sundquist, *Home as Found: Authority and Genealogy in Nineteenth-Century American Literature* (Baltimore, 1979).

laborers and capitalists is, in fact, a fated, determined means of subordinating laborer to owner, thus reproducing the master/servant hierarchy at the heart of capitalism. In fact, it is the way in which capitalist ideology mystifies these master/servant relations as much as the different historical and economic conditions that distinguishes capitalist class relations from feudal hierarchies.

Another, more complicated and more subversive method of normalization, however, occurs in the diverse forms and institutions of everyday life that have little apparent connection with the means of material production. What Louis Althusser has described as the process of *interpellation* and Antonio Gramsci as hegemonic discourse approximates the complex means by which ideological values are internalized and psychically lived by apparently "free" individuals under capitalism.[5] The family is, of course, one of those social forms, even though it is directly involved in social production and reproduction. In an elementary sense, the labor force depends upon the production of the family. Yet because its means of production seems so self-evidently *natural* and *biological*, the family is an especially attractive medium for disguising ideological messages and thus contributing to the naturalization of new social relations. Engels' *The Origins of the Family, Private Property, and the State* is the classic Marxian work on the relation between private, psychological relations and ideology, but both Marx and Engels treat the family as secondary to the mode of production. As Poster observes, for Marx and Engels, "the family is epiphenomenal compared to the mode of production. In general their writings relegated the family to the backwaters of superstructure."[6]

Engels' note to the third German edition of *Capital* makes clear that the origin of the family was a troublesome issue for Marx: "Subsequent and very thorough investigations into the primitive condition of man led the author to the conclusion that it was not the family that originally developed into the tribe, but that, on the contrary, the tribe was the primitive and spontaneously developed form of human association, based on consanguinity, and that out of the first incipient loosen-

5. Louis Althusser's "Ideology and Ideological State Apparatuses (Notes toward an Investigation)," in Althusser, *Lenin and Philosophy and Other Essays*, trans. Ben Brewster (New York, 1971), provides the most extended discussion of interpellation. Antonio Gramsci develops the notion of hegemonic discourse in *The Prison Notebooks*. See Gramsci, *Selections from the Prison Notebooks*, trans. and ed. Quintin Hoare and Geoffrey Nowell Smith (New York, 1971).

6. Friedrich Engels, *The Origin of the Family, Private Property, and the State* (New York, 1942); Poster, *Critical Theory of the Family*, 43.

ing of the tribal bonds, the many and various forms of the family were afterwards developed."[7] As sketchy and sometimes contradictory as Marx's critical remarks on the family are, they focus with some consistency on the *bourgeois* family. Yet even the vulgar Marxian distinction between economic base and ideological superstructure permits Marx and Engels to comprehend the mystification of economic motives as *natural* attachments and the legitimation of a deceptive "individualism" achieved in the bourgeois family. For in its reflection of capitalist alienation, the bourgeois family is where the "private individual" is at home, rather than in the more public groups Marx associates with the historical origins of social organization. As Raymond Williams observes, "the dominance of the sense [of the family as a] small kin-group was probably not established before the early nineteenth century."[8] In effect, the *biological* legitimacy of the "family" belongs to nineteenth-century capitalism, and such modern kin relations are integrally related to historically contemporary conceptions of the individual.

Hegel has a great deal to say about the family, in part because his own philosophical project so explicitly attempts to legitimate bourgeois individualism. Hegel understands the family as the active and historical mediation between individual and social forms of self-consciousness. The very centrality of the family in Hegel's philosophy reflects his emphasis on individual self-consciousness, which would serve nineteenth-century American capitalism as a convenient philosophical justification for entrepreneurial practices. Nevertheless, the main thrust of Hegel's idealism was toward a concept of "self-consciousness" that would find its dialectical realization in a larger social self-consciousness rather than in the mere exchange of the father's authority for that of the capitalist or ruler. In Hegel, the family is the virtual unconscious of man's social impulse and the historical process by which such an unconscious achieves conscious form involves the transformation of the family's privacy into public forms of social existence. For Hegel, the state does not merely imitate the structure of familial authority, it dialectically transforms that authority with the aim of achieving the ultimate self-governance citizens would achieve in Hegel's ideal community. In the course of such transformation, the limited authority of the family is negated.

In *Pierre*, Melville seems to criticize urban America for having

---

7. Karl Marx, *Capital*, trans. Ben Fowkes (3 vols.; New York, 1977), I, 471*n*26.
8. *Ibid.*, 472; Raymond Williams, *Keywords: A Vocabulary of Culture and Society* (Rev. ed.; New York, 1983), 133.

forgotten or neglected the significant social role played by the family. In the pastoral world of Saddle-Meadows, social life is organized around such ruling families as the Glendinnings. In New York, Pierre encounters unruly mobs, decadent aristocrats, eccentric artists and philosophers. The carnivalesque world of the city is distinguished by the alienation of different groups and individuals, as well as by the absence of those family ties that offered Pierre some stability in the country. Even in his rebellion against his family, Pierre attempts to create a surrogate family, composed of Lucy, Isabel, and Delly, as if to compensate for the isolation they all experience in the city. In this view, Melville's social criticism appears to be quite conventional; Pierre's "fall," like that of industrial America, is his loss of those stable family associations that ought to have been the bases for his initiation into social life.

Pierre's rebellion against his family and his rejection of the stability of Saddle-Meadows, however, cannot be so easily allegorized as urban America's repudiation of the stable, preindustrial family. Like Hegel, Melville understands family and social relations to function dialectically. Melville devotes a great deal of attention to the Glendinnings' structured and closed world in order to prepare the reader for Pierre's discovery of Isabel's illegitimacy and his subsequent rejection of his heritage. The father's sin is not just his adultery with Isabel's mother but his even more pernicious refusal to accept publicly his responsibility for Isabel: that is, to establish visible signs of kinship with her. The customs and practices that encourage such secrecy are those of the preindustrial family and the class relations governed by a landed gentry. Thus it is understandable that Murray finds Melville's social criticism in *Pierre* unmotivated. Rather than exploring the significance of the Glendinnings' fatal flaw in the particular social world they govern, Melville seems to change the subject from rural to urban social issues, from aristocratic to bourgeois discursive registers. By the same token, the landed aristocracy represented by the Glendinnings seems hardly a worthwhile object for Melville's criticism. Given the rapid change from rural to urban economies in Jacksonian America, Melville's attack on an outmoded form of aristocratic rule seems unnecessary. In fact, the Glendinning family and its "secret" refer more tangibly to the plot of some European romance than to concrete social problems in nineteenth-century America.

Viewed from the perspective of Hegel's conception of the family as the "unconscious" of the state, however, Melville's concentration on the preindustrial, aristocratic family may be an indirect approach to his criticism of American capitalism. Melville stresses the European character of the Glendinning family, as if reminding democratic Americans that they might be working to produce a society that will merely repeat the hierarchical class systems of Europe. Nineteenth-century Americans were familiar with the ways southern planters imitated the pretensions of the European aristocracy. Northern industrialists frequently justified urbanization as a way of encouraging democratization and overcoming the inherent hierarchies of landed estates. By the same token, the common nineteenth-century American assumption that agrarianism and industrialism constituted two distinct spheres is by no means historically accurate. As Carolyn Porter has shown, "farming was no more impervious to the forces of specialization, rationalization, and commodification than was household manufacture or urban life, once we recognize that America was not merely a predominantly agrarian society, but a *capitalist* agrarian society."[9] American capitalism had a vested interest in promoting the different mythologies of the country and the city, preindustrial feudalism and the "free exchange" of labor under capitalism, Old World aristocracy and American democracy. By developing the narrative contiguity of country and city, aristocratic family and democratic mob, Melville may be suggesting in *Pierre* that the origins of urban corruption are to be found in the well-ordered estates of the landed gentry.

Hegel's idealist treatment of the family's relation to the state may help us formulate this problem in terms pertinent to the romantic ethos of *Pierre*. According to Hegel, the ultimate function of the family is to serve the state, virtually by acknowledging the insufficiency or limitation of the family structure as an enduring historical principle. Hegel's version of Oedipal triangulation is supposed to effect the rite of passage from family to state, from biological repetition to historical time and change. Within the narrow family, Hegel's unrealized self is metaphorized as "brother and sister," both of whom remain in bondage to an external, abstract notion of authority that is at once the father and the divine. In the family, the dialectic of self and other is worked out in terms of brother and sister, precisely because "the brother . . . is in the

---

9. Carolyn Porter, *Seeing and Being: The Plight of the Participant Observer in Emerson, James, Adams, and Faulkner* (Middletown, Conn., 1981), 65.

eyes of the sister a being whose nature is unperturbed by desire and is ethically like her own; her recognition in him is pure and unmixed with any sexual relation." [10]

In one sense, Hegel here repeats the nineteenth century's ideology of the ideal, chaste, unsexed "family," which served the purpose of repressing and controlling those sexual energies threatening a rational social order. In this regard, Hegel's metaphor of "brother and sister" for the familial dialectic of self and other merely reinforces the ideology's spiritualization of family relations in the manner Rogin has analyzed so well: "Family ideologists sought not only to intensify the bonds between mother and son, but also to spiritualize the relations of husband to wife. Pierre's game of brother and sister is supposed to establish the closeness of this son to his mother. But it also calls attention to those family reformers who, purifying the marriage bond of power and appetite, modeled the relations of husband and wife on those of brother and sister." [11] Pierre's habit of calling his mother "sister" certainly follows this ideology of the family. The spiritualization of family relations helps maintain a sharp distinction between the "proper family" and the impropriety or illegitimacy associated with sexuality. Melville's use of the conventions of the fair lady and dark woman to represent, respectively, Lucy and Isabel suggests how feminine propriety depended upon the repression of the sexual. In keeping with Melville's general critique of American transcendentalism, *Pierre* identifies idealization and spiritualization with psychic and cultural repression of basic drives and appetites. This idealization of family relations is the object of Melville's critique of ideology in *Pierre*, because it is one of the principal means of disguising the ruling class's legitimation of its right to rule. By doubling Pierre's treatment of his mother as "sister" and his incestuous relation with Isabel, Melville renders extremely ambiguous the customary distinctions between the proper family and illegitimate sexual relations. [12]

10. G. W. F. Hegel, *The Phenomenology of Mind*, trans. J. B. Baillie (New York, 1967), 477.

11. Rogin, *Subversive Genealogy*, 164.

12. Williams, *Keywords*, 132, explains that the precapitalist family was often understood as "the household," rather than in terms of specific kinship relations. There is much disagreement among scholars concerning Williams' assumption that the nuclear family and the rise of the bourgeoisie are historically contemporary developments. I am not qualified to resolve these disputes, but I am struck with the central concern in the modern novel with adultery, illegitimacy, and thus the definition of "proper" family relations.

Hegel's interpretation of the unsexual relation of brother and sister as a model for familial self-consciousness thus appears to work in accord with those nineteenth-century family ideologists criticized by Melville. In terms of his larger social argument, however, Hegel stresses this relation of brother and sister in order to identify the limitation of the family and its necessary transcendence in the social order. Dividing unrealized self-consciousness into brother and sister, Hegel establishes an unsexual relation of self and other that is the abstract model for proper citizenship in the state. Within the narrow circle of the family, the metaphors "brother and sister" are reminders of the self's dependence on external authorities—God, father, Nature. Hegel wants to demonstrate that the apparently self-moving history of the family does not produce genuine historical growth and change but merely reproduces the same structure. Given the ways the European aristocracy based its power on complex family genealogies, Hegel's argument has immediate relevance for the changing class structures of early nineteenth-century Europe. The *desire* of the family remains purely sexual or reproductive—natural and thus not yet spiritual (or self-conscious) in the proper sense of historical *Weltgeist*. Within the family, the individual remains in bondage to natural authority, which rules that the "individual" has no particularity beyond his/her identification with the species reproduced. The *unsexual* relation of brother and sister signifies for Hegel that neither brother nor sister possesses an independent and reproductive power equivalent to the natural sexuality that continues to govern the family.

By the same token, the apparent authority of the father and mother is equally dependent upon the law of biological reproduction, which they merely follow. No matter what venerable origins or trappings of power the family employs to claim its independent identity, it continues to perform the same subservient function: the reproduction of the species. Within the family form, the child's rebellion is thus always doomed merely to repeat what it attempts to escape: the hierarchical relation of the individual to an external law. *Working* at that relation, *laboring* to overcome such externality—father, God, Nature—the son or daughter merely reproduces it in the subsequent role of husband or wife. Insofar as the son's Oedipal aggression fails to negate

---

Capitalism's judgment of ethical questions often involves the settlement of property rights. Kinship relations in the novel are almost always a function of property rights and the orderly transmission of those rights, rather than the other way around.

the family and transform it into the larger forms of social law and citizenship, the son must experience his transformation into a father as incestuous. Metaphorically, *spiritually*, such philosophical incest does weaken successive generations, since it reminds the individual that his "freedom" is already fated, that his "rebellion" is merely natural, that his "self-consciousness" is simply a biological mirage rather than a genuine product of human reason. The consequence of recognizing such a limitation to individuation in the reproduction of an unchanging and external natural law can result only in what Hegel terms "unhappy consciousness," which is his own version of philosophical madness, of absolute "ambiguity."

The "illegitimacy" of the family depends upon its failure to bring its own natural legitimation to self-consciousness: the transformation of natural law into social practice. The son realizes this potential in the family by rebelling against the father and discovering his destiny as a citizen: "The individual who seeks the 'pleasure' of enjoying his particular individuality finds it in the family life, and the 'necessity' in which that pleasure passes away is his own self-consciousness as a citizen of his nation." In short, rebellion against the family works ideally to transform the natural and biological family into the more populous social "family," insofar as Hegelian dialectics may be read in organic, evolutionary terms. Within the natural family, there are only sons and daughters, fathers and mothers; the son doubles the father, the daughter the mother. Within its own reproductive cycle, then, the natural family always grows more abstract and general, working against the destiny of the human spirit to individuate itself, to realize and complete natural law as human history. What remains purely external to the "son" within the confines of the family ought to become the internal and self-regulating principle of ethical authority within the well-ordered state: "It is knowing the 'law of his own heart' as the law of all hearts, knowing the consciousness of self to be the recognized and universal ordinance of society: it is 'virtue,' which enjoys the fruits of its own sacrifice, which brings about what it sets out to do, viz. to bring the essential nature into the light of the actual present,—and its enjoyment is this universal life."[13]

For Melville as well, the nineteenth-century family is an inadequate substitute for a truly democratic society. Melville understands,

13. Hegel, *Phenomenology*, 479.

however, how the family deceives the individual with the illusion of its own self-sufficient "community" and how it is also the primal site of transformation—from self to other, nature to culture. In the former case, the "family" remains a formalist work; in the latter case, the "family" is an active social and historical force. These different functions of the "family" may be understood primarily in the ways they organize the labor of those identified with the elementary "society" of the family. Indeed, it is the labor *of* the family—in the double sense of what the family produces and what is the social consequence of a certain family structure—that Melville recognizes as an indirect means of understanding the power and function of nineteenth-century ideology.

By her own account, Isabel achieves her initial awareness of herself as a consequence of her labor:

> "I must have been nine, or ten, or eleven years old, when the pleasant-looking woman carried me away from the large house. She was a farmer's wife; and now that was my residence, the farm-house. They taught me to sew, and work with wool, and spin the wool; I was nearly always busy now. This being busy, too, this it must have been, which partly brought to me the power of being sensible of myself as something human. Now I began to feel strange differences. When I saw a snake trailing through the grass, I said to myself, That thing is not human, but I am human."[14]

Indeed, Isabel's sense of the "old bewilderings" that haunted her adolescence are certainly associated with her sense of alienation from a stable human community. When she has grown and become a burden on the farmer's family, she asks the farmer's wife to " 'hire me out to some one, let me work for some one' " (124–25). Knowing little of the ways of the world, Isabel still senses that her departure from even this adoptive family requires some change in the conditions of her labor. Whereas her labor for her adoptive family had seemed to her equivalent to the physical and psychological maintenance the family gave her, her adult labor involves her in an exchange economy, in which wages mark the difference between the labor that produces the self (labor *for* the self) and the work that produces *society*. Melville uses "The Story of

14. Herman Melville, *Pierre, or The Ambiguities* (Evanston, Ill., 1971), 122, hereinafter cited parenthetically in the text by page number.

Isabel" to present a critical reading of the conventional paradigm for romantic self-consciousness. In her spiritual and physical growth, Isabel—unlike Wordsworth in *The Prelude*—learns how integral concrete labor is to the development of a psychological personality. And she experiences as well the first consequences of the alienation of the worker from her proper labor, her only true product: that sensuous human activity realizable only within a social community.

Isabel's mystical guitar is a metaphor for the sort of social product that ought to issue from such human labor. Isabel tells Pierre that she bought the guitar from a peddler who "had got it slyly in part exchange from the servants of a grand house." It is especially important, I think, that Isabel specifies that "with part of my earnings, I bought the guitar. Straightway I took it to my little chamber in the gable, and softly laid it on my bed" (125). A few sentences earlier, Isabel also indicates just what sort of labor had earned her the means of buying the guitar: "My work was milking cows, and making butter, and spinning wool, and weaving carpets of strips of cloth." These bucolic labors are conventional enough, except that in series they offer a little genealogy of human labor from agrarian activities to cottage industry. Measured against Isabel, Pierre is especially inexperienced in the ways of ordinary labor, particularly those involving even the most elementary manufacturing. His "labor" in the course of the novel includes his work as a writer, occasional hunting, and the "work" of honor, which is to say the labor of melodrama.

Nevertheless, Isabel's labor does not signify some growth in the direction of social integration, even though the development of the series clearly suggests such socialization. Milk produces butter, just as wool produces cloth for carpets. Like Hester Prynne, Isabel is often shown sewing, and her labor as a seamstress seems nearly to objectify in the work of her hands the weaving and vining of her black hair. All such labor, however, fails to produce her "own" image, as labor in Hegel's ideal society promises. Exchanging money for the guitar, Isabel is prompted by some intuition or identification with the instrument, even though she confesses she "had never seen a guitar before." "There was a strange humming in my heart," she says, and it is this claim (and many others like it) that convince us that she is some version of Hawthorne's mystical women. As it turns out, the guitar is a crucial figure in the melodramatic plot, because it contains the mysterious, gilt signature, *Isabel*, which Isabel takes as her *own* name. And in Melville's romance of coincidences, the guitar is revealed to have been acquired by the peddler from the mansion at Saddle-Meadows, fueling Isabel's intuition that it was her *mother's* guitar. This would account for the guitar being in the possession of the servants, to whom it must have been given by Mary Glendinning in some equally intuitive understanding of its illegitimate associations. The peddler acquires it from the servants "slyly," suggesting some cheat in the exchange, as if the guitar must perpetuate its illegitimacy in its repeated circulation: the economy of illegitimacy. The peddler, of course, lives upon an exchange economy, insofar as he makes nothing in his own right. His "slyness' is precisely his "craft," because perfectly honest, market-value exchanges would leave him penniless. To the value of the goods he offers, he must add the "cost" of his labor, which more than anything else amounts to his "slyness."

Ironically, Isabel's wages are part of an exchange economy in which the *need* to purchase some means of self-expression (the guitar) reflects the fact that Isabel's actual labor is alien, not an integral part of her spiritual and psychological development. Indeed, Isabel's sense of her alienation from *any* society may well be her intuition of the conditions governing the laborer in such an exchange economy. And it is this sense of alienation that provokes her not just to "uncover" her family origins but also to imagine that family to be the means of *protecting* her from a hostile, alienating world. It should not surprise us, then, that guitar and family origins are so intimately related in the plot: art as a "leisure-time" expression of the inner self and the family as a "private" validation of the self are related defenses against alienating labor. Isabel's regression from socialization to the narrow circle of her lost family heritage may also be understood as her rebellion against the romantic ideal of *Bildung* that her own story tries to sketch out. And this regression, like Pierre's own failure to grow "beyond" the love or conflict of the Glendinning family, expresses the failure of the larger social order to overcome (or at least *use productively*) the alienation of its workers.

What the guitar does for Isabel is effectively swerve her labors from her own socialization (from cows to carpets, Nature to Culture) in the direction of a self-expression that is at once sexual and illegitimate. In the context of the explicit sexual themes of *Pierre*, Isabel's first act of placing the guitar on her bed reminds us of the feminine form of the instrument. Insofar as it hides Isabel's own *assumed* name beneath a removable panel (I assume this is a decorative cover of the opening in the sound-box: a sort of hymen), the guitar serves as a sexually sugges-tive metonymy for Isabel herself. In this regard, we might conclude that her labor has provided her the concrete means (wages) of achieving self-expression that may communicate with the world.

Unlike the Memnon Stone, which is a mere ancient "gimmick" that simulates the voice of the divine, and unlike Westervelt's "trick" of the "Veiled Lady" in *The Blithedale Romance*, Isabel's guitar represents a genuine artistic desire to give objective, and thus communicable, form to her self-consciousness. By transforming work into wages, then into the music of the guitar, Isabel's labor initiates the transformation of individual activity into a social function, of mere existence into socially significant being. This constant metamorphosis is Emersonian, and it would place metaphor at the *heart* of the human project of bringing the world to self-consciousness. As a genuine "product" of Isabel's own labor, the guitar assumes a "real body," much in the manner of Whit-man's poetic body, insofar as it "embodies" those universals by which human beings recognize each other as fundamentally social. Yet we must remember that the guitar is initially *not* the product of Isabel's own labor. The guitar *becomes* her own only as she *labors* upon it, learn-ing how to make the music by which her story is told to others.

The guitar "plays," however, as if independent of Isabel herself, the dreamy story of her life, and Isabel understands the music to have only one purpose: to establish contact with her "brother," Pierre. In this sense, then, the music of the guitar merely plays the *family tune*, thus guaranteeing that Isabel will "legitimate" the name within the gui-tar as her "origin," her "mother." As such, the guitar does not serve the higher function of art in Hegel of mediating between citizen and di-vine, between social history and universal order, but merely "mysti-fies" and "enchants" Isabel and Pierre in the magic circle of the family. In effect, the guitar negates Isabel's more earthly labors, and it does so precisely by serving as a fetish for her *absent* family. This lost family is Isabel's imaginary compensation for her lack of social integration. The nineteenth-century sentimental romance used plots like Isabel's story to suggest the uniqueness of the illegitimate child's social exclusion; Melville's more encompassing plot eventually transforms Isabel's eccen-tric fate into the repressed story of respectable sons and daughters. By the end of the narrative, virtually every important character will have been revealed as inherently *illegitimate*. A substitute for her social la-bor, the guitar offers two compensations in place of a true democracy.

In the plot, the guitar divulges the secret of Isabel's family lineage and origins. As a musical instrument, it provides the spiritual and ideal pleasures of art in compensation for labor that within this social context fails to produce any psychic or social growth.

Without claiming much knowledge of nineteenth-century guitar production in America, I want to suggest that the name in the guitar may well be simply a trade or model name. Even in cottage industry, the name inside a guitar would normally be taken as that of its producer rather than its owner, except in the case of some expensive, custom guitar designed for a titled aristocrat. The cottage industry serving a feudal aristocracy like that at Saddle-Meadows could *only* sign the *same name* for producer and owner, since the lord or lady of the tenant lands "owns" both the means of production and the identity of the producers. The landed gentry gives titles to all the products of its lands, legitimating those products only with its signature. One of the functions of art in such feudal societies is to provide the tokens of that name, ranging from the architecture of the manor house to the trophies and objets d'art in the great hall.

Yet the secret signature in the guitar is an *illegitimate* name, even if we assume that it is *not* the real name of the elder Pierre Glendinning's Frenchwoman. The unconscious of the aristocratic Glendinning line is its very illegitimacy, which is not to say simply that the veneer of respectability is maintained to hide the unauthorized affair of the father. Critics as various as Murray, Milton Stern, Sundquist, and Rogin have called attention to the genealogy of the Glendinnings out of Pierre's paternal great-grandfather, who, "mortally wounded, had sat unhorsed on his saddle in the grass, with his dying voice, still cheering his men" in battle against the Indians in the French and Indian War (5–6). This event, of course, gives its *name* to Saddle-Meadows, which continues to be haunted by the usurpation that initiated this American aristocratic line. As Carolyn Karcher observes, "Melville in fact comments on the double irony that America may have sold her democratic birthright for an aristocratic mess of pottage, and that the ingredients constituting that pottage—lineage, title, landed property—are all tainted."[15]

The history of aristocratic pretensions is described by Melville in

---

15. Carolyn L. Karcher, *Shadow over the Promised Land: Slavery, Race, and Violence in Melville's America* (Baton Rouge, 1980), 94.

terms of those "incessant restorations and creations" designed to mask their artificial origins, which on close examination generally betray the theft, piracy, and military conquest that Marx considered the means of the precapitalist accumulation of capital (10). Critics have often connected the Glendinnings' aristocratic pretensions with Pierre's fantastic conception of himself and the melodrama that such a self-image seems to require. More interesting is Melville's contention that the rise of the bourgeoisie, which he generally traces to the execution of Charles I and the exile of Charles II, leads, not to an authentic democracy, but merely to the manufacture of new and explicitly arbitrary titles in the place of those social institutions that would transcend the family and thereby *realize* a larger human community. The history of the English peerage is a chronicle of such artificial titles: "For not Thames is so sinuous in his natural course, not the Bridgewater Canal more artificially conducted, than blood in the veins of that winding or manufactured nobility" (10).

Anticipating subsequent critics who would complain that his aristocratic romance has little to do with American democracy, Melville calls attentions to the Dutch patroons, like the Gansevoorts, whose lineages dwarf the more limited spans of their English equivalents, "those grafted families" who "successively live and die on the eternal soil of a name" (10). The difference between these American aristocrats and the English is that the former stake their claims to nobility on the property that they possess, whereas the English gentry make vain appeals to the past, often to fictionalized lineages: "But our lords, the Patroons, appeal not to the past, but they point to the present. One will show you that the public census of a county, is but part of the roll of his tenants. Ranges of mountains, high as Ben Nevis or Snowdon, are their walls; and regular armies, with staffs of officers, crossing rivers with artillery, and marching through primeval woods, and threading vast rocky defiles, have been sent out to distrain upon three thousand farmer-tenants of one landlord, at a blow" (11).

Murray points out that Melville is recalling in this passage the militiamen who set out from Albany on December 9, 1839, to subdue "a strong force of anti-rent farmers assembled on the Helderbergs" (435). The Anti-Rent protests in New York between 1839 and 1846 give strong historical credibility to Melville's argument that America does indeed have a powerful feudal aristocracy. The conventional reading of this passage as Melville's effort to defend America against English jibes at its "newness" and its "lack of history" does not address Melville's curious insistence on the appeal by American aristocrats to the present rather than to the past. Melville foresees in this passage the peculiarly American aristocrat who by the end of the Civil War would be known in caricature as "the Tycoon." This aristocrat makes no appeal to the past but relies instead on the accumulated wealth that quite literally expands his present, giving him authority over the historical moment. Indeed, this aristocrat's power is essentially antihistorical, bent as it is upon turning the "resources" of the past into the enduring image of this master. In this regard, the urban capitalist and the landed patroon have much in common.

Melville stresses the size of these feudal Dutch estates in New York by observing that they often exceed county boundaries and may include greater populations on their "rent rolls." The very mountains of the region serve as the "walls" of these estates, suggesting that the patroons' rule is not simply extensive but presumed to be *natural*. In Melville's landscape, the New York State Militia enters the picture in response to the provocation of the Anti-Rent agitators. It would not have been lost on the mid-nineteenth-century reader that such rebellion parallels quite explicitly the motives for the American Revolution.

Melville specifically associates this American aristocracy with Eastern and pre-Christian cultures: "These far-descended Dutch meadows lie steeped in a Hindooish haze; an eastern patriarchalness sways its mild crook over pastures, whose tenant flocks shall there feed, long as their own grass grows, long as their own water shall run. Such estates seem to defy Time's tooth, and by conditions which take hold of the indestructible earth seem to cotemporize their fee-simples with eternity. Unimaginable audacity of a worm that but crawls through the soil he so imperially claims!" (11). On the one hand, Melville merely seems to make these associations to stress the unexpectedly venerable character of these American princes. On the other hand, he understands how these Dutch patroons imitate the chaotic and irrational despotism that nineteenth-century westerners popularly associated with the "mysterious" Orient. Hegel is a familiar figure of this "orientalizing" by which nineteenth-century Europeans rationalized their ethnocentrism and imperialism, and he repeatedly uses India to represent the moral anarchy of the East: "If China may be regarded as nothing else but a State, Hindoo political existence presents us with a people but *no State*. Secondly, while we found a moral despotism in *China*, whatever may be called a relic of political life in *India*, is a despotism *without a principle*, without any rule of morality and religion: for morality and religion (as far as the latter has a reference to human action) have as their indispensable condition and basis the freedom of the Will. In India, therefore, the most arbitrary, wicked, degrading despotism has its full swing." [16] Melville stresses the military claims to rule both of the Glendinnings and the Dutch patroons he considers typical of an American landed aristocracy. Like Hegel's Indian monarchs, Melville's American princes are products of a social situation lacking any rational political principle that might coordinate the various and conflicting claims to power and authority. This seems confirmed by the New York State Militia, on order of Governor Seward, acting as if it were the private army of these threatened landowners.

Hegel considers the "history" of India to be no history at all, merely the record of the acts and possessions of different princes and their numerous wars. In particular, Hegel stresses how family genealogies take the place of the public events we normally associate with history: "It is the struggle of an energetic will on the part of this or that prince against a feebler one; the history of ruling dynasties, but not of peoples; a series of perpetually varying intrigues and revolts—not indeed of subjects against their rulers, but of a prince's son, for instance, against his father; of brothers, uncles and nephews in contest with each other; and of functionaries against their master." [17] For Hegel, the Hindu prince merely serves as a fetish for the still-struggling spirit of social self-governance—a spirit that Melville understands as America's democratic dream. Hegel's Hindu genealogies of princely families find their equivalence in Melville's conception in *Pierre* of the *image* or *portrait* of the father as the ultimate product or fetish of a patriarchal aristocracy. The patroon or patriarch is possible only as a consequence of a fragmented, essentially unpolitical society, like the anarchic New York that Pierre discovers on his first evening in the city with Delly and Isabel. Just this chaos of the urban realm gives special credibility to the apparently pastoral order represented by the Patroon's country estate.

In *Capital*, Marx develops Hegel's arbitrary Hindu despot as a historical and rhetorical figure for the development of capitalism.

16. Hegel, *The Philosophy of History*, trans. J. Sibree (1899; rpr. New York, 1956), 161.

17. *Ibid.*, 165.

Sketching the history of cooperative labor, Marx notes, "The colossal effects of simple cooperation are to be seen in the gigantic structures erected by the ancient Asiatics, Egyptians, Etruscans, etc." For Marx, cooperation in the labor process of precapitalist societies generally depends upon "the common ownership of the conditions of production." In Marx's own myth of social origins, cooperative labor reminds us of the essentially collective motives for socialization. On the other hand, Marx recognizes that the "sporadic application of co-operation on a large scale in ancient times, in the Middle Ages, and in modern colonies, rests on direct relations of domination and servitude, in most cases on slavery." Marx is careful to distinguish this cooperation of slave-labor from capitalist cooperation, which seems to begin with the "free wage-labourer" selling "his labour-power to capital." This mystified "free-exchange" enables the capitalist to make "coordinated labor" appear to be a consequence of his ownership and management of the labor-power that he has purchased.[18] Less explicit because more subtly contrived as a "free exchange" in the rhetoric of capitalism, the capitalist's exploitation of labor nonetheless finds a precedent in the forced labor of slaves in ancient times rather than in the tribal cooperation of primitive hunting tribes or agrarian societies.

In particular, Marx calls attention to the "colossal works" of this coordinated slave labor in terms designed clearly to gloss his theory of surplus value. The monumental projects undertaken by such coordinated labor forces are generally made possible by large state surpluses often generated by military conquests. These monuments are thus testaments to the surplus value on which the ancient despot based his political power—the "capital" of domination. Indeed, the labor force is itself often composed of just such a "surplus," insofar as the slaves committed to such great works were often the spoils of war. In addition, the monuments built by such despots often serve no other purpose than to represent that arbitrary power in the form of such purely ceremonial structures as tombs, pyramids, and obelisks. Failing to recognize that it is their coordinated labor alone that produces such objects of wonder, these workers take such productions as symbols for the despot's power and authority. As such, these ancient monuments—so often appropriately dedicated to death and/or a religious or military ideal—are testaments to social waste as well as dramatic illustrations

18. Marx, *Capital*, I, 451, 452.

of the kind of reification that will be the ultimate product of capitalism. Having quoted a long section of Richard Jones's *Textbook of Lectures* on the economics of such colossal projects among the ancients, Marx concludes by making explicit the implications of such despotism for the rise of capitalism: "This power of Asiatic and Egyptian kings, of Etruscan theocrats, etc. has in modern society been transferred to the capitalist, whether he appears as an isolated individual or, as in the case of joint-stock companies, in combination with others." [19]

The colossal works of Hegel's and Marx's ancient despots have a curious association with Terror Rock, or the Memnon Stone, in *Pierre* and with the *name* of the Glendinning estate, Saddle-Meadows, which memorializes Pierre's great-grandfather's subjugation of the Indian. In subtler ways than the oriental despot, however, Melville's American aristocrat legitimates his usurpation of Nature, "savage," and tenant-farmer by means of those signs and symbols (representational forms) that constitute his "estate" or "property." It is thus little wonder that on the eve of his break with his family Pierre burns the "'mementoes and monuments of the past'" that he had so fondly collected over the years. With special deliberation, he burns the chair-portrait of his father, whose image now seems to speak to him only of the father's adultery and illegitimate child, Isabel: "'It speaks merely of decay and death, and nothing more; decay and death of innumerable generations, it makes of earth one mold. How can lifelessness be fit memorial for life?'" (197). What the coordinated labor of soldiers, tenant-farmers, artisans, and painters produces is merely the *personality* of the ruler. And that personality is already a fetish for the labor of others that has actually produced such an image: the portrait of a father or the military saddle of a great-grandfather. This transformation of the living labor of the community into "heir-looms" is precisely a labor that "speaks merely of decay and death," a subtler version of Marx's "commodity fetishism" and an anticipation of Lukács' more developed conception of reification in *History and Class Consciousness.* It is a lineage without a proper history, insofar as it merely repeats the illegitimate authority of the ruler. Viewed in this manner, Pierre's grandfather's patriotism in defending "a rude but all-important stockaded fort, against the repeated combined assaults of Indians, Tories, and Regulars" during the Revolutionary War can no longer be understood as an unqualified valor

19. *Ibid.,* 452.

in the name of democratic ideals (6). Reread according to the aristocratic lineage that such "patriotism" has produced, the grandfather's sacrifice serves to maintain only his family's power rather than the ideals of a social democracy. The grandfather merely repeats the conquering will—and its antihistorical bias—that the great-grandfather initiated in his combat with the Indian during the French and Indian War. In the course of making these close associations between the acts of "founding" the American Glendinnings by the great-grandfather and the "founding" of America in the Revolutionary War, Melville renders ambiguous the presumed "origin" of America's break with its European heritage. And by suggesting an ironic repetition of such "origins" in the New York State Militia's supression of the Anti-Rent protesters in 1839, Melville transforms the democratic revolution into the secret consolidation of a new, American aristocratic power.

Pierre's own gesture of rebellion, including the burning of these fetishes, ought to involve some self-conscious rejection of the limitations of the family in favor of a larger social relation. But like most "young Americans," Pierre bids instead for radical individualism: "'Henceforth, cast-out Pierre hath no paternity, and no past; and since the Future is one blank to all; therefore twice-disinherited Pierre stands untrammeledly his ever-present self!—free to do his own self-will and present fancy to whatever end!'" (199). In his own will-to-power, Pierre hardly restores America to the social revolution in which it ought to have found its origin; Pierre merely repeats that illusory "revolution" by which his ancestors supplanted the authority of others with that of their own family name.

The truth of "descendedness," Melville argues, involves an infinite regression: "For as the breath in all our lungs is hereditary, and my present breath at this moment, is further descended than the body of the present High Priest of the Jews, so far as he can assuredly trace it; so mere names, which are also but air, do likewise revel in this endless descendedness" (9). As radical breaks with the past, his ancestors' militarism and Pierre's rebellion against his family repudiate the *history* that is carried in every "name." Even as Pierre destroys the fetishes of the past, he begins to reproduce the rhetoric of such fetishism—of the oriental despot, the English aristocrat, the Dutch patroon—in his vainglorious self-reliance. For Melville, the only genuine nobility derives from our involvement in the process of constructing a human community, not from those apparently ahistorical "images" that monumentalize the family or the self. Our shared air, which circulates in the very breath of our speech, is the guarantee of a shared humanity, of a "family of man," whose only proper labor is the construction of a social habitation—that is, a *history*—for such being. For the American, such historical labor (labor *as history*) ought to involve the production of a *new* relation to Europe rather than a simple break with that inescapable past. This, I take it, is the function of the "recognition scene" near the end of *Pierre*, when Isabel and Pierre encounter "another portrait of a complete stranger—a European," which "was as much the father of Isabel as the original of the chair-portrait" (353). This scene is actually a crucial scene of *méconnaissance*, insofar as it seems to plunge Pierre into despair regarding his folly in assuming a portrait to be evidence of actual bloodlines. On the other hand, the portrait of the stranger is used by Melville not merely to absolutely mystify family origins for the sake of plot reversal or some philosophical quandary; the portrait of the European stranger reminds us how every "origin," every tradition, every *history* is the product of our social labor—whether such labor be "imaginative" or "material": "But perhaps there was no original at all to this second portrait; it might have been a pure fancy piece; to which conceit, indeed, the uncharacterizing style of the filling-up seemed to furnish no small testimony" (353). As "a pure fancy piece," the portrait serves to expose the unconscious of Pierre's determination to legitimate Isabel through his own artistic labor. Yet, as the coordinated work of the historical and social imagination, the portrait may serve as a figure for the relation to Europe that American democracy ought to be working to produce.

What inhibits this historical labor is thus not just the family, oppressive as it is represented in the lineage and fortunes of the Glendinnings, but also individualism and its contemporary cant for Melville: Emersonian self-reliance.[20] Hegel's philosophical labor and Marx's

20. In *Pierre*, Melville makes a number of puns on Kant's surname as part of his more general critique of transcendental idealism. Speaking of the idealists of various sorts—painters, sculptors, students, German philosophers—inhabiting the upper floors of the tower in the Church of the Apostles, Melville jibes: "While the abundance of leisure in their attics (physical and figurative), unites with the leisure of their stomachs, to fit them in an eminent degree for that undivided attention indispensable to the proper digesting of the sublimated Categories of Kant; especially as Kant (can't) is the one great palpable fact in their pervadingly impalpable lives" (267). Yet the purely *negative* palpability of Kantian idealism—its cant is its can't—finds its habitation in the "Titanic" tower that rises out of the stores and law offices into which the old church has been divided. Elsewhere, Melville judges these "theoretic and inactive" transcendentalists to be "there-

more material labor both insist that the individual can realize himself only in and through an otherness that he works to produce, transform, and ultimately internalize as his own social bond. Social history is just this perpetual process of self-transcendence as the means of self-realization. In capitalism, however, the dialectic of self and other is transformed into a dualism between worker and owner, wages and capital, change and repetition, materiality and idealism, other and self: horologicals and chronometricals. Marx's theory of surplus value describes the ways that the capitalist steals the labor-power of the worker by manipulating the working day or mystifying the amount of capital actually consumed in production. The aim of surplus value in capitalism is for Marx, however, considerably more significant than the simple accumulation and expansion of capital. The first aim is to establish the most elementary class distinction: the laborer stakes his being on his physical body, which is successively "used up" in the production process; the owner finds his being in capital, whose very accumulation is a psychic defense against his fear of illegitimacy, a constant reminder that he has a material identity that "grows" in time rather than shrinks (as does the laborer's labor-power). And because it "grows" without the capitalist's labor, surplus value assumes the appearance of a natural organicism, a simulation of the Nature that industrial capitalism displaces. This chimerical organicism finds its pre-capitalist precedent in the peculiar pastoralism of Saddle-Meadows and the special brand of American aristocracy enshrined there.

In *Pierre*, physical labor is always at odds with individual identity, with an ideal of "self-reliance." Isabel's romantic imagination equates self-consciousness with productive labor, but Isabel experiences only the alienating effects of her own labor. Indeed, the nearly mystical art of her guitar seems to be a compensation for the failure of her daily labor to produce the identity (spirit) she desires. Charlie Millthorpe's father, "a very respectable farmer," illustrates this discrepancy between what Henry James, Sr., called "doing" and "being": "Pierre well remembered old farmer Millthorpe:—the handsome, melancholy, calm-tempered, mute, old man; in whose countenance—refinedly ennobled by nature, and yet coarsely tanned and attenuated by many a prolonged day's work in the harvest—rusticity and classicalness were strangely united. The delicate profile of his face, bespoke the loftiest

---

fore harmless," but as neighbors with the commercial and legal powers of the modern city these transcendentals must be said to serve some more active and dangerous ideological purpose, even if such a purpose depends on their apparent ineffectualness (262).

aristocracy; his knobbed and bony hands resembled a beggar's" (275). Melville uses farmer Millthorpe to illustrate the general observation that "the political and social levelings and confoundings of all manner of human elements in America, produce many striking individual anomalies unknown in other lands" (275). These "anomalies," of course, ought to be the signs of an authentic American revolution, which would transform the illegitimate family of the aristocrat into a genuine democracy. But in this context, the signifier of poverty is labor; the signifier of wealth is idleness. The wear and tear of honest farming is considered *unnatural*, already hints of incipient death: "knobbed and bony hands." The "undiluted" transmission, the sheer repetition, of genetic traits is assumed to be the result of a mere inheritance that is more properly the *work of nature:* a "countenance . . . refinedly ennobled by nature."

The Millthorpes, themselves dependent on the aristocratic and feudal authority of Saddle-Meadows, "loosely and unostentatiously traced their origin to an emigrating English Knight, who had crossed the sea in the time of the elder Charles" (275). Thus, farmer Millthorpe's labor is considered a degradation of such ancestry, and it is little wonder that his poverty and death are rumored to be consequences of drunken dissipation. Insofar as the wear and tear of human labor results in nothing but the apparently enduring identity of the aristocrat, labor is quite literally dissipation and effectively "unnatural"—*other* than itself. Given these circumstances, then, it is hardly surprising that Charlie Millthorpe aspires "to be either an orator, or a poet; at any rate, a great genius of one sort or other. He recalled the ancestral Knight, and indignantly spurned the plow" (279).

Oratory, poetry, "great genius of one sort or other," we know involve Pierre's own project to "gospelize anew," to write the infernal book that would declare his rebellion against the Glendinnings' hypocrisy and assure his fortune and reputation. Indeed, the "labor" of writing is given considerable attention by Melville, both in his representation of Pierre's anguished struggle at the Church of the Apostles and in his general observations on the differences between physical and intellectual labor. Even before he rebels against his family and departs Saddle-Meadows for New York, Pierre himself has worked and earned, after a fashion, by virtue of his trivial lyrics: "The Tropical Summer: a Sonnet," "The Weather: a Thought," "Life: an Impromptu," "The late Reverend Mark Graceman: an Obituary," and so on. Like the "heir-looms" he burns, Pierre's poems are mere fetishes for his poetic self. Both literary formalism (a sonnet) and philosophical idealism (a thought) reify nature and thus speak only of the death of spiritual grace that they have helped to produce ("The late Reverend Mark Graceman: an Obituary"). The name "Reverend Mark Graceman" seems to anticipate "Mark Winsome" in *The Confidence-Man*, who quite clearly is a caricature of Emerson. The actual products of Pierre's juvenile imagination parody the idealizations of Nature and death that characterize literary transcendentalism. More specifically, Pierre's poetizing may indicate that the labor of idealism often produces the *death* of the spirit that the poet and scholar hope to *realize* in their works.

Emerson repeatedly affirms the dignity of labor that unites intellectual and manual work: "I hear therefore with joy whatever is beginning to be said of the dignity and necessity of labor to every citizen. There is virtue yet in the hoe and the spade, for the learned as well as for unlearned hands." Yet what unites different kinds of labor for Emerson is their mutual concern with the production of a spiritual self. Emerson is quick to warn us that work performed without regard for the soul it serves may well be enslaved by other temporal masters— convention and fashion: "And labor is everywhere welcome; always we are invited to work; only be this limitation observed, that a man shall not for the sake of wider activity sacrifice any opinion to the popular judgments and modes of action."[21] Emerson characteristically gives heavier weight to the work of *man* than to the work of the world. Because the "dignity of labor" requires a spiritual understanding of man's role in a natural economy, the labors of idealists—"of the poet, the priest, the lawgiver, and men of study generally"—have special authority in Emerson's division of labor. In "Man the Reformer," his address to the Mechanics' Apprentices' Library Association of Boston in 1841, Emerson seems to take perverse pleasure before such an audience in distinguishing between "intellectual exertion" and "the downright drudgery of the farmer and the smith": "I would not quite forget the venerable counsel of the Egyptian mysteries, which declared that 'there were two pairs of eyes in man, and it is requisite that the pair which are beneath should be closed, when the pair that are above them per-

21. Ralph Waldo Emerson, "The American Scholar," in Emerson, *Nature, Addresses, and Lectures*, ed. Robert E. Spiller and Alfred R. Ferguson (Cambridge, Mass., 1971), 62, Vol. I of Joseph Slater and Douglas Emory Wilson, eds., *The Collected Works of Ralph Waldo Emerson*, 4 vols. to date.

ceive, and that when the pair above are closed, those which are beneath should be opened.'" The manual laborer is all too quickly deceived by the apparent reality of the products of his labor and thus lured to accumulate and possess objects that ought to be mere symbols of the soul. The genius of the poet and scholar finds its wealth in its own activity; when genius confuses earthly and transcendental rewards, then it falls as Bellerophon did:

> He may leave to others the costly conveniences of housekeeping and large hospitality and the possession of works of art. Let him feel that genius is a hospitality, and that he who can create works of art needs not collect them. He must live in a chamber, and postpone his self-indulgence, forewarned and forearmed against that frequent misfortune of men of genius,—the taste for luxury. This is the tragedy of genius,—attempting to drive along the ecliptic with one horse of the heavens and one horse of the earth, there is only discord and ruin and downfall to chariot and charioteer.[22]

Emerson's description of the discipline and worldly privation of the man of genius is parodied in Melville's description of Pierre at work in his bare, cold room in the Church of the Apostles. And Emerson's warning that genius must not confuse the "horse of the heavens" with the "horse of the earth" or the eyes that "are above" with the eyes that "are beneath" is caricatured in Plotinus Plinlimmon's pamphlet, "Chronometricals and Horologicals."[23]

---

22. Emerson, "Man the Reformer," *ibid.*, 152, 153.

23. Many critics agree that Plotinus Plinlimmon and his lecture on "chronometricals and horologicals" is Melville's intended "satire on all shallow and amiable transcendental 'reconcilers' of the 'Optimist' or 'Compensation' school," as Willard Thorp put the matter in his Introduction to *Herman Melville: Representative Selections* (New York, 1938), lxxxii. Extracted as Plinlimmon's lecture is from a series of "Three Hundred and Thirty-three Lectures" and qualified as "*not so much the Portal, as part of the temporary Scaffold to the Portal of this new Philosophy,*" Plinlimmon's very form parodies the Emersonian lecture. The title itself, "'*EI*,'" is paronomastic of Emerson's identification of the "eye" and the "I," as well as the spiritually generative qualities Emerson attributes to the crossing of the "eye" and the "I," which involves the third paronomasia: "das Ei" or "egg," as in *ab ovo*. Connecting all of these puns is, of course, their mutual philological source, the Greek philosophical term *eídos*, which variously links appearance, constitutive nature, form, type, species, and idea. I cannot recount here the complicated history of *eide* in even the restricted classical tradition from Plato to Aristotle and Plotinus, but I will simply remind the reader that classical philosophical debates concerning the relation of immanence to

Melville criticizes Emerson's idealist foundations for human labor by suggesting that the special work of the intellect may serve merely to preserve us from the more difficult and concrete labor of producing a workable society. Emerson's labor of and for the self might require privation and "unworldliness" precisely because such alienation is its secret product. Transcendental idealism thus may be viewed as an elaborate system of psychological defense against the alienating consequences of more material labor in capitalist America. Until he faces the exigencies of earning a living for his own "family" in the city, Pierre has spent all of his literary earnings on cigars, "so that the puffs which indirectly brought him his dollars were again returned, but as perfumed puffs; perfumed with the sweet leaf of Havanna" (262). Melville parodies romantic idealism by transforming the spiritual activity of Emerson's genius or the human desire for transcendence in Wordsworth's image of "wreaths of smoke / Sent up, in silence, from among the trees" into the ephemeral vapors of self-reliant man—what T. E. Hulme terms the "circumambient gas" of romanticism.[24]

"This towering celebrity," Melville writes, "—there he would sit smoking, and smoking, mild and self-festooned as a vapory mountain" (263). This ironic identification of Pierre-as-juvenile-author with the Memnon Stone suggests that *this* formalist conception of poetic spiritualization is designed principally to obscure the self, to give it a protective outer wrapping (literally, a "white jacket" of smoke) that would protect it from the mob. Unlike the music of Isabel's guitar, the smoke from Pierre's poems and cigars protects and isolates the self, rather than serving as its virtual embodiment and medium for communication: its externalization, in Hegelian terms, in and for sociohistorical circulations.

In its own way, this figuration of Pierre as poet is the equivalent of the chair-portrait of his father. Both conceal a secret of illegitimacy

---

transcendence often focused on the particular status of *eide*. F. E. Peters in *Greek Philosophical Terms* (New York, 1967), 50, notes that by Aristotle's postulation of "the *eide* as the thoughts of God, a position that continues down through Plotinus . . . into Christianity, and at the same time . . . as immanent formal causes with an orientation toward matter, . . . an at least partial solution to the dilemma of immanence vs. transcendence was reached. But the problem continued as a serious one in Platonism, discussed at length by both Plotinus . . . and Proclus."

24. Wordsworth's lines are from "Tintern Abbey," ll. 17–18. T. E. Hulme, "Romanticism and Classicism," in *Critical Theory since Plato*, ed. Hazard Adams (New York, 1971), 769.

that is related to their equally false claims to authority. The father's adultery is discovered in his mysterious smile in the portrait in the same way Pierre's plagiarism from other authors is revealed in his own ambitious work. Melville's description of Pierre as a "vapory mountain" also helps explain his paradoxical act of burning the chair-portrait. What Pierre intends as an act of rebellion serves as the means of protecting his father from exposure, insofar as Pierre finds in the portrait some family resemblance to Isabel:

> Painted before the daughter was conceived or born, like a dumb seer, the portrait still seemed leveling its prophetic finger at that empty air, from which Isabel did finally emerge. There seemed to lurk some mystical intelligence and vitality in the picture; because, since in his own memory of his father, Pierre could not recall any distinct lineament transmitted to Isabel, but vaguely saw such in the portrait; therefore, not Pierre's parent, as any way rememberable by him, but the portrait's painted *self* seemed the real father of Isabel; for, so far as all sense went, Isabel had inherited one peculiar trait nowhither traceable but to it. (197)

The curiously prophetic quality of the chair-portrait, whether it be an effect of the painter's genius or merely Pierre's excited imagination, suggests an artistic function different from the defenses of Emersonian idealism or Pierre's protective veil of poetic smoke. The portrait of the father brings together the aristocrat's conscious desire for authority and the unconscious illegitimacy that fuels such desire.

Like his ancestors, Pierre wants to turn himself into an enduring figure in the landscape, precisely by protecting himself from the "mob" (such as the one that assaults Delly, Isabel, and Pierre in that infernal first night they spend in the city) and at the same time rebelling against his predecessors by willfully "authoring" his own unnatural family of Isabel, Delly, and, ultimately, Lucy. It is a family composed of nothing but "sisters" and a "brother," we are quick to notice, recalling our earlier remarks about the relation of brothers and sisters in the metaphorics of the Hegelian family. Contemptuous of the various efforts of vanity presses and journals to exploit his minor celebrity, Pierre himself merely reproduces, even in his haughty denial of their overtures, the cult of authorial "personality" these publishers *labor* to produce. Like the aristocrat and capitalist, he vainly tries to father himself and a family to render honorable such imaginative incest.

Melville's representation of Pierre as some "vapory mountain" also associates him with the natural landmark at Saddle-Meadows, Terror Rock or the Memnon Stone, which later in the narrative will come to mythic life in Pierre's dream of Enceladus, the earthbound Titan. Earlier, I interpreted the Memnon Stone as a version of those colossal monuments Hegel and Marx associated with the despotism of Asiatic and Egyptian rulers. Although a natural formation, the Memnon Stone is discovered by Pierre, "the first known publishing discoverer of this stone, which he had thereupon fancifully christened the Memnon Stone" (132). The stone becomes Pierre's colossus, his monument to the *natural* surplus the genius ought to have in reserve. The cavity at the base of the rock and its general phallic suggestiveness make the Memnon Stone a figure for a hermaphroditism that is particularly appropriate either to the false self-sufficiency of the Glendinnings or to Emerson's self-reliant genius: American aristocrat or radical individual. It is interesting to note that the Church of the Apostles' architecture is the urban equivalent of the rock, insofar as the new tower where Pierre has his rooms rises out of the courtyard of the old church. The hermaphroditism of the rural and urban forms—the former associated with the aristocracy of the Glendinnings and the latter with either Pierre's writing or the law and commerce in the buildings below—suggests the self-generative powers of the "original character" in *The Confidence-Man:* "The original character, essentially such, is like a revolving Drummond light, raying away from itself all round it—everything is lit by it, everything starts up to it (mark how it is with Hamlet), so that, in certain minds, there follows upon the adequate conception of such a character, an effect, in its way, akin to that which in Genesis attends upon the beginning of things."[25]

Yet, such an "original" in both *Pierre* and *The Confidence-Man,* whether literary character turned author or citizen turned despot, remains Melville's grandest illusion—the secret passion of the idealist not merely to *participate* in nature's economy but to *originate* and thus *dominate* that economy. Such self-procreative and ahistorical formalism belongs only to the impossible realm of the "chronometrical," and as such

---

25. Herman Melville, *The Confidence-Man: His Masquerade,* ed. Elizabeth S. Foster (New York, 1954), 271.

it is as "self-consuming" as it is "self-producing." It is, in a word, an *incestuous* form of artistic production that merely produces its own obscurity, weakness, and ultimate death. By the same token, it obscures its actual origins, which in the case of Pierre's writing must be termed the historical conditions—necessities and exigencies—under which he must work. The unified religious authority of the old Church of the Apostles has been replaced by the apparent dualism of material *vs.* ideal, utilitarian *vs.* transcendental. The lawyers and shopkeepers in the renovated church exercise their very real powers over the workers in the city by maintaining the *illusion* of freedom represented by the dreamers and freethinkers occupying the tower. The "freedom" of such idealism (of Emerson's self-reliant genius) is, in Melville's scrutiny, merely a double of the servitude it hopes to escape; it is a *reflection* of the poverty and alienation of those who work to preserve such masters.

Such an interpretation of Pierre's art as the idealist version of the oriental despot's colossal monuments—testaments to his arbitrary power, accumulated economic surpluses, and exploitation of labor—revises considerably the conventional reading of Melville's oft-quoted glimpse into the pyramid of the human soul:

> The old mummy lies buried in cloth on cloth; it takes time to unwrap this Egyptian king. Yet now, forsooth, because Pierre began to see through the first superficiality of the world, he fondly weens he has come to the unlayered substance. But, far as any geologist has yet gone down into the world, it is found to consist of nothing but surface stratified on surface. To its axis, the world being nothing but superinduced superficies. By vast pains we mine into the pyramid; by horrible gropings we come to the central room; with joy we espy the sarcophagus; but we lift the lid—and no body is there!—appallingly vacant as vast is the soul of man! (285)

Generally interpreted in the context of Melville's nihilism or as his existential affirmation of the groundlessness of being, this passage deals less with man's essential nature (his "geology," as it were) than with the "nothingness" he produces by way of his labor to idealize the world in the service of material interests. In this passage, Melville not only indicts transcendental idealism for offering us an absolutely elusive notion of "spirit" or "soul," he also connects such idealism with those idealizing arts of political rulers who would mask their illegitimate power and their exploitation of workers in the form of majestic symbols of their supernatural authority. This political mystification initiates a historical process of labor through which we quite literally *unmake* ourselves and transform the natural energies of our bodies into alien, unnatural objects. "Nothingness" is not for Melville the essential condition for being that it would become for the twentieth-century existentialist; the vacancy in Melville's pyramid is the consequence of specific historical acts of social labor made to serve perverse gods.

Melville distinguishes Pierre's labor from that of farmer Millthorpe and even that of Isabel:

> The mechanic, the day-laborer, has but one way to live; his body must provide for his body. But not only could Pierre in some sort, do that; he could do the other; and letting his body stay lazily at home, send off his soul to labor, and his soul would come faithfully back and pay his body her wages. So, some unprofessional gentlemen of the aristocratic South, who happen to own slaves, give those slaves liberty to go and seek work, and every night return with their wages, which constitute those idle gentlemen's income. Both ambidexter and quadruple-armed is that man, who in a day-laborer's body, possesses a day-laboring soul. (261)

The spiritual slavery that Melville describes here connects Pierre's life-denying artistic idealism with the institutions of southern slavery, just as the feudalism of the Dutch patroons is associated with oriental despotism. The passage suggests that the "division of labor" in modern bourgeois culture more subtly replicates the explicit exploitation of labor in slave-holding societies. Porter considers the mythic oppositions of country and city, pastoralism and industrialism, to be characteristically American means of forgetting capitalism's deep roots in the feudalism of aristocratic class structures: "Perhaps it is partly due to a long-standing confusion in the minds of Americans over the difference between capitalist and aristocrat that they have never really been able to resist altogether the plantation myth's attractions."[26] In particular, the Transcendentalist's rejection of economic materialism often results in the substitution of an ideal economy of the self that comes dangerously close to the values and customs of the landed gentry. By explicitly

26. Porter, *Seeing and Being*, 228–29.

feminizing Pierre's "soul" ("pay his body her wages"), Melville also returns this reflection on art and everyday labor to the psychosexual themes centering on Pierre's incestuous relation with Isabel, whose guitar plays as he writes. The "mystical" communion of Isabel and Pierre, like the spiritual "friendship" so prized by Emerson and Thoreau, is for Melville an inadequate substitute for the social product that ought to result from the coordinated labor of politically committed citizens.

Melville's association of Pierre's labor as a writer with the master-slave relation of southern slavery begins with the Emersonian cliché that writing transcends ordinary labor by coordinating physical and spiritual functions. But Melville then suggests that the function of writing may be precisely to protect its "author" from the physical depletion of ordinary labor. In this regard, authorship is explicitly related to the ownership of slaves and the idleness of the aristocrat, but with the interesting qualification that this relation between master and slave gives the slave the *illusion* of "liberty to go and seek work." That this exploitation of the slave's desire for freedom also involves the slave's desire to do his/her "own" labor is important for Melville's parable of writing. The illusion that the soul can work independently ("freely") from the body, which stays "lazily at home," is fundamental to Emersonian idealism: "Nature is the incarnation of a thought, and turns to a thought again, as ice becomes water and gas. The world is mind precipitated, and the volatile essence is forever escaping again into the state of free thought. . . . Man imprisoned, man crystallized, man vegetative, speaks to man impersonated."[27] Melville effectively reverses the terms of Emerson's triumphant transcendentalist vision, transforming the essentially free mind into a slave to the physical master, who after all *still speaks to*, or governs, this presumptively "free" spirit.

The separation of the "self" from its "labor," and the separation of physical from spiritual production, is the fundamental alienation operating in aristocratic families and in the romantic "arts" designed to "naturalize" such aristocracy. Insofar as the family does nothing but project the concept of a remote, external "law" of authority, which cannot be internalized but merely reproduced as alien and external, the family produces nothing other than alienation itself, that pure negation (*Verneinung*) that Hegel himself equated with the death of the Spirit.

27. Ralph Waldo Emerson, "Nature," in Emerson, *Essays: Second Series*, ed. Alfred R. Ferguson and Jean Ferguson Carr (Cambridge, Mass., 1983), 113, Vol. III of Slater and Wilson, eds., *Works*.

The move from family to society, from the Law of the Father to the internal law of self-governance, is the negation of negation, the transformation of stony externality into the self-moving principle of *Geist* as its historical movement: the *Bildungsweg* of Hegel's social theory that Marx could appropriate from an otherwise bourgeois apologist.

Pierre's "labor" in writing his "infernal book," his new gospel, is designed to reproduce this portrait of the stony self, of the Self as distinct from man's social dependency and the labor required to maintain the historical relation of self and society. We read little directly of Pierre's grand work, except those quotes from "the last sheet from his hand" and the slips he has cast to the floor. Still, we learn enough of "his apparent author-hero, Vivia," to recognize that Pierre has "directly plagiarized from his own experiences" (302). These fragments do not speak of self-consciousness as self-knowledge, as we would expect from this romantic author. Instead, Vivia speaks only of his contradiction and despair, of his hatred of life and his impotence—what Nietzsche would term his *ressentiment:* "Yet that knowing his fatal condition does not one whit enable him to change or better his condition. Conclusive proof that he has no power over his condition" (303). What Pierre/ Vivia cannot know is that he has merely given objective form to a "soul," a suffering "self," produced by those contradictions in his family history that are also the disabling contradictions of a promised social democracy based upon radical individualism, whether such individualism assumes the form of the father, the military leader, the mythic hero, the Dutch patroon, the capitalist, or the visionary author.

In this regard, then, Pierre/*Pierre* reproduces the aristocratic law of the Father by means of one of those "arts" that capitalism employs for similar purposes of naturalizing and legitimating its own founding contradictions: between "self" and "society," "owner" and "laborer," "ideal" and "historical," chronometrical and horological. The art of the novel gives us a "labor" that we as readers perform only to *use up* our bodies (and our time) in the service of reproducing the "genius" of the author: Herman Melville or Pierre Glendinning. That always-absent "author" governs and controls our labors in order to take the place of the social and communal relations our work of reading ought to yield.

In *Capital,* Marx argues that it is the *identity* of the capitalist that is the true fetish, an alienated metonymy for the "labor-power" stolen from his workers in the form of "surplus value." Indeed, the growth of surplus value, the incessant drive for accumulation, seems some desperate desire on the part of the capitalist to disguise what he recognizes to be the inauthenticity of his identity: that which represents "him" is never "he himself." In a similar sense, Pierre's book is "filched" from those "vile atheists," Lucan and Voltaire, among others, who ought to remind Pierre of the impossibility of "authoring" anything outside the complex genealogy of literary and social forces. The infinite regress of *literature* and the infinite regress of *descendedness* that Melville uses to subvert aristocratic pretensions are both the preconditions for negating myths of self-reliant man and aristocratic authority in favor of that more enduring and integrated product: a social collective sustained by the labors of men and women.

Neither the aristocratic ruler nor the American capitalist wants *that* dispersed, displaced, collective authority. In *Pierre*, Melville attempted to kill romance, to take it to its ultimate extreme as a formalist prop for the ideology of America's secret aristocracy of the Spirit: economic capitalism and philosophical transcendentalism. Rogin concludes that the "self-referentiality that takes over *Pierre* brings the book's narrative to a halt" and "explains its own failure, for it is the appropriate literary form for the claustrophobic family. *Pierre* is the victim of the domestic relationship which brings both storytelling and therefore life itself to an end." [28] In this regard, we can judge Pierre's swerve back into the chivalric action of the duel and the melodrama it stages to be merely the "proper" ending for the "novel" he has written, the "infernal" new gospel of capitalist individuation as sustained by the rhetoric of literary authority. It is altogether fitting that melodrama should be Pierre's choice in the face of his literary "failure." Pierre's final "actions," however, by no means compromise his own conception of literature; such action is perfectly consistent with Pierre's literary project: the realization of romance in experience, the substitution of the author's self for the worker's active labor. Such realization—life imitating art at last—merely enables Pierre to succumb to the "romance of the real" that is told by the authors of capitalism and enacted by their "characters," whether intellectual or manual laborers.

Yet just as the chair-portrait of Pierre's father *reveals* his kinship with Isabel and thus the very secret the portrait artist attempted to conceal with the conventional "nobility" of his subject (and the conventions of the portrait genre), so *Pierre* represents its own unconscious

28. Rogin, *Subversive Genealogy*, 179–80.

and thus *escapes* fleetingly its identification with Pierre and his fragmentary monument, his unfinished colossus. By so ruthlessly connecting his own craft of fiction and his own will to literary authority with the political wills of despots, aristocrats, and capitalists, Melville completes his book by undoing his own claim to legitimacy and by *characterizing* himself in his parody of an author, Pierre. Insofar as Melville accepts the social anarchy he finds at the heart of the Glendinnings' and the Gansevoorts' conceptions of "democracy," he must be "humiliated" by a literary vocation that merely serves that ideology's effort to rationalize its contradictions. Melville does not accept these conditions for labor; his rebellion is exemplified by his refusal of the customary alternatives of philosophical idealism or the "world elsewhere" of art. The "unconscious" of *Pierre* is, like the unconscious of the chair-portrait, no mystical effect of artistic intuition; it is the ideological analysis that results from deconstructing those apparently self-evident distinctions we assume govern our everyday reality: ideal and material, self and other, author and reader, owner and worker, master and servant, state and family. That Melville understands these distinctions to have special roles to play in reconciling social democracy with radical individualism makes his labor in *Pierre* especially pertinent to Jacksonian America.

Rogin and others have judged *Pierre* to be work symptomatic of Melville's ultimate self-referentiality as an author, his resignation to the delusions that later would define twentieth-century modernism. Melville deconstructs in *Pierre* the "democratic" pretensions of American capitalism by exposing the relation of radical individualism to the incestuous and claustrophobic closure of the aristocratic family. And Melville further deconstructs the new "authority" of Emerson's expressive self, both subject and object of its own labor, by revealing how literary authority participates in the naturalization of capitalist contradictions. Given his own complicity with the principal subjects of his critique, Melville can hardly be said to have mastered the problems his narrative uncovers. *Parody, irony,* and *satire*—mere literary terms, after all—hardly begin to address the force of Melville's critique in *Pierre.* In one sense, *Pierre* is Melville's farewell to the romance and the novel—to "literature" as he had attempted to practice it in his previous works. Yet *Pierre* is by no means the expression of incipient madness, despair, or nihilism. Quite the contrary, the book raises those questions about the ideological consequences of literary production that motivate the more socially and politically focused work of *The Confidence-Man*. Melville's critique of literary production may have devastating consequences for his own sense of vocation, but it also makes possible the active study of the genealogy of social values that Melville's Ishmael futilely attempts to "understand" from his detached vantage and by means of his romantic "negative capability" in *Moby-Dick*. By means of the deconstructive "failure" of *Pierre* as literature, Melville could make the leap from Ishmael to the confidence men, whose agitations and subversions enter the social drama, provoking the "labor" of their interlocutors, of their *readers*, either to *reproduce* the Wall Street World— America as the "tomb" of its past—or *produce* the carnival of an authentically democratic society. In *Pierre* and *The Confidence-Man*, Melville developed a mode of writing that left "literature" behind and anticipated the cultural criticism of our own present moment.

# Whitman's "Convertible Terms"
## America, Self, Ideology

· · · · · · · · · · · · · · · · · ·

*Kathryne V. Lindberg*

> Walt Whitman is the greatest poetical representative of German philosophy.
>
>> —Walt Whitman, January 13, 1884, Camden, N.J. newspaper fragment

> The meaning of America is Democracy. The meaning of Democracy is to put into practice the idea of the sovereignty, license, sacredness of the individual. This idea gives identity and isolation to every man and woman.
>
>> —Walt Whitman, Introduction to *Leaves of Grass*

To consider seriously the relationship between Whitman and Hegel is to pose a series of questions about reading and influence and, more importantly, to explore the boundary conditions of the discourses of literature and philosophy—and, not to be redundant, *ideology*—for all of these become involved in Whitman's poetry and the self of which it sings. Both self and song affirm the priority of voice to writing, poetry to philosophy. Whitman is the poet whose very *corpus* was introduced in the 1855 edition of *Leaves of Grass* by a frontview etching of nearly the whole of his person. This bodying forth of the "literatus of the modern" apparently excludes the authorial signature and challenges other literary conventions of epic form and presentation. *Corpus* and body are puns marking, rather than effacing, contradictions between perfection and historical change, spontaneous poetry and textualized self.

The etched imprint, underscoring Whitman's assertion that he "who touches this [book] touches a man," rests rather tenuously on a pun: written body of work, an author's corpus, and the corporeal presence of the man behind, or represented in, "Song of Myself."[1] Thus his book, while claiming to be both an organic poem (it does, after all, grow during the writer's life) and the living man himself, rests upon the sort of accident of language this figure of speech would preclude. This pun is also a metonym, because like a mark or signature on a legal document, it stands in for, names, the man or the representative citizen. Whitman deliberately chose this particular image rather than signing the poem or providing an ornate, aristocratic, author's cameo in the convention of the frontispieces of older special editions (one might recall Alexander Pope figured as a Roman bust or as the great head in poet's hat so admired by Dr. Johnson). Representing himself as an American laborer, in work clothes with cocked hat and open shirt, seductively inviting or confirming the solidarity of writer and citizen, Whitman revises the old relationship of the author to the common, contemporary American. Thereby he enters, he does not escape, the play of rhetoric and the economy of textual transmission.

The author's signature, even if coded in revisionary portraiture, engages the logic of the signature and the communication system over which philosophy, poetry, and other discourses exercise illusory territorial control. The signature authorizes a writer's statements and the exchange value of an original work, guaranteeing a presence behind, and the singularity of, an original work; at the same time, it signals the absence of its signatory and his voice or testimony.[2] And as Whitman's own thefts of great names suggest, signatures and names can be borrowed to endorse projects their owners would have questioned. Such will be the status of "Hegel" in Whitman's text: that of a philosophical endorsement or legitimation of the poet's own ideas about self, history, and democracy. So the American poet hoped merely to ornament his critical essays with that German name. In fact, as I will argue, he incorporated more of Hegel than he might have recognized when he availed himself of what was then the current name (metonym) for philosophy itself. Put another way, Whitman gave a name to the tendencies and ideas that one might have recognized as Hegelian anyway;

1. On the prevalent metonyms, metaphors, and other figures of speech that became figures of thought for nineteenth-century American writers, see Henry Sussman, *The Hegelian Aftermath: Readings in Hegel, Kierkegaard, Freud, Proust, and James* (Baltimore, 1982), 1–14.

2. On the question of signatures in the text of philosophy, see Jacques Derrida, *Margins of Philosophy*, trans. Alan Bass (Chicago, 1984), 307–30.

certain words, including *spirit*, *self*, and *history*, already bore Hegel's signature.

To conquer or appropriate tradition in its most abstract and potent form, that of metaphysics or continental speculative philosophy, Whitman enlists all the dangerous powers of rhetoric and the literary and philosophical institutions he ostensibly sought to overcome. This is one nexus of contradictions he acknowledged, built upon, yet felt compelled to repeat in what he eventually called "the theory of America." This "theory" grounds or projects the culmination of the past and the promise of a future in one organic poem, and/as the perfected man, at once incorporating and superseding philosophy and religion. Whitman's insistence on "theory" also marks his affiliation with Hegel. When the American poet became acquainted with German philosophy, he read in—or into—it his own desired "poetry of the future" and a particular doctrine of the union of self and nation. As I hope to show, his "literatus of the modern" shares something with Hegel's speculative philosopher, the acme of the progress of the world historical spirit. Whitman's America and its bard are always on the horizon as an integration of reader and writer, as the summa of poetry and politics. So is Hegel's philosophy of the future a prospective sublation of history and metaphysics. But here I begin to preempt the development of Whitman's not unprofitable exchanges with philosophy—the subject of this essay.

Just as Whitman's America is its own greatest poem, the "literatus of the modern" will himself *be* its theory/idea/poet. He proclaims the various contradictions of his belated, yet prospective, nation and poetic mission by repeated metonymic substitutions of his "Self" for "America," of history for eternity. Such tentatively resolved contradictions can be charted in a series of what, in *Democratic Vistas*, he calls "convertible terms": "America and democracy," "Soul and LITERATURE."[3] Such terms are translated and transposed among his various prosaic and poetic self-presentations and manifestos. As unacknowl-

3. Walt Whitman, *Democratic Vistas*, in Whitman, *Prose Works, 1892*, ed. Floyd Stovall (2 vols.; New York, 1963–64), II, 413. Subsequent quotations from Whitman's works will be taken from the New York University Press series The Collected Writings of Walt Whitman, ed. Gay Wilson Allen and Sculley Bradley, and will be noted parenthetically in the text with the following abbreviations. *Corres.—The Correspondence*, ed. Edwin Havilland Miller (5 vols.; New York, 1961–69); *LG—Leaves of Grass*, ed. Harold W. Blodgett and Sculley Bradley (New York, 1965); *PW—Prose Works, 1892*, ed. Floyd Stovall (2 vols.; New York, 1963–64).

edged borrowings from philosophy and other disciplines, these and other tropes of repetition and substitution constitute a culturally hegemonic poetry that masters all selves under the sign of Whitman, "a cosmos" and "rough." The classic example or intimation is "Song of Myself, Sec. #51":

> The past and present wilt—I have fill'd them, emptied them,
> And proceed to fill my next fold of the future.
>
> .  .  .  .  .  .  .  .  .  .  .  .  .  .  .  .  .  .  .
>
> Do I contradict myself?
> Very well then I contradict myself,
> (I am large, I contain multitudes.)
>
> (LG, 88)

Cataloging and containing workers, women, soldiers, children, the types and representatives of America en masse, Whitman's poems and other writings also address science, philosophy, music, and other discourses. He had to acknowledge the great contradiction between the single, solitary self and its democratic (or was it merely the imperialistic?) inclusiveness. Therefore, against the often-articulated hope for the integrative power of poetry stands the barely repressed despair of *Democratic Vistas*, expressed in a recurrent and urgent contradiction that persists after the writing of most of *Leaves:* "the origin-idea of the singleness of man, individualism, asserting itself, and cropping forth, even from the opposite ideas. But the mass, or lump character, for imperative reasons, is to be carefully weigh'd. . . . The two are contradictory, but our task is to reconcile them" (PW, II, 373).

The masterful and mastering gesture be which Whitman contains "multitudes" and writes a poem that is a "man" does not mark a break with philosophy, or even with literary tradition. The two discourses met over the desire to create mastering systems. Not content with placing limits on the speculative and ideological capacities of language and especially of poetry, the Americans followed the British Romantics— and necessarily their German informants—out of the immediate neighborhood of poetry and into philosophy. At a strained pitch, nineteenth-century philosophy shares with poetry the desire to unite all thought in a single concept or construct and to create an organic system that would transcend the vicissitudes of time and the limitations of language. Whitman mentioned all these philosophers by reference to their main ideas—Kant's Idea, Fichte's Self, Hegel's Spirit. He several times acknowledges that only Hegel, only "the Hegelian formulas" profiled in the anti-Carlylean *Democratic Vistas*, were "fit for America." He thus appropriated for himself a master word, if not a system: the Self, which, as we will see, owes much to the stature, if not always to the rigor, of Hegel's thinking about the "I"—not precisely that of *I*dea.

Hegel also invoked images of the ideal writer and of his natural style. But that philosopher's organic artwork was his System, not a poem, and his most real or vital man was, not the divine literatus, but the speculative philosopher. In a sense, then, Hegel's "Idea" corresponds to Whitman's more poetic "Self"; it is at least circular and organic, the origin and telos of philosophy. So Hegel figures man, the philosopher, in his 1820 "Berlin Introduction to the History of Philosophy": "Thus developed, philosophy is built up within itself. There is *one* Idea in the whole and in all its members, just as in a living individual *one* life, one pulse beats in all his limbs. All the parts arising in it, as well as their systemization, emanate from the one Idea. . . . Thus the Idea is the centre, at the same time the periphery."[4]

Whitman's attempts to create a self that would be somehow convertible into a visionary American State and represented by his organic poem were overdetermined by influences, including Hegelian formulas. There was for the self-proclaimed American bard more than simple or even interested misunderstanding; there was Whitman's desire for a legitimate grounding to his announced "theory of America," a desire itself not innocent of philosophical and poetic precedents. Hegel, too, placed his national culture and its philosophical language in a position of priority.

Whitman continually re-presented his expanding, yet whole, poem, *Leaves of Grass*, through its various editions, spanning and interpreting the stretch of history that coincided with his life. Contrary to his advertisements, he did not write spontaneously but massively revised both his poem and his public persona for the greater part of four decades. Over the years, he presented different pictures—both literal portraits and idealized images—of himself in, and as accompaniment to, the poem. There is the 1855 portrait of the Whitman persona, a figural composite of the poetic journeyman and innovator of Free

4. G. W. F. Hegel, *Introduction to the Lectures on the History of Philosophy*, trans. T. M. Knox and A. V. Miller (Oxford, 1985), 21.

Verse, lounging in the frontispiece. In later years and subsequent editions, he would be pictured as the Wound Dresser or the Good Gray Poet, by then signing souvenir portraits and endorsing his work as "Walt Whitman." Whitman insists on this evolving but multifaceted and much-revised persona, tying it to the alleged transparency of his language and the living, organic—even human—character of *Leaves of Grass*. He offers his Self, his person, as a presence in defiant opposition to the distance and abstraction often associated with philosophy and high art—as in, for example, "So Long," a short poem that in various editions closed one or another section of *Leaves:*

> My songs cease, I abandon them,
> From behind the screen where I hid I advance personally solely
>     to you.
>
> Camerado, this is no book,
> Who touches this touches a man.
>
> (*LG*, 505)

This apparent iconoclasm or effacement of literary authorship, by which Whitman claims to stand bodily before or alongside his reader, partakes of a long philosophical tradition of discomfort with mediation and writing. He offers, not a complete or static "book," but Leaves. These organic fragments are presented as body and person, not as sign; still, this is the familiar Christian—even Socratic—gesture of "Ecce homo." Western philosophers from Plato and Aristotle through Kant and Hegel similarly attempted to ground System in a Nature prior to and more real than language, often representing or personifying the truth they sought. Philosophical decorum and the monumentality of his System precluded Hegel from asserting himself in more obvious ways in his account of the journey of Spirit through self-consciousness back to simple wholeness. Whitman, feeling no such constraints of decorum, took a more obviously autobiographical turn or shortcut through Hegel's protracted journey. Perhaps one can read it differently, in the light of Whitman, but Hegel maps the journey of the Spirit thus:

> What Spirit prepares for itself in it [the *Phenomenology of Spirit*,] is the element of [true] knowing. In this element the moments of Spirit now

spread themselves out in that *form of simplicity* which knows its object as its own self. They no longer fall apart into the antithesis of being and knowing, but remain in the simple oneness of knowing; they are the True in the form of the True, and their difference is only the difference of content. Their movement, which organizes itself in this element into a whole, is *Logic* or *speculative philosophy.*[5]

If philosophers have chosen to privilege abstract essence, or Soul, over appearance, or Body, Whitman's reversal of—ambivalence about—these priorities does not fundamentally change them. As we will see, his abjuring of the proper name and other proprieties of literary production and rigorous argumentation was not a rejection but a personal appropriation of tradition. In a sense, Whitman has merely literalized or overstated the organic metaphor for Art and System, going beyond the ideal of the exact coincidence of form and content, beyond philosophical self-presence, to the presentation of the Poet himself as "simple, separate person."

With successive self-presentations, from the representative "I" to a "Me/Myself" that encloses all the questions and answers of the philosophers and priests of the past, the Whitmanesque self loses its historical specificity in order to become transcendent or, like the Hegelian world historical spirit, translatable—yet Whitman also insists on being "untranslatable." Just so, mergers of chauvinism and egotism into what Quentin Anderson has termed the "imperial self" were already apparent in the 1855 Preface.[6] The prospective American poet outdistances all others (even as he appropriates Plato): "philosophy speculates, ever looking towards the poet, ever regarding the eternal tendencies of all toward happiness, never inconsistent with what is clear to the senses

---

5. G. W. F. Hegel, *Phenomenology of Spirit,* trans. A. V. Miller (Oxford, 1977), 21–22. This is one passage that justifies the characterization of the *Phenomenology* as a *Bildungsroman,* as do its numerous citations of *Wilhelm Meister* and *The Sorrows of Werther.* This claim was most convincingly made by Jean Hyppolite, *Genesis and Structure of Hegel's "Phenomenology of Spirit,"* trans. Samuel Cherniak and John Heckman (Evanston, Ill., 1974), 10–17.

6. Quentin Anderson, *The Imperial Self: An Essay in American Literary and Cultural History* (New York, 1971), especially "Consciousness and Form in Whitman" and "Coming Out of Culture." Anderson further develops the argument of the antisocial/apolitical self with regard to Whitman's bullying revisions of friends' early criticisms of the poet. See *Walt Whitman's Autograph Revisions of the Analysis of "Leaves of Grass,"* introductory essay by Quentin Anderson, textual notes by Stephen Railton (New York, 1974).

and to the soul. For the eternal tendencies of all toward happiness make the only point of sane philosophy" (*PW*, II, 448). This posture of poet before or against philosopher, which Ezra Pound would later characterize as "Disney against the Metaphysicals," seems to be Whitman's major contribution to the American "tradition" of antitraditionalism. This aversion is not limited to the Whitmanian wing of the American canon, for Poe dismissed the too-speculative Transcendentalists with the epithet "Frogpondians."

With ample support from *Leaves*, as well as from his often self-promoting criticism and correspondence, Whitman's poetic heirs and most of his critics have taken such claims at face value. Part of an American resistance to aesthetic conventions, or at least to theory, this legacy of "the unexamined life" persists. In his irreverence and experimentation, Whitman does seem thoroughly American, and perhaps we do need a founding poet—if only to reject for his crudity (as T. S. Eliot and Pound were compelled to acknowledge "the pig-headed father," in Pound's phrase). It might, then, seem excessive to consider the philosophical substrata of Whitman's work—and in so doing, to subject his mythic self to the sort of scrutiny generally reserved for systematic thinkers and political propagandists. Yet, even in the terms, and with the tools, of traditional literary scholarship, it is clear that from the beginning of his poetic career and increasingly in his literary and cultural criticism, Whitman tried to incorporate or translate current and traditional philosophy with all its sophistry and mediations into a poetry that so loudly—if disingenuously—proclaims its difference from all things systematic and traditional. He did, though, advertise himself as "representative of German philosophy," as the first epigraph to this essay suggests.

Thus, in "Song of Myself," he is "a kosmos, of Manhattan the son" (*LG*, 52), "an acme of things accomplish'd, an encloser of things to be" (*LG*, 80). These familiar announcements were made after Whitman wrote the unpublished, but much-cannibalized, long poem "Pictures," which presents a gallery of philosophers and poets he would, sometimes stealthily but at other times boastfully, claim to assimilate and supplant from 1855 onward.

In "Pictures," Whitman offers a sort of prolegomena to the longer *Leaves of Grass*. It is a gallery of philosophical and poetic luminaries repressed in the later, recognizably Whitmanesque work. This poem—

whose 126 lines take up part of a 29-page notebook from which Whitman, much more the self-quoter than the spontaneous writer, sometimes drew lines for poems appearing in *Leaves*—is an early statement of poetic purpose and ambition. In it, Whitman runs through a catalog of "pictures" of modern America and, more importantly, of the great prophetic, philosophical, and artistic figures that serve as models or precursors for "the poetry of the future" or the primordial utterance he calls his own "barbaric yawp." The poem begins:

> In a little house pictures I keep, many pictures
>     hanging suspended—It is not a fixed house,
> It is round—it is but a few inches from one side of it to the other side,
> But behold! it has room enough—in it, hundreds and thousands,—all the
>     varieties;
> —Here! do you know this? This is the cicerone himself;
> And here, see you, my own States—and here the world itself,
>     bowling
>     rolling   through the air;
> And there, on the walls hanging, portraits of women and men, carefully
>     kept.
>
> (*LG*, 642)

Here he is but a generic guide through the imaginary picture gallery or library of his own reading and memory; the gallery that is "not a fixed house, / It is round—it is but a few inches from one side of it to the other side" is surely Whitman's head. This poem is descriptive or presentational; its verbs are intransitive, and its staged observers (both poet and his implied reader) are passive. Still, some of the elements and even the paratactic style of the catalogs are in place. Whitman is observer and commentator, not the subject and object of the poem, not, as he would later become, the poem itself. In later poems, he, as Whitman, accompanying the reader or waiting one step ahead, will visit the States and mockingly defy the "questioners" or priests and philosophers of the old ideas. He will "contain multitudes" in a strange historical yet timeless unity—or is it merely an uneasy contradiction? Here, he points at Old World heroes, positioning himself behind that modest particle, the demonstrative pronoun. *This, that*, and *there* become useless when the self is everywhere.

A few lines further on in "Pictures," he pays homage to the great intellectual and artistic works of the past, not merely as tributes brought to America—let alone as the minor characters and props that must exit the stage of history when, as *Democratic Vistas* proclaims, the divine literatus enters—but as prophets and precursors of his own more humble words. Here Whitman is content to allude to pictures already painted; that is, to poems and prophecies he has not already appropriated for his own nationalistic or personal boasts. And though the dramatic situation of the poem hardly rings true, he is willing to share the world-historical, if not the poetic, stage with his precursors:

There is a picture of Adam in Paradise—side by side with him Eve, (the
    Earth's bride and the Earth's bridegroom;)
There is an old Egyptian temple—and again, a Greek temple, of white
    marble;
There are Hebrew prophets chanting, rapt, extatic—and here is Homer;
Here is one singing canticles in an unknown tongue, before the Sanskrit was,
And here a Hindu sage, with his recitative in Sanskrit;
And here the divine Christ expounds eternal truth—expounds the Soul,
. . . . . . . . . . . . . . . . . . . . . . . . . . .
And here, the questioner, the Athenian of the classical time—Socrates, in the
    market place,
(O divine tongue! I too grow silent under your elenchus,
(O you with bare feet, and bulging belly! I saunter along, following you, and
    obediently listen;)

                                     *(LG,* 643)

This passage is remarkable for the specificity of proper names; though these are metonymies for whole cultures, Whitman seems content to tell the story of the past without rejecting it outright. Later, his expansive self will brook no competition or contention. It is significant that Whitman admits being silenced by Socrates, to whom he obediently listens. I would emphasize that our guide is stunned by the great dialectician's *elenchus,* a strange word but not one of Whitman's own coinage. *Elenchus,* a Greek word, can mean refutation in general, but it refers specifically to an argumentative strategy by which one asks questions to draw out contradictions in such a way that an opponent refutes his or her original thesis. Whitman, who boasted of contradictions and disdained analysis or philosophical scrutiny, would of necessity have to eliminate such lapses, even such words, from subsequent poems and from much of his prose. I would argue, however, that philosophy, especially certain anxieties about dialectics and contradiction, were barely repressed in Whitman's work. Indeed, he protests too much their irrelevance to his expansive vision. Therefore, questioners—"askers" of all kinds, historians and philosophers among them—have a particularly hard time of it as they become incorporated into the Whitmanian self or poem. Section #4 of "Song of Myself," for example, shows the expanding self transcending the nattering details of life:

Trippers and askers surround me,
People I meet, the effect upon me of my early life or the ward and city I live
    in, or the nation,
. . . . . . . . . . . . . . . . . . . . . . . . . . . . . . . . . . .
These come to me days and nights and go from me again,
But they are not the Me myself.

(LG, 32)

More than once, and in marked contrast to "Pictures," *Leaves of Grass* presents this acquisitive "I," which by miniaturizing the other creates a suprahistorical self, a kind of grossly physical Spirit of America that as the "Real Me Myself" will in turn stand apart from the material concerns it has incorporated and transformed or translated into its own terms. "Salut au Monde!" for example, owes much to the historical cataloging of "Pictures." But in the later poem, first published in 1856 as "Poem of Salutation," Whitman culturally, if not geopolitically, colonizes the world "in America's name" (*LG*, 148) and under the authority of his own vision and persona. The poem begins, "O take my hand Walt Whitman!" The major answers of the poem are prompted by an importunate and characterless shill who repeatedly calls the poet by name. "What do you hear Walt Whitman?" and "What do you see Walt Whitman?" precede lengthy lists begun with his favorite personal pronoun and his most characteristic trope, the anaphora, "I see," "I hear," and finally, "I am":

I see the cities of the earth and make myself at random a part of
    them,
I am a real Parisian,

I am a habitan of Vienna, St. Petersburg, Berlin, Constantinople,
. . . . . . . . . . . . . . . . . . . . . . . . . . . . .
I descend upon all those cities, and rise from them again.

(*LG*, 144)

In this exchange, the cities, the whole world outside the poet's idea of his American self, lose historical specificity; they not merely are incorporated into Whitman's vision but are introjected or transformed into parts of the living whole, the monstrous and sublime Whitman who also figures (in) the manifest destiny of America:

Within me latitude widens, longitude lengthens,
Asia, Africa, Europe, are the east—America is provided for in
    the west,
. . . . . . . . . . . . . . . . . . . . . . . . . . .
Stretch'd in due time within me the midnight sun just rises above
    the horizon and sinks again,
Within me zones, seas, cataracts, forests, volcanoes, groups,
Malaysia, Polynesia, and the great West Indian islands.

(*LG*, 137–38)

Whereas in "Pictures" historical figures and images from his reading inhabit the confines of Whitman's cranium, here he, and presumably more of his body than just his head, widens to include all continents. Perhaps this metaphorical imperialism, this theft of the world's natural and cultural riches, is not quite so innocent of complicity with a certain manifest and Westerning destiny by which the United States began, prior to the Civil War, to play out its industrial ambitions on this and other continents. In any case, Whitman was hardly innocent of the philosophical—even the American Transcendental—formulas by which the details of history could be made to fit a unified pattern. Eventually, the great expense of suffering during the Civil War will be swept up into his poem as a moment of abstract struggle and dialectical opposition by which history progresses.

Here too Hegel, as Whitman creatively misread the positive or unilaterally progressive force of the dialectic, was most helpful. One senses a certain maintenance of contradiction alternating with simple assertions of unity throughout Whitman's works as he declares his individuation from the masses and his embrace of them. In troubled moments of "Sea-Drift," for example, a certain tragic ebb and flow of the poetic self make for some of the most stunning modern self-reflexive poems. Perhaps in the "Sea-Drift" poems, where Death and the threat of the loss of mastery and selfhood are greatest, Whitman is his closest to meditating on Hegelian negation and the dialectic. Although there is no necessary textual link between the "Lordship and Bondage" section (B:iv) of the *Phenomenology of Spirit* and the dialectical relationship between loss of mastery and the birth of self-consciousness in the "Sea-Drift" poems, Whitman allows one to read the full negative force of Hegel's dialectic in the submission of self to the absolute otherness of Death, the master overcome by the poet's merging of the origin and end in the mystical union of Death, which, in "Out of the Cradle Endlessly Rocking," is tamed by being named. But that was part of Hegel he did not know or recognize, since the *Phenomenology* had yet to be translated. Only recently, after several crossings of influence, including those from Emerson to Nietzsche and back through French readings of Hegel, has the full logical and existential negativity of the dialectic been appreciated.[7] Whitman makes quite clear that his Hegel was an optimist whose System solved contradictions and enlarged the democratic self. Therefore, when Hegel appears in the 1881 edition of *Leaves of Grass*, he names the inspiration or hope of a mystic unity beyond history:

> *Roaming in Thought*
> *(After reading* HEGEL.)
> Roaming in thought over the Universe, I saw the little that is
>     Good steadily hastening towards immortality,
> And the vast all that is call'd Evil I saw hastening to merge itself
>     and become lost and dead.
>
> *(LG, 274)*

Often, where Whitman most seems to reject the past, and specifically to reject philosophy, if not reason altogether, he merely represses his poetic and intellectual influences. And, as I will argue, this very act

---

7. The seminal existentialist reading of Hegelian formula is suggestive in this regard. See Alexandre Kojève, *Introduction to the Reading of Hegel: Lectures on the Phenomenology of Spirit*, trans. James H. Nichols, Jr., ed. Allan Bloom (1969; rpr. Ithaca, N.Y., 1980), 31–70.

of denial or lying for the sake of originality depends on the dream of system and dialectical resolution Whitman sought or imagined in Hegel. "Chanting the Square Deific," another of Whitman's didactic or propositional poems, first included in the *Leaves* of 1865, also works through familiar material from Hegel's "Introduction to History" toward a unity in Whitman's version of how Spirit, progressing through religions from East to West, ends as the integrated Self or corporeal soul:

> Life of the great round world, the sun and stars, and of man,
>     I, the general soul,
> Here the square finishing, the solid, I the most solid,
> Breathe my breath also through these songs.

(LG, 445)

"Hegel," the name of the master philosopher, appears in Whitman's text as the promise of a philosophy great enough for America and worthy to be mastered by its poet. And, quite apart from American resistance to—or repression of—continental philosophy, which has been well documented since Tocqueville's time, Hegel himself stands for the philosopher who would exceed the limits of the tradition he inherited. Whitman was especially drawn to the philosopher of all philosophers, the creator of THE SYSTEM, Hegel, and precisely because that German philosopher had ideas—or the philosophical IDEA—big enough for the American poet, or the Idea of America, to sublate. Indeed, whether or not Whitman knew it, Hegel predicts, even preempts, Whitman's "Poetry of the Future" when, in the Introduction to *The Philosophy of History*, he announces the death of his own philosophy and its rebirth as the yet unknown American Future:

> America is therefore the land of the future, where, in the ages that lie before us, the burden of the World's History shall reveal itself—perhaps in a contest between North and South America. It is a land of desire for all those who are weary of the historical lumber-room of old Europe. Napoleon is reported to have said: "*Cette vieille Europe m'en-nuie.*" It is for America to abandon the ground on which hitherto the History of the World has developed itself. What *has* taken place in the New World up to the present time is only an echo of the Old World— the expression of a foreign Life; and as a Land of the Future, it has no

interest for us here, for, as regards *History* our concern must be with what has been and that which is.[8]

The teleology of Hegelian World History is commensurate with the development of self-consciousness out of oriental servitude into the freedom of pure Spirit—or what has been called the "White Mythology" of pure philosophical speculation.[9] This ethnocentric destiny is traced as the development of Western thought—and not just symbolically or metaphorically but in that other rhetoric by which one creates and justifies abuses of the Other.

Moreover, the dialectic, as Whitman read it, provided a resolution to certain contradictions that Carlyle and others noted in democratic government and American culture. This is not to say that Whitman was a Hegelian in the sense of someone who had read carefully and believed. Nevertheless, in what he read he found the confirmation of his own beliefs; the Hegelisms he fashioned for himself are fundamental to his notion of modernism as well as to his definition of the American (poetic) self. It is in response to Carlyle, whom Whitman came to realize as a personal and intellectual obstacle between himself and Emerson, that the poet deployed what he took to be Hegelian optimism, which he terms *"the most thoroughly American point of view I know"* (*PW*, I, 262).[10] Interestingly, his adoption of Hegel, mentioned here in a footnote in "Carlyle from American Points of View" (in *Specimen Days*), did not mark an acceptance of tradition or of Old World influence:

> In my opinion the above formulas of Hegel are an essential and crowning justification of New World democracy in the creative realms of time and space. There is that about them which only the vastness, the multiplicity and the vitality of America would seem able to comprehend, to give scope and illustration to, or to be fit for, or even originate. It is

8. G. W. F. Hegel, *The Philosophy of History*, trans. J. Sibree (1899; rpr. New York, 1956), 86–87.

9. Derrida, *Margins*, 213.

10. In a letter of February 21, 1883, to William D. O'Connor, Whitman first speculates that Carlyle had helped turn Emerson against him (*Corres.*, III, 326–27). It would be reductive to attribute his late attacks upon Carlyle to efforts to redeem himself in the eyes of Emersonians, but upon reading the Carlyle-Emerson correspondence, Whitman seemed to express personal resentment for the Englishman's influence.

strange to me that they were born in Germany, or in the old world at all. While a Carlyle, I should say, is quite the legitimate European product to be expected. (*PW*, I, 262)

Indeed, if his adoption of Hegel might be deemed barely legitimate for reasons of linguistic and philosophical competence, Whitman's use of what he called "the Hegelian formulas" displays many excesses of Western philosophical humanism, including the abusive potential of the World Historical, which is to say, both nationalistic and individualistic development of Spirit (*Geist*). And, notwithstanding Whitman's ostensible attack upon Carlyle's and others' aristocratic and cultural strictures, the American Self he fashioned, in part from Hegelian tags, is ultimately repressive and deceptively ideological because of its apparently apolitical and otherwise disinterested character. But let me go more slowly here, following carefully the path of the literary historian before I begin to speculate on the implications of the disguised or potential Hegelian or philosophical Whitman.

What of Hegel did Whitman actually know? What made Hegel so attractive? What did Whitman take from or make of this proper name for "modern" German thought? Whitman's use of Hegel remains a clouded issue about which critics and intellectual historians will continue to disagree.[11] Filling in the map of Whitman's misreadings will not get us any closer to a clear picture of influence, but it will disturb the image of the poet who claimed to be above both propaganda and poetry. The indisputable fact that the American poet knew the German philosopher only second- or thirdhand through summaries and poorly translated fragments hardly prevented Whitman from capitalizing both on Hegel's image and on certain hints that endorsed his own ambitions for American poetry. One has also to deal with Whitman's proud announcements of his antisystematic reading and writing procedures. At about the time (from 1874 to 1882) that *Hegel* began to appear in his works, Whitman explains, however self-consciously, how he might have read Hegel or any book for that matter:

11. There is a stunning range of disagreement about the influence of Hegel on Whitman for which reasonable and contradictory support can be gathered. At one extreme is Robert S. Hartman's equation of Hegelian statism and Whitmanian democracy in the Introduction to his much-used translation of *Reason in History* (Indianapolis, 1953), xv. Contrast this to Olive W. Parsons, "Whitman the Non-Hegelian," *PMLA*, LVIII (December, 1943), 1073–84, which denies Whitman's Hegelianism on the grounds that he never exhibited any knowledge of the Hegelian dialectic.

here printing from my impromptu notes, hardly even the seasons group'd together, or anything corrected—so afraid of dropping what smack of outdoors or sun or starlight might cling to the lines, I dared not try to meddle with or smooth them. Every now and then, (not often, but for a foil,) I carried a book in my pocket—or perhaps tore out from some broken or cheap edition a bunch of loose leaves; most always had something of the sort ready, but only took it out when the mood demanded. In that way, utterly out of reach of literary conventions, I re-read many authors. (*PW*, I, 293–94)[12]

One cannot fail to notice that the metaphor of leaves—his textual metaphor for the concrete and universal individualism of his poems, his words, his thoughts—is there invoked for reading as well as for writing. Notwithstanding the careful construction of that version of originality, spontaneity, or randomness, Whitman elsewhere gives a more whimsical, but no less disruptive, treatment of books, influence, and, more specifically, Hegel. Again contrasting Hegel and Carlyle, he says:

Although neither of my great authorities during their lives consider'd the United States worthy of serious mention, all the principal works of both might not inappropriately be this day collected and bound up under the conspicuous title: "*Speculations for the use of North America, and Democracy there, with the relations of the same to Metaphysics, including Lessons and Warnings (encouragements too, and of the vastest,) from the Old World to the New.*" (*PW*, I, 262)

Hegel can thus be seen to provide both the subject matter and the method—a grand myth of America and the dialectic—by which Whitman could contain even philosophy and the threat of continental, artistic, and political influence. It was in this light, and as a way of composing his own vast (anti) theory for America, that he appropriated Hegel.

One can assume that, like nearly everyone else with intellectual pretensions, let alone with fairly steady jobs as book reviewers—like anyone "in the know" from London to New York to Cambridge to

12. To this proclaimed antiphilosophical, antisystematic spontaneity, contrast *PW*, II, 722–23, in which Whitman acknowledges his career-long submission to the ruling ideas of Plato and "the German philosophers."

Ohio—Whitman probably knew something of Hegel around the time *Leaves* started appearing, but our poet was not always the best scholar or the worst plagiarist. For the sake of economy, and a certain sense of scholarly hygiene, let me just list the Hegel available to Whitman—at least the books he acknowledges by citation. First, Frederic H. Hedge's *Prose Writers of Germany*, an anthology of fragments translated from German classics beginning with Martin Luther and ending with Adalbert von Chamisso's story of Peter Schlemihl, was published in Philadelphia in 1847 and was probably the first introduction for most Americans to Hegel. It affords Hegel twelve pages: one page of bio-bibliography, nine and a half pages from *The Philosophy of History*, and two pages of a joke from Hegel's miscellaneous writings that, by way of defending philosophy from charges of obscurity, ironically indicts folk expressions and gossip for excessive abstraction. So, if the real Hegel was often compelled to borrow literary or figurative language to make his grave system accessible, this American Hegel was already brief and perhaps too homespun. There was of course other summaries, translations, and adaptations of Hegel available, many of which were even more fragmented and indirect. Whitman himself, in a footnote to a passage also written about 1881, cited Joseph Gostwick's 1854 anthology, *Outlines of German Literature*, as his chief Hegelian source. Gostwick schematizes German thought from 380 to 1870, affording Hegel nineteen pages in which he attempts to lay out Hegel's major themes and texts by summary, with only about a page of translation. Most quotations are drawn from the Introduction to the *Encyclopedia* and from *The Philosophy of History*.[13] These passages define key formulas and emphasize freedom as the motive and telos of the Great German

13. William H. Goetzmann, *The American Hegelians: An Intellectual Episode in the History of Western America* (New York, 1973), gives a history of Hegelian ideas in America during Whitman's time. There were numerous English summaries of Hegel available from the 1840s, but the earliest translations of whole volumes of Hegel's works, which also reflected the textual complexity of compiled lectures, are *Hegel's Lectures on the Philosophy of History*, ed. John Sibree (London, 1857), *Hegel's Logic, Being Part One of the Encyclopedia of the Philosophical Sciences*, trans. William Wallace (Oxford, 1873), and *The Philosophy of Art, Being the Second Part of Hegel's "Aesthetik,"* trans. William McKendree Bryant (New York, 1879). There is no reason to believe that Whitman knew these books, but one knows from footnotes and acknowledgments that he used Frederic Henry Hedge, *Prose Writers of Germany* (Philadelphia, 1847) and Joseph Gostwick, *Outlines of German Literature* (Philadelphia, 1854). Curiously enough, the copy of the latter at Harvard's Widener Library is inscribed to Thomas Carlyle.

Spirit in its battle against the oriental past. They also happen to include some of Hegel's more nervous or self-reflexive defenses of method.

Whitman's direct references to, and invocations of, Hegel and the American Hegelians occur late in his career as attempts to defend his version of America on philosophical grounds and to enlarge his audience from his few confirmed Whitmanians to English and Continental patrons and academics. Therefore, before recognizably Hegelian gestures appear—or *reappear* under Hegel's name—in his poetry and prose of the 1870s and 1880s, Whitman was already styling himself a Hegelian. The most telling debuts of this new persona are in Whitman's letters to potentially friendly reviewers whose essays he previewed or influenced in his great self-promotional campaign. For example, in a letter of January 16, 1872, to Rudolph Schmidt, a German professor who translated and reviewed Whitman's poetry, we read: "The central purpose of 'Democratic Vistas' is to project & outline a fresh & brawny race of original American Imaginative authors, with *moral purpose*, Hegelianism, underlying their works, poems—& with Science and Democracy—also thoroughly *religious*—(not ecclesiastical or sectarian merely)" (*Corres.*, II, 151).

A few days later he wrote a similar letter to Edward Dowden, editor of London's *Westminster Review.* Here, again, *Democratic Vistas,* which he rightly characterized as his most sustained critical and nationalistic statement, occasions his belated Hegelian affiliation:

> In "Democratic Vistas" I seek to make patent the appalling vacuum, in our times & here, of any school of great imaginative Literature & Art, fit for a Republican, Religious, & Healthy people—and to suggest & prophesy such a Literature as the only vital means of sustaining & perpetuating such a people. I would project at least the rough sketch of such a school of Literatures—an entirely new breed of authors, poets, American, comprehensive, Hegelian, Democratic, religious—& with an infinitely larger scope & method than any yet—(*Corres.*, II, 154)

To the Englishman, perhaps by way of acknowledging Carlyle's and Arnold's attacks upon the former colony's cultural poverty and nearly anarchical habits, Whitman was more defensive than in the earlier letter.

He also claimed, despite evidence of increased sales and public recognition, to be the prophet despised in his own land. He planted the following biographical details—or fleshed out his international and/ or Hegelian persona—in letters to Schmidt, William Rossetti, Anne Gilchrist, Moncure Conway, and other foreign publicists. The letter to Dowden, exemplary of this genre of Whitmanian self-promotion, continues: "There is one point touched by you in Westminster criticism that if occasion again arises, might be dwelt on more fully—that is the attitude of sneering denial which magazines, editors, publishers, 'critics' &c. in the U. S. hold toward 'Leaves of Grass.' As to 'Democratic Vistas' it remains unread, uncalled for here in America" (*Corres.*, II, 154). Whether it was for his new public/academic image or his private edification, Whitman also corresponded with William Torrey Harris, head of the St. Louis Philosophical Society, superintendent of public schools, and editor of the *Journal of Speculative Philosophy*, to which the poet probably subscribed.[14] While visiting family in St. Louis in 1879, Whitman apparently saw Harris several times and perhaps attended meetings of the Hegel society, or so he reported to John Burroughs, in a letter of November 23, 1879, devoted largely to Burroughs' "Nature and the Poets":

> I saw in the Library a late London *Fortnightly* in which J A Symonds, touching briefly but very commendingly & mentioning my name, made quite an extract from Dem. Vistas (summing up the general spirit of British literature as being markedly sombre & bilious)—A B Alcott is expected here, to talk—I may see him—This is quite a place for the most toploftical Hegelian transcendentalists, a small knot but smart— the principal of them, W T Harris, editor of *Speculative Philosophy*, has been often to see me, has been very kind, & I like him much. (*Corres.*, III, 171)

It is noteworthy that Whitman numbers Alcott among the toploftiest of Hegelians. Alcott admired Whitman's notion of "personalism" and introduced the term into American philosophy. In a letter to the editors of the *Galaxy*, Whitman described the essay bearing this strange word for its title:

---

14. In a letter of September 28, 1880, Whitman thanks Harris for a copy of his journal, which is also mentioned elsewhere (*Corres.*, III, 187–88).

[It] sketches the portrait of the ideal American of the future—also characterizations of the American woman—overhauls the Culture theory, shows its deficiencies, tested by any grand, practical Democratic test—argues that the main thing wanted for the literary, esthetic, & moral areas of the United States is to institute what must result in copious supplies, among the masses, of healthy, acute, handsome Individualities, modernized, & fully adapted to our soil, our days, city & country. The name of my piece is

*Personalism.*

Don't be alarmed at the (perhaps at first sight) oddity of the word—it is the right title for the article, and will justify itself, & remain. (*Corres.*, II, 19)[15]

This "theory," as it appears in *Democratic Vistas*, is a rather literal-minded humanism in which the individual is the primary ontological and ethical category. The point here is that the antiphilosophical poet, once rejected by Emerson because of the physicality of his verse, entered the polite society of Transcendentalist philosophers by a slightly different route. As we shall see, he also comes full circle to a version of self-reliance.

Although *Democratic Vistas* and two essays on Carlyle are Whitman's most serious published treatments of Hegel, we might recall another issue of this late philosophical conversion. There remains in the Whitman archive a set of animadversions composed of four brief, elementary introductions to the thought of Kant, Hegel, Schelling, and Fichte, entitled "The Sunday Evening Lectures," written, perhaps, in anticipation of the poet's appearance before some sort of philosophical society.[16] The lectures comprise fragmentary and palimpsestic notes,

15. *Democratic Vistas* first appeared in two issues of *Galaxy*: "Democracy," *Galaxy*, IV (December, 1867), 919–33, and "Personalism," V (May, 1868), 540–47. They were first issued as a book in 1871. It seems that whereas Emerson had little positive to say about Whitman in later years, Alcott was much impressed with the poet's doctrine of American individualism—so much so that he adopted Whitman's coinage and theory of "personalism."

16. Walt Whitman, *Notes and Unpublished Prose Manuscripts*, ed. Edward Grier (6 vols.; New York, 1984), VI, 2009. The textual headnote explains that the manuscript is missing and quotes Maurice Bucke to the effect that the manuscript "'is simply a series of fragments.'" The "lectures" exist in manuscript at the Humanities Research Center at the University of Texas at Austin. The editors of the comprehensive *Collected Writings of Walt Whitman*, however, say that the manuscript is not known to exist, though they include the lectures from the 1902 edition of *The Complete Writings of Walt Whitman* (ed. Maurice Bucke, Thomas B. Harned, and Horace L. Traubel).

some written in what appears to be Whitman's earlier, legible hand but most in his later, unsteady one. At least some of the layers containing editorializings and rereadings are in the familiar, barely legible scrawl of the older poet. These pages do form a sort of palimpsest in which reading and writing merge, or where we see the writer reading himself. They resemble the nearly illegible series of unpublished prefaces intended for various foreign editions of *Leaves* that Whitman revised annually on his birthday.[17] Perhaps Whitman did not similarly ritualize his afterthoughts on Hegel, but he certainly made characteristic mockery of such scholarly illusions as fixed sources and a stable line between reading and writing that prevents one from saying Whitman invented Hegel. We might demure at reading the poet out of his hand—or his handwriting—which might prove no more trustworthy than his portrait for determining his age and the proper shape of his literary corpus.

There is, however, no evidence that Whitman was ever invited to deliver these lectures. But they are the sort of thing one might lecture from or improvise upon; they certainly collate the quotations, allusions, and summaries that Whitman distributed elsewhere in published prose and poetry. Whitman's final intentions for these lecture notes, made lovingly into a book by Whitman's friend, Maurice Bucke, the mystic, psychologist, and literary critic—or, more simply, one of the poet's like-minded early disciples—are largely open to question. It is a leatherbound presentation copy or souvenir of the second delivery of the lectures at the Ninth Annual Banquet of the Walt Whitman Fellowship, held in New York in 1902. Before the Americanists, the New Critics, or even the Beats, all for their own reasons, managed to efface the signs of the philosopher, lecturer, and politician from his image, Whitman's old friends and new followers constructed a persona more in keeping with the face of the poet we have just seen presented to his European, academic, and Transcendentalist/Hegelian friends.

This curious little book, a collation of various sizes and shapes of leaves of scratch paper written over in ink or dull pencil, organizes Whitman's enthusiastic commentaries and his transcriptions from Gostwick and Hedge under biographical generalizations and summaries that Whitman culled from two popular encyclopedias. The book,

17. Some of the Prefaces are in collections of "Whitmaniana" at the University of California at Berkeley, for example. Several are collated in Clifton Furness, ed., *Walt Whitman's Workshop: A Collection of Unpublished Manuscripts* (1928; rpr. New York, 1964); p. 209 mentions the birthdate revisions.

despite careful trimming and mounting of penciled scraps of newsprint paper, remains mere leavings of Whitman's rather shallow but terribly interested reading. While far from certifying the poet's claim to philosophical rigor or high seriousness, these notes constitute a reading, or a creative rendering, of Whitman's American Hegel. Not surprisingly, this Hegel speaks directly to several of Whitman's abiding concerns, of which I will give only brief excerpts, since we will return to consider them in the expanded form as the principal themes of *Democratic Vistas*. I quote, from the Texas manuscripts, the opening of the section on Hegel:

> I will begin by impressing upon your attention the growing and greater particularity—with which the moderns use the words relating to philosophical inquiries. The realm of words is becoming more definitely bounded. This is one of the marked characteristics of our times. Precision is demanded. Though they inevitably run into each other, each term in the Category yet has its own exact limited area & [each?] writer conforms.[18]

Here, in the attempt to incorporate his four metaphysicians and translate their notions or categories of "Self," "Science," and "History," Whitman finds—projects—his own abiding concern with the power and plasticity of individual words. While he seems to approve philosophical efforts to keep words bounded by definitions, he also reserves for himself the poet's license to free them. In *Democratic Vistas* and throughout the poetry, he will elide whole categories by forcing one word, *America*, to stand in for the many contradictions he wants at once to ignore and to contain. He also claims a philosophical precedent for such rhetorical sleights-of-hand and discursive excess: "Theology, Hegel translates into science" (*PW*, I, 260).

His appropriation of the dialectic shows Whitman translating Hegel into a useful version of unilateral progress toward Unity or mystical Union:

> Penetrating beneath the shows of the objective world we find that in respect to human cognition of them all and several are pervaded by *the*

18. Walt Whitman, "The Sunday Evening Lectures" (MS in Humanities Research Center, University of Texas at Austin), 25. I have assigned numbers to the text pages as they are bound in the volume. The "pages," in fact, often comprise two or three fragments mounted or matted on the same page, apparently in the interest of design.

*only absolute substance* which is SPIRIT, endued with the eternal impetus of development, and producing from itself the opposing powers and forces of the universe. A curious, triplicate process seems the resultant action; first the Positive, then the Negative, then the product of the mediation between them; from which product the process is repeated and so goes on without end.[19]

In this way, "Hegel" sublates or even renders irrelevant the Socratic *elenchus* that Whitman had suppressed from the time of "Pictures." With this positive or progressive version of the dialectic the poet can read or revise the Civil War symbolically and ahistorically as a negative moment in the destined arc of the Union, as drawn in *Drum-Taps*. Negation, the irresistible motive force of the dialectic, becomes merely instrumental; sublation gives way to change and to the American dream of progress. As it happens, when Whitman writes of death and language in the self-reflexive poems of "Sea-Drift," he is closer to the full force of Hegelian negation than he is in his philosophical notation or his historical poetry.

In praising Hegel, Whitman makes clear his desire for a philosophically grounded notion of Self that can stand as dialectical resolution or sublation of subject and object, facticity and spirit. Indeed, this is the theme knitting together his remarks about Kant, Schelling, Fichte, and Hegel. He rejects Fichte's "spontaneous intuition" as too egotistical an answer to Kant's "distinction between the *I* and the *not I*." And while admiring Schelling's imaginative formulation of " '*the essential identity of the subjective and objective worlds*,' " he finds that Hegel "encloses all":

> Yourself, myself,—amid the baffling labyrinths—what am I, what are you here for?—give some suggestion (however indirect or inferential) . . . the world with its manifold shows—the beginning, endless wonder, Time—the other wonder Space—oneself, the darkest labyrinth, mightiest wonder. What triumphs of our kind out-topples this—that one, a man, has lived and bestowed on his fellow-men the Ariadne's thread to guide them through this maze?
>
> Only Hegel is fit for America—is large enough and free enough.

19. Whitman, "Lectures," 41.

The haunting contradiction of separate self and democratic masses (most pressing among "the varieties, contradictions, and paradoxes of the world and of life") he could face directly and discursively in *Democratic Vistas*.[20] This he does by mentioning the name of the greatest philosopher, for he does not elaborate his Hegelisms in that essay.

He does, however, transpose his notes on Hegel and theories of the Self from "Carlyle from American Points of View"—if it is possible to fix the thefts and transpositions among his own critical writings. With reference to the dismissal of Carlyle for the Hegelian integration of self and other, he says:

> The most profound theme that can occupy the mind of man . . . is doubtless involved in the query: What is the fusing explanation and tie—what the relation between the (radical, democratic) Me, the human identity of understanding, emotions, spirit, &c., on the one side, of and with the (conservative) Not Me, the whole of the material objective universe and laws, with what is behind them in time and space, on the other side? (*PW*, I, 258)

Since he believed his assertion of the equation or synonymity of America = democracy = poetry = Whitman, Whitman's defense of American democracy is also a defense of his corpus and/as "personalism." It is noteworthy that *Democratic Vistas* was written in response to Carlyle, specifically, as Whitman says, to Carlyle's 1867 pamphlet, *Shooting Niagara*, whose title was meant to suggest the foolhardiness of America's democratic government, in which high culture and Western civilization are as doomed to death as someone riding a barrel down Niagara Falls, that great American symbol of freedom and natural force. Carlyle asserted that the contagious American experiment and the imminent total collapse of aristocratic power and cultural values would be the necessary results of wider suffrage and increased democratization promised after the Civil War. Indeed, Carlyle's focus is on the degradation of the individual into the lowest common denominator of mob psychology. His pamphlet is remarkable for its racism, elitism, and Bismarckianism, and Whitman felt compelled to respond, not to Carlyle's politics, but to his persona, to his seductive prose, and to the related claim that democracy diminishes individualism. *Democratic Vis-*

20. *Ibid.*, 32, 35.

*tas* is his answer to the most influential conservative modern thinker and his assertion of his own poetic and philosophical powers. In this and other responses to Carlyle, Whitman takes his formulas from Hegel, but these are visions and vistas of personal and poetic—which is to say, ideological—mastery, not merely defenses of an American politics Whitman too found threatening. At the beginning of *Democratic Vistas*, he nearly echoes Carlyle by promising "not to gloss over the appalling dangers of universal suffrage in the United States." Indeed, he avers that he is writing "to admit and face these dangers" (*PW,* II, 363).

Critics have generally treated Whitman's essay as a manifesto of both nativism and egalitarianism. And the essay certainly does promote a certain brand of liberal optimism and populism in its alleged opening of literature and high culture to "the ungrammatical people." Yet, despite—or really because of—Carlyle's reactionary challenge, Whitman's response is more an assertion of his individual power and prerogatives than a defense of "the people." It is more an advertisement for the repressive or ordering potential of American culture than a revolution against inherited constraints. His ambition is transparent in a eulogy of Carlyle as the dyspeptic anti-hero who speaks unhappy truths. Admiration for Carlyle—or is it his desire for equal influence?—forced the American poet to give over his much-heralded democratic principles: "Who cares that he wrote . . . 'Shooting Niagara'— and 'The Nigger Question,' and didn't at all admire our United States? (I doubt if he ever thought or said half as bad words about us as we deserve.) How he splashes like a leviathan in the seas of modern literature and politics" (*PW,* I, 250–51).

Whitman certainly felt ambivalent about the powers of the supreme individual, of the monarchs and aristocrats who had always defined the way of the world and of the poets who celebrated them. He knew that he had to realign the power relations between culture and the state in order to make literature and democracy compatible. Therefore, he grudgingly acknowledges, "literature, strictly consider'd, has never recognized the People, and, whatever may be said, does not today" (*PW,* II, 376), and "the great poems, Shakspere included, are poisonous to the idea of pride and dignity of the common people" (*PW,* II, 388). But as we have seen, he wanted, by a variety of tropes, to overturn the old order only to ensure the supremacy of the perfect individual. This "New Man," a metaphor that had already become abusive in the eugenics movements of Whitman's time, had no clear model or precedent, yet Whitman reserved for himself the role of modeler. He was ready to write the history of the future of America, to account for the biography or at least the *conception* of what he called the "copious, sane, gigantic offspring." This gigantic offspring is in part the issue of the marriage of Carlyle's monumental history and Hegel's dialectic. Although Whitman prescribes, in some biological or physiognomical detail, the "race of perfect Mothers" and the strongest young men who will be the future of America, he gives precedence to the concept over the thing, or, in this case, abstract Idea of union over the Union. Here, by means of a pun that plays on both proper name and general idea, Whitman substitutes an Ideal—or Idea—of America for his troubled national state in the Reconstruction period:

> I say, the true nationality of the States, the genuine union, when we come to a mortal crisis, is, and is to be, after all, neither the written law, nor, (as is generally supposed,) either self-interest, or common pecuniary or material objects—but the fervid and tremendous IDEA, melting everything else with resistless heat, and solving all lesser and definite distinctions in vast, indefinite, spiritual, emotional power. (*PW*, II, 368)

If the true nationality is an idea of nationalism, a sense of belonging as an individual to the Idea of America, Whitman is dealing, not merely in abstractions, but quite deliberately in ideology, or, as I will argue, in a specific American ideology of the individual.[21] Sometimes this individual is simply a representative American, sometimes the "simple, separate person," sometimes the poet who cannot finally bridge the gap between his person and the masses.

At such moments, something like the Hegelian dialectic's introjection (or *Aufhebung*) of the warring opposites of Self and the Masses stands on the horizon as a yet-unfulfilled promise:

---

21. In *The Eighteenth Presidency!* Whitman argues that the training of young men, especially his own working-class comrades, should replace party politics and open elections. His rather strange support of John Frémont against the vested interests announces itself as the "Voice of Walt Whitman to each Young Man in the Nation, North, South, East, and West" (*The Eighteenth Presidency: A Critical Text*, ed. Edward F. Grier [Lawrence, Kans., 1956]), 19). Whitman's concern with the corruption ensuing from universal suffrage and graft-ridden party politics seems consonant with American populism's treble embrace of racism, individualism, and anti-elitism.

The question hinted here is one which time only can answer. Must not the virtue of modern Individualism, continually enlarging, usurping all, seriously affect, perhaps keep down entirely, in America, the like of the ancient virtue of Patriotism, the fervid and absorbing love of general country? I have no doubt myself that the two will merge, and will mutually profit and brace each other, and that from them a greater product, a third, will arise. (*PW*, II, 337)

Still, it seems clear that the "literatus of the modern," even traveling under several pseudonyms (including *Walt Whitman*), is a special individual, belonging to the future as the advance guard for a nation of representative individuals. For all his theorizing, and in the terms of his own argument, Whitman is already a practicing "literatus," an exception to the same average he represents—or an excess against which boundaries can be marked or overtaken.

Thus he resisted, at the same time that he wished to transform, the power of the heroic individual thematized in Carlyle's historicism; he says as much in "Carlyle from American Points of View": "My utmost pretention is probably but to offset that old claim of the exclusively curative power of first-class individual men, as leaders and rulers, by the claims, and general movement and result, of ideas. Something of the latter seems to me the distinctive theory of America, of democracy, and of the modern" (*PW*, I, 262). This theme is enlarged upon in *Democratic Vistas*: "I demand races of orbic bards, with unconditional uncompromising sway. Come forth, sweet democratic despots of the west!" (*PW*, II, 407). Whitman also felt that the theoretician of America or, more familiarly, the "literatus of the modern," had to master or incorporate what Hegel had come to represent. He would be prophet, poet, and philosopher, or, to quote Whitman: "not only possess'd of the religious fire and abandon of Isaiah, luxuriant in the epic talent of Homer, or for proud characters as in Shakspere, but consistent with the Hegelian formulas, and consistent with modern science" (*PW*, II, 421).

We have already seen what Whitman understood by Hegelian formulas: *Democratic Vistas* repeatedly deploys the integrative power of the dialectic of what he called Idea, to surmount acknowledged impediments to an American literature. Whitman announces both a new poetry and its grounding in a new metaphysics. Doubly belated, coming after the great literature of the past and after Hegel's formulation of the philosophical System, he desires mastery over both, and in so doing he hopes to capitalize on the complicity of poetry and philosophy in any national image: "In the prophetic literature of these States (the reader of my speculations will miss their principal stress unless he allows well for the point that a new Literature, perhaps a new Metaphysics, certainly a new Poetry, are to be, in my opinion, the only sure and worthy supports and expressions of the American Democracy)" (*PW*, II, 416). The trinity "religion/poetry/philosophy" is familiar enough from Hegel. Whereas most Hegelians are somewhat uncertain about literature's position as that which philosophy must eventually overcome, Whitman clearly asserts the historical priority and the privilege literature enjoys over philosophy and other discourses. By a dialectical or hermeneutical circularity, poetry is origin and telos of what is highest in Western culture. Therefore, America's "poetry of the future" subsumes or, because it answers requirements of the earlier discourses, "sublates" religion and philosophy rather than the other way round. By Whitman's account, "the Priest departs, the divine literatus comes. Never was anything more wanted than, to-day, and here in the States, the poet of the modern is wanted, or the great literatus of the modern" (*PW*, II, 365).

From the beginning of the essay, Whitman avoids both contradiction and precise definition by collapsing or troping one term into another. Just as poetry and philosophy become interchangeable parts mastered by the modern literatus, *America*, the proper name of nationalism in the United States, and *democracy*, a common name for participatory government, become synonymous: "To him or her within whose thought rages the battle, advancing, retreating, between democracy's convictions, aspirations, and the people's crudeness, vice, caprices, I mainly write this essay. I shall use the words America and democracy as convertible terms" (*PW*, II, 363).

Foremost among Whitman's other convertible terms are *Soul* and *Literature*. In his formulation, literature is both the vehicle and the goal of American culture. It takes the place of Hegel's Spirit, which is the ultimate manifestation of self-consciousness or the goal and cessation of historical change, as well as the motive force of history, which might also be called change or chance:

What an age! What a land! Where, elsewhere, one so great? The individuality of one nation must then, as always, lead the world. Can there be any doubt who the leader ought to be? Bear in mind, though, that nothing less than the mightiest original nonsubordinated SOUL has ever really, gloriously led, or ever can lead. (This Soul—its other name, in these Vistas, is LITERATURE.) (*PW*, II, 413)

Put crudely, the true mission of literature is to supply the ideology or jingoism by which the perfect individual, in the name of a portmanteau abstraction, America/Democracy/The Modern, will rule the world. One might notice that this formulation begins rather concretely in time and space, but the relative specificity of "age" and "land," as the here and now of Whitman's America, are quickly changed into "world" and "always." This essentializing or totalizing hyperbole rests on an old cliché—or dead synecdoche—of the Body Politic, for which literature, in this essay, is the soul. With Carlyle as leviathan, an embodiment of Hobbes's metaphor of the Body Politic, Whitman refers to the State on the model of the individual, that monstrous self, which so easily translates into the fascist—or, as Pound tragically punned, "factive"—individual.[22] Such repressed genealogies and intertextualities—running back from Whitman to Hegel and forward from both to high modernism—forever disturb Whitman's dream that the oxymoron "democratic self" could be happily made grammatical or tautological, at least by overemphasis on the latter term.

Can one simply leave this aside along with the strident imperialism implicit in Whitman's equations of democracy and America, of American and individual, of the translation of these into America making the world safe for democracy, free enterprise, and certain individuals, principally white males? The degree to which Whitman intended to allude to, or even to influence, the historical events of his time, from the annexation by the United States of larger parts of "America" according to the Monroe Doctrine, cannot, yet must, concern us here. Nor can the ideological force lines—sometimes distinguished as cause and effect or theory and practice—be fixed and overcome here more than anywhere else in the text of history. But we cannot ignore the function of literature in creating and controlling the individual, or *his* place in a certain American "ideology of the individual" according to which politics and history can be transcended by the Self and by Art.

22. Ezra Pound, *Guide to Kulchur* (1938; rpr. New York, 1970), 194. Here and elsewhere, Pound uses the notion of "factive personality," a pun on *factive—facere* (having the power) to make, and the fact as central historical factor/hero/anti-hero of an age—to index his political actors in history and fiction, including Jefferson, John Adams, Sigismundo Malatesta, Mussolini, and Dante.

The concepts or near antinomies with which Whitman has the greatest difficulty are "democracy" and "individual." Perhaps retaining something of Carlyle's horror at the unwashed masses while expressing his own fears of contact and the loss of personal identity, Whitman did not succeed in making the key terms of his argument convertible. He did, however, attempt several definitions—or de-definitions—of these terms in relation to each other:

> For to democracy, the leveler, the unyielding principle of the average, is surely join'd another principle, equally unyielding, closely tracking the first, indispensable to it, opposite, (as the sexes are opposite,) and whose existence, confronting and ever modifying the other, often clashing, paradoxical . . . plainly supplies to these grand cosmic politics of ours, and to the launch'd forth mortal dangers of republicanism, to-day or any day, the counterpart and offset whereby Nature restrains the deadly original relentlessness of all her first-class laws. The second principle is individuality, the pride and centripetal isolation of a human being in himself—identity—personalism. (*PW*, II, 391)

The individual is at once the measure of all things and the enemy of democracy, and despite the caveat that *America* and *democracy* are "convertible," Whitman cannot resolve the terms by rhetorical trope or, what might be the same thing, by dialectical sublation. He recites the familiar circular argument of humanism, if under his own term, *personalism*: "Even for the treatment of the universal, in politics, metaphysics, or anything, sooner or later we come down to one single, solitary soul"(*PW*, II, 394).

He remains unconvinced, unhappily contradictory. There is a great temptation, therefore, to allow Whitman his claim of representativeness, of the embodiment of profound contradictions. He seems to fit so well Lionel Trilling's brilliant formula for nineteenth-century cultural history: "in any culture there are likely to be certain artists who contain a large part of the dialectic within themselves, their meaning and power lying within themselves, it may be said, the very essence of the culture, and the sign of this is that they do not submit to serve the ends of any one ideological group or tendency."[23] Trilling does not,

---

23. Lionel Trilling, *The Liberal Imagination: Essays on Literature and Society* (New York, 1950), 9–10.

however, take us out of the problem of the superiority of the special individual, does not address questions of the elitism and paternalism of liberal cultural history, which still depends on its revolutionary heroes—Whitman being principal among them. Moreover, Whitman, like Trilling himself, came to recognize the impossibility of remaining outside ideology. The poet recognized that his focus on the self, the transformation of the common man into the superior individual, was an alternative to politics and thus wholly ideological.

Despite all his talk of the perfect and perfectible individual, Whitman keeps returning to the unhappy conflict between Self and Society—and the infelicitous locution of "Me Myself" and the "not me." This failure of language opens the space of poetry and marks the need for the unifying Idea supplied by Hegel's/America's poetry of the future to ensure its continued political or ideological utility. Thus, "[democracy] is a great word, whose history, I suppose, remains unwritten, because that history has yet to be enacted" (*PW*, II: 393). Poetry's task is to record and, in recording, to create the history of democracy and its modification by individualism. Although Whitman does privilege individualism by placing it on the side of Nature against the leveling tendencies of democracy and the mortal dangers of republicanism, individuality, too, must be restrained.

Unlike Hobbes and Carlyle, to name two political thinkers with whom Whitman was familiar, the American poet does not choose to restrain individualism by fixed class hierarchies or state repression and prohibitions. He has a certain notion of self-government and perfectibility. Yet he does not, as a fuller reading of Hegel might have allowed him to do, simply transform the individual into the State. Finally, as a supplement to poetry's forceful Idea, Whitman suggests that modern governments—and perhaps the convertible terms *America* and *democracy* still apply here—should provide certain training by example and/ or education. Before placing or naming this ordering principle, let me quote one of Whitman's less poetical summaries of the pedagogical and civilizing force of poetry and/as Idea:

> I say the mission of the government, henceforth, in civilized lands, is not repression alone, and not authority alone, not even of law, nor by that favorite standard of the eminent writer, the rule of the best men, the born heroes and captains of the race, (as if such ever, or one time out of a hundred, get into the big places, elective or dynastic)—but higher than the highest arbitrary rule, to train communities through all

the grades, beginning with the individuals and ending there again, to rule themselves. (*PW*, II, 379–80)

These "selves," modeled on Whitman's grandiose Self, were to be confident and expansive and, it would seem, above politics. Yet such a theory of selfhood, which is necessarily available only to the few, is essentially political and undemocratic. Self-definition or an ideology of the self must be imposed from above by the legislating poet, if not by the State. Whitman's poetic self-advertisements, his carefully crafted representative persona perform this task; so too does his prose bespeak this desire.

I have used the charged word *ideology* several times, by way of questioning the political or historical construction and ultility of Whitman's "Self," his use of Hegel in a politically and nationalistically determinative way. To do so is necessarily to make a sort of accusation, if not of malice and deception, at least of some sort of complicity in the evolving American projections of a wasteful and interested, if democratic, selfhood. This charge of complicity, an indictment of the representative or informing self, is inevitable if only because *ideology* has always been uneasily and defensively pejorative, and according to its own internal logic, "ideology always belongs to someone else." Yet, one must grudgingly admit that even the most excessive formulations of the Whitmanesque self are—like Prospero his Caliban—our own and deeply ideological. This is testimony to the power of Whitman's poetry and his persona, not a diminution of his imagination to the *merely* political, whose borders are easily crossed by the American poet, as he sometimes invites us to observe.

Ideology, while supplying the illusion of being beyond history, has a history, and in order to clarify what I have meant by Whitman's ideology, I will cite Louis Althusser's familiar schematic account of the rise of ideological "overdetermination," which has relevance for Whitman's ambitious poetics: "In the pre-capitalist historical period which I have examined extremely broadly, it is absolutely clear that *there was one dominant Ideological State Apparatus, the Church*, which concentrated within it not only religious functions, but also educational ones, and a large proportion of the functions of communications and 'culture.' "[24]

---

24. Louis Althusser, "Ideology and Ideological State Apparatuses (Notes and Investigation)", in Althusser, *Lenin and Philosophy and Other Essays*, trans. Ben Brewster (New York, 1971), 151.

In attempting to usurp the roles of priest, politician, and philosopher, Whitman claims for the poet a mastery of the goals and instruments of American culture. The poet renames and reinterprets old institutions to make them, in Whitman's particular watchwords, modern and American. It seems clear that Whitman knew Matthew Arnold's *Culture and Anarchy*, published in 1868, three years before *Democratic Vistas* began to appear. Whitman may not have been ill-disposed towards Arnold's argument for both the widening of culture to the lower classes and its utility in controlling those masses. In an extended redefinition of the word *culture*, which Whitman calls the enemy close at hand, *Democratic Vistas* frees American culture from the constraints of Old World discourses and, especially, of its elitist literature.[25] But this opening, a vista or horizon and not yet a fact, depends on Whitman's model of the "typical personality," that special democratic self abstracted from the masses and re-presented by the poet:

> I do not so much object to the name, or word [culture], but I should certainly insist, for the purposes of these States, on a radical change of category, in the distribution of precedence. . . . *I should demand of this programme or theory a scope generous enough to include the widest human area. It must have for its spinal meaning the formation of a typical personality* [emphasis added] of character, eligible to the uses of the high average of men—and *not* restricted by conditions ineligible to the masses. (*PW*, II, 396)

The typical personality of Whitman's poetic and critical corpus is wide, amorphous, if not aleatory. His American readers, so ready to reject history and politics in the name of an idealized individualism, have a special stake in appropriating or interpreting the self—the selves—he offers. "Song of Myself" alone is broad enough for most everyone to identify something of him or herself in the catalog of American types that Whitman calls "myself." The resulting construct—variously "Whitman," "I," "Me," "the real Me Myself," and even "you"—essentializes individualism and liberates the self from the very socioeconomic contingencies, the facticity, it seems to contain. In characteristic fashion, Section #15 of "Song of Myself" concludes its list of Ameri-

25. For further discussion of this problem, see my *Reading Pound Reading: Modernism After Nietzsche* (New York, 1987), 214–18.

cans particularized by occupation, class, and familial relationships ("the carpenter," "the quadroon girl," "the connoisseur," "the prostitute") with a version of the poet's self to which we all are offered access:

> And these tend inward to me, and I tend outward to them,
> And such as it is to be of these more or less I am,
> And of these one and all I weave the song of myself.
>
> (*LG*, 44)

Whitman seems here to acknowledge the artistry and artifice of the self he is about creating. "Weave" is a textual metaphor as old as Homer's Penelope; "song of myself" is both the poem's title and the name for the union of self and other(s) it promotes. Nevertheless, Whitman did not single-handedly create the American self or found the doctrine of individualism. To say so would at once remove him from the history that forms, and the previous poetic and philosophical texts that informed, his poem. He does, however, present a special plea for the primacy of the individual in American culture. In this he can be said to be *our* poet, the American ideologist par excellence. He invites us to imagine ourselves as slaves and workers in a poetry intended to "cheer up slaves and horrify despots," but perhaps the identification of oneself between these categories, rather than the active questioning of both, adds to their permanence. However, though his fantasy of a large readership of slaves and workers did not materialize in his own lifetime, there has always been a large underground, nonacademic audience for Whitman's poetry, a fact that somehow confirms his status as role model for America's national poet. Oddly enough, while many academic readers reject the poets' Whitman, only recently have critics begun to find him worthy of—or amenable to—examination along lines other than that he dictated by calling himself democratic, American, original.

Ideology works by identification. Among its tools are the definition of personal identity and/as individualism—as against, for example, identification of oneself as a worker. There is much to quarrel with in Althusser's writings, particularly with his own belief in individual volition, but his definition of ideology as that which grounds and projects the individual in society is particularly suggestive of Whitman's project: "Ideology represents the imaginary relationship of individuals to their real conditions of existence. . . . What is represented in ideology is therefore not the system of the real relations which govern the existence of individuals, but the imaginary relation of those individuals to the real relations in which they live." [26]

As I have suggested, Whitman brilliantly offers several accounts of the American individual, or a template for that elusive prize of the Me/Myself, which is necessarily in danger of being lost in that democratic majority. With heavy philosophical artillery—or was it only a fabricated philosophical ancestry?—he followed and exceeded Emerson in refuting Tocqueville's old charge that "in democratic communities each citizen is habitually engaged in the contemplation of a very puny object, namely himself." If the Whitmanesque self does not "contain multitudes," it certainly is not puny, and it undermines the idea of the inclusive democratic self it would corporeally represent as Whitman embracing his people. In single combat against the anti-democratic and aesthetically conservative forces represented by Carlyle, the European philosophical tradition (Hegel being a stunning exception), the despotic East, and all the other(s) outside his American self, Whitman played an exemplary role. This is to say that he appropriated for himself and for his category of the American self all the rhetorical and repressive powers of the aristocratic self he denied. He was, as his recognition of the utility of Hegel's formulations suggest, hardly innocent about the dangers of his mission. If one is more likely to think of rock musicals (*Hair*'s "I Sing the Body Electric") and Rambo in connection with the individualistic "rough," this does not mean Whitman can be dissociated from a certain Western ideology that yet finds its grounding in a philosophical tradition for which Hegel remains an important signatory.

26. Althusser, *Lenin and Philosophy*, 162, 165.

# The Nothing That Is
## Wallace Stevens' Hegelian Affinities

· · · · · · · · · · · · · · · · · ·

*Judith Butler*

In twentieth-century reflections on history and metaphysics, Hegel's romantic postulation of the dialectical unity of opposites has come to seem irreconcilable with the assertion of human finitude, the ineluctability of temporal experience, the hermeneutical fusion of cultural horizons, and the refutation of language as a closed system of signs. And yet, true to its own logic of inversion, the dialectic reemerges within the confines of twentieth-century thought, deprived of the possibility of synthesis, of systematic closure, and of the claim to ontological truth. As a persistent wish, the structure of a metaphysical longing, the dialectic survives as that precise metaphysical possibility that can no longer be realized.

In his *Logic*, Hegel argued that the dialectic consisted in the unity of apparent opposites—more precisely, in the logical and ontological relation of mutual implication that persists between ostensibly oppositional terms.[1] When the dialectic no longer denotes the ontological unity of opposites or the logical principle of dialectical reversal, it no longer maintains its conventional meanings. The invocation of the dialectic becomes instead a performative moment in a language, an occasion in which the loss of metaphysical moorings clears the way for a poetic affirmation of what is. For Wallace Stevens, the appearance together of discordant things initially recalls the possibility of a unity, that romantic symbolization of opposition in which difference is forever repaired through the emergence of unforeseen unities, affinities, and continuities. For Stevens, the impossibility of the romantic iden-

The author offers grateful acknowledgment to the Institute for Advanced Study and the American Council of Learned Societies for supporting this work.

1. All citations are from *Hegel's Logic, Being Part One of the Encyclopedia of the Philosophical Sciences*, trans. William Wallace (1873; rpr. Oxford, 1975). Hereinafter cited parenthetically in the text as *Logic*.

269

tification of opposites constitutes one of the modern predicaments of metaphor. Within the terms of Stevens' poetry, the possibility of a return to an ontological fusion of discordant things is opened through metaphor, and invariably foreclosed. What relation exists between opposites, now that their unity cannot be presupposed but only invoked momentarily, under the sway of a poetic delusion?

Stevens' poetry everywhere affirms the disjunction between the terms of a metaphor with a self-consciousness that makes that affirmation suspect. He writes against the temptation to conflate the disparate things compared, and yet he makes the comparison and evokes it as an identity. The poetry dramatizes the desire for a metaphorical redemption of difference only to withdraw from the conceit and thematize— poetically—its inevitable failure. The poems become, in part, a curative for Romantic symbolism, engaging the illusion only to dispel it all the more fully. In "Re-statement of Romance," Stevens begins with a denial that indirectly reveals the voluptuous fusion of landscape and self he knows he is no longer able to concede:

> The night knows nothing of the chants of night.
> It is what it is as I am what I am:
> And in perceiving this I best perceive myself
>
> And you . . . [2]

He enumerates the separateness of the night, the chants, the self, dramatically separating the "I" and the "you" through the spatial interruption of the stanza break. The act of separation becomes a moral imperative, and the metaphorical fusion, a dangerous romanticism to be painstakingly resisted. Indeed, at such moments Stevens appears to be involved in a poetics of positivism, defending the beauty of enumerated things and the impossibility of a connective relation between them. Upon closer scrutiny, one realizes that enumeration itself is the enacted mode of their relationship. In "The World as Meditation," the Romantic fusion of image and thing is engaged only to initiate a drama of disillusionment that marks a decidedly post-Romantic poetic sensibility. The poem opens with a question, "Is it Ulysses that approaches

---

2. Wallace Stevens, *The Collected Poems of Wallace Stevens* (New York, 1954), 146, hereinafter cited parenthetically in the text as *CP*.

from the east, / The interminable adventurer?" (*CP*, 520). The matter seems swiftly settled in a Romantic vein as the hopeful affirmation of his impending arrival takes over for several lines; the landscape everywhere affirms his presence: "The trees are mended. / That winter is washed away." The sudden resolution of pain, the clear evidence of a landscape that is the visible sign of apocalyptic change, is interrupted by the insistent introduction of uncertainty once again: "Someone is moving on the horizon"—not Ulysses, not yet, but someone who seems to be Ulysses, but may not be. He appears and disappears, "lifting himself above" the horizon, as if he were a phantom after all, a godlike manifestation that takes leave of the world of physical evidence. The certainty of the landscape as a sign of presence gives rise to an ambiguous distinction between what is in the landscape and what is beyond it; the landscape now transcended no longer seems to be the sign of this reality's presence; the locational and ontological status of the image becomes questionable. Despite this ambiguity, however, the affirmation of presence persists:

> A form of fire approaches the cretonnes of Penelope,
> Whose mere savage presence awakens the world in which she
> dwells.

The "form of fire" at first appears to approach her garment from the outside, but it is unclear whether the fire is conjured from the weaving, her artistry. The phrase "whose mere savage presence" refers to the fire (which may be the body's passion beneath the garment) or to Penelope, thus suggesting a conflation in which her fiery weaving invokes the presence she desires.

The next stanza begins in the mood of strained waiting and resignation; Penelope seems to know that it was not him, that whatever seemed a premonition of his presence is now gone: "She has composed, so long, a self with which to welcome him." And then, as if the poem suddenly confesses its own central conceit, Ulysses becomes a name for the poetic process itself. He is "companion to his self for her, which she imagined." But is the companion "him," Ulysses, for whom she has composed the self, or is the companion that very "self" that she has composed? If the second reading is (also) right, then the composed self is a "companion to his self," an imagined presence that accompanies him. The line continues, however, with "for her," suggesting that the self she composes is at once for him and for her, a solitary imagining of herself with him because she requires it. Read in the alternative way, he is his own companion, and that reflexive love is the act of composing himself for her. The ambiguity over what is a reflexive relation and what a relation to each other suggests Stevens' "re-statement of romance." In the poem so entitled, he writes,

> you and I, alone,
> So much alone, so deeply by ourselves,
> So far beyond the casual solitudes,

> That night is only the background of our selves.

As one might expect of love in a post-Hegelian time, each person reflects the other without that reflection constituting an identity: "Supremely true each to its separate self, / In the pale light that each upon the other throws" (*CP*, 146).

In the second stanza of "The World as Meditation," the encounter is already past, and retrospectively the question is posed, "But was it Ulysses? Or was it the warmth of the sun / On her pillow?" The moment of a confused metaphorical identification is laboriously (and ascetically) unpacked, and in the following lines, we see that Stevensian use of poetry as a curative for romanticism: "The thought kept beating in her like her heart. / The two kept beating together. It was only day." It was only day, only the sun, and since it was either the sun or Ulysses, it was not Ulysses.

But the poem refuses to close on this tone of syllogistic defeat. Although the rational deconstruction of the metaphorical identification results in the enumerated separateness of things, a paradoxical affirmation begins the second to the last stanza: "It was Ulysses and it was not." Here a distinction emerges between Ulysses the man and Ulysses the name of a presence conjured by desire. The final image appears to be one of thorough reflexivity: Penelope "would talk a little to herself as she combed her hair, / Repeating his name with its patient syllables." But even this apparent solipsism, this closed circle of reflexivity, is contested by the ambiguous location of *patient*. Is it her patience displaced onto the name, or the patience of the name itself, waiting for its referent perhaps, or possibly both? She repeats the name with its long vowels and soft consonants as an incantation of presence; indeed, the name, as a linguistic materiality, produces through repetition the fullness of sounds that approximates and eventually preempts the awaited referent. She waits, but in the poetic muttering that closes the poem she appears, on the one hand, to create a kind of aesthetic self-sufficiency eclipsing the absent object that was the occasion of the poem. On the other hand, it is very much his absence and his presence as an absence that structures both her desire and its proximate linguistic satisfactions. She repeats his name, "never forgetting him that kept coming constantly so near." And yet what kind of presence is this? Not the presence of a memory of him who once was there, but the temporally present experience of his absence, what Sartre (in Hegelian fashion) might have called his presence in the form of absence. The "he" who is gone is there in the mode of being-gone, and insofar as he is there, this being-gone constitutes a specific modality of presence. Rather than remain restricted to a notion of being-there that limits all 'thereness' to the empirical being of things, Stevens defies the syllogistic conclusion (itself tied to the positivist reading of beings) that Ulysses was not there and expands the repertoire of thereness to include those objects that are locationally indefinite but that sustain a kind of thereness or presence that is the defining or configuring presence of absent things.

Hence, "It was Ulysses and it was not." And both are true, but only because the two instances of the existential proposition "it was" are used in very different senses. Quick to dismiss the tempting identification of "the idea of the thing with the thing itself," Stevens insists that no Ulysses was there, and that absence remains unredeemed by the play of linguistic presence that follows. Indeed, precisely because Ulysses is not there is he there in the second sense, as a linguistic feat that conjures a presence sustained through repetition, an intermittent presence with no inherent continuity. Although Ulysses is empirically absent, his presence is not wholly a production of the imagination, a subjectively wrought projection played upon the landscape as an essentially indifferent medium. There is an objectness to Ulysses' presence, to his very present absence, and it is in the landscape as the structures of configuration. Stevens' language refuses to reduce Ulysses either to a subjectively imposed image or to an empirical object. Hence, to say "it was Ulysses and it was not" is to claim not only that Ulysses had an imaginary presence without an empirical reality but that the same way in which it was Ulysses is a kind of structuring absence.

The title of the poem, "The World as Meditation," suggests that ambiguity, for it is unclear whether the meditation, which we might expect to belong to some meditating agent, has come unmoored from that agency, making the world a kind of free-floating meditation, like Penelope's monologic muttering that creates intermittent presences through the repetition of the long vowels of Ulysses' name. If the world is the agent of meditation, or the activity of meditation conceived without an agent, then it is this curious presencing that, having no inherent temporal continuity, reveals itself in inadvertent and transient ways. In the fourth stanza, the organic world seems involved in its own self-reparation, the kind of self-loving reflexivity that characterizes Penelope's reassuring words to herself as she combs her hair: "The trees had been mended, as an essential exercise / In an inhuman meditation, larger than her own." Here it seems that the reparative and generative exercise of meditation is a movement of the world that characterizes both Penelope and the landscape but that issues from neither one exclusively; indeed, we might expect a divine agent to occupy the originating point of that meditation, but instead we find the activity regenerating itself, without an agent and without a teleological purpose.

In the quotation from Georges Enesco that opens the poem, meditation is the "essential exercise" of the musician, a constant composing of the self for the act of composition. Experience in the mode of meditation is a "permanent dream" in which the distinction between night and day no longer applies. Within the poem, meditation at once transcends and embraces the oppositions that appear insuperable in the nonaesthetic mode: night and day, the human and the inhuman world. Meditation is "inhuman" in the sense that the natural world is exercised by that activity, but also because it is indifferent, even cruel, and without a final purpose. Although Enesco refers to meditation as an activity of self-involvement, his withdrawal is a preparation for a disclosure of the world; meditation thus affirms the separateness of human and inhuman worlds as the condition of the mutually revelatory relation between them. The separateness of both terms is clear, and yet the melancholy revelations they occasion, each about the other, appear to be the post-Romantic consequence of this peculiar dialectic of meditation in which it is the separateness of things that constitutes their sameness. The two worlds are, of course, not identical, and yet their difference occasions the revelation of their specificity, their common finitude. Penelope is protected neither by the landscape nor by the metaphorical illusions that it configures: "No winds like dogs watched over her at night." The self composed is the "deep-founded sheltering," a separateness that not only affirms itself, but also is affirmed through the world that is greater than that self. In "The Man with the Blue Guitar," Stevens writes, "the discord merely magnifies," and here it seems that discord constitutes the musical tone of meditation, the metaphysical melody that refuses synthesis but consummates the momentary revelations of difference: "But play, you must, / A tune beyond us, yet ourselves" (*CP*, 165).

"Negation," one of Stevens' most self-consciously philosophical poems, suggests other possible meanings of "the world as meditation" and comments implicitly on the course of a dialectic alarmingly detached from a divine origin and an eschatological plan. The poem greets its reader with a familiar "Hi!," a Japanese *yes* (*hai*), which affirms that the poem and the reader are old and intimate friends. The line continues, "The Creator too is blind," and here the reader is implicated in the sightless company of the poet and the Creator, assuming for the moment that the two are distinct. As the stanza continues, the Creator parodies the Absolute Spirit of an idealist dialectic, a force that embraces oppositions only to transcend them and continuously to constitute ever-greater unities. I cite the stanza in full:

> Hi! The Creator too is blind,
> Struggling toward his harmonious whole,
> Rejecting intermediate parts,
> Horrors and falsities and wrongs;
> Incapable master of all force.

Stevens' wry mockery of the principle of dialectical progress as a constant effort to subordinate and tame the negative is resonant with a number of post-Hegelian positions. In *Writing and Difference*, Jacques Derrida claims that *Aufhebung*, the activity by which external differences are canceled, transcended, and preserved, is a strategy of "mastery" that conceals its own anxiety in the face of unsystematizable experience. The subordination of all negation to an overarching unity of rational knowledge and metaphysical plenitude implicitly refuses to accept insuperable difference. Derrida invokes Georges Bataille's critique of Hegel as resistant to excess of any kind, that which exceeds the bounds of reason and refuses reassimilation into its terms.[3] Stevens

3. According to Gilles Deleuze, the Hegelian hostility toward difference is the consequence of an anti-erotic project of total and totalizing control. See Deleuze, *Neitzsche and Philosophy* (New York, 1985).

affirms that the dialectic is conceived as negative toward negation by the subordination of that litany of negation, "Horrors and falsities and wrongs," into a progressive history that promises the ultimate dialectical redemption of the negative. Stevens imagines the dialectic as the blind struggle of an incapable master whose project of dialectical advance is delusional.

And yet this mockery is self-mockery as well. The Creator who is blind is nevertheless "meticulous," and the "evanescent symmetries" that he creates recall the reparative/generative exercises of the world as a meditation. In the second half of the poem, Stevens affirms the "evanescent symmetries" as the ultimate principle of transience (and hence of negation) and seems to suggest that we endure brief lives because of the necessary transience of the poet's creations.

> Too vague idealist, overwhelmed
> By an afflatus that persists.
> For this, then, we endure brief lives,
> The evanescent symmetries
> From that meticulous potter's thumb.

Subordinate to his construction, the idealist becomes another negativity taken up by the continuing dialectic deprived of teleological closure. The Creator appears to be the vague idealist, but his creation takes on a life of its own, finally turning upon its originator. The "afflatus that persists" at first appears to be the "hot air" of idealist metaphysics, but it plays upon the *conatus* of Spinoza's Ethics, the desire to persist in one's own being. But the most probable philosophical association here is Schopenhauer. In an essay, "A Collect of Philosophy," Stevens poses the question of whether there can be intrinsically poetic philosophical ideas and considers Schopenhauer's "eccentric philosophic apparatus on the grand scale in the *World as Will*."[4] The "apparatus" of Schopenhauer resonates with the "afflatus" of metaphysics in the poem, but cause for further association is confirmed later in that same essay. Stevens quotes from Arthur Kenyon Rogers' summary of Schopenhauer's philosophy in *A Student's History of Philosophy:* "The eternally striving, energizing power which is working everywhere in the universe—in the

---

4. Wallace Stevens, *Opus Posthumous*, ed. Samuel French Morse (New York, 1957), 190, hereinafter cited parenthetically in the text as *OP*.

instinct of the animal, the life process of the planet, the blind force of inorganic matter—what is this but the will that underlies all existence" (*OP*, 192). This "blind force" of the will is further figured by Rogers, and quoted by Stevens, in terms that seem to prefigure the poem: "the blind man carrying on his shoulders the lame man who can see" (*OP*, 193).[5]

5. For a further discussion of Stevens' uneasy relation to philosophical texts, and to Schopenhauer in particular, see Richard Macksey, "The Climates of Wallace Stevens," in *The Act of the Mind: Essays on the Poetry of Wallace Stevens*, ed. Roy Harvey Pearce and J. Hillis Miller (Baltimore, 1965), 185–223. Apart from showing Stevens' use of imagery from Schopenhauer, Macksey makes use of various phenomenological themes to explore the philosophical dimension of Stevens' poetry as well as Stevens' resistance to systematic philosophy. Citing Hegel, Heidegger, and Merleau-Ponty, among others, Macksey suggests a reading of Stevens that maintains an insuperable tension between moments of experience and their linguistic determination, an opposition that institutes a relentless temporality (198). This sense of temporal nonclosure is what I have tried also to suggest as the sense of a dialectic without finality. For a further discussion on Stevens' relation to Schopenhauer, see Frank Doggett, *Stevens' Poetry of Thought* (Baltimore, 1966).

Some other attempts to understand Stevens' relation to philosophical texts tend to situate Stevens within "the linguistic turn" of contemporary philosophy, arguing, for the most part, not that Stevens was influenced by such intellectual currents, but that his work sustains significant resonances with that of Wittgenstein and some of his followers. See J. Hillis Miller, "Stevens' Rock and Criticism as Cure," *Georgia Review*, XXX (1976), 5–31, 330–48, Gerald Bruns, *Modern Poetry and the Idea of Language* (New Haven, Conn., 1974), and Charles Altieri, "Why Stevens Must Be Abstract, or What a Poet Can Learn From Painting," in *Wallace Stevens: The Poetics of Modernism*, ed. Albert Gelpi (Cambridge, Eng., 1985). Altieri suggests that "the metaphysical machinery" of Hegel and Heidegger is inappropriate for understanding Stevens' specific use of metaphoric language as producing multiple moments of tentative similarity; he suggests that Wittgenstein's notion of *seeing as* illuminates Stevens' use of metaphor.

Readings of Stevens in terms of Heidegger tend to center on the poetry as the revelation of being or the emergence of linguistic affirmation after the death of the gods. A reading in terms of some existential themes, perhaps more Sartrian than Heideggerian, can be found in J. Hillis Miller, "Wallace Stevens' Poetry of Being," in *The Act of the Mind*, ed. Pearce and Miller. A more recent work is Paul Bové, "Fiction, Risk and Deconstruction: The Poetry of Wallace Stevens," in Bové, *Destructive Poetics* (New York, 1975).

Joseph Riddel's review (in *boundary 2*, I [1972], 79–97) of Helen Vendler's book on Stevens, *On Extended Wings: Wallace Stevens' Longer Poems* (Cambridge, Mass., 1969), underscores the problem of reading Stevens as a simple dialectician, where *dialectic* is understood as a process in which the final and full telos is implicit at the outset of that process. In fact, such a notion is closer to the meaning of *teleology* in the Aristotelian sense than either *dialectic* or *phenomenology* in the Hegelian sense. Vendler appears to accept the notion that Stevens' poems are like "circles gathering beginning into end," that they are evolving forms that gradually and inexorably recapitulate their beginnings in their endings. Both Riddel and Miller have argued, however, that Stevens' later poems resist precisely that formal closure that Vendler assumes to characterize the poetry generally. Sig-

In the poem, the will becomes the Creator who is blind, the "afflatus" that persists and surpasses the "brief lives," as though a blind dialectic takes up individual lives for no reason and for no ultimate purpose. If the Creator "too" is blind, then the directionless struggle to redeem the negative within the emerging contour of life's unity is the struggle of poet and reader as well, one that might well be a universal existential problematic. The "this" for which "we" endure brief lives seems, then, to be precisely the idealist conceit deprived of its teleological principle, an open dialectic that inevitably overwhelms us, overtakes us, "an inhuman meditation" larger than our own. But there is no synthetic closure to this particular dialectic, only the perpetual creation of "evanescent symmetries," Penelope and the evanescent Ulysses, "Two in a deep-founded sheltering, friend and dear friend."

Blind, vague, and incapable, this Creator/master is nevertheless an artisan/"potter" (close enough to "poet") whose transitory creations are "meticulous." The casual and mocking tone of the opening line gradually reverses until the final two lines seem reverent, even awestruck. The transitory creations of the potter's thumb are the imperfect offerings of an imperfect god, "symmetries" that form a temporary polarity in tension, the very structure of metaphor, whose unifying force necessarily fades. The potter's thumb, like the poet's thumb supporting his pen, constructs the "evanescent symmetries" of metaphorical comparisons. Finally, then, the dialectic is less a progressive "afflatus" than a principle of transient perfections, momentary aesthetic redemptions in which similarities are metaphorically constituted and then dissolved. The "afflatus" of the imaginary conflates disparate things only to see the terms of that conjunction disjoin and scatter: "the night knows nothing of the chants of night" (CP, 146). The potter's work is, then, the poetic inception of metaphor, conceived as a dialectical unity in which separate things are offered together in a temporary unity and then dispersed without the possibility of preserving that "failure" as a moment of a more inclusive unity.

---

nificantly, Riddel's move to a deconstructive reading of Stevens, as well as Michael Beehler's *T. S. Eliot, Wallace Stevens, and the Discourses of Difference* (Baton Rouge, 1987), suggests not only the lack of formal closure but the refusal to claim a linguistic adequacy to being, the possibility of an authentic linguistic presencing, to be at the core of Stevens' poetry. On the other hand, Vendler's reading becomes the point of departure for Klaus Martens' metaphysically optimistic reading of Stevens as delineating a utopian future through the act of negation in *Negation, Negativität und Utopie im Werk von Wallace Stevens* (Frankfurt, 1980).

"Negation" mocks an unwieldy idealism only to affirm finally a less ambitious version of the same. Not a system of ideal relations, the poem offers instead a discontinuous series of momentary symmetries that compel belief. In "Connoisseur of Chaos," Stevens writes, "a law of inherent opposites, / Of essential unity, is as pleasant as port," subordinating through an ironic juxtaposition the metaphysics of dialectical idealism to a more pleasurable headiness (dialectic as dessert wine). Slightly less irreverent is the subsequent subordination of metaphysics to the aesthetic gesture: "As pleasant as the brush-strokes of a bough." And then, as if to vindicate the poetic capacity to affirm particularity over and against philosophical abstraction, he finishes the stanza with the line "An upper, particular bough in, say, Marchand." In the next stanza, he disavows the "theory" offering "the pretty contrast of life and death" and proving "that these opposite things partake of one." Without equivocation he writes, "We cannot go back to that." And though the metaphysical structure has become too extravagant and unwieldy for the modern sensibility, some remnant of that metaphysic remains:

> And yet relation appears,
> A small relation expanding like the shade
> Of a cloud on sand, a shape on the side of a hill.

Is this the dialectic freed of the trappings of totality, a set of evanescent relations that constitute the ruins of an idealist metaphysics? Stevens contends in *The Necessary Angel* that poetry is "a phase of metaphysics," and in "Connoisseur of Chaos" poetry appears to be the last phase; dialectical unity appears as an imaginary construction, temporary, compelling, false, and yet a source of poetic meaning. But the metaphorical "relations" that appear are not for that reason wholly subjective. The act of poetic transfiguration is nevertheless constrained by that which it transfigures; indeed, it is "the mere being of things" that configures in advance the terms by which it is poetically encountered.

And yet the "being" to which Stevens subscribes is not a self-identical empirical being. Not only was it Ulysses, and it was not, but this being and not-being in their uneasy conjunction constitute a different modality of being, not the "afflatus" of dialectical idealism, but a dialectical truth nonetheless. In "A Primitive Like an Orb," the inhuman meditation, the "tune beyond us, yet ourselves" is redescribed as

> the huge, high harmony that sounds
> A little and a little, suddenly,
> By means of a separate sense. It is and it
> Is not and, therefore, is. In the instant of speech,
> The breadth of an accelerando moves,
> Captives the being, widens—and was there.
>
> (*CP*, 440)

As part of that huge, high harmony, Ulysses is there and is not, and poetry, that late phase of metaphysics, affirms the reality of that truth of transience. The moment of the poetic utterance, "the instant of speech, / . . . Captives the being," a peculiar verb formation that suggests both that the words are captivated by the being and that the words (in a reverse moment) are understood to capture the being, whereby poetry becomes a kind of willing bondage to "being," which, in its submission, exercises its own subordinating power. This peculiar inversion of the lines of referentiality constitutes the unresolvable ambiguity of the poetic gesture that neither invents not represents being but embraces, in a momentary "symmetry," the chord, the resonance, the metaphysical enlargement that this being makes possible. The instant of speech "Captives the being, widens"—and here again it is both the speech that widens or enhances that being into its metaphysical thereness and the being that itself widens in response to that enhancing poetic gesture. Immediately after that reciprocal "widening," Stevens inserts a dash, a rupture, the "sharp flash" of metaphor (*CP*, 288), and affirms "and was there." This second presence, this wider, more inclusive sense of being, only exists for us in the moments of its poetic inception. The language that asserts its presence always comes too late, for the grammar of substances that describes the empirical thereness of things never "captives" that elusive moment of reciprocal exchange.

In resolving the contradiction "It is and it / Is not" with that Hegelian conclusion "and, therefore, is," Stevens affirms a kind of passing being that encompasses the narrower play of presence and absence, the melodic synchronicity of dissonant chords. In Hegel's *Logic*, this simultaneity of opposition is articulated as the paradox of determinate negation. In "The Doctrine of Being," Hegel gives what might count as a philosophical rendition of Stevens' poetic lines above: "In Being (determinate there and then), the determinateness is one with Being; yet at the same time, when explicitly made a negation, it is a Limit, a Barrier. Hence, the otherness is not something indifferent and outside it, but a function proper to it" (*Logic*, 136). That which is, in the simple and determinate sense of being, is self-identical only in virtue of the limit or barrier that demarcates that being from that which it is not. The barrier performs the "is-not" that simple identity requires to exist. Functioning as a distinguishing and mediating barrier, negation is here determinate negation, *i.e.*, it posits the self-identity of being through the act of a specific and specifying negation. Indeterminate negation, on the other hand, is a free-floating nothing that does not operate in the service of demarcating some manner of being. In Hegel's *Logic*, there is no meaningful sense of negation as indeterminate, for even the notion of "Nothing" operates in the service of a dialectical exclusion from "Being" and so remains essentially tied to the latter term. In an exposition that later proves central to Heidegger's "What is Metaphysics?" Hegel argues that negation is always a negation of something and that this intentionality is the manner of being that pertains to the not-being: "If we take a closer look at what a limit implies, we see it involving a contradiction in itself, and thus evincing its dialectical nature. But, again, the limit, as the negation of something, is not an abstract nothing, but a nothing which is what we call an 'other'" (*Logic*, Part VII, Sec. 92, p. 136).

Hegel's affirmation of "the nothing which is" parallels Stevens' own poetic assertion in "The Snow Man" of "the nothing that is":

> For the listener, who listens in the snow,
> And, nothing himself, beholds
> Nothing that is not there and the nothing that is.

The listener is ontologically "nothing," and yet at the same time, this vacant self conditions the beholding of "Nothing that is not there," alternately understood as "everything that there is" or "the Nothing that is not there, but somewhere else" or, even, as the closing phrase indicates, "the nothing that is." These swift equivocations of being and not-being nowhere constitute a stable and mutually exclusive set of oppositions. Hegel's emphasis on the dialectical unity of opposites as a movement suggests that the only way to understand the unity of these terms is in the moments of their transition into one another. That the unity is momentary is true for Hegel and Stevens alike; the "evanescent symmetries" in Stevens are similar to the transitional moments that are, for Hegel, only knowable through speculative thought: "Wherever there is movement, wherever there is life, wherever anything is carried into effect in the actual world, there Dialectic is at work" (*Logic*, 116). This unity is manifest in the collapsing of terms, which constitutes the movement of transition: "The Speculative stage, or stage of Positive Reason, apprehends the unity of terms (propositions) in their opposition—the affirmative, which is involved in their disintegration and their transition" (*Logic*, 119).

Stevens' well-known formulation that "death is the mother of beauty" suggests that the limitation and barrier that determines and distinguishes beings, that affirms that they are these beings rather than those, is the occasion of a variegated and specified ontology. Without negation, *i.e.*, without distinction, there would be no beauty, for there would be no specificity and no change (no temporal experience, none of the "exhilarations of change" [*CP*, 288] and no metaphysical melodies), only an unspecified, homogeneous mass, Parmenidean Being. Hegel makes the same point in the *Logic*:

> In all other cases of difference there is some common point which comprehends both things. Suppose e.g. we speak of two different species: the genus forms the common for both. But in the case of mere Being and Nothing, distinction is without a bottom to stand upon: hence there can be no distinction, both determinations being the same bottomlessness. . . . [I]t is natural for us to represent Being as absolute riches, and Nothing as absolute poverty. But if when we view the whole world we can only say that everything is, and nothing more, we are neglecting all specialty and, instead of absolute plenitude, we have absolute emptiness. (*Logic*, 128)

Hegel subscribes to a rationalist account of this dialectical inversion, which puts him at a distance from Stevens' realistic insistence on the primacy of being. Hegel argues, for instance, that "the limitations of the finite do not merely come from without . . . by its own act it passes into its counterpart. . . . [L]ife, as life, involves the germ of death" (*Logic*, 116–17). In other words, for Hegel, there is a law of dialectical inversion that resides as an organizing principle of being, such that not-being issues forth from being as a law of inexorable necessity. For Stevens, however, being is itself prior to any reason, teleology, or dialectical necessity.

The mere being that is poetically revealed and affirmed is, within Stevens' poetic world, "irrational," but is not for that reason without the possibility of a meaningful affirmation. The conflation of the rational or intelligible with the meaningful suggests that meaning comes first from the acts of the mind, that the domain of particular beings receives its meaning only after being filtered through the cognitive grid of a rational agent. But for Stevens, there are clearly moments where what "is" has its meaning in virtue of a kind of primary and precognitive "isness." The mere being that is the "palm at the end of the mind," the light, the sound, the "being still / . . . some skreaking and skrittering residuum" (*CP*, 160), is the "mere" or "still" of being, not trivial at all, but the ground of a kind of Aristotelian wonder that there are things rather than no things. Here we see that what does not exist, what is gone, or what has never existed continues to configure being as a signifying absence and provides the even more necessary ground for the experience of that which has "mere being." Here it is not just the mere being that is clearly some thing and not no thing, but the ground that lets mere being come into view, a ground that is nothing and so is identical with groundlessness. But this is a groundlessness that "figures," quite literally, what is, is essential to what is, and so is wherever being is.

The way in which absence works, the way in which history persists, the way in which all manner of "not being" organizes experience and allows for the poetic affirmation of mere being, these are affirmations of "the nothing that is" that in no way rely upon the rationalist teleology of being and not-being encoded in Hegel's *Logic*. Hence, it seems that there can be a dialectical inversion of opposites without assuming that the oppositional terms exist as immanent or internal features of each other. For Stevens, both being and nothing escape reason or, rather, they set the terms within which all intelligibility occurs.

In a series of letters from 1942 to 1943 between Wallace Stevens and Jean Wahl, the French philosopher who introduced an existential Hegel to France with his 1929 book, *Le Malheur de la conscience dans la philosophie de Hegel*, Wahl insists that Stevens is a "realist."[6] Wahl cites "Notes Toward a Supreme Fiction" in support of his contention: "The

6. The following quotations are from the collection of Wallace Stevens' correspondence with Jean Wahl housed in the Huntington Library in San Marino, California. Jean Wahl published *Le Malheur de la conscience dans la philosophie de Hegel* in 1929 (the

first idea was not our own . . . the clouds preceded us." And the clouds, the first things, have an ontological weight and presence prior to the human acts by which they are known; indeed, they have a fullness and specificity, a "mere" yet sufficient being that determines the form of the epistemological encounter. In "Notes," Wahl finds this realist presumption of the self-sufficiency of being described in "a thing final in itself and therefore good."

For Stevens, the priority of being reveals the limits of language and compels poetic description to disavow its own claim to a transpar-

---

text is currently available in a 1951 reprinted version through Gérard Monfort). Influenced by Hegel's early theological writings, particularly the essay on love, and by Kierkegaardian themes, Wahl introduces an existential Hegel to France. Less a systematic philosopher than an existential theologian, Hegel appeared in Wahl's text as a believer in necessary paradoxes, one who refused the rationalist or metaphysical appropriation of experience. Stevens corresponded with Wahl prior to Stevens' lecture at Mount Holyoke College in August of 1943. Wahl was visiting Holyoke for the year, and the two communicated about the possible convergences of philosophical ideas and poetry. The correspondence continued after that lecture as Stevens prepared a lecture for the University of Chicago, what later became "A Collect of Philosophy" in *Opus Posthumous*. In a letter dated December 9, 1942, Wahl responds to Stevens' question, later to become the focus of that essay, whether there are intrinsically poetic ideas. Wahl's answer suggests his own interest in existential themes: temporality, life, freedom, anguish, and insurpassable subjectivity. First, Wahl asks Stevens whether he has read Hegel's early poem "To Eleusis." He then enumerates the following among a larger list of possibly poetic ideas: the infinity of the world; the idea of the reality of evil; Whitehead's allusion to Wordsworth's suggestion of the eternal quietness of nature, and to Shelley, on the eternal passage of nature; Schopenhauer's "Will," the *élan vital*; the idea of freedom; *les vérités éternelles*—Malebranche; Condillac on sight; Descartes—I think therefore I am; to be or not to be; Samuel Alexander on Space, Time, and Deity; Bradley's *Appearance and Reality*—space and time as the stuff of things; the enormous a priori in Husserl.

There is no reason to assume that Stevens read Hegel in any depth or that he had any desire to read him. In a letter to Ted Weiss dated November 14, 1944, Stevens refers to Hegel as one of the "divinities of the Styx," a phrase that will no doubt give pleasure to some Nietzschean readers of Hegel who have argued that the "bad air" of German metaphysics is a sign of its essential decadence. But the question nevertheless remains whether the unsystematic Hegel defended by Wahl did not in some way resonate with the kind of poetic ideas that Stevens clearly sought. After all, in Wahl's rendition of Hegel, language is destined to fail in its effort to determine being, and in its failure, it provides for the possibility of a certain kind of *showing* rather than *saying*. Clearly, one might also consider the common interest of Wahl and Stevens in the philosophical gesture toward a temporality that can never be stayed within the terms of philosophical language. This constant failure of philosophical referentiality indicates precisely the kind of open temporality underscored by Richard Macksey, referring to Stevens' late poetry: "the tactic is to let the poem become its own answer, to push the words toward their own antitheses; change for Stevens, as for Hegel, depends upon the dialectic of continuing negation" (*The Act of the Mind*, ed. Pearce and Miller, 202).

ent revelation of what is. The poetic word is inevitably belated; the being that resides has no meaning without the widening effects of the poetic gesture. Stevens poetically tells us everything poetry is not, no longer is, and in this denial we receive the intimations of a poetic rendering of reality that relies on the discrepancy between word and being as "the discord [that] merely magnifies" (*CP*, 169). With the operations of difference now essential to poetic signification itself, the claims of symbolic closure no longer structure the poetic task.

The chord struck between language and being is forever discordant, and in the poem, it is the falsehood by which meaning itself is mobilized. Although what Sartre called Hegel's "ontological optimism" is no longer in place for Stevens, that figure of unity and metaphysical closure is reconstituted as the vital illusion of poetic metaphor, the illusion that Stevens' poetry constructs only to expose and renounce.

> Slowly the ivy on the stones
> Becomes the stones. Women become
>
> The cities, children become the fields
> And men in waves become the sea.
>
> It is the chord that falsifies.
> The sea returns upon the men,
>
> The fields entrap the children, brick
> Is a weed and all the flies are caught,
>
> Wingless and withered, but living alive.
> The discord merely magnifies.
>
> Deeper within the belly's dark
> Of time, time grows upon the rock.

(CP, 170–71)

The first four lines of "The Man With the Blue Guitar" reiterate the conceit of an effective transubstantiation, an ontological synecdoche, that not only relates disparate things through analogy but confirms the relationship as their unity in being. The conceit is promoted, though almost listlessly, only to be interrupted by the modernist insight into the poetic construction of this ontological fiction: "It is the chord that falsifies." But rather than diminish the power of poetry to reveal ontological relationality, the poem appears to begin again, in the aftermath of that illusion, to make the insurpassable difference between elements into its postmodern theme. Less a return to nominalism than an attempt at a poetics of enumeration, the poem makes negation itself into an illuminating act of separation. Not only separating "men" from "waves," "women" from "cities," the poem separates itself, down the middle, from conceits of poetic ontology that no longer hold. Significantly, the poem does not remain rooted in a nostalgia for the ontological harmonies of the past but moves to the meditation of difference as the very condition of a postmodern affirmation.

Gilles Deleuze has argued that the move beyond Hegel in contemporary critical theory locates and releases difference without reassimilating it into the orbit of an all-inclusive ontology. As the exemplar of this totalizing gesture, Hegel is the name for the project of conceptual mastery that Deleuze seeks to supplant with a Nietzschean movement of affirmation. Recently, Deleuze has argued that the description of the world outside of totalizing metaphysics ought not to rely on the copula at all, that one must "substitute the AND for the IS. A *and* B." The last seven lines of Stevens' "The Man With the Blue Guitar" employ conjunctions, commas, and disjunction to dissolve the ontological illusion and to recast being within the terms of a poetic empiricism. Deleuze appears more entranced by the figure of being than does Stevens, but his redescription of what ontology might mean articulates the generative possibilities of negation that Stevens enacts in the second half of his poem. According to Deleuze, "The AND is not even a specific relation or conjunction, it is that which subtends all relations, the path of all relations, which makes relations shoot outside their terms and outside the set of their terms, and outside everything which could be determined as Being, One, Whole."[7]

Although Deleuze seems to return to a plenitude of relations that preexists the language tracing its terrain, Stevens' project is less metaphysically ambitious. And yet the conjunction works for Stevens, not merely to enumerate separate things, but to make enumeration itself into a rhythmic operation of ambivalence, one that recapitulates the

7. Gilles Deleuze and Claire Parnet, *Dialogues*, trans. Hugh Tomlinson and Barbara Habberjam (New York, 1987), 57.

loss of older harmonies and yet affirms the possibility of "evanescent symmetries." Neither Deleuze nor Stevens is far from Hegel's own insight into the generative possibilities of negation, its capacity to circumscribe some domain of relationality not yet articulated. Although Hegel is figured as the philosopher who subordinates all difference to Being, he is also the philosopher, defended by Wahl, Jean Hyppolite and others, who proclaimed the impossibility of language to fix the negative with a name, who sought to criticize the (Kantian) Understanding for its inability to think the thought of the infinite, the fundamental openness of time. The totalizing Hegel is only one dimension of his philosophical contribution; the other is decidedly less easy to caricature. His philosophy of language, of history, and of the logical operation of negation are yet to be fully reconsidered within contemporary criticism, but these dimensions of his work will reveal a Hegel who knows the limits of what can be said or thought, and who sought a mode of thinking that would not capture its object but let it live.

On the one hand, Stevens' poetry can be read as interrogating the aftermath of metaphysical illusions that characterize the romanticism of thinkers such as Hegel and Coleridge, but on the other hand, Stevens and Hegel converge in their affirmation of negation as a source of possible meanings. Stevens' poetry is partially a project to mourn the loss of an illusion of metaphysical harmonies and to affirm sometimes meditatively and sometimes playfully the multiple and fluid significations that emerge in the wake of this disillusionment to shift continually the terrain of ontology itself. The loss of linguistic adequation diminishes the poet's claim to omniscience, but the loss of grandeur ushers in an infinitely more variegated world. The negative cannot be superseded by form, but one can poetically enact the desire to master the negative as well as its inevitable defeat—as well as the pleasures that follow in the possibilities of a poetic enumeration immersed in time and the significant separateness of things.

# Notes on Contributors

MITCHELL BREITWIESER teaches American literature at the University of California at Berkeley. He is the author of *Cotton Mather and Benjamin Franklin: The Price of Representative Personality* and *American Puritanism and the Defense of Mourning: Religion, Grief, and Ethnology in Mary White Rowlandson's Captivity Narrative*, as well as of essays on Whitman, Thoreau, Melville, and Jefferson.

JUDITH BUTLER is associate professor of humanities at Johns Hopkins University and the author of two recent books, *Subjects of Desire: Hegelian Reflections in Twentieth-Century France* and *Gender Trouble: Feminism and the Subversion of Identity*.

BAINARD COWAN teaches English and comparative literature at Louisiana State University. He has written *Exiled Waters: "Moby-Dick" and the Crisis of Allegory* and articles on Hegel, Walter Benjamin, and Melville. He is also co-editor of a new series at LSU Press, Theoretical Horizons in American Culture.

GREGORY S. JAY teaches in the modern studies graduate program at the University of Wisconsin/Milwaukee. The present essay was completed during his tenure as a Fellow at UWM's Center for Twentieth Century Studies. He is the author of *T. S. Eliot and the Poetics of Literary History* and *America the Scrivener: Deconstruction and the Subject of Literary History*.

JOSEPH G. KRONICK, associate professor of English at Louisiana State University, completed his essay with the aid of a grant from the National Endowment for the Humanities. He is the author of *American Poetics of History: From Emerson to the Moderns* and of articles on Heidegger, critical theory, and American literature. He is co-editor of the new LSU Press series Theoretical Horizons in American Culture.

KATHRYNE V. LINDBERG is associate professor of American literature at Harvard University and is the author of *Reading Pound Reading: Modernism after Nietzsche* and articles on Eliot, Joyce, and Pound. In 1989 she won a fellowship year at the Humanities Institute at the University of Wisconsin, Madison.

JOSEPH N. RIDDEL teaches at the University of California at Los Angeles and is the author of numerous essays on modern American poetics and critical theory. Two of his books, *The Clairvoyant Eye: The Poetry and Poetics of Wallace Stevens* and *The Inverted Bell: Modernism and the Counterpoetics of William Carlos Williams*, are being reissued in new augmented editions by Louisiana State University Press.

JOHN CARLOS ROWE is professor of English and comparative literature at the University of California, Irvine. He is the author of *Through the Custom-House: Nineteenth-Century American Fiction and Modern Theory* and *The Theoretical Dimensions of Henry James*, as well as of many articles on classic and contemporary American literature and literary theory.

HENRY SUSSMAN teaches English and comparative literature at the State University of New York at Buffalo. He is the author of *The Hegelian Aftermath: Readings in Hegel, Kierkegaard, Freud, Proust, and James* and *High Resolution: Critical Theory and the Problem of Literacy*. Recently he has also published *Afterimages of Modernity: Structure and Indifference in Twentieth-Century Literature* and co-edited a collection entitled *Psychoanalysis and . . .*

# Index